Your Child's

Development

from birth to

adolescence

Richard Lansdown

PhD, FBPsS, C. Psychol.

Marjorie Walker

PhD, MS Ed, BS Ed

FRANCES LINCOLN

For Harry
- R.L.

To my son, Michael Walker,
and to my parents, Miriam and Mike Girsh
- M.W.

Frances Lincoln Limited
4 Torriano Mews,
Torriano Avenue,
London NW5 2RZ

First paperback edition 1996
Your Child's Development
Copyright © Frances Lincoln Limited 1991
Text copyright © Richard Lansdown and Marjorie Walker 1991
The right of Richard Lansdown and Marjorie Walker to be identified as
the authors of this work has been asserted by them in accordance with the
Copyright, Designs and Patents Act 1988.
All photographs, except those on pages 48, 79, 104, 178 and 308,
copyright © Anthea Sieveking 1991

British Library Cataloguing-in-Publication Data
A catalogue record for this book is available from the British Library

ISBN 0 7112 1114 0

Set in 11/12 Bembo by Ace Filmsetting Limited, Frome, Somerset
Printed and bound in Hong Kong

9 8 7 6 5 4 3 2 1

Your Child's
Development

from birth to
adolescence

Photographs by Anthea Sieveking

Contents

We have adopted the convention of using 'she' in one chapter, 'he' in the next.

Introduction

This is a book about all the children in the world. No matter how they differ in size, in colour, in gender or in temperament, no matter what variation there is in skill or ability, children have similar needs, for love, respect, care and attention.

It is also a book about the unique child, for all children are themselves, with their own personalities, their own strengths, their own vulnerability.

Above all it is a book about children and their parents (or those who fill that role), for it is in the interaction between children and parents that we see a young person flower or, sadly, fail. The best people to help children are parents: we hope that this book will help you along that path.

The authors' standpoint

The history of the study of childhood is rife with opinions posing as facts. While it is our hope and belief that any view put forward in this book is firmly based on empirical evidence, we have to acknowledge that we are no more likely than anyone else totally to escape the influence of fashion. So that readers may know where we start from, we record here our standpoint on five major themes.

The general theoretical standpoint is that sometimes referred to as lifespan developmental psychology: the development of any child can only be understood within a context of human ecology. Children are influenced by, and in their turn influence, their families; they and their families are the product of the geographical, historical, social and political setting in which they grow up. No child is an island.

Nature and nurture

The nature/nurture debate, centring around the relative contributions of what a person inherits and how he or she is treated, has now largely subsided, the consensus being that both are of crucial significance. Few would now contend that a child is automatically doomed by his or her genetic inheritance; nor, on the other hand, is it widely believed that a good environment will necessarily overcome every natural obstacle.

Interactions

The process of development involves an interaction between children and their world: children affect those around them, including their parents, just as they are themselves affected.

The interaction between a mother and her baby begins before the baby is born: an active baby in the womb constantly reminds her of its presence, demanding attention and provoking comments and talk. This fetus will emerge at birth as an already acknowledged presence. Later, the way in which a baby responds to the attention of others will determine how and whether that attention is repeated; in turn, the response to the child will influence the child once more, and so the process continues, at school, in the community, throughout life.

Individual differences

Each child has an individual temperament in which the inherited component is likely to be considerable but not total. Some say that children differ in their inborn resilience as well: there are wide variations in the ability to cope with change and adversity. Whether these variations are fundamentally a result of inheritance is still an open question, but it is certainly the case that resilience can be nurtured, or sapped, by a child's experience.

Maturation

Maturation is the process of growth, development and ripening which takes place naturally and is little if at all affected by practice or learning. There is no point in asking a child to do something for which he or she has not yet developed the physical or neurological equipment.

The effects of maturation have been explored through studies of identical twins. In one study, for example, one twin from each pair was given systematic toilet training after the first few weeks of life. These children did not become clean and dry any earlier than their twins, whose training did not begin until they showed themselves to be ready for the process.

This is not to imply that children all mature at the same rate. The boundaries of normal development are wide, and children progress according to their own schedules. It is important to recognize, too, that psychological readiness to perform a task is relevant, as well as physical maturity.

Critical periods

There are certain times in children's lives when they can acquire particular skills easily and naturally – for example, children under the age of about twelve can learn languages much more easily than those who are older. It is sometimes asserted that if this key time, referred to as a critical period, is missed, it will be difficult, perhaps impossible, to acquire the skill. Critical periods have also been invoked by theorists in the emotional development of children. Pediatricians Marshall Klaus and John Kennell have argued that if baby and mother do not become bonded in the first hours of life the child will have trouble developing subsequent close relationships. While we would agree that there are sensitive periods when learning is easier, we cannot accept the idea of a rigid critical period, after which learning is no longer possible.

All the ideas introduced here are referred to throughout this book. Some other influential theories are discussed in the first chapter, where we consider the major influences on children.

1 INFLUENCES ON DEVELOPMENT

In this chapter we look at some of the many influences that go to shape children. Some of them are inherent in the children themselves: they are what the children bring with them into the world – their genetic inheritance. Others come from the family and from the society in which children grow up, that is, from their environment.

Our aim, here and throughout the book, is to bring together theory and practice in order to show how an understanding of the influences on your developing child can help you, both in your everyday dealings with him or her, and in periods of crisis.

The Biological Birthright

The human being begins life as a single fused cell containing within itself a complex programme, instructing it how to develop. To understand how the programme works we have to know something of genetics and in particular of the chemical DNA, the agent of change.

The genetic blueprint

In every body cell there are forty-six chromosomes, made up of twenty-three pairs of thread-like structures, which contain genes. These genes

The genetic mix comes up with some intriguing differences alongside similarities. In each of the two brother and sister pairs here the hair colour is the same but one child has straight hair, the other curly.

carry the genetic blueprint in the form of DNA (deoxyribonucleic acid). The cells that we are talking about are infinitesimally small. Think of 28 g/1 oz of the chemical DNA, and imagine one millionth part of that; then imagine one millionth part of that millionth. That is how much DNA there is in a single human cell; that minute amount of chemical is enough to produce a baby consisting of a trillion cells.

Twenty-three chromosomes coming from the father's sperm and twenty-three from the mother's ovum join to make the baby's first cell. A baby's personal genetic code can be read by blood sampling. The DNA carries this code and it is as unique as fingerprints. Many characteristics are inherited: hair colour is one of the more obvious examples of pure inheritance – there is nothing we can do before, during or after birth to alter the natural colour of a baby's hair. There is, however, a certain amount of chance involved even in something as apparently simple as the inheritance of hair colour. The genes on each pair of chromosomes are thoroughly shuffled before being passed on, so every egg or sperm carries a unique set, which explains why no two people – not even 'identical' monozygotic twins, derived from a single fertilized egg – are ever exactly alike.

Genetic effects are not all evident at birth. Genetic influences continue to play a part in human development right into old age and, indeed, may be predominant in determining the nature of a person's death. It is often not appreciated that genes can lie dormant for many years, to be triggered by changes in the body.

How gender is determined

In Ancient Greece it was believed that the more excited a man was during sexual intercourse, the more likely he was to produce a male child. Geneticists study gender determination in a rather more prosaic way. The first major discovery was the role of the X and Y chromosomes. (Most chromosomes are identified by numbers but those to do with gender are named X and Y.) The male sperm has both an X and a Y chromosome, the female has two Xs. If the male passes on a Y the baby will be a boy, if the male passes on an X the baby will have two Xs and will be female.

Genetics and temperament

Temperament refers to a person's persistent, prevailing mood. Babies often display evidence of a particular temperamental bent within the first months or even the first days of life.

For many years it was believed that a person's temperament was formed entirely by environmental influences: a warm, loving home produces a warm, loving, placid baby. However, studies of twins give some support to the idea that there is a strong genetic element in temperament: identical (monozygotic) twins, whether they are brought up together or apart, show much more consistent similarity of temperament than fraternal (dizygotic) twins.

Genetic abnormalities

Genetic abnormalities may occur when a single chromosome or a part of a chromosome is missing, duplicated or out of place. The most common abnormality is Down's syndrome, caused by an extra chromosome at position 21 (or, much more rarely, by an extra piece of chromosome 21 being attached elsewhere). Some single-gene abnormalities are confined to one sex: haemophilia affects only boys, Turner's syndrome is only found in females.

However, most of the variation between individual children's development results from multiple-gene effects, rather than being caused by a deficiency in a single gene. For example, there is a wide range in the ages at which children become clean and dry. To some extent this is due to different patterns of genes. This example also provides a good illustration of the way that parental handling can play its part along with genetic factors: with sensitive care parents can train a child who is genetically disadvantaged at about the same time as others.

Genetic counselling

The best protection against genetic problems is to know your own genetic history and build family planning around this information. A family history consists of the medical and psychological history of your closest relatives: your parents and grandparents, brothers and sisters, aunts and uncles. Your partner will need to seek out this information, too. It is advisable to do this well before you decide to conceive.

Genetics tomorrow

In the 1960s the nature/nurture debate was in full swing: it was accepted that one had to look to genetic influences to explain purely organic factors, hair and eye colour for example, but it was fashionable in some circles to decry any contribution from inheritance to psychological aspects such as intelligence or personality.

Today a more balanced view prevails. A 1991 review of the topic sees behavioural genetics as being at the dawn of a new era, developing at a breathtaking speed; but at the same time the authors acknowledge that non-genetic influences can be at least as significant as genetic inheritance.

There is more to it than a simple redressing of the balance, however. In the last five or ten years our understanding of genetics as related to behaviour has advanced in leaps and bounds and we are on the edge of even more exciting discoveries, leading, it is hoped, to the drawing up of a complete human-gene map, enabling us to identify sets of specific genes that account for genetic variations in behaviour. New techniques make it possible to cut DNA into small pieces, thus allowing a minute examination of the details; this gives the opportunity to track a fragment of DNA as it passes from parent to child. One example of the practical use of these new techniques is found in the case of Duchenne muscular dystrophy, an inherited condition. Until recently, the only safeguard that could be offered to a woman who came from a family in which this condition occurred, and who might be a carrier, was amniocentesis during pregnancy and then a termination if the baby were found to be affected. Now genetic explorations can establish before conception whether a woman is actually a carrier or not.

Research is also now taking place into intra-uterine marrow transplantation and gene replacement. There is even discussion of manipulating the genes of very early embryos, which will allow the correction of inborn errors of metabolism that affect the central nervous system. Some day geneticists may be able to predict the susceptibility of an individual to a variety of common disorders such as premature vascular disease, diabetes, and cancer. It may even be possible to select such characteristics as height or hair colour – a prospect that has led some geneticists to warn against the development of 'designer children'.

The development of such techniques will not make the choices for parents any easier than they are now – far from it. When the likelihood of handicap can be predicted with a high degree of accuracy early in pregnancy or even before conception, sensitive issues arise. Children with disabilities can lead full, happy lives. Do we need a perfect child every time? Who decides such questions, individuals or society?

We are, however, a long way from a complete mapping, from the ability to point to certain genes, or combinations of genes, and to link them to certain behaviour. And even if the mapping were complete we would still have only part of the picture; for the full story we will still have to consider environmental features.

Genetics or Environment

Of all the areas in which genetic and environmental influences interact, two in particular have generated heated controversy. These are differences in general between boys and girls; and the role, nature and origin of intelligence. They are dealt with here since they form a bridge between influences that can be labelled primarily genetic and those that are principally social.

Gender differences

Males are more vulnerable than females: 120 males are conceived for every 100 females, but because male embryos are more delicate and are more likely to be miscarried, by the time babies are born the differential has been much reduced: 106 boy babies are born for every 100 girls.

Male vulnerability remains throughout life. Boys and men are more susceptible than girls and women to a wide variety of disorders including cerebral palsy, ulcers, mental retardation and some learning difficulties. Males are also more likely to have various sex-linked disorders such as colour blindness. One explanation of this vulnerability may be that the XY chromosome combination does not have as strong an immune system as an XX combination. In any case, the greater male vulnerability is clearly genetically determined.

There are also good grounds for assuming that differences in behaviour and preferences between the sexes are biological in origin. However, here there is an equally strong argument on the other side: boys will be boys and girls will be girls because they are taught to be so. Adults expect children to behave in a sex-stereotyped way and, generally, children obligingly do so.

In one series of experiments adults were introduced to a baby who, in appearance and dress, could be taken as either a boy or a girl. When they were told they were with a boy they were more likely to play and speak in a rough, horse-play fashion; when they believed the child was a girl they were more gentle.

If stereotyping begins as early as this, it is clearly not going to be easy to sort out the relative importance of the influence of genetics and environment. This subject will come up again in the course of this book. For the moment, let us stay with the judgement of John Money, who has researched and written widely in this field. His conclusion is·that hormones predispose towards certain sex-related behaviour but a child's experience will either facilitate or diminish hormonal influences.

Intelligence

The subject of intelligence, like that of gender stereotyping, lends itself to prejudice and misunderstanding, to fury well beyond the normal bounds of academic discussion. In this case, discussion is often bedevilled by a failure to grasp that the problems surrounding the notion of intelligence and those related to intelligence testing are not identical. We will try to unpack these two ideas.

The definition of intelligence

Here we run into an immediate stumbling block: there is no accepted definition of the word, yet we all think we know what it means. Various

Fathers are often less likely to engage in rough and tumble with their daughters than with their sons – but this little girl and her father are not hampered by stereotypes.

attempts have been made: in 1921 fourteen psychologists contributed to a symposium on the topic and produced fourteen definitions. Some suggestions have been:

- the ability to perceive relationships
- the ability to discriminate (that was Cicero)
- the ability to think about abstract notions
- the aggregate or global capacity of the individual to act purposefully, to think rationally and to deal effectively with his environment
- attention, adaptability and learning capacity

It is all too easy to fall back on an approach that is dangerously circular: intelligence is what is measured by intelligence tests. Intelligence tests, in turn (and here we may avoid the worst of the circularity) are judged in part by how well they predict attainment in school, so we can say that intelligence tests assess those mental qualities that underlie school success.

Immediately there are gaping holes: what about success in other areas? Do intelligence tests predict who will be good at business or at holding down a job, any job? Are they any help in discriminating between those who will have successful and unsuccessful marriages? No, they are not, because they are not designed to do these things. What is more, even as far as school attainment is concerned, they measure what is necessary but not sufficient, that is they do not take into account qualities such as persistence, application and drive, which also play a large part in academic achievement. For this reason, if no other, there can be no one-to-one relationship between measured intelligence and school success; the most we can have is a clear trend.

One commonly accepted approach which has practical value is to see intelligence not as a single whole but rather as a collection of components. Some psychologists assert that we are dealing with two broad factors: a general, underlying intellectual ability and a set of specific abilities. The existence of a general ability explains why there is a tendency for people who are good at one thing also to be good at others. On the other hand, this is no more than a trend, there are plenty of exceptions; and the notion of specific abilities allows one to explain why, for instance, some people are magnificent when dealing with words and hopeless when faced with a mathematical problem.

Critics of this approach argue that on the one hand it is simplistic: mathematics, for example, is a skill to which many different attributes contribute. And on the other they say that if we were to follow the specific abilities argument to its logical conclusion we would end up with hundreds of specifics, which would be unworkable.

A further complication is that some knowledge systems are immensely complex and yet seem to function similarly in all human beings. For example, even the severely retarded have no difficulty in perceiving the three-dimensional nature of an object, despite the fact that they receive the information in a two-dimensional form.

What contributes to intelligence

Setting aside the difficulties of definition, assuming that we can agree that there is such a phenomenon as intelligence, we can begin to look at the factors underlying it. In general there are two main contributors to intelligence: inheritance and environment. It is the opposition of these two in the past that has led to such controversy.

Supporters of the inheritance position point out that skin colour, build and other physical attributes are inherited: why then should the brain be excluded from this pattern? They refer to studies which indicate that identical twins have more similar intelligence profiles than fraternal twins.

The environmentalists will have none of this. They look to the way that children's all-round development, including height and weight, is affected by environmental influences such as nutrition, health care and the level of education offered. They point out that the neural characteristics of a brain can be altered by environmental factors. They say, rightly, that measured intelligence can be increased, for example by means of good preschool education. And they declare that environment explains all.

What can we make of this?

It seems reasonable to say that genes determine the maximum potential of a person's intelligence but that environmental influences determine the extent to which that potential is reached. This ducks the essential question: by how much can environmental influences alter a person's final intelligence? The only honest answer to this question is that we do not know and we are unlikely to know in the near future.

Intelligence testing

Those who construct modern intelligence tests do not attempt to isolate specific skills, they look for broad categories. So the Wechsler Scales, the most commonly used intelligence tests in the world, produce two overall scores related to verbal and non-verbal abilities. The most recently published tests covering the whole age range from two upwards, the fourth edition of the Stanford Binet Scale, has four domains: verbal reasoning, spatial reasoning, memory and mathematical ability.

The process of constructing a test goes as follows.

First, psychologists devise a series of questions and tasks related to reasoning, vocabulary, visual perception, memory, attention and fine motor skills, all of which are seen as being related to academic achievement.

Next, they give these tests to a random selection of children. Some tests are tried out only on fairly limited samples, but the most widely used tests, including both Wechsler and Stanford Binet, have been given to very large groups of children, taken from widely varying populations. The performance of these random samples provides a standard by which to judge others. The scores obtained from an intelligence test are usually expressed in terms of an intelligence quotient, or IQ. An IQ of 100 is average: 68 per cent of people fall into the range 85 to 115; 13.5 per cent have IQs between 115 and 129; another 13.5 per cent come between 70 and 84; 2.5 per cent are below 70 and 2.5 per cent above 130.

Tests are valid only for those children who closely resemble the group on whom the test was standardized. It is not valid to use an American test on African children because there is such a disparity in experience between the two groups. It is, however, more or less reasonable to use an American test on British children because the two cultures, although different in many ways, are sufficiently similar.

We should also point out that, to have any credence at all, a test must be administered by a properly trained professional.

A question that is often asked relates to the variation in test scores: if we test a child today and find an IQ of 100, will the score obtained in future also be 100?

If there are variations in the emotional or physical states of the child there may be differences in test scores. A child who is even mildly unwell may not be up to concentrating on matching patterns. Again, psychologists and others who administer tests do differ in their ability to bring out the best in children, though adequate training should minimize inconsistencies.

Even if the child is well and cheerful and the person giving the test well trained, there is still an expected margin of error of about seven points either way, so in the best of all conditions, when we repeat our test on a child who had a score of 100 we may get anything from 93 to 107. In terms of psychological testing, this is in fact a very small variation.

IQ tests are often criticized as being of no practical use. How does it help a teacher faced with a child who cannot read to know that he or she has an IQ of 95? While a precise score may be of little value, it does help in the production of a complete picture. In this particular case, the teacher, with evidence that the child's intelligence is normal, might want to try a different approach to the task of teaching the child. If it happened that the test also showed a marked discrepancy between verbal and non-verbal scores, this would certainly be useful information.

Of greater concern is the charge that a test result may be used to label a child and then, through the mechanism of the self-fulfilling prophecy, may come to determine his or her future. Label a child as unintelligent and you may well get an unintelligent performance.

It is not reasonable, however, to condemn intelligence tests out of hand because – like other useful tools – they may be misused. And we would say that, on balance, intelligence tests *are* useful tools. Provided that the person giving a test understands its limitations, provided that he or she has been properly trained, provided that the test chosen is appropriate for the child and for the questions that are being asked about the child, an intelligence test can yield valuable information.

The Social Context

In this section we deal with how children are influenced by society at large and, especially, by home and school. Each aspect is discussed separately; in practice, of course, they all interact.

Cultural differences

As the world becomes smaller, ideas, fashions, even languages become more widely shared. But the society into which a child is born still has much influence: each country, each subculture within a country, has its own way of treating babies and children, its own set of expectations.

Some differences are immediately visible – those related to food preferences being an example. Others are visible but harder to disentangle. Learning to walk, for instance, is a universal skill. But in many parts of Africa children learn to sit, crawl, stand and walk earlier than they do in the West. Arguments still continue on the origin of this difference, with one camp putting forward a genetic explanation and the other pointing to rearing patterns: it certainly seems that when African children are brought up in the same way as western children they learn to walk at the same rate.

Vast differences are observable, throughout the world, in the ways in which the newborn child is treated. In one culture, for instance, the baby's face is seen only by the mother for the first three months of life. There is also wide variation in the age of weaning, this generally coming later in poorer countries.

Some cultures give babies and toddlers a life without restraint. Then, suddenly, usually when a brother or sister comes along, they are cast out from this Garden of Eden and treated with harsh discipline. (It has been said that this is one reason for the repression of women in some cultures – they have never been forgiven for their treachery.)

Most nations, through their school system, exert on children pressures which tend to encourage those characteristics that are valued in their culture. In Chinese nursery schools children are encouraged to join in group activities; there is little evidence of individual efforts being valued. In Japan, children are under pressure to conform to a rigid school regime. In Britain, the United States and Australia, parents and teachers often try to maximize individuality and creativity.

Social background

Usually, anyone who knows a particular culture well will be able, on quite a brief acquaintance, to identify an individual's social background. Different societies have their own cues – accent, use of language, manner, dress. From this initial placing it is often possible to predict something of a person's choice of food and drink, holiday venues, reading matter. More importantly, membership of a particular social class may be associated with self-esteem or the lack of it, with good or ill health, with success or failure in school and work, with delinquency or propriety.

Generalizations about the influence of social background on child development are as fraught with problems as are most other generalizations: there are always exceptions and it is easy to oversimplify. However, most people would agree that there do tend to be marked differences in attitude in certain key areas between the members of different social classes. These attitude differences underlie the observable variations in lifestyle. Broadly speaking, the higher the class the more likely is the individual within that class to have his or her material needs satisfied, to have a sense of power and to be confident that he or she can influence those in positions of authority. As one moves down the social scale the struggle to survive becomes harder; and, not surprisingly, the sense of control may diminish.

We are speaking of general tendencies here. Even if success be considered only in the most worldly of terms, we can all point to successful people of humble origin and members of the upper classes who have, apparently, thrown away all the advantages of their background. Social class is one among many factors that interact with the individual characteristics of the child in shaping his or her development.

The family

Over the last twenty or thirty years, the average family size in many countries has diminished and structure has become much more variable. In the United States and Australia, for instance, approximately one in five children under the age of eighteen lives in a one-parent family. None the less, in most, if not all, parts of the world the majority of children still live in families with two parents who have been married only once.

Family style and atmosphere

Every family has its own individual lifestyle, its own rules about the way things are organized and decisions are made. However, some basic patterns may be distinguished. Some of the most illuminating research into family style was conducted by American psychologist Diana Baumrind at the University of California in the early 1970s. She identified four basic parental styles: authoritarian, permissive, authoritative and indifferent.

Authoritarian parents expect children to follow the rules set them without question. They look for respect for authority, especially their own.

Permissive parents see themselves as accepting their children as they are. Family rules are few and not always enforced. Such parents like to think of themselves as a resource to whom children can turn rather than shapers of minds.

Authoritative parents see the need to control children but they try to do so in a rational way that makes sense not only to them but to the children as well. Within limits, they encourage individual freedom and initiative.

Indifferent and uninvolved parents have little interest in what their children do and are often not even aware of where the children are.

Various studies have been done evaluating the influence of the different styles: the results strongly indicate that authoritative parents are by far the most likely to produce well-balanced, socially aware and successful children. The children of parents who adopt one of the other three styles tend, for different reasons, to show greater anxiety and insecurity and lower self-esteem.

The members of this family are clearly taking a great delight in the new baby, and in each other's company.

Labels within the family

Parents can affect their children a great deal simply by the way they talk about them. When they constantly call a child bright, tough, beautiful, lazy, easily bored, hyperactive, slow, dyslexic or clumsy, they are creating a label which, by gradually changing the child's perception of him or herself, can easily become a self-fulfilling prophecy. Though occasionally labels can be of value in reinforcing desirable behaviour, too often they emphasize the negative aspects of the child's personality and exaggerate problems. Even the most positive label can have a negative effect. For example, to call a child a genius, talented or gifted when he is none of these can lead to frustration or guilt if he does not achieve at a high level. The child may then, despite real natural ability, be turned off the activity in question.

Scapegoating is a particular form of labelling. It is often seen in families who have tensions and anxieties which they cannot express openly: the parents don't argue, or work out their frustrations directly – to do so would be to threaten the family's stability. Instead, usually quite unconsciously, they dump all their frustrations on one child, who is seen as a relatively safe outlet. This child then acts out the family's tensions and problems for them. A child who is made a scapegoat can become very disturbed and may eventually feel, and indeed be, excluded from the family.

To break this cycle, parents need to learn to be sensitive to the way they are treating this child. They also need to learn to express their feelings directly and appropriately – no easy task. Often it is a brother or sister who is the first to realize what is going on, but it is only rarely that a child, acting alone, is strong enough to change the family pattern. The family is likely to need outside adult help – perhaps in the form of family counselling – if it is to learn other ways of coping.

Mothers

'Unique, without parallel, established unalterably for a whole lifetime as the first and strongest love object and as the prototype of all later love-relations for both sexes.' So Freud, in *An Outline of Psychoanalysis*, defines the importance of the mother.

There are some who say that we are none of us truly adult until our mother has died and even then we go on, subconsciously perhaps, trying to please her.

These views are extreme, and would not hold true in every case. We cannot accept, for instance, that the mother is inevitably the strongest love object for all people. None the less, the central importance of the mother in most children's lives is indisputable. Various aspects of mothering are considered throughout this book. Here we pick up on just one: how children are affected when mothers work outside the home.

Throughout the world substantial numbers of mothers with preschool and school-age children are employed outside the home. The effects on children have been widely documented in many countries, including Britain,

The mother – source of love and security.

Israel, the United States and the Soviet Union; and generally, if not always, no unfavourable effects have been found.

Children of working mothers are no less healthy, physically, mentally, emotionally or socially. Indeed, in one study children whose mothers went out to work before they were of school age were found at the age of seven to be socially rather better adjusted. No difference has been shown in delinquency rates; evidence on school performance is inconclusive.

Of course, when comparisons are made between the children of mothers who work outside the home and those whose mothers do not, various other conditions have also to be taken into account. These include family size, social class, the mother's educational level, her attitude to work and to her children and the nature of the alternative care provided. Children whose alternative care arrangements are inconsistent or of a poor quality, for example, certainly suffer.

Fathers

Looking at older texts on child development one might be forgiven for thinking that fathers did not exist before the 1960s, when they suddenly became visible. The pendulum has swung and many eminent authorities now insist that fathers have a unique role to play in bringing up children and that any child who has to grow up without a father or a father figure is deprived. This is still not a universally accepted view, however.

Studies on the early relationship between father and baby are relatively few. John Bowlby's pioneering research on emotional attachment (see pages 141–8) laid the main emphasis on the role of the mother, and the popular interpretation of his work reinforced this. However, subsequent inquiry has shown that a child may form a primary attachment to the father; and that, in any case, children tend to form multiple attachments, seeking to have different needs met by different people.

Much more work has been done on tracing children's progress in terms

A warm and supportive father will contribute enormously to a child's confidence and self-esteem.

of the relationships they had with their fathers. The evidence is that a powerful positive influence is exerted by warmth and closeness in a father. Boys with fathers who are caring, competent and seen to contribute actively to family life are more likely to grow up self-confident and academically successful. Girls, too, show greater confidence in themselves, and there is evidence that both men and women who have had a strong and loving father are more likely to form good relationships with others and to make satisfying marriages.

So research evidence supports the assumption we might naturally make, that the child with a loving father is at a psychological advantage. We should beware, however, of assuming from this that the child living without a father will necessarily be psychologically crippled. Studies of families where fathers are absent have shown that this disadvantage can be overcome. This is far more likely to happen, though, in a family where mother and children have strong emotional support from a man – perhaps a grandfather, an uncle or a family friend – who can take over something of the father's role. History records instances where such a father figure has given more to children than many a natural father ever does. 'Father' in this context is not a biological term.

Position in the family

First children are born into a privileged position: they enjoy the undivided attention of their parents. If they remain only children they will continue to have their parents to themselves and never feel the pain of being displaced by a brother or sister.

First-born children are different in many ways from others. They are under more pressure to achieve and often do achieve at a higher level. Perhaps because their parents have more time for them, and there are greater possibilities for a relationship on a more adult level between adult and child, on average, they develop more complex language skills at an earlier age than others, they have a higher measured intelligence, and they seem to be more ambitious and more resilient to stresses, even to physical demands. One study of undernourished children has shown that the influence of a poor diet was less marked in first-born children than in others, as though being born first gave some kind of protection. Parents certainly tend to be, and to remain, more protective and more restrictive and overprotective of their first child than they are of subsequent children.

Only children tend to have the characteristics of the first born, to an even more striking degree.

Brothers and sisters

The relationship with a brother or sister may be the most long-lasting of one's life. In the normal course of things, parents die many years before their children, and relationships with partners are usually not formed until adulthood. Brothers and sisters are often an important part of each other's lives from earliest childhood into old age. These relationships have a strong influence on a child's development: a warm, caring relationship can have a very positive effect, a hostile brother or sister can influence the degree to which a child in turn becomes hostile to others.

When brothers and sisters have a good relationship they can be a great support to each other, especially when family problems arise. For example, quarrels between the parents can sometimes leave children feeling emotionally abandoned by both mother and father. In such a situation a brother or sister often provides a degree of emotional protection and may even, to some extent, substitute emotionally for the parents.

A myth of child development is that all brothers and sisters fight, or fluctuate back and forth between love and hate. Some do, but others consistently remain firm, close friends. There is another myth that older children are always jealous of their younger brothers or sisters. Sometimes they are, but jealousy may also go the other way, from younger children to older; and there are families in which jealousy does not exist. A wide range of behaviour is evident, with differences both between and within families.

It would, however, be foolish to say that rivalry between brothers and sisters is not common. In the first months, when the baby becomes a reality and begins to take up the family's time and attention, most older children exhibit some signs of disturbance. They may regress, becoming naughty especially when parents are giving attention to the baby. They may be demanding, unable to settle down and play. Such behaviour is not difficult to understand. Even in the most loving and understanding of families, an older child is almost bound to feel to some extent displaced by the new baby. This feeling is likely to be reinforced by the practical difficulties of life with a baby. The mother has to respond to a whole new set of demands from the baby at a time when she is still feeling physically and emotionally exhausted by the birth, and almost certainly suffering from lack of sleep. She is, therefore, less likely to find the time or the energy to play with or pay attention to an older child. She may well find the child's demands something of a last straw and, as well, be guilty about feeling so. It is hardly surprising that during the period after the birth of a baby mothers tend to give more orders to their older children, to have more confrontations and to initiate fewer conversations and games. The father's attitude can make all the difference here: if the father can both give support to his partner and pay extra attention to the older child the family is more likely to emerge from this difficult time relatively unscathed – indeed, it may even be strengthened.

Once the initial reaction to the new baby is over, more mature behaviour, the beginning of social awareness, may gradually emerge in the older child. Even at a very young age – eighteen months to two years – a child may become concerned about the baby and may be able to empathize with and interpret a brother or sister's moods and needs. Toddlers often know exactly what to say to babies, how to get their attention, how to distract them and how to get them to understand short sentences. When the baby cries it may be the toddler who gives comfort. Even teasing requires some understanding. Knowing exactly what irritates a brother or sister is one demonstration of an appreciation of the other's personality.

Middle childhood brings a greater equality in the relationship: during this period brothers and sisters may spend almost half their time with each other, more than with anyone else. Later, as one child reaches adolescence before the other, a divide can often open up, to be bridged as the younger one reaches a similar stage.

There is no conclusive evidence that problems are more or less likely to occur between children of the same sex. Children under five are more likely to be upset by the birth of a brother or sister than those who are older; however, once the few months around the birth have passed, it does not seem to make much difference whether children are close together in age or widely spaced.

A moment of closeness shared by brother and sister, reflecting the warmth of a friendship that may endure throughout their lives.

Temperament is a more reliable guide: children of similar temperament tend to get on better than those who are different – although there can also be problems if they are too alike. When considering relationships, it is always worth asking whether two children would have been friends if they had not happened to be born in the same family.

At the same time, as British psychologist Judy Dunn points out, we can understand the relationships between brothers and sisters only when we look at them in the context of the emotional climate of the family as a whole. Perhaps the strongest influence on the way children relate to each other is the way their parents behave towards them. If children feel that their parents are unfair, or favour one child more than another, there will almost inevitably be problems between the children. This does not mean that you should go to extremes to make sure you treat all your children exactly alike. In fact, parents never do manage to treat their children in precisely the same way, and when they try to, they invariably make a botch of it. As always, parents need to aim at sensitivity to the needs of each child as an individual. Conflict is far less likely to arise between children where both perceive themselves as loved and valued, and consider that they are fairly treated.

The brothers and sisters of sick or handicapped children have recently received attention from researchers, and the possible effects of being in this position have been shown to vary widely. Sometimes other children in the family seem to suffer psychologically more than the sick child; in other cases they gain in that they grow to be more understanding of the needs of others (there is some tendency for the brothers and sisters of sick children to join one of the helping professions). Much depends on the extent to which the healthy children have to shoulder burdens that are too much for their years, much on the support available to their parents. If the parents have a network of help they are more likely to be able to sustain their healthy children as well as the sick one, and will not need to lean too heavily on younger members of the family.

Grandparents

In many cultures, grandparents are honoured as the dispensers of wisdom. The Roman Catholic Church has added a special prayer for grandparents to the service of baptism – perhaps in recognition of their influence. Grandparents indeed often have a very special place in passing on cultural and religious values; but while it can be a great benefit to have a wise grandparent who knows and helps with traditions, carried to an extreme the influence of the grandparent can lead to difficult situations. If a grandparent is of an authoritarian bent and wishes to subordinate both parents, as well as the child, to his or her wishes, the effect can be disastrous. Particularly in a cross-cultural or inter-faith marriage, an authoritarian grandparent who insists on certain cultural or religious observances can cause great tension.

The kind of grandparents that people become is to quite a large extent

There is often a special bond between children and grandparents, a particular warmth and understanding in their relationship.

culturally determined. In some traditions grandparents are expected to remain more or less remote, in others it is not unusual for the grandmother to be handed the baby at birth. Present lifestyle also influences an individual's response to grandparenthood. If grandparents are alone, with few outside interests, their grandchildren may become the centre of their lives.

Grandparents who go so far as attempting to take over the parents' role can pose a serious threat to both parents' self-esteem: it is no accident that cultures with a tradition of powerful grandmothers have a string of jokes about the awfulness of the mother-in-law. Ironically, mothers who have allowed their own children to be taken over in this way are the most likely to try to take over themselves when their own grandchildren are born.

For other people, being a grandparent is more a matter of juggling time and schedules to take on this new responsibility. Once in a while they may appear and take their grandchild out on a special outing or provide a special treat. But they never interfere, never become personally involved with everyday problems and do not give advice.

Most grandparents fall somewhere between these two extremes. And, whatever the grandparenting style, it does seem that there is often a special bond between grandparent and grandchild. It can appear, to wondering parents, that the generation gap has disappeared, and that grandparents understand their grandchildren better than they ever did their own children. This may be because they usually do not need to deal with their grandchildren on an everyday basis, or to be involved in disciplining them. They can be indulgent and generous and relaxed in a way they might not have been able to be with their children.

When the family breaks up

Much of our understanding of the effects on the family of death and divorce have come from two large-scale studies carried out in the United States by E. Mavis Hetherington and her colleagues and by Judith Wallerstein. The overall, perhaps surprising, conclusion is that, in general, children seem to suffer more disturbance when their parents divorce than they do when they lose a parent through death.

This may be, in part at least, because there is frequently more support available to a child whose father or mother has died than to the child of divorced parents. Other family members and friends often feel a great desire to offer love and caring to the child who has been bereaved, while divorce, on the other hand, may cut the child off from many members of the wider family, as well as from the parent who has left. Again, the loss brought about by death is irrevocable. Terrible though it is, it must be accepted, and so it is accepted. Divorce can always be revoked, and the children of divorced parents often yearn for their parents to come together again – a longing which keeps the wound open. Feelings of anger and guilt are also stronger in the children of divorced parents. And it must be remembered that divorce may have been preceded, and may also be followed, by a lengthy period of discord between the parents, which can be deeply disturbing for the children.

Judith Wallerstein, in her study on children of divorced parents in California between 1970 and 1980, found that 90 per cent of the children she interviewed showed, immediately after the break-up, acute distress and a wish that parents would reunite. Five years later there was evidence that children could recover psychologically, providing that they had sufficient emotional support within the post-divorce family. Ten years later, as they entered adulthood, they tended to be very concerned lest they, too, should repeat the pattern and make unhappy marriages.

She also traced certain behaviour patterns shown by children around the time of a divorce. Children who are very young when the divorce occurs, up to about five or six, tend to regress, showing sleep disturbances in particular, and seeming to fear abandonment by the parent they are living with – to the extent that they may want to keep him or her always within reach. A child of this age may refuse to go anywhere without the parent and may resist when the parent wants to go out alone. Depression is seen in seven to eight year olds, who grieve for the absent parent and often continue to hope for a reconciliation. Conflicts of loyalty are high at this age. Between nine and twelve children seem to feel the need to take sides. In all these age groups children tend to do less well at school than before. The picture at adolescence is more varied.

What parents can do

When parents divorce, children are often left very much in the dark about the whole business. The adults involved can be so preoccupied by their own problems that talking to their children seems beyond their capacity: but for the children's sake they must make this effort. The children need to know what is happening and why – especially why. It is essential to get across a clear message about the reasons, for otherwise there is the risk that the children will blame themselves.

Once the divorce has taken place, children cope best if they are allowed and encouraged to maintain good relations with both their parents, to forgive them. They also need to come to terms with the permanency of the situation. Young children often hope and imagine that their parents will come together again. There is no need to be brutal about putting an end to this daydream – if children fantasize it is probably because they need to. At the same time, it is important not to encourage the idea that it is likely to happen. It is usually best to say something like 'Yes, it would be lovely, wouldn't it, but . . .', implying that there is a question mark over the event.

Single-parent families

Following divorce or the death of a parent, the task of raising a child successfully takes on a new dimension. Physically, emotionally and economically, the strains of being a single parent can be considerable. None of these problems can be considered in isolation. For example, in order to bring in an adequate income for the family, a single parent may have to become more involved in work and thus have far less time and energy for being a parent; the parent may feel guilty about paying less attention to the child but resentful of the financial burden. Children, too, can feel resentful and blame the parent for the situation, yet guilty because they perceive that he or she is making sacrifices on their behalf.

At the same time, people who divorce may want more than ever to be successful in their role as parents. Single parents who have chosen to raise their children alone may feel a need to justify their choice by demonstrating how satisfactory a life they can offer. On the positive side, parent and child often become very close. They provide companionship for each other, make plans together, worry about problems together. The child sees the value in his or her contribution to family life and often takes on more responsibilities. Unfortunately there can be a negative aspect to this closeness too, as parent and child can become overinvolved, and sometimes the child may need to take extreme steps to break free at adolescence.

Stepfamilies

When, for whatever reason, the original family breaks up, one possible outcome is the setting up of a new family, with a stepmother or father and possibly stepbrothers and sisters. No matter how good the intentions of everyone concerned, a stepfamily can never be the same as the original unit, and there are often additional strains: memories, good or bad, of the departed parent will to some extent colour the attitudes of those who knew him or her. Again, remarriage often brings together people who are at different stages in their own developmental timetable: a young mother may have to cope simultaneously with the birth of her own baby and the transition into adolescence of stepchildren. Establishing new family rules and customs takes time, a new financial arrangement may cause stress, settling into a new home can be even harder. On the other hand, there can be advantages: parents can share responsibilities, the hitherto single person will have a new source of support, stepparents can bring much to the children they are caring for.

Studies so far conducted indicate that, despite all the possible problems the remarriage of a parent brings, in most cases it has no discernible adverse effects on children's development. Most children do no worse or better at school than before and the majority enjoy satisfactory home relationships. For some, though, there is strain. When the remarriage follows divorce, the extent to which the children remain in contact with the parent who has left continues to be highly significant. Generally, children cope with their lives much better if they can retain contact with both parents; and this is so even when the parents are still in conflict with each other.

Adoption

The development of the adopted child is in most dimensions no different from the development of the child living with his or her biological parents. None the less, adoption does raise some special difficulties, which must be recognized.

The pull between nature and nurture may have a poignant meaning for you if you are adoptive parents, for you may have only the sketchiest information about the biological parents of your child. Even when details are available they are often not passed on as freely as might be wished. This may mean that you do not have a full medical history, which can have serious implications, particularly if there is any possibility of genetic problems. The more information you can gather, from social workers, doctors or other sources, the better able you will be to anticipate your child's health needs, and to inform the child as he or she approaches adulthood.

As adoptive parents you are even less likely to have any indication of what your child's native talents or inclinations might be, so you will need to be open-minded and make sure that he or she is exposed to a wide variety of experiences. But, really, this is just as it should be for parents bringing up a child who is biologically their own – who may make guesses based on their own preferences and family history, but are also unable to predict their child's abilities with any certainty.

Temperamentally, an adopted child may well be different from any member of the immediate family; having a child with a different temperament can be a demanding experience, but, provided that the family is flexible in its approach, it may also be an enriching one.

No matter what age a child is when he or she is adopted, the initial period of adjustment can be difficult. All the members of the family, including any other children, natural or adopted, need preparation. Counselling is sometimes available for adopting families, and can be extremely helpful.

If you are adopting a baby you are unlikely to have the full nine months to prepare for the arrival, and when the child comes you may not be sure that you will be able to keep him or her permanently. Babies need to be given the chance to form a close attachment with their adoptive parents, and this may be difficult if the process of adoption is not finalized and parents are reluctant to invest their emotions completely . If a child has been in hospital or with the biological mother for even a few days, he or she may react to the change by fussing, not sleeping, or refusing to feed. But most babies, adopted or not, have problems of this kind at some stage, and, given time and care, will settle down.

Toddlers or preschool children may remember traces of their former life and may go through periods when they have trouble eating and sleeping and are fearful or wary of you. They may need to test your limits, and will feel more secure when they know the rules and what boundaries you draw. Again, all children need limits, but it may be particularly difficult to set them when you want to be totally accepting.

Taking an older school-age child into your family can be even more demanding. Children who are adopted at this age have often had great difficulties to cope with – they may have had to contend with abuse, in one form or another, or have suffered the loss of their parents. They may feel angry, depressed and be in need of counselling. Helping children who have been through deeply damaging experiences calls for great love, patience and skill. None the less, with the security of a permanent home and caring family, they may be able to overcome past problems and move on to a more confident adolescence.

All adoptive parents are faced with the difficult task of making a child their own, while being honest about the fact that he or she is not their own. It is important for children to know from the beginning that they are adopted: if they believe that they are the natural children of their adoptive parents and find out later that they not, this can result in deep feelings of distrust and resentment. Many adopted children, when they become adults, try to find and meet their biological parents. Most of them say their desire to do this stems from a need to fill in some of the blanks in their sense of identity; it should not be taken as in any way a rejection of their adopted family.

The impact of education

Of all social influences, it is certainly the family that has the strongest effect on how children develop. The relative impact of education is a more controversial matter. A question sometimes asked in educational and political circles is whether schools really make much difference in the long run to how children turn out as adults. Another question follows on: if schools do have an influence, is one school really much better than another?

When there is a match between the expectations and values of the home and the school the question of schools making a difference scarcely arises,

The quality of education children receive is inevitably of great concern to parents.

since one complements the other. When there is a mismatch, however, we may wonder to what extent one can counteract the other.

In the 1960s, there was in many countries a strong lobby to the effect that the power of the family was so all-pervasive that school could have relatively little influence. However, research undertaken since then has provided a counterbalance to this argument.

Over the last twenty-five years or so there has been wide-ranging debate on the value of preschool education for disadvantaged children. The centre of this discussion has been the United States, where it was thought, hoped, in the 1960s, that Project Headstart, the most extensive (and expensive) set of preschool programmes the world has ever known, was going to provide poor children with compensatory education to allow them to take their place as equals in the school system.

Early results were exciting: measured intelligence went up and children seemed to be learning more. Later came a period of disillusion, for the gains in IQ washed out within a few years and the children who had received the extra help seemed no better off than a control group who had received none. But later still, when the children who had had the extra help were in their late teens, studies showed that those who had been through well-designed preschool programmes had in fact done better in school and, even more importantly, they had had fewer brushes with the law and were more likely to be employed.

Impressive preschool provision has also been made in India through the Integrated Child Development Scheme, which provides extra nutrition and the teaching of basic hygiene as well as preschool education. This scheme is not perfect, it has not solved all the problems of Indian education, but, over and over again, evaluations have shown that children benefit from taking part in it.

At the other end of the school age scale, some research into the effect of secondary schools has also shown interesting results. In 1979 the psychiatrist Michael Rutter and his colleagues published the results of their research into the degree to which individual schools varied in their effect on children's academic progress, behaviour in and out of school and attendance. Their conclusion was that in all these areas the school environment was influential. More recently, an analysis of public examination results in Britain in 1989 found wide differences between the results achieved by schools taking pupils of similar ability.

We look at education in more detail later in this book. There is one further point that should be made here: it is an unfortunate fact that major decisions about educational matters are frequently made by politicians, who base their conclusions on ideologies rather than on an understanding of education and of children. Too often it is the ballot box, rather than the classroom, that determines what kind of education is offered. On the evidence we have looked at here, it certainly seems that education makes a difference to our children. We all need to do what we can to ensure that they receive the best education that is available.

Resilience

Why are some children so much better equipped than others to face problems? How is it that some withstand so well the effects of poverty, divorce, the death of a loved one? Why do some transcend their backgrounds while others are pulled down?

These are challenging questions. There is no doubt that some children do seem to manage difficult situations better than others. They are resilient where others are vulnerable, they emerge, apparently indomitable, from situations which have defeated others.

The roots of resilience

If we could discover where the roots of resilience lie, could we perhaps help children to be more resilient? In John Bowlby's view, an important difference between vulnerable and resilient children can be found in the quality of their early relationships, particularly their attachment to their mother or to a mother figure: warm, continuous, intimate early relationships bring a sense of security. Children who develop the confidence that parents will be there when they are needed repeat this confident behaviour pattern in their relationships with other people and have a firm base to act from when faced with adversity. In contrast, children who are rejected by their parents learn to expect to be turned away if they look to people for comfort. They do not develop sufficient confidence to attempt to make relationships with anyone, and they will have little to support them when under stress. They may become very unhappy adults.

However, while acknowledging that patterns of attachment tend to persist over a lifetime, at no point does Bowlby say that these patterns are necessarily irreversible. On the contrary, he is optimistic about the potential for change, since each person's life is what he calls 'a unique pathway'. The infant may be born into unfavourable conditions, but if he or she later passes into a nurturing environment, the vulnerable child can become a resilient adult.

Other theorists favour a multifaceted explanation. Michael Rutter contends that temperament and intelligence both contribute to resilience, as does the patterning of stressful experiences themselves.

Resilient children, it is argued, may receive messages from their genetic system that are different from those received by the more vulnerable child. When some children feel stressed, their system triggers a high anxiety response and they literally feel different from those who receive other messages. The way children express their feelings in a crisis can be a valuable pointer to the way they are likely to cope in the long term. Those who can openly express their emotions of grief or anger tend to survive better than those who close up.

Intelligence seems to be a factor in children's ability to cope with adverse social conditions: clever children are less likely to be pulled down even by an emotionally impoverished home and family life. This may be because of their greater skill in problem-solving, or it may be that they are treated better at school and in other social situations, which compensates in some degree for the inadequacy of what they receive at home. Most probably, each makes some contribution.

The more successful children are at school, the more rewarding their friendships, and the more worthwhile they feel in themselves, the more likely they are to be resilient. This is hardly surprising, for clearly such children have more resources to sustain them. In particular, we know from adult studies that people with close relationships are less likely to have mental breakdowns. They have people to turn to for help; and it may also be that the qualities which make children or adults able to form close relationships are the very qualities that are needed for resilience.

The timing of stress may be important too, since children are more resilient to particular experiences at different stages of life. We have already mentioned the way divorce appears to have different effects on children of different ages. Separation from the mother incurred by a stay in hospital is known to have more negative effects on children between six months of age and four years than it does on younger babies and older children.

The cumulative effect of multiple stresses should also be considered. Children who suffer a number of stressful situations may simply be worn down by the successive blows. It may not be the first stressful situation which finds a child unable to cope, but the second or third.

Fostering resilience

In part at least, resilience is a learned response. When children are uncertain they look to their parents for clues which signal the parents' feelings, and then they react accordingly. So children's interpretations of the situation they live in come largely from their parents. Resilient parents may model successful coping methods for their children. Parents can also help their children to cope by preparing them for stressful situations.

The protective power of preparation

In everyday life children need to learn to cope with many potentially stressful situations as part of growing up, learning to take responsibility and becoming independent. It is not usually the new situation in itself which makes children over-anxious, it is the fear of what is to come – the unknown and the uncontrollable. If you prepare them in advance for what is going to happen, they will almost always be much better able to cope.

Moving house

In lists of life-events which cause stress in adults, moving house rates high. It is a stressful event for children too. A young baby is not likely to be unduly disturbed by a move unless it disrupts the parents' routines, but it is not long before babies have a sense of their surroundings and come to recognize changes. Toddlers and small children know their surroundings, they have created special places for themselves: they know the shelf that they can reach for pots and pans to play with, the stairs they love to climb, where they and their parents sleep. For school-age children a move may well involve not only leaving their familiar home, but also changing school; most troubling of all, it will probably mean moving away from their friends.

Something else to remember is that moving is often part of a chain of disturbing events. If a house move has been brought about as a result of a divorce or a death in the family, or even because the birth of a new baby means that more room is needed, the change of surroundings is going to be part of a cumulative pattern of stress for the child.

Even when there are no such related problems, but especially if there are, you need to prepare children for a move. Explain to them why you are going to a new house, talk about the house you are going to, show them photographs. Talk to them about leaving their friends and suggest ways they can keep in touch. Take them on a tour of the neighbourhood, and, if you can, arrange for them to meet some children in the area before you move. You should certainly organize a preliminary visit to a new school. You might consider taking them around the house too – but think carefully: other people's furniture, or no furniture, can give a false picture.

A new baby

If you are expecting a baby, you should start preparing your other children early in the pregnancy. There is nothing to be gained by putting off telling them until the birth is imminent, and risking their finding out at second hand or by accident. Most children are sensitive to changes taking place around their mother, they will be conscious that something is going on and if they begin to feel anxiety building up they may worry.

Once they know what is happening, most children are fascinated to see the 'bump' growing and are interested in hearing about how babies are born and how they themselves were born. They want to feel included in the plans. Talking about the baby, reading books together, watching television programmes about babies being born all help.

It is worth remembering that 'a new brother or sister' may mean one thing to parents and quite another to children. Most children imagine a

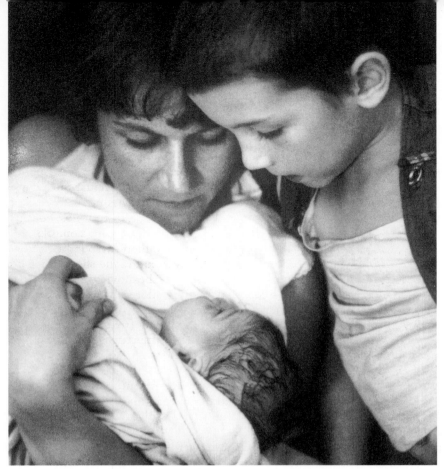

Preparing your child for the arrival of the new baby will help him to feel involved.

playmate – understandably, especially as they may have heard their parents saying, for months or years, 'Jane needs a playmate – she should have a brother or sister.' They will not expect that the baby will be demanding and helpless unless they are prepared for it.

Preparing for hospital

A frightened child alone in a hospital bed, not knowing what is going to happen, surrounded by unknown people, without even familiar toys to play with, is a heartrending sight – and yet, in the midst of worry, the need to make arrangements, pack pyjamas, talk with doctors, organize a home and the care of other children, it is no wonder that parents often do not find time to prepare a child for the hospital or remember to pack favourite toys.

When hospitalization occurs unexpectedly there is often no time for preparation, so it is important to discuss hospital with your children even if there is no immediate reason to think they will be ill. Books about hospitals are available at bookshops and often from hospitals. Films and videos about children going into hospital can also be helpful, especially if you can watch them together and explain what is happening.

If there is prior warning, it is well worthwhile asking the hospital if you and your child (not forgetting brothers and sisters) may visit the ward, to meet the staff and to become familiar with the surroundings and the layout of the rooms. Whether there is warning or not, do remember to take a favourite toy or two, to help your child feel more at home.

Preparation should not stop when the child is on a ward. Once there he or she is likely to be bombarded with a succession of events which can be more worrying for a child than the illness itself. Psychiatrist and author Elisabeth Kübler-Ross has described with sensitivity and understanding the needs of the child in hospital.

'We are of the belief that children should be dealt with honestly and openly, that they should not be promised toys for good behavior, that they should be told when a procedure is going to hurt. Not only should they be told what is going to be done, but they should also be shown. We very often use a doll or teddy bear and allow the children to do the procedure on the teddy bear or the doll, so they know exactly what they have to face. This does not mean that they don't cry . . . but they know that you have been honest with them and they will accept the procedure much more easily than if you had lied to them at the beginning of a serious illness.'

Preparation for death
There are two myths about young children's response to the death of a loved one: that they do not understand what death is and that they are not capable of feeling deeply sad.

The concept of death is complex, made up of many components. Young children, indeed, with their limited experience, tend to have only a hazy concept of death. They often expect dead animals and people to come to life again. George Sand recalled how she was told at the age of four that her father had been killed in a riding accident; next day she asked her mother, 'Is papa still dead today?' The fact that children can have such misunderstandings is all the more reason to talk to them about death and, most importantly, to allow them to ask questions.

Children are going to come across death whether we like it or not. It is sad when a pet dies, but you can use their loss to help them come to a greater understanding. Have a simple ritual and bury the body, marking the grave; allow them to grieve; and answer questions truthfully.

Gradually the concept of death develops. By around five or six most children have some idea that death is universal. Almost all children of eight or nine have something quite close to an adult understanding.

Preparing a child for the death of someone known to be ill may seem at times to be beyond adults who are themselves caught up in their own anticipatory mourning. But there is good evidence that children who have been carefully prepared, and who have had a chance to talk through their feelings, cope better with the loss when it occurs.

After the death, going through the ritual of a funeral or a wake can be a help to children. And, again, children need to ask questions and have them answered in a direct way. Telling children that the person who has died has 'gone to sleep' only serves to make the situation worse – they may well become terrified of going to sleep themselves, or of the idea of anyone they love going to sleep. Children's greatest fear is that they will be abandoned, left uncared for and alone. This, for them, is the worst of the threats associated with death and they need a lot of help and reassurance to deal with it.

The death of a parent

It is when a parent dies that the threat of abandonment comes closest. But even in these devastating circumstances, children can be helped to cope. John Bowlby found that there were three conditions that helped children to cope with the death of a parent: a secure relationship with both parents before the death; prompt and accurate information about what has taken place; the comforting presence of the other parent or another loved and loving adult.

If a parent has an illness which is likely to end in death, children need to be told, by someone they know and trust and in language they will understand, that their mother or father is extremely ill and may die. Any questions they may ask should be answered honestly. They should be assured that everything will be done to make their mother or father comfortable – but that everyone does die sometime. In these circumstances there is a great temptation to reassure children, but it is not fair to them to make a promise which cannot be kept.

Whether or not a dying parent sees a child must be up to the parent. Some want to spend their last moments with their child, others feel they wish the child to remember them as they were before they became so ill. But provided that the parent is willing, and depending on how sensitively such visits are approached, they can help children cope with their feelings, and have a more accurate picture of what is happening.

If the death is sudden there is no time for preparation, but children still need to be told, with sensitivity but honesty, what has happened.

After the death, children, like adults, need to mourn, although they may not express their grief in an adult fashion. Attending the funeral may give them an opportunity to share and express their sorrow and to see others showing their feelings. If the family are comfortable with the idea of the child seeing the body, this can help too; children who have seen what the parent looks like in death are less likely to be troubled by disturbing fantasies. If at all possible, through all this time of death and mourning, there should be a sensitive and loving adult readily available to support and care for the child. If the surviving parent is for the time unable to manage this, or only able to be available to the child to a limited degree, a relative or a family friend can sometimes take on this role.

The ways in which children express their feelings after the death of a parent will of course be dependent on their age at the time of the death. Especially if it is the mother who has died, it can be very difficult to settle a baby with a new caregiver. In extreme cases, a baby may sleep poorly and lose all interest in feeding, or in the surroundings. This is not surprising – the child must miss his or her mother desperately, and there is no way of explaining what has happened to a little baby. However, provided that they are treated with steadfast, loving care, most babies will go on to form an attachment to the new caregiver, and will develop normally.

Preschool and young school-age children mourn, but not as an adult would. They may be crying, in the depths of despair, and a few minutes later be out playing, apparently cheerfully. This is not an indication that their grief is shallow, only that their concentration span is shorter than an adult's. It is important to remember, too, that for children play is often a way of expressing deep emotions.

Older children begin to understand the loss intellectually, but their comprehension is still limited, and so it is particularly important that they should be told the facts as clearly as possible. If they are left in confusion they can easily come to feel that somehow they have caused the death or that their father or mother died because he or she did not want to be with them. If they seem anxious and worried, they need to be encouraged gently to talk. Sometimes a clear, authoritative description of their parent's death can help a lot, setting their minds at peace.

Talking about the dead person, sharing memories and feelings, showing photographs – all these simple means help children, as they do adults, gradually to come to terms with their loss. As questions come up they should be given clear and truthful answers. Children need to be helped to remember their dead mother or father in realistic terms: there is no necessity to turn a dead parent into a god or a saint.

The death of a child

When it is the child who is dying the task of preparation can seem insurmountable. How on earth can you communicate with a child of six about his or her own death? The answer to this question is more straightforward than you might think: what you need to do is to open the way for the child to talk. Most children over the age of five or so (some say even younger) who have been very seriously ill for any length of time know that there is a chance that they may die. They have probably known other children with the same condition who have died, they are more than likely to have overheard adults' conversations. Their big anxiety is that they will be separated from their loved ones. If adults refuse to talk about it they are in danger of increasing the child's anxiety since there may be so many worrying questions unanswered.

A six year old in a London hospital provided a moving example of how talking openly about death can help a dying child. The little girl knew she was dying, and one night she told her mother that she was worried about going to heaven because she thought she would be lonely there, she did not know if her parents could visit heaven like they had visited hospital. After a long talk with her parents, she made plans for how she would be able to play in heaven with her good friend Adam, who had died in the bed next to her in hospital a few months before. She slept peacefully that night and died, also peacefully, a few days later.

Adolescents facing death can have a harder task, for they share many adult perceptions. 'It's all such a waste, I won't even take my exams now,' said one sixteen year old. They too need to be given an opportunity to talk – but may prefer to remain silent.

In the brief review above we have touched on a number of influences that impinge on children in both the long and the short term. A question that is often put is the extent to which early experiences go on affecting children or adults. How continuous are they?

Continuity and change

The child, it is said, is father of the man. We are not, it is also said, prisoners of our past. These views exemplify one of the constant tensions in developmental psychology: how do developmental processes bring about stability on the one hand and change on the other? Can we argue that stability overrides change, that one's adult psychological state is somehow fixed in childhood, or is this too simplistic a view?

In the 1950s many people believed that personality was consistent. Some commentators thought that inadequate mothering, for example, led to irreversible psychological damage. Examination of the evidence led to a different view: the long-term effects of early experiences are to a large extent dependent on subsequent experience. The New Zealand psychologist Jack Tizard has contributed to our understanding of this. In his view, continuities do occur but there is a constant interplay between the characteristics of the person, built up over the years, and the present influences impinging on him or her.

A 1989 review of the evidence, by Michael Rutter, emphasizes the importance of considering humans in their social context, a context which includes key phases in adult life – marriage and child-bearing being only two – as well as in childhood. Within this context, both continuities and discontinuities are to be expected. At puberty, for example, there are large-scale physical developments associated with psychological change, but the adolescent brings with him or her a pattern of thought, a set of attitudes, which will to some extent determine how he or she responds to the challenges of physical change. In some ways this exemplifies the whole argument: the outcome of developmental transitions is partly, but only partly, determined by previous experience.

Opposing views on nature and nurture have now merged into consensus; it is likely that the debate on continuity and change will reach a similar resolution. If we are going to understand children we must adopt a balanced view of this as of other controversies. In the chapters that follow we aim to take a broad perspective on children's development.

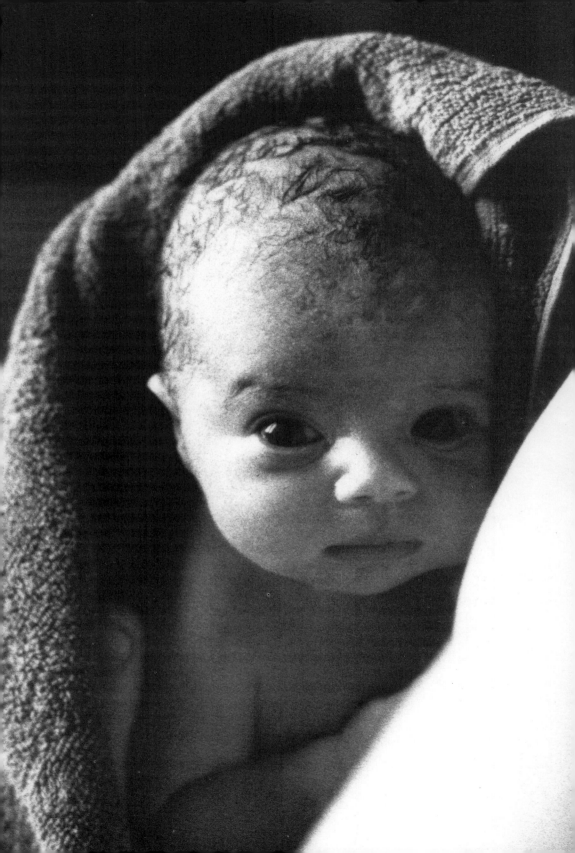

2 THE NEWBORN CHILD
the first weeks of life

Let us begin at the beginning – tracing a baby's development from the earliest hours in the womb to the first days after birth. From the moment of fertilization, your baby's first cell contains, encoded in genetic instructions, all the ingredients needed to make this particular human being. Your daughter or son is already an individual. At the same time, even in the womb, her or his development may be affected by you, the parents.

Before Birth

There has been much debate, among parents, doctors, philosophers and politicians, on the question of when human life begins. Some hold that a human being exists from the moment of conception; others that the fetus should be considered as human from the time when, if it were to be born, it could survive outside the womb; a third group asserts that a baby becomes truly human only at birth. We would like to put forward another idea: human life begins when the parents begin to consider the baby as a human being. This notion might perhaps seem fanciful, but it has serious implications: there is a world of difference between the attitude of parents to a wanted child and to one who is unwanted; feelings towards a child who has been desperately wanted for years are different again. And, as we shall see not only in this chapter but throughout the book, parents' attitudes count.

So, it is our belief that, psychologically, human life begins at that moment when one of the parents becomes aware of the baby as a developing person. For almost all mothers, this recognition comes at some time during the pregnancy; for some fathers it does not happen until after the birth.

Physically, however, the beginning is conception. From fertilization, development is a continuous process which can be divided into prenatal and postnatal periods with the event of birth marking the division. The long journey begins with this critical nine-month period.

In the womb the fetus develops minute by minute: it seems fully protected, and yet is sensitive to changes experienced by the mother. There has never been any doubt that parents influence their growing child's health and well-being; yet it is a relatively new idea that parents take an active part in orchestrating pregnancy, birth and the first days of their baby's life.

Conception

We say that a baby is conceived as if it happens all at once – in a burst. Actually, conception is a process. It begins when a male sperm cell, the smallest cell in the human body, penetrates a female ovum, the largest cell – which is about 90,000 times heavier than the sperm. In spite of the disparity in size between the sperm and the ovum, they contribute more or less equally to the baby's inheritance.

How many weeks pregnant?
Doctors date pregnancy from the first day of the mother's last menstrual period. It is assumed that fertilization has taken place about fourteen days after that (though, of course, sometimes it happens earlier, or later). The average time from fertilization to birth is 266 days or thirty-eight weeks, but two weeks is added to this time when doctors talk about how many weeks you are pregnant – so pregnancy becomes 280 days or forty weeks long. In describing pregnancy we use the same method of counting weeks as doctors do, that is dating it from the last period, so, for example, week eighteen of pregnancy falls sixteen weeks after fertilization.

The sperm and the ovum unite to form the baby's first cell, which is called the zygote.

In the first twenty-four to thirty-six hours after fertilization the zygote swims down the fallopian tube to the womb. As it goes it divides and doubles, forming first two identical cells, then four, then eight, and so on. By the third day it is a solid ball of sixteen cells, called a morula. The morula enters the uterus and fills with fluid, dividing again. It is now called the blastocyst. Some cell differentiation is already occurring: the inner cells of the blastocyst become the embryo and the outer cells the placenta. Six to eight days after fertilization, in week three or four of the pregnancy, the cell mass begins to implant itself on the uterine wall. By the time the blastocyst is firmly implanted, two more weeks have gone by; the process of conception is now complete, and you are in the fifth week of your pregnancy.

The embryo

During the embryonic phase, which begins with implantation, rapid cell division continues and more differentiation occurs.

Some cells form a sac of membranes, inside which the embryo floats in a liquid, the amniotic fluid. The embryo is attached by the umbilical cord to the placenta, which develops gradually during the embryonic period and through which oxygen and nutrition are supplied to the developing baby and carbon dioxide and other waste products pass back to the mother. The placenta thus performs the functions of lungs, digestive system, liver and kidneys for the baby. It also acts as a partial barrier between the mother's circulatory system and the baby's, filtering out some potentially harmful substances: most drugs and anaesthetics, however, do cross the placenta, and so do many disease organisms.

By week five of pregnancy (three weeks after conception) the embryo is 10 mm long – just under half an inch. During this week the cells differentiate into the ectoderm (the outer layer) and the endoderm (the inner layer); in week six the mesoderm (the middle layer) is formed. In the weeks to come the outer layer will develop into the skin, the spinal cord, the nervous system, the sense organs and some of the glands; the middle layer will

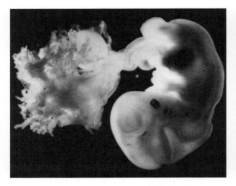

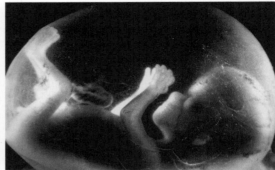

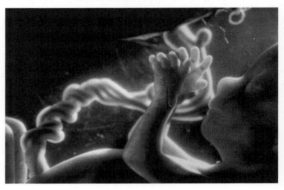

Above left *The embryo at four weeks of pregnancy, two weeks after fertilization.*
Above right *The fetus at twelve weeks.*
Right *The fetus at fourteen weeks.*

become muscle, bone, connective tissue, blood vessels and urinary and reproductive organs. The inner layer will differentiate into other internal organs, including the heart and liver.

By week six (four weeks after conception), the embryo has developed from a flat disc into a rounded form. The heart has formed and now supports a rudimentary circulatory system. The two distinct hemispheres of the brain are in existence in their earliest, most primitive form. The head and trunk have formed, and the jaw and mouth are developing. Limb buds can be seen and ten primary teeth buds have appeared. The embryo does not yet look human, but is recognizable as a mammal.

Week seven (five weeks from conception) sees rapid development of the limb buds, which start to look like minute arms and legs, with indentations where the fingers and toes will eventually grow.

By eight weeks the developing embryo is about 38 mm/1½ inches long and has swellings which eventually become the ears, markings which look like eyes and a mouth that opens and closes. The arms have a recognizable elbow and wrist, and the hands have ridges which indicate the fingers. By ten weeks the fingers and toes are distinct. The embryo has some liver and kidney function and a spinal cord. Brainwaves can be measured electronically and the first reflex activity can be observed. The embryo is now about 45 mm/1¾ inches long.

The fetus

Twelve to twenty weeks

By some time between the twelfth and the fourteenth weeks, all the major organs, including the testicles or ovaries, have formed, and the circulatory system is complete. The fetal period, which follows, is one of growth rather than the development of new structures.

At twelve weeks the fetus looks human, although the large head appears fantastically out of proportion to the body. Measured from the top of the head to the rump the fetus is about the width of an adult palm; the head takes up half of this space. The child's sex can be determined – it is even possible to see a boy's sex organs on an ultrasound scan, if he happens to be lying in the right position. The face has formed and the eyelids are present; the toes and fingers are there and the nails are beginning to grow. The ribs and spine, which were cartilage or soft bone in the embryonic stage, are now turning to hard bone. The muscles too are developing and the fetus is moving freely within the womb.

Between the eleventh and the fourteenth weeks of pregnancy the fetus begins to make urine. It is excreted into the amniotic fluid: some of this is swallowed by the fetus as it passes over its face, and reabsorbed. The rest of the urine passes out through the placenta into the mother's circulation.

By thirteen weeks individual differences between the faces of fetuses have become apparent.

Between fifteen and eighteen weeks growth is very rapid. The limbs are lengthening and the head looks smaller in proportion.

Twenty to twenty-six weeks

The fetus has been moving vigorously for many weeks, but at some point between sixteen and twenty weeks will come the moment when, for the first time, the mother feels her baby kick against the wall of the womb. And at twenty weeks the fetus may actively suck when hungry: some babies even suck their thumbs in the womb.

At twenty-two weeks the fetus is approximately 25 cm/10 inches long: it has reached half its birth length. Its eyebrows and head hair are visible. Fine, downy hair known as lanugo is covering the body.

The nerve cells, or neurones, are continuing to develop. The organs which control balance are in place, and have achieved an adult level of maturity. Within the womb the baby turns slowly, rather like an astronaut in space; its control of movement is improving and it appears to land more often with the heavy head down. By now fetal movements are felt more strongly; the fetus will often appear to be moving very actively when the mother is at rest.

By twenty-four weeks the fetus is about 32 cm/13 inches long from head to toe and weighs around 500 g/18 oz. The nervous and respiratory systems are usually still not mature enough for survival outside the womb, but some babies born at twenty-four weeks have proved capable of surviving, with intensive care in a special unit. At this stage the body is thin and the skin is wrinkled, but fat starts to appear in the tissues beneath the skin.

Twenty-six to thirty-two weeks

By twenty-six weeks the lungs are beginning to produce surfactant, a foamy substance which prevents them from collapsing. The skin, which is now noticeably thicker and more opaque, is covered with a film of vernix, a mixture of sebum and skin cells.

It seems that by about twenty-six weeks, though probably not before, the fetus can hear. In research carried out in Japan, tones were played directly to the fetus through earphones put up against the mother's abdomen. During the last three months of pregnancy 110 out of 123 fetuses reacted to the tones with a quickening of the pulse. This is not, of course, to say that they hear with the same intensity or in the same way as they will after birth. The auditory system is still immature and, in addition, sounds are muffled by the amniotic fluid.

At twenty-eight weeks the fetus is about 35 cm/14 inches long and weighs around 900 g/2 lb. There is still little fat under the fetal skin, which means that a baby born at twenty-eight weeks lacks insulation against the cooler world outside the womb.

By thirty weeks a layer of fat is forming under the skin. The lungs are well developed and the central nervous system has reached a stage where it can control rhythmic breathing movements. Babies born now are capable of breathing air and, given skilled care, have a 60 to 70 per cent chance of survival.

Around thirty-one weeks most fetuses position themselves head down in the womb. By this time fetal movements are so pronounced that it is often possible for other people to feel them. Even before birth it is possible to detect differences between one baby and another, for they vary in their activity levels. It might at first seem that this is incontrovertible proof that at least some characteristics have a genetic basis, for how can the environment influence a baby in the womb? The answer is that the influence can come from the mother. Her physical state has an effect on how well the baby develops in the womb, and her baby may respond by movement to her mental state – possibly because hormones produced in the mother when she is depressed or elated are transferred through the placenta to the baby.

Thirty-two to forty weeks

In the last couple of months of fetal life there is rapid development of the systems that will come into play at birth.

Babies born during this period usually survive. By thirty-two weeks their fingernails reach the tips of the fingers. By thirty-six weeks the toe-

Tests on the baby in the womb

Various tests can be done on the baby in the womb, to check that development is normal. Among these, AFP screening, ultrasound scanning and amniocentesis are widely available. Chorionic villus sampling, introduced more recently, is now also becoming fairly common.

AFP screening

Alpha-feto-protein is a substance which is produced by the fetal liver and finds its way into the mother's bloodstream. Levels of AFP can be checked by a simple blood test, administered in early pregnancy. An unusually high level of AFP may indicate the presence of a fetal abnormality, such as spina bifida, but the proportion of AFP can also be high for other reasons (for example, there will be a high reading if a woman is expecting twins, or if her pregnancy is more advanced than had been calculated). These days some obstetricians prefer to dispense with AFP tests and offer routine ultrasound scanning instead; however, AFP screening is still quite widely used.

If you do have an AFP test and the level seems abnormal you will be offered further investigations, such as ultrasound or amniocentesis.

Ultrasound scanning

In ultrasound scanning very high frequency sound waves are used to produce a picture of the baby in the womb. A scan will provide information that can be used to establish the age of the fetus, to detect certain abnormalities and to check if the placenta is functioning and healthy. Scans are routinely administered before amniocentesis and chorionic villus sampling.

Amniocentesis and chorionic villus sampling

Amniocentesis and chorionic villus sampling are two methods of screening for chromosomal abnormalities, such as Down's syndrome. Either test will also reveal the sex of baby – useful information if there is a risk of a sex-linked genetic disorder such as haemophilia. In amniocentesis a hollow needle is inserted into the uterus and about 20 ml of amniotic fluid is drawn off; in CVS tissue is taken from the developing placenta. Tests are then done on the cultured sample.

CVS is usually done at between eight and eleven weeks of pregnancy. Amniocentesis is usually not done before sixteen weeks, but some hospitals are able to offer it as early as ten weeks.

nails reach the toe tips – this is one of the criteria doctors use to make a quick judgment about the degree of maturity. Between thirty-six and forty weeks there is considerable weight gain: a baby may be gaining up to 28 g/1 oz a day at this time. In particular, there is an increase in the proportion of fat – which at thirty-two weeks accounts for 7 to 8 per cent of body weight and by the time a baby is born is about 16 per cent of weight. At thirty-four weeks a fetus has reached half its full-term birthweight. By thirty-seven weeks babies look plump and are strong enough to have a firm grasp.

Usually between thirty-six and forty weeks, the baby's head (or with a breech baby the buttocks) descends into the pelvis, in preparation for the birth. Because the baby now almost fills the space in the womb, fetal movements tend to be more limited.

So much having happened, with something of a personality perhaps already formed, 266 or so days after conception, your baby is ready to be born.

Nutrition in pregnancy

If you are a pregnant mother you will want to do all you can to contribute to the well-being of your developing baby. One very important way to help is by making sure you have a healthy diet: your baby's nourishment depends on what you eat.

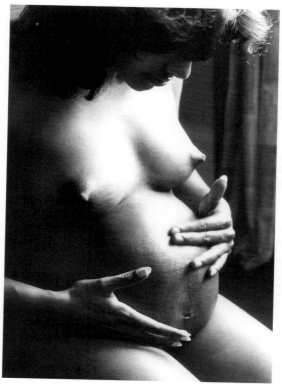

Late pregnancy – a time when you may feel both a deep sense of contentment and an urgent longing for your baby's arrival.

So long as you eat well-balanced regular meals you should not need to make significant changes in your diet because you are pregnant, nor is there any reason to increase the amount of food you eat or the quantity of fluid you drink. You should not need to take dietary supplements, either. You should, though, be certain that your intake *is* adequate and well-balanced. The five basic food groups include bread and cereals, vegetables and fruits, meat (or, if you are vegetarian, alternative protein foods), milk and milk products, and fats. You and your baby need a balanced daily selection from each of these groups (see pages 496–7).

Women experience very different responses to food during pregnancy: some find that they are extremely hungry and need to eat frequently, others feel so nauseous, especially in the early months, that they do not want to eat, and may even be unable to hold down food. If you are anxious that you may not be able to provide sufficient nourishment for yourself and your baby, you should talk the problem through with a dietician.

Substances which should be avoided

Drugs

Most medicinal drugs, including many which are commonly prescribed and others which are freely available over the counter, cross the placenta and may affect the baby – as also do social drugs such as alcohol and cannabis. If you think you might be pregnant, or even if you are intending to conceive, it is best to avoid taking any drug unless it is absolutely necessary. Make sure that any doctor who is treating you is aware of the situation.

Some women, however, have to continue taking drugs throughout pregnancy, for chronic conditions such as diabetes, epilepsy, or severe asthma. If you are in this position you need to discuss the matter with your doctor, ideally before you conceive.

Alcohol

It is generally thought best to limit alcohol intake when pregnant. Although many women do continue to drink in moderation, it is as well to be careful, for the amount of alcohol which can safely be consumed has not been determined. Some women metabolize alcohol better than others: if a woman does not metabolize alcohol well, a single bout of heavy drinking early in pregnancy may seriously harm the baby's development. Excessive drinking at any stage can certainly lead to problems, some of which may be severe.

Smoking

Nicotine narrows the blood vessels in the placenta, so that the passage of oxygen and nutrients to the baby is restricted. Babies born to women who smoke are on average 200 g/7 oz lighter than babies born to comparable non-smoking mothers, and the more cigarettes consumed per day the higher the chance of having a low-birthweight baby. Smokers also have more complications of pregnancy and labour, including bleeding during pregnancy and premature birth.

It is, nevertheless, often difficult to stop smoking during pregnancy (or at any other time). If you are a heavy smoker you may find it useful to join a self-help group or take part in an anti-smoking programme. If you give up smoking before the twentieth week of pregnancy your risk of having a low-birthweight baby will be no higher than that of a non-smoker. If you find you cannot give up smoking entirely, cut down.

The Birth

Birth choices

Some of the first decisions you make for your baby concern where and how she is to be born. Will it be better for her to be born at home or in hospital? Will it matter to her, now or in the future, who is present at her birth? Does the birth experience have a long-lasting effect on a child? Will it make any difference to her if she has a natural birth, without any medical intervention, or a high-technology, obstetrically managed delivery? If you take pain-relieving drugs, how will they affect her?

All these are important questions not only in their own right but also because they raise a crucial matter of general principle. *In itself no single event or condition has an inevitable effect on a child's development*. What matters is, in general, the overall pattern of a child's life; and, in particular, how any given event or condition is handled. Many parents blame themselves for one act which they think has ruined their child's life. Human development is far more complex than that: one act can have many possible outcomes.

Caesarian deliveries provide a good example. Being born by a surgical process in itself carries no long-term benefit or harm, what is important is the skill with which the operation is performed and the quality of care before and after the operation. Similarly, when a baby is born drowsy from drugs, if the mother is able to understand the reason for the drowsiness and can wait a while for the baby to recover, they will probably then be able to relate well to each other. If, however, disappointed by the initial lack of response, the mother becomes guilty or resentful, and remains so, then relating will be harder.

This is not to imply that the choices parents make are unimportant. Though a single event in itself may not be critical, single events add up to make a whole: it is how they add up that really counts.

Where should your baby be born?

In Britain, the United States and Australia today less than 2 per cent of births are planned home deliveries. In some countries, however, the situation is very different. For example, in the Netherlands about one third of

Your baby is here – a miracle, a mystery.

deliveries occur at home. And the Netherlands has one of the lowest rates of perinatal mortality (that is, deaths around the time of birth) in the world – far lower than British and North American rates. Studies also indicate that, in the Netherlands as in many other countries, those mothers who have their babies at home experience fewer problems during delivery and after the birth.

From the parents' point of view, the great advantage of a home delivery is that they remain in control of their own lives. The mother can have family and friends around her, move about the house, read her favourite books, listen to music, take a bath when she wishes. The father is likely to feel more at ease, and more comfortable in supporting his partner, than in a hospital. Their child will be welcomed into her own home, and they can care for her themselves from the beginning.

It might seem reasonable to conclude, then, that any healthy woman with a normal pregnancy, so long as she is assured of adequate medical care, would do well to opt to have her baby at home.

On the other hand, many women feel more secure giving birth in a hospital where they know that medical back-up is available if it is needed – where if the pain becomes too much there is the option of an epidural anaesthetic, where a baby in distress can, if necessary, be delivered by Caesarian section, where a baby at risk can be given expert medical care as soon as she is born. And a number of women are just glad to be removed from the responsibilities of home.

Ultimately, decisions of this kind can be made only in terms of a balance between personal preference and medical risk. If there is any indication that expert medical or surgical intervention is likely to be needed during the birth, or if it is thought that either the baby or the mother will require special care, then it will be best for the baby to be born in hospital. Parents also need to be aware that even when it seems safe to predict a straightforward delivery, an unexpected emergency can occur. The risk is small, but it is there. If, in the course of a home birth, your labour becomes prolonged, or changes in the baby's heart-rate indicate that she is distressed, or you bleed heavily after the delivery, a rapid transfer to hospital may be necessary. One factor in coming to a decision about a home birth should be the ease with which medical help can be obtained should it be needed.

In some circumstances, a compromise may be acceptable. Although giving birth in hospital is never going to be the same for a mother as being in her own home, many hospitals have gone some way towards providing home-like surroundings, warm, supportive staff and a degree of freedom and choice for parents. Some hospitals have special birthing rooms, birth units or birth centres for those who want a gentle, natural birth. In some parts of Britain another possible alternative is offered by the Domino scheme: in this system a community midwife cares for the mother throughout her pregnancy, brings her into hospital for the birth, delivers the baby and carries out the follow-up care. If there are no problems mother and baby are back in their own home within hours.

Who will be there?

Another decision has to do with who should be present at the birth. In particular, of course, should the baby's father be there?

The presence of her partner can be a great support to a woman in childbirth, and many couples feel that their relationship is enhanced by sharing the experience of the birth of their child. However, while many fathers want to attend the birth, others feel uncomfortable at the whole idea. And while many women find it helpful to have the father there, others want their mother, or perhaps a sister or a woman friend, instead – and some prefer to have no one but a midwife.

There is a simple answer to this question: it is entirely up to you. There is no evidence to show that one combination of people present at a birth is any better than any other, for the baby, the mother or the family. If your partner would like to be with you, and you feel happy about it, go ahead. Do not feel you should succumb to social pressure – either way.

A rather more complex question is whether the baby's brothers and sisters should be there – an option which is usually only available if you are having a home birth. There are two aspects to this: one is whether they should be physically present in the room; the other is whether they should even be in the same house.

It is impossible to be dogmatic on the first point. In making a decision about whether children should attend a birth, there are so many variables to consider: the way the family functions, the emotional and intellectual state of the children, whether they want to be there, how the mother feels about it, what everyone expects will take place. Parents should be warned, however, that young children may find the process less than interesting; they may even be bored by an event that is so far outside their normal experience. If you decide that you want your children to be present, you should make sure that someone is there for them – a friendly adult who has nothing to do other than pay them attention, answer their questions, and take them away if they want to go.

There are no rules about whether they should stay in the house, either. However, we can be quite firm about the general principle which should guide all these decisions: what children need at this time, as on any other important occasion, is the recognition that they exist as individuals. Ample thought should be given to preparing them for the event, and to choosing who will be looking after them when the time comes. Who they are with is far more significant than where they are.

What sort of birth?

Decisions about where a birth should happen and who should be there are only the start: the birth process itself can be handled in different ways. You may hope that your child's birth will be gentle and natural, and as much as possible under your control; or you may be happy to feel that the process can be taken over by medical staff, with the support of modern technology.

It must be acknowledged here that births do not always go exactly as planned. It is your right and your responsibility to make decisions now and throughout the period of your child's development; none the less, there are times when it is sensible to share decisions with others whom you trust. One such time is when it becomes apparent, during the birth process, that mother or baby is at some risk. As there may be no space then for much discussion on what is best from everyone's point of view, it is important to know that you can trust whoever is looking after you to do what is best for you and your baby. You will feel more confident if during your pregnancy you have discussed with your midwife or doctor both how you hope the birth will go and what the options are if there should be complications.

Intervention in the birth

There are various ways in which medical staff can intervene in labour. They can induce or accelerate the process by introducing hormones into the mother's bloodstream, through an intravenous drip or by using pessaries; they can speed things up by artificially rupturing the membranes that surround the baby. Episiotomies – cuts made to enlarge the birth opening – are common practice. Obstetric forceps or a vacuum extractor may be used to help the baby out. In a difficult delivery, an obstetrician may take over entirely and deliver the baby by Caesarian section (see page 60).

Pain relief in labour

Any decision about pain relief must be the mother's. Most women experience pain in labour, and all are different in their sensitivity to pain. What they have to decide is how they will cope with it.

Many mothers prefer, if they can, to avoid drugs, for themselves and for their babies – almost all drugs cross the placenta. Some women (though not all) find effective methods of controlling pain, or even eliminating it almost entirely, without drugs.

You can reduce levels of pain considerably just by moving around freely and changing position during labour. Finding a comfortable space allows you to work with the pain.

When left to choose their own birth position, women often elect to squat, sit on a birth stool, or go down on all fours. All of these positions relieve pressure and generally make for an easier delivery.

Massage is another effective way of working with pain and helping to relieve it. A birth partner can help by massaging your back. Touching and stroking are often helpful ways to provide comfort.

Self-hypnosis, visualization, patterned breathing may also be worthwhile and can be learned with practice. Listening to music is a good way of taking your mind off your pain.

Floating or semi-floating in warm water can be an effective means of pain relief, and in some countries specially made shallow pools can be hired – they may even be installed, in a progressive hospital. The baby may also

During labour all feelings are of great intensity. A partner can give comfort and support and help you work with the pain.

be delivered in the water, though this is something you would need to discuss at an earlier stage with whoever is looking after you.

Drugs used during delivery

You may not find that any of the self-help methods described above work sufficiently well for you, and want to use drugs to assist pain relief. Three types of drug are commonly offered to mothers during delivery: sedatives, such as valium, given to reduce anxiety; analgesics (for example, pethidine or gas and oxygen) to ease pain; anaesthetics, either local or general, to block pain. Epidural anaesthesia is a popular and effective form of local pain block that removes sensation from the waist down.

It has to be said that virtually any obstetric medication in general use will cross the placenta and influence the baby. Gas and oxygen, a mixture of nitrous oxide and oxygen which is inhaled by the mother, is cleared from the baby's system with her first breath. Newborns whose mothers have received any other kind of drug during delivery may be born more sluggish, more sleepy and less likely to suck vigorously. Some have respiratory problems. All these effects are relatively short-term and seem to pass within the first month.

Caesarian delivery

By no means every birth is straightforward. Some babies are awkwardly positioned for delivery, sometimes a baby's head is too large to pass through the mother's pelvis, some babies become short of oxygen, either in the womb or during the birth. A mother may have a condition – such as a severe kidney problem – which means that the normal birth process could put her at excessive risk. Some of these problems are apparent well before the birth; others do not become evident until the mother is advanced in labour.

On these or other grounds it may be decided, either before or during the birth, that the safest course is to deliver the baby by Caesarian section, that is through surgical incisions made in the abdominal wall and uterus. It is often said (and probably truly) that the Caesarian section has greater potential for the preservation of life than any other major surgical operation. However, no operation is without its hazards, and in recent years Caesarians have sometimes been performed too readily. In the United States, the frequency of the operation has quadrupled since 1968; in 1987 one in four of the babies born in the States was delivered by Caesarian. Many of these babies could have been delivered quite safely through the normal birth process. The mothers would have avoided the risks and the after-effects of a major operation. Would a normal birth also have been of benefit to the babies?

Immediately after birth babies delivered vaginally breathe with more vigour than babies delivered surgically. It seems that the squeezing of the chest as the baby passes through the birth canal has a positive effect in clearing the lungs and making it easier for the baby to breathe. By six hours after the birth, however, babies born by Caesarian are breathing as freely as vaginally delivered babies.

Being born

To the child, birth brings sudden, dramatic change. In her mother's womb, which performs many of her bodily functions for her, the baby has been curled inside a sac of supporting fluid. Now the uterus contracts to propel her out into the world. As she passes through the tight birth canal she is pushed, squeezed, stretched and massaged; for her own part she twists and turns, adapting herself to her mother's shape and negotiating her way out. She emerges into a world where she is going to have to breathe, take in food and excrete for herself – all in an environment very different from the one she has known.

She meets a rush of air, and her lungs inflate with her first breath.

Having lived in total darkness, for the first time she is exposed to light: even low levels of light make newborns squint.

She has to cope, too, with a change of temperature. Inside the womb she has been accustomed to a constant temperature of 37°C/99°F. At birth she emerges into a comparatively cool room.

Sound is perhaps less of a surprise, for the womb, penetrated by noises from inside and outside the mother's body, does not provide a quiet environment; nevertheless, the range of sounds experienced at birth is greater than any the baby has previously encountered.

Then for the first time she experiences being handled: she is picked up, put down, generally moved around with a briskness that is quite different from the gentle motions, cushioned by amniotic fluid, that are all she has so far known.

It is difficult to avoid the speculation that birth must be an overwhelming experience for the newborn. Some writers talk of the 'birth trauma' as an experience that inflicts a psychological scarring that lasts a lifetime. Some even go so far as to suggest that people who are psychologically troubled need to re-live the experience of their birth in order to come to terms with it. However, speculation is all it is: just because an adult would find it distressing to be squeezed and pushed through a narrow passage, and shocking to be assaulted by dramatic changes in movement, light, sound and temperature, all occurring at once, it cannot be assumed that this is so for babies. It may be that there is some inborn mechanism which helps the newborn to cope with these changes. We do not know.

Checking the baby

Immediately after birth the baby's general appearance is observed to see if she is healthy, her breathing, heart-rate and movement are checked and her reflexes are tested. All these are assessed according to the Apgar score, a numerical scoring system devised in the 1950s by an American anaesthetist, Virginia Apgar.

Using the Apgar score, a rating of 0, 1 or 2 is given to each of the following observations: *a*ppearance, *p*ulse, *g*rimace (response to stimulation), *a*ctivity (muscle tone) and *r*espiration. A score of 2 indicates that there are no problems, 1 that there is some cause for concern, 0 that there are serious deficiencies in the area rated. For example, a pulse-rate of over 100 is given a score of 2; a pulse that is present but below 100 is given 1; a score of 0 indicates that the pulse is absent. Babies in generally good condition usually have a total score of 7 or more; less than 7 indicates that the baby may be at some risk; 4 or less, that she is in a critical condition. The rating is usually made immediately after birth and again when the baby is five minutes old; the second score is often much higher than the first – indicating that the baby is already recovering from the birth and adapting to life outside the womb. If the second score is low the test is repeated at ten minutes, and perhaps again at fifteen minutes.

The Apgar score is a useful tool that helps medical staff to make a rapid assessment of a baby's condition in the vital first moments after birth. A low overall score, or a low score in a particular area, is an indication that the baby has a problem. More detailed investigations can then begin and, meanwhile, the baby can be provided with any special care she may need.

The newborn baby's spine, mouth and genitals are also closely inspected; the legs are rotated to make sure there is no dislocation of the hips; and the weight and length are recorded.

At some point in the first six to nine days after birth a nurse will prick the baby's heel and take a few drops of blood to be tested for phenylketonuria (PKU), hypothyroidism and certain other diseases (all rare). A day or two after birth a doctor will check the baby's reflexes; during this examination you should have the opportunity to ask any questions you want to put about your baby, and mention anything that may be worrying you.

Gentle birth

Speculative descriptions about how babies must feel when being born have led some people to argue that for the sake of the baby we should make birth as gentle an experience as possible. The French obstetrician Frederick Leboyer has been particularly influential in this area. In his book *Birth Without Violence* he advocates the use of reduced light, delayed clamping of the umbilical cord, gentle massage and a warm bath for the baby. Early reports of the effect of this approach noted superior development in babies born into this more gentle world. However, most of the later, more systematic enquiries have failed to show significant differences in the infants' behaviour in the first hour of life, or at twenty-four or seventy-two hours or eight months – though in one controlled study researchers found that, during the first days after birth, babies delivered by the Leboyer method spent more time lying quietly awake.

It seems, on the whole, that Leboyer's claims remain unproven. On the other hand, there is no evidence that a gentle birth can harm a baby; and any method of childbirth that might tend to produce more quietly alert babies deserves consideration – as does any method that may enhance the experience for the parents.

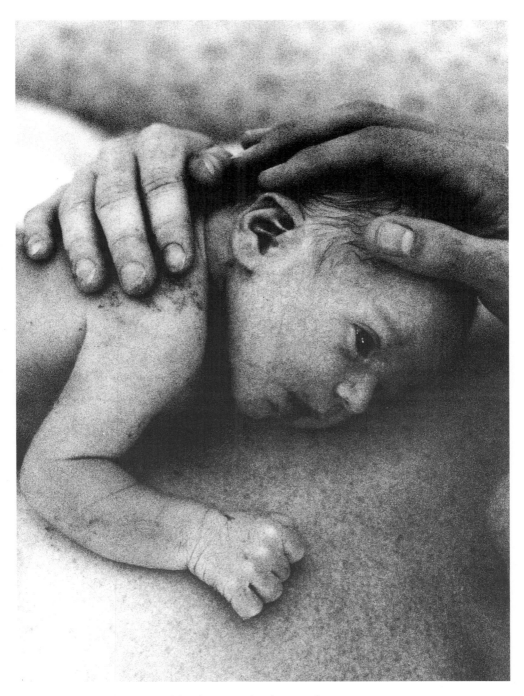

The newborn seems so vulnerable, almost too fragile to touch – yet you are overwhelmed by the need to protect, to cradle her.

The New Baby

Your baby has been born. She may seem very mysterious to you, as she lies there in your arms – and indeed she is a mystery, which will only gradually unfold. Little by little, you will come to know this person. Meanwhile, though, are there any clues that will help? How about newborns in general? What do they look like? What can they do? How do they relate to their parents? How do their parents relate to them?

The baby's appearance

Size at birth

There are wide individual variations in babies' size at birth, so the following figures should be taken as no more than a rough guide, but, just for interest, 95 per cent of babies of West European or European-American origin born at full term weigh between 2.7 kg/6 lb and 4.5 kg/10 lb and are 46–56 cm/18–22 inches long. The average weight for boys is 3.3 kg/7 lb 6 oz, for girls 3.2 kg/7 lb 4 oz. A twin weighs on average about 680 g/1½ lb less than a single baby, a triplet about 340 g/12 oz less than a twin.

Most babies with a birthweight of over 4.5 kg are big simply because their parents are big, and they are going to be big people. Because of their size, these babies can have problems in passing through the birth canal and surgical intervention may be needed. Once born, however, they should have no special difficulties.

At the other end of the scale, some small babies are genetically small, but most babies with a birthweight of less than 2.25 kg/5 lb will probably need some special care (see pages 86–8).

Because after birth babies lose some fluid and have their first bowel movement (the meconium), and because their food intake is at this stage limited, it is normal to lose up to 10 per cent of birthweight over the first few days of life. Most babies have regained their birthweight by the tenth day and from then on they gain weight rapidly (see pages 96–7).

A trio of new babies – all born with different lengths and weights, yet all well within the normal range. Small defects caused by the birth process soon disappear and wrinkled skin fills out.

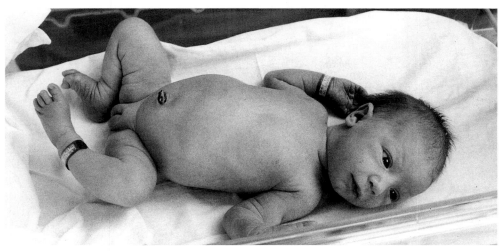

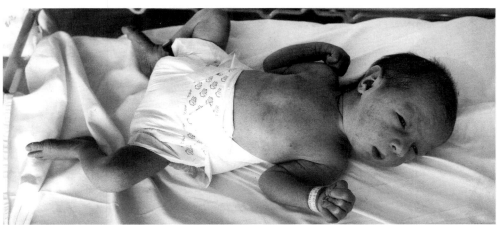

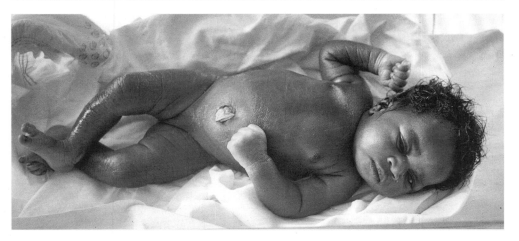

The head

The head makes up almost a quarter of the entire body length. The biggest difference in proportion between newborns and adults lies in the area above the eyes: in the infant the ratio between this part and the whole face is 8:1; by adulthood this has changed to 1:2.

As a new parent you may be alarmed by the form of your baby's head, for during the birth process the skull is often moulded into a very odd shape. Moreover, the newborn's face may look squashed, and the ears may even be lying in the wrong direction. There is no need to worry. These are only temporary misshapings; by the time your baby is twelve hours old she will be looking a lot more normal.

You will notice the diamond-shaped soft spot, or fontanelle, on top of your baby's head; there is a similar, smaller spot on the back of the head. They will disappear as the skull bones join together within the first two years of life.

Especially if labour was prolonged, the baby may have a swelling on her scalp (*caput succedaneum*). This is caused by the pressure of the dilating cervix against the baby's head, and it will generally disappear within the first twenty-four hours.

There may be a cyst-like swelling (*cephalhaematoma*) on one side of the

---

Birthmarks

Birthmarks can be a major source of worry to the parents of a newborn. However, usually they are only a short-term problem. Many blemishes disappear entirely; others become less noticeable with time. Your doctor will be able to give you specific information and advice.

Salmon patches (*naevus flammeus*) on the eyelids are the most common birthmarks – they are found on about 15 per cent of all newborns. Similar marks may occur at the root of the nose, on the upper lip, or the nape of the neck. All those on the face will disappear or fade considerably within the first eighteen months. Why they tend to remain on the neck is a mystery.

Bluish-black areas, sometimes called mongolian spots, over the baby's back, buttocks or genital area have usually gone within a few years.

Strawberry marks – small red lumps that are present at birth or come during a baby's first few weeks – will generally disappear during childhood.

The pinkish flame-shaped marks called port wine stains can be more permanent. A dermatologist will be able to give advice on the natural course of the mark and about possible steps to take, which may include laser treatment.

On one point you can be reassured: far the majority of parents report that after a short period, sometimes only a few hours or days, they stop noticing any blemish. Some parents, though, find it hard to accept their baby's birthmarks; talking this through with a member of the hospital staff can be helpful, provided that the hospital has staff equipped to carry out this type of counselling – by no means all hospitals do. Organizations of parents whose children have similar problems can help a lot.

baby's head. Again this is usually caused by pressure during labour, and it will go during the first six months.

Electrodes fixed to the scalp for fetal blood sampling or for monitoring during labour can leave a small round scar on the top of the head. This too will gradually disappear.

The skin

At birth your baby's skin may look quite loose and wrinkled; don't worry – she will soon fill out.

It is quite likely that during the first week of life the baby's skin (and the whites of her eyes) will develop a yellow tint. This 'physiological jaundice', which is seen in about 50 per cent of babies, is a result of a breakdown of excess red blood cells that occurs after birth. During this process a yellow pigment called bilirubin is produced, and it is this that causes the yellowish tinge. It normally disappears within a week or ten days. Putting the baby in a sunlit position in a warm room helps. Treatment with ultraviolet light is usually effective if anything more is needed.

Parents can get very anxious about blemishes and irregularities that appear on the skin. It is quite common for spots or pimples to break out on the skin during the first week of life; and sometimes small white pimples appear on the baby's nose. None of these spots are of any significance; they don't seem to bother babies, and they will disappear within a few days.

The eyes

Most newborn babies have blue eyes, even if their permanent eye colour will be different. The colour will change, if it is going to, during the first six months.

The eyes are sometimes bloodshot at birth. This is as a result of pressure on the head during labour and delivery, and usually clears up fairly quickly without any special treatment.

A yellowish discharge from the eyes may indicate an infection; a doctor should check this.

Genitals and breasts

New babies' sexual organs often look swollen, and sometimes babies (both boys and girls) have milk in their breasts. Both swelling and milk production are caused by hormones that have passed from the mother's body. The swelling will subside and the milk cease to flow without any treatment. Hormone activity may also cause vaginal bleeding – a pseudo-menstruation – in baby girls. Again, no treatment or special care is necessary: it will stop within a few days.

This is what they look like. More controversial, and far more important from a developmental point of view, is what the newborn can do.

The World of the Newborn

Parents have always, instinctively, gazed at and talked to their newborn babies – and have often been ridiculed for doing so. Why try to make eye contact with a baby when she cannot really see you? Why talk to her when she cannot understand?

Now, with more advanced methods of observation, a picture of babies' abilities is emerging which shows the view intuitively held by parents to be the one closer to the truth. Newborn babies can see, hear, feel and do a lot more than used to be thought possible. And, certainly, they respond.

A mother instinctively tries to make eye contact with her new baby, and wants to talk and croon to her.

Perception in the newborn

Sight

Give anyone a baby to hold, and he or she will almost certainly try to achieve and maintain eye contact. This seems to happen instinctively and clearly meets a deeply felt need, at least for the adult.

The visual system of a newborn baby is limited because it is immature. The eye itself is only one-third of its adult size, and though the receptor cells, which receive images, are fairly well developed, the fovea – the central part of the retina, where receptors are closely packed together – is still rudimentary. Within the brain the visual cortex, which controls the eyes and interprets the images they take in, is still in the process of development, and many of the essential connections between the cells are lacking.

Any description of what the newborn sees must, in the end, be speculative. We cannot know what a new baby sees: we can only draw inferences from observation, and from information about the stage of development of the eye and the visual cortex.

Newborn babies search, even in a dim light, opening their eyes widely and scanning the surrounding area. They are attracted by edges, where there is a contrast between light and dark, and by movement. Most of all, babies like to look at the human face. Given a choice, they almost invariably choose to look at a face (especially the mobile eyes and mouth) or, failing that, a face-like pattern. This attraction clearly has adaptive value – a baby's desire to seek out the key distinguishing feature of a person who will protect her is a powerful weapon in the battle to survive.

It seems that newborns focus best at a range of about 20–30 cm/8 to 12 inches – so they are well equipped for what is at this age their most important visual activity: looking at the mother's face while feeding. But this early vision, even for close objects, is not perfect. Researchers at the University of Rotterdam tested babies of various ages by showing them patterns of black and white stripes. They found that at one week the babies could see stripes roughly 12 mm/½ inch wide at 30 cm/12 inches away. (At this distance, an adult with normal vision can see stripes thirty times finer.)

A newborn cannot synchronize her eyes as an adult can: the visual cortex is not yet well enough developed to keep both eyes focused on the same thing. It may be that the baby sees double – or, possibly, she may suppress the image from one eye while she is using the other. What she cannot do is combine the image from one eye with that from the other.

The peripheral vision of new babies is also poor: babies younger than two months can see little from the right side of the left eye, or the left side of the right eye.

A fairly recent discovery is that newborn babies do have some perception of colour, albeit limited. At birth they can distinguish yellow, red, green and turquoise from grey and discriminate between red and green, though they do not seem able to tell the difference between yellow and green or yellow and red. What we do not know, of course, is just what the colours look like to a baby.

In summary: babies can see a lot more than used to be thought, but their vision still has marked limitations. However, while sight as poor as a newborn's would be a serious handicap to an adult, it could be an advantage for the young baby: it might be that if babies could see as well as adults do they would be bombarded with more images than they could possibly cope with. During their first weeks of life babies tend to close their eyes whenever they are presented with a sight of any complexity – an indication, perhaps, that they have a need to protect themselves from excessive visual stimulation.

Hearing and balance

Newborn babies hear well – a great deal better than they can see – though their hearing, too, has limitations. Externally, the ears of a newborn child are almost as well developed, on a tiny scale, as those of an adult; the internal parts, however, are still immature. It seems that the softest sound the newborn can hear is about 10 decibels louder than the softest sound that would be heard by an adult. So while a new baby can hear someone talking in a normal tone of voice, she is unlikely to pick up a whisper. Moreover, babies are more sensitive to the higher ranges of sound. And the sound they respond to most readily is the human voice – particularly a high-pitched voice (for this reason, they tend to process female voices more effectively than male). Infants aged twelve hours to two days synchronize their movements to human speech sounds in both English and Chinese.

Babies less than a week old seem able to recognize their mothers' voices:

Perception in newborns	
Sight	Makes eye-to-eye contact Sees best at 20–30 cm/8–12 inches Looks mainly at the edges of faces and objects Responds to light and dark, and movement Can distinguish some colours from grey, and red from green Cannot synchronize eyes Has poor peripheral vision – cannot see what is around her
Hearing	Discerns human voice Recognizes mother's voice at less than one week Hears better in higher ranges Cannot hear very soft sounds
Taste and smell	Prefers sweet tastes to sour Prefers sweet smells Recognizes smell of own mother's milk and prefers this to other women's breastmilk
Touch	Skin is sensitive, but she may not respond to a very light touch Feels pain such as a prick in the heel

already at this age a baby will turn her eyes towards her mother when she hears her voice. In one experiment a story was read to babies three days old by their mothers and by other women. Each baby seemed to like the story better (she listened to it for longer) when it was read by her mother. It seems likely, indeed, that, if a baby can hear in the womb (see page 50), she already has some familiarity with her mother's voice before she is born.

The organs of balance in the inner ear are the only parts of the human body to reach maturity during the period of gestation: by twenty-two weeks of pregnancy they are already adult in size and shape – and, tumbling about in the womb, the baby puts them to use. As your newborn baby is carried, pushed, rocked or turned over, she probably feels the motion in much the same way as you would.

Taste and smell

Babies have a full set of 10,000 tastebuds from birth. It will be some years before these tastebuds are fully mature, but even at one day old babies will suck faster on something sweet, and make a wry face at a sour taste. Breastmilk, of course, has the sweet taste that babies prefer.

Just as babies favour sweet tastes, they also prefer sweet smells. Very young babies will turn their heads towards sweet smells, such as those of banana and vanilla, and away from ammonia and liquorice.

The pediatrician Aidan MacFarlane presented babies with two pads, one soaked in the milk of each baby's own mother, and one soaked in the milk of another woman. At two days, babies did not seem to make any distinction between the two pads. By six days, however, two-thirds turned towards the pad with their mother's milk, and by eight to ten days three-quarters turned towards their mother's pad.

Touch

The nerve endings in the newborn baby's thin skin are as numerous and as well developed – though of course not as large – as an adult's. Moreover, the somatosensory cortex, where the messages of these nerves are processed, is more mature than any other sensory area of the brain. This being the case, we would expect the newborn to be extremely sensitive to touch. And indeed, many babies, premature babies especially, will respond to the gentlest touch.

Rather surprisingly, though, there is evidence that some babies may not be able to feel a very light touch. In one experiment the palms of babies two to three days old were tickled with weak electric currents. The babies did not respond at all until they were exposed to three times the amount of current an adult could feel.

Generally, girl babies appear to be slightly more responsive to touch than boys. Both boys and girls will feel you blowing on their tummies – but girls often respond to a lighter puff of air than boys.

Feeling pain

Until recently it was widely believed that newborns did not feel pain. It was thought that their response to painful stimuli was purely reflexive – that, for example, a baby who moved when pricked by a needle did so automatically, not because of any feeling of discomfort.

The current view is less simple. Physiologically, the newborn's system for transmitting pain messages to the brain is not fully developed – which might suggest that new babies would not be likely to feel pain, or would feel it only to a limited extent. However, a growing body of evidence based on observation indicates that babies feel pain to a far greater extent than had been supposed. Researchers have observed babies as young as four hours to see how they respond to a prick in the heel: they report that the babies display physiological signs consistent with those exhibited by adults who describe themselves in pain. One study showed that at four hours old seven out of ten babies actively used the unaffected leg to swipe at the one that had been pricked: this suggests a far greater ability to localize pain than had been thought possible.

A baby's reflexes are tested soon after birth. Below *He is startled by a loud noise.* Right *She involuntarily grips her father's thumbs.*

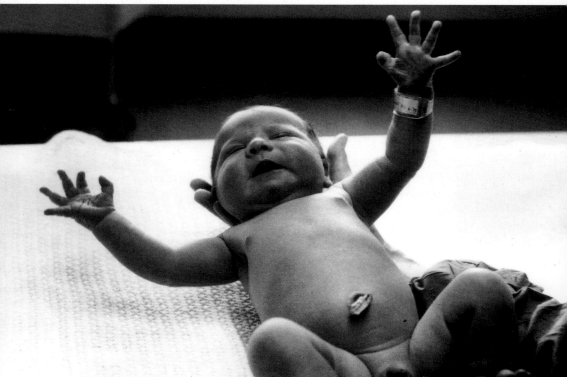

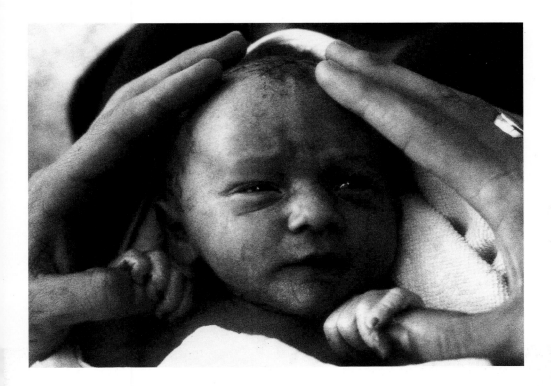

Reflexes

Newborn babies have a wide range of reflexes, that is involuntary responses to stimulation, as distinguished from skills which have to be learned. Some, such as those which govern breathing and sucking, the baby needs in order to survive. Others, such as the stepping and grasp reflexes, are primitive mechanisms that are of no practical use to the human baby but remain from earlier stages of evolution. Some reflexes are permanent – the breathing reflex, for example; but others, such as the Moro or startle reflex, disappear after a few months (see chart on page 74).

Pediatricians use reflexes to help build up a picture of a baby's development. The first check is to assess whether they are present at or just after birth. Stimulation of the feet is part of the test for the Apgar score, administered as soon as a baby is born (see page 61). Other reflexes, including the startle, grasp and stepping reflexes, are tested a day or two later. The absence of the expected response is an indication that all may not be well, and that further investigations should be carried out.

Reflexes can also be used to help pinpoint the degree of any possible prematurity, since the age at which each reflex appears prenatally is known.

Equally useful is the fact that reflexes disappear in a more or less predictable sequence. If there is a marked delay in the disappearance of a reflex, that is also an indication that further investigation may be required.

73

Some of the reflexes present in a newborn baby

Reflex	Way of testing	Baby's response	Duration
Blink	clap hands close to the baby's face	closes eyes	permanent
Swallowing		instinctively knows how to breathe while swallowing, though this is not well coordinated in the first few weeks	permanent
Gagging		coughs automatically if milk goes down the windpipe	permanent
Rooting	stroke the baby's cheek with a finger or nipple	turns his head towards the finger or nipple	until 3–4 months
Sucking	put the tip of a finger in the baby's mouth	sucks rhythmically	until 4 months when awake; until 7 months when asleep
Stepping	hold the baby upright with the soles of his feet touching a flat surface	makes walking movements	until 2–3 months
Startle or 'Moro'	make a sudden change in the baby's position so that his head drops backward; or create a sudden loud noise	throws out his legs and arms and arches his back	until 3–4 months
Palmar or hand grasp	press lightly on the palm of the baby's hand	grasps finger	until 3–4 months
Plantar or toe grasp	press lightly on the sides of the baby's foot	toes curl under	until 8–12 months
Babinski	stroke the side of the baby's foot	curls his big toe and fans out other toes	usually until 12 months

A new person in the family

The first meeting with someone you feel you have known a long time can be a strange experience. For several months this creature has been moving in the womb, kicking with a certain rhythm, often at predictable times – you may even have felt that some of the kicks were in response to the sound of your voice. You may have heard a heartbeat, even seen her picture on a scan. She is an old friend, she is a stranger.

However much you have anticipated this first encounter, there will still be some surprise. The rush of emotions can be overwhelming. So too can the sudden feeling of responsibility – the realization that you will be caring for and about this person for years to come. During these first hours and days of parenthood you may feel you are on an emotional roller coaster moving between elation and sadness, doubt and confidence, anxiety and fulfilment.

It is hardly surprising if a new mother is overcome by extremes of feeling. Not only is she meeting a most important new person in her life, the meeting is taking place at a moment when she is intensely vulnerable. The birth process is a major event, physically and emotionally; even a perfectly managed, uneventful delivery is exhausting, and a more complicated, stressful birth can leave the mother in a state of shock.

What is more, during the first hours and days after giving birth the mother's body is flooded with hormones. It has not so far been possible to pinpoint with any certainty the precise effect of postpartum hormones on the mother's emotional state, but while it appears unlikely that the biochemical changes actually cause feelings, it does seem that they play a part in increasing the intensity of emotions.

While the new father does not have to cope with the physical after-effects of pregnancy and birth, he, too, may be confused by mixed reactions to the situation – and the baby. Even when there has been plenty of preparation, a father can feel out of place and useless during the birth, and may be far from feeling full of joy and confidence when the baby comes. His first meeting with his child may be awkward – though, on the other hand, especially if the mother needs time to recover, it may be the father who gives the newborn her first warm, loving welcome into the world.

If during these first hours after the birth you are more conscious of fears and uncertainties than of love for your child, remember that while some parents fall in love with their baby immediately, for others coming to love is a more gradual process.

In the words of Sheila Kitzinger, a social anthropologist who has studied and written extensively about birth, 'It is just like any other kind of love affair. Sometimes you fall head over heels in love immediately, but you can also have an on-and-off love affair, or one which reveals itself slowly over time. You suddenly realize you do love your baby. It can come as a surprise that you feel so strongly.'

A new baby alters the balance of the family. Don't be surprised if you all feel rather vulnerable at first.

Bonding

In the mid-1970s, a period when most hospital-born babies spent their first days in a nursery, separated from their mothers, two American pediatricians, Marshall Klaus and John Kennell, startled the world of child psychology with their theory of bonding. They claimed that the first moments of a newborn's life are critical in the formation of the relationship between mother and baby. If a mother is parted from her baby during the first hours after birth there will be (it is alleged) an adverse effect on the relationship, on her parenting, and on the subsequent development of the child.

The key aspects of the theory are that:

- there is a bond from the mother to the child

- this bond can only be formed in the first hours after birth

- bonding helps a woman to be a loving, caring mother to her child

---

Postnatal depression
During the first few days after giving birth as many as 50 per cent of women go through a period of feeling emotionally distraught. A new mother may be horrified to find herself crying uncontrollably, even feeling, momentarily, that she hates her baby. This state is commonly referred to as the 'baby blues', and in more technical language as postpartum or postnatal depression. In nine out of ten of the mothers affected this dramatic mood dip passes within a week or so, but in a few it lasts longer. If it goes on for more than a week, medical advice is needed.

There is a school of thought that considers postnatal depression to be directly caused by biochemical changes. However, in most cases, the explanation seems to lie in a combination of the increased vulnerability of the woman who has just given birth and the social circumstances of her life.

If a woman has financial worries, or if she is unsupported by her partner, or if she has cause for anxiety about her baby or her other children, she is at far greater risk of suffering from postnatal depression. Women who deliver at home are less likely to become depressed than those who give birth in hospital (it is probably significant that these women are generally at low risk of complications at or surrounding birth). Mothers with babies who are immediately responsive are less likely to become seriously depressed; and so are women who have a good network of emotional support. This last gives a clue to the best way to help: women suffering from postnatal depression recover more quickly if they are encouraged to talk, to voice their feelings and their fears.

In considering the likely effect of a mother's depression on her baby, various factors have to be taken into account: probably most significant are how long the depression lasts and whether there is someone to take over the care of the baby. In a mild bout of depression lasting a few days the danger of any enduring effect on the baby is slight. However, the child of a single mother whose profound depression lasts for years is at physical and emotional risk.

Over the years since Klaus and Kennell published their study things have changed a lot. In most hospitals it is now normal practice for the mother to have her baby beside her. Certainly this seems to be a happy development for mothers – and, one might guess, for babies. But does early closeness or separation have an inevitable effect on their relationship?

There have been many studies in which researchers have observed mothers and babies who have been together from birth and those who have been separated. It has been found that mothers who have had early contact with their babies tend to breastfeed for longer than those who have not. There is also evidence that early contact may help mothers who are from very deprived backgrounds to care for their babies. For most mothers, however, there is no hard evidence that an early brief separation has any effect on their subsequent relationships with their babies.

No mother who wants to be with her baby should be deprived of the opportunity. But many mothers cannot be with their babies immediately after birth: the stresses of anaesthetics or the effect of a complex birth procedure (such as a Caesarian section) may make it impossible. A mother may simply be too exhausted. Babies, too, sometimes need to be separated from their mothers for sound medical reasons. And babies who are to be adopted are of course highly unlikely to be with their adoptive mothers in the hours immediately following birth. All the research results available suggest that these mothers and babies soon make up for lost time when they do meet, and there is every reason to believe that they can go on to establish a close attachment (see page 141).

Temperament

Newborn babies have many characteristics in common; but they also differ from each other, not only physically, but also in the more subtle ways we group under the heading of temperament or personality. These differences will become more evident over the months and years to come, but it is already possible to observe, among the youngest babies, variations in energy level, in the amount and vigour of kicking and general movement, in the quantity of crying and fussing, and in the readiness with which they adapt to a new situation. Moreover, certain types of behaviour are frequently found in clusters: for example, babies who quickly develop a regular routine tend also to adjust easily to new experiences; irritable, fussy babies are often difficult to feed and slow to adapt to changes.

Various ways of categorizing the different aspects of babies' temperaments have been suggested, but the most influential has been the formulation of the psychiatrists Stella Chess and Alexander Thomas, who began researching this topic in the 1970s. Chess and Thomas found that the babies they studied fell into four groups. Most (about 40 per cent of their sample) were what they described as temperamentally easy. Easy babies are characterized by regularity and adaptability. Within a few days or weeks they establish a routine more or less by themselves, sleep regular hours, eat at

As you get to know your baby you will learn how to respond to her needs.

predictable intervals and have bowel movements at regular times. They also react positively to new experiences – visiting other people's homes, for example. Such babies are relatively easy to look after and reinforce parents' confidence in their ability to care for their child.

Only 10 per cent of the Chess and Thomas sample fell into the second group, difficult babies. The difficult baby is slow to develop any regular routine. As soon as you think she has settled into a pattern of eating or sleeping, this baby will alter it. If she sleeps through one night, she will keep you awake for nights after. Just when you think you know her daytime sleep pattern, and arrange your chores around it, she will stay awake all day. Difficult babies tend to be irritable and to cry a lot, they resist new experiences and are upset by change.

The third group, slow-to-warm, made up about 15 per cent of the sample. Whereas difficult babies react aggressively to strange situations, slow-to-warm babies withdraw. Though they do not take easily to new people, new places or new foods, they do not show strong resistance either. They are less irritable than the difficult babies but they can still be hard work, for they need to be stimulated or coaxed into every new experience.

The remaining 35 per cent of babies in the sample shared certain characteristics of two or three of the basic types. They might be easy in some circumstances, difficult in others.

In further studies, Chess and Thomas found that these early patterns tended to some extent to persist throughout childhood, and even into early adulthood. We are certainly not arguing here (nor do Chess and Thomas) that temperament is in any way fixed at birth. In our view there can be no doubt that innate temperament is shaped and altered, and can even be counteracted, through life's experiences. However, a recognition that even the youngest babies have their own temperamental tendencies may help parents to fit their approach to their children's needs.

Compatibility of temperament

Life is a lot easier if parent and child are temperamentally compatible. They need not necessarily be similar in temperament; but it is important that they should be capable of adjusting to each other.

Expectations can play a large part here. For example, not all difficult babies are perceived by their parents as troublesome. Some parents expect babies to be unsettled and cry a lot, and take a baby's fussing calmly, as all in the day's work. Others seem to find it hard to cope even with the demands of a baby who appears to outsiders to be reasonably easy. If parents like these have a difficult child, they may be thrown into turmoil; and their baby is likely to respond by becoming even more unsettled.

In most families, compatibility between parents and baby is achieved over time, with compromises being reached on three sides. Babies do an impressive job of adapting to their parents' lifestyle, and even those parents who, before the birth, protested that the baby was 'not going to make any difference to our lives' find themselves making adjustments.

A world of activity

In the first few hours and days of life, your new baby's behaviour may seem haphazard and unpredictable. Gradually – quite soon if you have an easy baby, more slowly if she is temperamentally difficult – you will see a pattern emerge. As this becomes established you and your child will be able to work towards a rhythm of living.

Sleeping

During the first few days of life a newborn baby may spend twenty-three hours out of twenty-four asleep. By two weeks the average baby is sleeping

Feeding, sleeping, looking, hearing, crying – the pattern of your new baby's life starts to emerge and gradually you will both establish your own rhythms and ways of doing things.

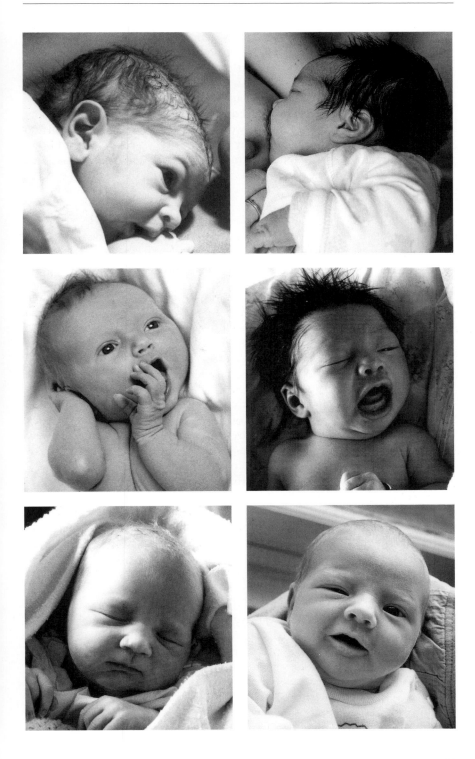

sixteen to eighteen hours out of twenty-four – though there is wide variation in the amount of sleep babies need, and it is not unknown for a baby a couple of weeks old to sleep for as little as eight hours. The usual pattern is one of sleeping sessions three to four hours long interspersed with short bursts of wakefulness, scattered throughout the day and night.

In the early weeks babies have no control over their sleeping and waking states, and they move between the two apparently at random. There is no point in expecting your newborn baby to sleep for long stretches: her brain will probably not be sufficiently mature to regulate her sleeping patterns until she is at least three months old. (See also pages 169–73.)

Feeding

In the womb a baby receives nutrition from her mother, through the placenta, with no effort on her part. Now, out in the world she has to acquire her food for herself, by sucking. Fortunately, with her strong sucking reflex, she is well equipped to do so.

This all sounds very simple; and, on the whole, it is. However, while many babies and mothers find feeding comes easily and naturally, some babies, and some mothers, have to learn how to do it. Decisions have also to be made on whether to feed by breast or bottle, or, just possibly, a combination of the two.

Learning to feed

For the baby, there are two instinctive processes at work: the automatic turning of the head towards a touch on the cheek, and the urge to suck when presented with a nipple. If a baby is breastfed her cheek will naturally brush her mother's breast; it will help a bottle-fed baby if whoever is feeding her touches one cheek gently before offering the teat.

If you are breastfeeding you may find that the baby needs to be encouraged to suck on a good mouthful of breast (sucking just on the nipple itself may make the breast sore). If the baby seizes the nipple only, inserting a finger in the side of her mouth will break the suction. Gently stroke her lips with the nipple to encourage her to open her mouth and take in more.

Breast or bottle?

This is another of those early decisions you will make for your baby. The balance of the dietary evidence is firmly in favour of breastfeeding: breastmilk is perfectly suited to a baby's digestive system and it changes its composition, during each feed and over weeks, to adapt to the baby's changing needs. It also provides a measure of protection against many diseases, since the mother passes antibodies to the baby in her milk and, especially, in the colostrum, the yellowish fluid secreted by the breasts in the earliest days, before the milk comes in. Moreover, breastfeeding can be intensely pleasurable to mothers and, it seems, to babies. The close contact can help to create an early attachment between mother and child.

But the case for breastfeeding is not so simple. There are mothers for whom breastfeeding is difficult or impossible: a mother may need to be away from the baby for lengthy periods, she may be in poor health, she may, for medical reasons, need to take drugs which could harm her baby. This last raises a consideration that has wider implications: a breastfeeding mother passes on to her baby some of everything she herself takes in. So, for example, if she smokes, her baby will absorb some nicotine; if she drinks alcohol, so will the baby. A sense of proportion is necessary here – an occasional glass of wine will not do irreparable harm. But when deciding what she is going to consume, a breastfeeding mother needs to consider her baby's needs as well as her own.

Babies whose mothers cannot breastfeed, or choose not to, are not necessarily deprived. Most babies do well on formula milk. Bottle-feeding also has the advantage that others can share in the feeding.

It is certain, though, that however you choose to feed your baby, the way she is held and loved during feeds is important to her well-being. What babies (and parents) thrive on is skin-to-skin and eye-to-eye contact, in a relaxed atmosphere. You may have to work harder to achieve these when bottle-feeding, if only because a bottle is not so tactile as a human breast.

Whose schedule?

Parents are often very concerned (and are certainly given a good deal of conflicting advice) about whether to feed on demand or to a schedule. You may find it helps to clarify the issue if you think about the learning process the baby has to go through. In the womb she was fed more or less constantly; once born, she has to learn to accept that there will be times when she feels full and times when she is empty. This is a big change: it is hardly surprising that it takes most babies some time to adapt.

Normally, newborn babies do best when they are allowed to feed according to their own individual rhythms. These rhythms vary a lot from baby to baby, and a particular baby's pattern may change from day to day – or hour to hour. During the first day of life demands for food are usually infrequent; on succeeding days some babies seem happy to leave an interval of four hours between feeds (a new baby who goes longer than four hours without a feed may need to be woken to be fed); but most babies want to be fed much more often than that – some, as often as every hour.

Mothers used to be advised to divide feeding time equally between the two breasts. If the second breast is uncomfortably full of milk you may need to move the baby over, for your own sake. However, in general it is probably best to let the baby decide when she wants to come off the first breast. Over the course of the feed the fat content of the milk increases, while the rate of flow decreases. At the beginning of a feed the baby takes in a large volume of low-calorie milk; at the end, she takes a smaller volume of high-calorie milk. If a baby is transferred from one breast to the other before she has finished at the first, she may end up taking in too little of the high-calorie milk, and need to be fed more frequently.

Crying

On the whole, newborns cry rather less than slightly older babies, though, of course, there are wide differences between individual crying patterns. In the first three days of life most normal babies cry between 2 and 11 per cent of the time. But new parents, particularly, can find even a small amount of crying quite worrying: does it mean that their baby is unhappy? It may help to remember that crying serves important functions for a baby.

Crying helps develop the child's respiratory system and circulation. This does not mean that it is good to leave a baby to 'cry it out', to develop her lungs. A little cry goes a long way, and protracted crying is exhausting for everyone. What is even more important, crying is your baby's main form of communication. She needs you to respond swiftly when she cries. Parents sometimes worry that by reacting immediately to their babies' cries they will encourage them to cry more. The evidence is, however, that babies whose parents are sensitive and responsive to their cries actually cry less overall. Perhaps they become generally more comfortable and contented.

Smiling

In some photographs taken of babies in the womb, the fetuses look as if they are smiling. Certainly, babies seem to smile from birth but as far as we know, these are not social smiles. They do not involve the eyes and seem to be reflex actions. During the first two weeks babies tend to smile when they are drowsy: as their muscles relax a smile appears. If they are startled they will be aroused again and the smile will vanish; soothe them and the smile returns.

In their second two weeks some babies can be induced to smile when they are awake, if they are gently stimulated. By the time they are about six weeks most babies will smile if they see a face smiling at them, or if they hear a familiar voice. Now their eyes smile and their faces light up – these are true 'happy' smiles.

Learning and teaching

From birth, babies are constantly learning. Here you, the parents, have an essential role to play. If you offer your baby consistent signals, and respond with sensitivity to the signals she sends, you can help her to develop ever more complex skills and to build the basic blocks of language and thinking. Perhaps most important of all, you can help her to learn that she is loved, valued and protected.

For an example of the kind of response we are describing, watch a mother breastfeeding her baby. As the baby breaks off from sucking she gazes at her mother, who bends closer and strokes her cheek, encouraging her to suck again. It is an intense conversation, with both mother and baby actively participating. While mothers embark on these 'conversations' for their own sake, they constitute an early example of teaching and learning: the mother is teaching her baby to anticipate certain acts and the baby learns that feeding can be satisfying emotionally as well as physically.

Memory in the newborn

There can be no learning without memory. And, once again, recent research has revealed that even a young baby's memory is better than we might think.

A newborn baby will watch her mother's face for a few seconds and then lose interest – or so it seems. Actually, what is happening is quite complex: as the baby responds to a new stimulus – looking at a face or listening to a repeated sound – the nerve cells in the brain become active. The baby can stand the excitement of a new stimulus for only a short time, and then the nerve cells appear to switch off, and cease to register the message.

Can the baby remember an image or sound she has experienced for such a short time? Research indicates that babies less than a month old can remember either a visual image or a sound for up to twenty-four hours, but only if it is repeated over and over again. Some images and sounds (the parents' faces, the baby's name) are, naturally, often repeated. Quite soon, your baby will learn to remember them. You and she have begun on the long journey of teaching and learning.

Imitating

Example is, of course, among the most powerful of teaching methods – and, from the outset, babies are able to imitate. Babies as young as twelve hours can copy adults who open their mouths wide or stick out their tongues. Within a few days they can raise their eyebrows and wriggle their noses in imitation, and even copy happy, sad and surprised expressions.

If you try to test this out on your baby, you may be disappointed. Researchers involved in this type of study build special environments for their experiments, to block out all distractions. What is more, a baby's response is not always easily recognized: sometimes it can be seen clearly only in a slow-motion recording. But you can be sure that your baby is learning to imitate you, even if you are not able to read her responses.

Conditioning

It appears that very young babies can learn that certain actions bring rewards. Their feeding behaviour may be, in part, an example of this. The baby's sucking reflex is activated by a touch on the cheek and the presentation of a nipple (see page 82). When her sucking is rewarded by a gulp of warm milk, she sucks more vigorously.

Of course, babies find sucking enjoyable in itself. In one study newborns were given a suck on a dummy as a reward when they turned their heads. In response they tripled the number of head turns. In a later experiment the same babies were given the dummy when they did not move their heads – and they learned to turn them less often.

When All Is Not Well

Babies needing special care

All newborns thrive on warmth, love and affection. Some need medical attention as well. Babies whose birthweight is less than 2.25 kg/5 lb, those who have severe or persistent breathing difficulties and those whose bodily functions are immature are likely to require attention in special care baby units. All sick babies will, of course, need special care, as will some of those born with defects or disabilities.

Most antenatal care is aimed at helping babies reach full term in a healthy state at an average weight. Babies born early will have missed the last stages of development and will not be well equipped to cope with the world outside the womb. Any birth before thirty-seven weeks of pregnancy is regarded as premature.

Sometimes a baby comes early because the placenta is not functioning well, or because the mother is in poor health or ill nourished. In about half of all cases of prematurity, though, the cause is unknown.

Any premature baby is at risk, as the basic mechanisms for survival may not be working properly. Breathing difficulties, for example, are common. Most babies born early also have immature heat-regulating systems, and insufficient of the subcutaneous fat which helps them retain heat; because of this, extra care has to be taken to keep them at a constant warm temperature. Preterm babies may also have feeding problems because their sucking and swallowing reflexes have not developed. Again, during the last few weeks of a full-term pregnancy antibodies are transferred to the fetus which help the newborn form immunities. A baby born too early will not have received these antibodies, and so will be more susceptible to infection.

Low birthweight is one of the results of prematurity, but there are other causes for babies being born small. One is genetic: the babies are normal, they just have small parents. Unless there are other problems, these babies should not need any special care. There are babies, though, who weigh significantly less than would be expected for their gestation period and their parents' weight. These babies, called 'small-for-dates', do need special care. Their small size indicates that something is not right: it may be that they suffered from malnutrition or from a reduction in blood flow while they were in the womb.

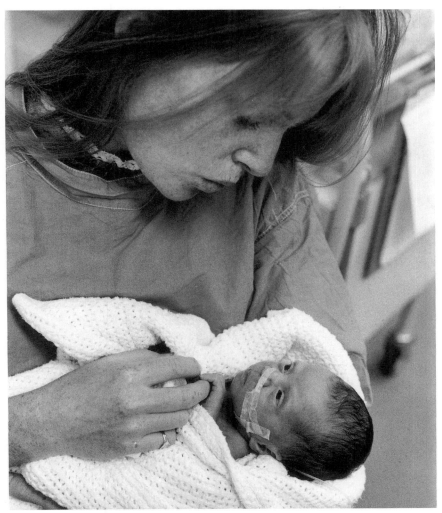

Babies need human contact. Even if yours is in a special care unit, you should try to touch her, feed her and cuddle her.

What parents can do

If a baby has to stay in a special care unit for any length of time, it can be hard for the parents to form a relationship with her. Fortunately, most hospitals are now aware of how much baby and parents need each other, and encourage the parents to spend time with their child. You should be with your baby as much as you can, and, even if you feel nervous initially, try to feed her, touch her and cuddle her. The father often has a particularly important role to play when a baby is in special care, the more so if the mother has had a difficult delivery when he may be the most readily available person in the family.

Even when you have your baby home and are caring for her yourself, you may find some difficulty in relating to her. She may be less responsive than most babies, she may look so small and scrawny that you feel afraid to hold her, she may be restless and have a plaintive, wailing cry. It helps if you can remember that prematurity is not an illness: your baby is developing all the time, at her own rate.

For the first couple of years, the development of premature and small-for-dates babies tends to lag behind that of other children of the same chronological age. If they are brought up in a constant, loving environment where they receive adequate nutrition and medical care, there is no reason to expect anything other than generally normal development once the first two years have passed. However, low-birthweight children from unstable or impoverished homes tend to remain smaller than other children, to have more emotional problems and to do less well in school. Once again, it is not a single event or condition that counts, so much as the way the condition is treated, and how it fits into the general pattern of a child's life.

The child with a disability

All parents, before their baby is born, harbour hopes and fears for the child. After the birth, some have to face the fact that their baby has an evident disability. For example, one baby in 600 has cerebral palsy; one in 700 has Down's syndrome; three in 10,000 have a significant sight loss. (These figures are all approximate. The occurrence of disabilities varies from country to country, and the reliability of the figures depends partly on the accuracy of reporting and partly on the stringency of definitions.)

In responding to the birth of a child with a disability, most parents, though of course not all, tend to go through a series of recognizable stages.

The first response is one of shock, and possibly of revulsion. This is an entirely natural, human reaction. It is not one to be ashamed of. Parents may also have to accept that, in these early days and later, their attitude towards their child will swing from deep love to loathing and back again.

Next comes a searching – for causes and explanations, and, often, for someone to blame. At this stage parents are frequently racked with anger – at each other, at themselves, at their doctors, at fate, at they don't know who or what. Some parents say too that in these early days they are mourning the loss of the perfect child they had hoped to have.

The third stage is seeking out what can be done, medically and educationally, trying to establish what the outlook is for the future, what the prospects are that the child and the family may lead a normal life.

Some parents come to terms with the problem rapidly, and are soon able to recognize what their child has to offer. Others may take longer. A small minority, perhaps feeling that they – or the family as a whole – will not be able to cope, refuse to acknowledge the child. Even at this early stage the baby's responsiveness is telling. If you can communicate with your baby, no matter how great the disability, you will have something to build on. For this reason it is particularly important to get advice if your baby is blind or has some other problem that might impede communication.

A disability is another example of an event or condition whose effect on children is largely determined by the parents' response. One indication of the attitude of parents (and others) is the way they describe their child. Older children often say that they dislike the term 'disabled child', preferring 'a child with a disability'. This is not a matter of playing with words, but of setting priorities.

Bringing up a child with a disability is not easy. Some well-meaning people will tell you that the children bring great rewards. They do, but compared to the effort and the stress associated with the task, the rewards can often seem hard-won.

Parents can feel isolated – they may even believe that friends and colleagues are shunning them. To some extent, this can be true. Some people are frightened by the thought of any disability; others simply do not know what to say, and, embarrassed, avoid the issue. But sometimes parents themselves must take a measure of responsibility for their loneliness: preoccupied with their problems, or feeling that no one will understand, they isolate themselves.

There is help available – medical, social and personal – for children and for their families, but parents may have to work hard to find it. On the medical side, the family doctor or a pediatrician should be able to answer basic questions, and to direct parents to specialists in the field of their child's disability. The doctor can also put the family in touch with those branches of the social services which may be useful.

It often helps to meet parents of children with similar disabilities early on. They can provide information and advice; what is perhaps even more important, they will know something of what you are feeling. Many self-help organizations have been established which you may find very useful.

Grandparents, friends and neighbours can be a source of support – don't refuse their help, thinking you are strong enough to cope on your own. On the other hand, they can add to your burdens. Grandparents are sometimes so shocked that they cut themselves off from the new baby. Friends may make insensitive remarks. It helps to be ready to give a clear explanation of the baby's condition and to correct any misconceptions.

In the last few pages we have discussed babies who have needs that are special in the medical sense. However, all children – the healthy full-term infant and the child with a disability alike – share the same fundamental needs. The British psychologist Mia Kellmer Pringle summed up the needs of children under four headings: love and security; praise and recognition; new experiences; responsibility. Responsibility can come later; the first three are relevant to all babies, everywhere.

3 TOWARDS INDEPENDENCE up to eighteen months

To the new parent, the transformations that occur in the first eighteen months of a child's life seem miraculous. Over this period your son or daughter will change from a dependent baby to a walking, talking toddler. You will be able to watch him learn to control his body, so that he can sit, stand and walk; he will also become a social being, able to recognize and respond to the people and things around him. But you will not simply be observing while all this is going on. You are a partner in your child's development. What is more, as he develops and you respond to his altering needs, you too, as a parent, will be changing.

Physical Development

An understanding of the way development proceeds will enable you to appreciate all the small steps that lead to such major feats as walking and talking – and should also help you to avoid unrealistic expectations of your child.

There are two basic laws relating to the physical development of children at this time.

• Development proceeds from top to bottom (the cephalocaudal law). Babies' heads grow first, which is why, during the first years, their heads look enormous in proportion to their bodies.

• Development proceeds from the inner parts to the extremities (the proximodistal law). This explains why babies' hands and feet look so tiny compared with their bodies. By the time they are starting to walk, their chests, as well as their heads, may appear too large for their legs to carry, which can make them look awkward.

Children grow faster during their first year of life than they ever will again. A baby can be expected to gain 25–30 cm/10–12 inches in length and about 7–8 kg/16–18 lb by the first birthday, with the most rapid increase happening during the first six months. Changes in proportion are also occurring. For example, a baby's head at birth accounts for 25 per cent of the length of the entire body and almost 33 per cent of the body's volume, while the arms and legs make up only 8–16 per cent. These proportions gradually alter during childhood: the average adult's head is just under 10 per cent of the body length. At birth a baby's head circumference is greater than that of his chest; before the end of the first year, the two measurements are much the same.

Height

Height is mostly determined by heredity. Though factors such as nutrition also have an effect, in families where nutrition has been adequate for several generations a child's ultimate height usually approximates to an average of the height of the parents. However, at any point of childhood, but especially during the first two years, children may be considerably taller or shorter than their parents were at the same age.

The average length of a full–term baby is about 50 cm/20 inches. The length increases by 25–30 cm/10–12 inches during the first year and another 12.5 cm/5 inches in the second year. During the first two years the average boy tends to be slightly taller than the average girl. Perhaps a reminder is necessary here, that these are averages, and there are few average children; moreover, the figures are based on samples of European and North American children and do not relate accurately to the children of other nationalities, who may differ in stature. However, most children in developed countries will fall within the range specified on the charts on pages 94–5. Usually, if a child is extremely short or tall, the explanation is that he is taking after his parents, who are similarly short or tall. However, if, for no obvious reason, your child's height falls well outside the range indicated on the charts, it would be sensible to seek medical advice. The doctor will want to monitor your child's rate of growth for a time before taking any further steps; if the growth pattern indicates that there could be a medical problem, he or she may undertake further investigations, and recommend treatment if that is thought to be appropriate. For example, short stature is sometimes caused by a growth hormone deficiency, which may be corrected by administering supplementary hormones throughout childhood and adolescence, until growth is completed.

As a general rule, however, if your child is well, vigorous and energetic, there is no need to worry about height.

Weight

Weight is less predictable than height. Though the influence of heredity is significant, it can be counterbalanced by nutritional and psychological factors, and general health. Weight is also far more likely to alter quickly over a short period. This is one of the reasons why it is a good indicator of changes in a baby's well–being.

Weight gain is a result of changes in bone, muscle and fat. Bones increase in number, size and weight during this period, while the muscle fibres, though virtually all present at birth, grow in length and thickness. Most of the fat component of the body is found immediately under the skin. Some is laid down before birth and fat cells continue to develop rapidly during the first year, reaching a peak at about nine months.

The average boy weighs 3.3 kg/7 lb 6 oz at birth; at 3.2 kg/7 lb 4 oz, the average baby girl is a little lighter. Babies normally lose up to 10 per cent of their birthweight during the first three days after birth, regain their birthweight by about the tenth day, then go on to gain weight very rapidly during the next six months, increasing their weight by about 900 g/2 lb a month. At six months weight gain slows to approximately 450 g/1 lb a month. Towards the end of the first year weight gain reduces again, to settle at about 280 g/10 oz a month for the second year. (See the charts on pages 96–7.)

Length chart for boys aged 0-18 months

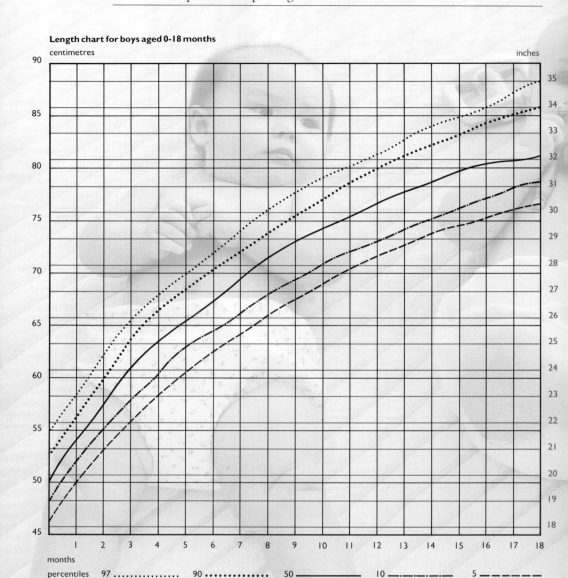

months

percentiles   97 ·············   90 ••••••••••   50 ——————   10 —·—·—·—   5 — — — — —

Length 0–18 months

Measure your baby lying down, stretched out straight, using a steel measuring tape. To use the charts, find the age, in months, at the bottom of the chart and the length in centimetres on the left or inches on the right; mark where the age and length cross. If you note your child's measurements regularly, and join the marks to make a curve, you will be able to plot the pattern of growth.

The charts are based on data collected by measuring a number of children at regular intervals. If your child's length is on the 50th percentile, he or she is longer than 49 per cent, and shorter than 50 per cent, of the boys or girls of the same age who were measured. If the length is

94

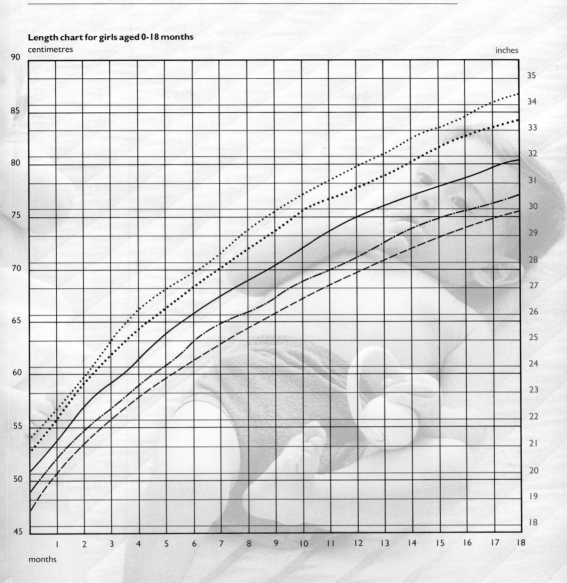

Length chart for girls aged 0-18 months

centimetres

inches

months

on the 10th percentile, the child is longer than 9 per cent of the children measured, shorter than 90 per cent.

The range of the normal is wide. Even if your child does seem short (or long) when compared with the average length, provided he or she is otherwise well, there is probably no reason to be concerned. In most cases where children are unusually short or long, they are just taking after their parents. However, if, for no obvious reason, your child's length is below the 5th or above the 95th percentile it is worth checking with your doctor. It is also wise to seek advice if there is a significant change in the growth pattern, or if there is a marked discrepancy between length and weight.

Weight chart for boys aged 0-18 months

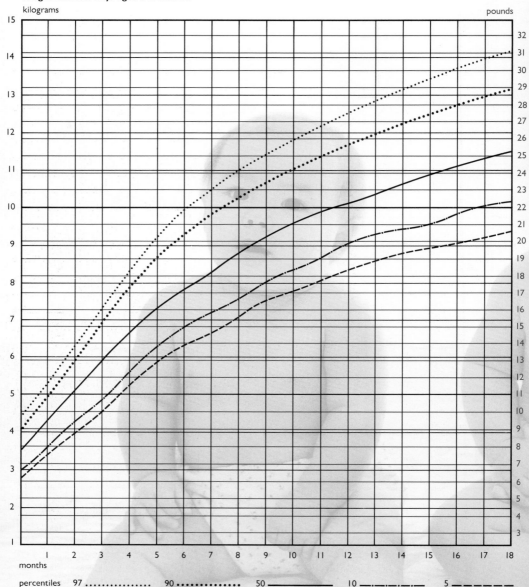

kilograms

pounds

months

percentiles   97 ················   90 ••••••••••••   50 ———————   10 —·—·—·—·—   5 — — — — —

Weight 0–18 months

Babies are generally weighed as part of their routine clinical examinations. If you want to weigh your baby at home you will need to use special baby scales. If possible, weigh the baby naked before a feed.

The weight curve can be plotted on the charts above following the same instructions as those provided for the length charts.

A baby may lose up to 10 per cent of birthweight during the first three days after birth, regaining the

Weight chart for girls aged 0-18 months

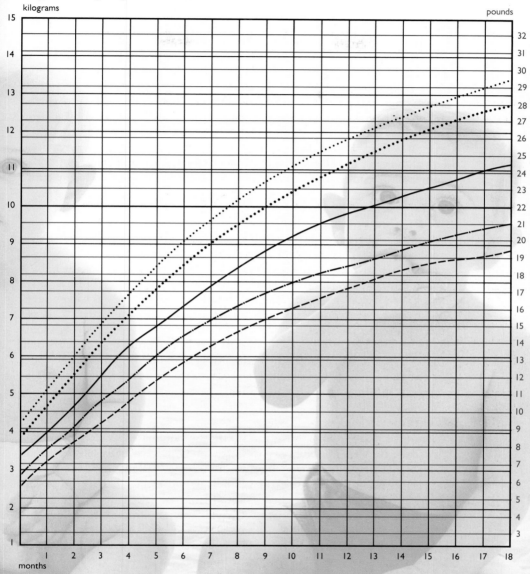

kilograms

pounds

months

birthweight by about the tenth day. After this he or she will gain approximately 28 g/1 oz a day. The birthweight has generally doubled by six months, trebled by a year.

You should check with your doctor if your child's weight changes markedly or goes below the 5th percentile or above the 95th percentile. He or she is most likely to be on the same percentile for both weight and height; if there is a wide discrepancy here you may want to discuss it with your doctor.

Nutrition

Nutrition plays a significant part in determining whether or not a child ultimately reaches the potential weight (and height) that his genetic endowment offers. However, in countries where food is generally plentiful there seems to be only a crude connection between the amount babies eat in the first fifteen months of life and the amount of weight they gain. Certainly, a baby who is starved will be underweight, and a baby who is grossly overfed will be overweight, but in normal circumstances most babies are good at regulating their food consumption so that they take what they need. A baby's level of activity also makes a difference. A thin baby who is awake a good deal of the time and cries and moves a lot, may well eat and drink as much as a quieter, heavier baby; he puts on less weight because he burns up more calories.

Breast- and bottle-feeding

There is a slight tendency for bottle-fed babies to be heavier than those who are breastfed. This may be because breastfeeding mothers are more inclined to allow babies to regulate the amount they take. When the baby is satisfied, he stops sucking. The mother doesn't know exactly how much milk he has had, but, usually, she will simply accept that he has had enough. When a parent is feeding a baby from a bottle, on the other hand, there is a temptation to encourage the baby to 'finish the bottle'. There is also some evidence that variations in the composition of breastmilk may actually help a baby to know when he has had enough. Depending on how hungry he is the baby can choose to take in more or less of the richest milk, which comes at the end of the feed.

Weaning

Weaning marks a major transition for mother and baby – emotionally and physically. Giving up the breast or bottle on which the baby has depended since birth brings satisfaction in terms of increased independence, but it has its painful side too, as mother and baby surrender their early closeness.

Both babies and mothers need a lot of time to make this adjustment, so weaning needs to be a slow process, extending over months rather than days or weeks. When you begin, and how you proceed, is up to you and your baby. If you are sensitive to your baby's signals, he may be able to show you when he is losing interest in feeding from the breast or bottle; but your own feelings, too, need to be considered.

For example, some parents find the night feeds very satisfying: they enjoy the opportunity to have an uninterrupted cuddle with their baby. Others, though, find it difficult to cope with broken nights, and for them weaning the baby from night feeds is likely to be a priority. If they are lucky, their baby might start sleeping through the night when he is a couple of months old. However, at three months many babies are still waking at least once during the night, and possibly more often.

A breastfeeding mother who wants to drop the night feeds can start to wean her baby by expressing breastmilk and putting it into a bottle, which can be offered to the baby during the night – by the father, preferably, or by someone else who is prepared to help. The baby is more likely to accept it if it comes from someone other than his mother, from whom he expects the breast. As the baby gets older, water can be substituted for milk in night feeds.

At around four or five months, as the baby becomes intensely interested in his surroundings, he may be ready to be distracted from one of his day-time feeds. Again, when the teeth start to come through, usually at around six to nine months, a baby may start to bite or play at the breast. This may be a cue to start curtailing, and ultimately to drop, one or more of the remaining daytime feeds.

The bedtime feed will probably be the last to go, as most babies continue to need the comfort of sucking until late in the first year. However, if this comfort feed is gradually made briefer, most babies can gently be weaned from it by the time they are a year old. If you and your baby want to continue for longer, that's fine.

Some breastfed babies lose interest in the breast and wean themselves. This can be emotionally difficult for a mother who enjoys breastfeeding. However, though she may feel unwanted when her baby rejects feeds, she should be assured that her baby still needs her. Her relationship with him is more, far more, than a matter of physical nourishment.

Introducing solid food

For the baby, the introduction of solid foods brings many new experiences. In taste, texture and consistency these foods are very different from the milk which is all he has so far known. Different skills are called for: chewing and swallowing need to be learned, whereas sucking was an instinctive response.

The introduction of new foods happens in parallel with weaning, and should be an equally gradual process. However, it is a mistake to see it as the same process. It is quite possible to supplement breast- or bottle-feeding with solids rather than shifting completely from one to the other.

For the first six months, the only food most babies need is milk: this meets all of their nutritional requirements. However, you can start introducing tastes of solid food from the time your baby is about four months old. By the time a baby is six months old the stores of iron with which he was born are used up; milk does not provide enough iron for his requirements, so he needs other foods.

Cereals and vegetable or fruit purées are probably the most common early foods, but you don't have to limit your baby to these. It is important not to give him any food with added salt, as this could put a strain on his kidneys; nor should he have foods with extra sugar or additives. Eggs, cow's milk, wheat, fish and chocolate can all cause allergic reactions, so they should be added with circumspection. If you or your partner have any history of food sensitivity, or if the baby suffers from eczema or any skin rash, you need to be particularly careful. Otherwise, introduce foods as you like, but always one at a time (so you can immediately identify and avoid anything that disagrees with the baby) and, at first, in tiny quantities and purée form. Physiologically, most babies can chew and swallow little pieces of food by the time they are four months old, but there is no reason to try this out. It is an effort for the baby and, while the food can be chewed and swallowed, it may not be digested very well.

Around six months, when the first teeth have just started to come through, your baby will probably begin to like holding something in his hand and mouthing it. His chewing will not be very effective, but he will enjoy going through the motions with a rusk or a crust of bread. As he gets older and his teeth appear, he will become increasingly adept at coping with food of different textures. He will no longer need to have his food reduced to a smooth purée; it will be enough if you mash it, increasingly roughly. By the time he is a year old even mashing should be unnecessary, as he will be able to manage small chopped pieces of most foods.

Give your baby time to get used to foods with different tastes and textures: he may find them exciting, but equally he may at first be suspicious, rejecting or indifferent. Many babies spit out their first solid or semi-solid foods. This is not necessarily because the baby doesn't like the food. He may be sensitive to the flavour or smell, but it may simply be that his tongue, which is large in relation to his mouth, forces the food out. So far, the only motion the tongue has known is a sucking one. The baby has to learn how to take food in and chew it. This is a complicated exercise, and he will need lots of practice, over many meals, before he can manage it with any efficiency.

A healthy diet

So long as your baby is taking in substantial amounts of breastmilk or vitamin-enriched formula, you can be confident that the milk is supplying most of what he needs. Once he is weaned, you will, of course, want to make sure that he continues to have a healthy diet. The chart on pages 496–7 gives guidance on essential nutrients. The best way to ensure that your child gets them, in a form that he likes, is to provide a wide variety of different kinds of foods, both uncooked and cooked in various ways. Don't take it too seriously if a particular food is rejected. He may accept this food happily enough if he is given another chance after a reasonable lapse of time.

However, do make sure that you offer food, in small quantities, fairly frequently. As a rough guide, a young child needs to be fed twice as often as an adult. Between his main meals he should be offered nutritious and attractive finger foods which he can easily handle and control. When he is recovering from an illness, he may need an extra meal a day for as many days as the illness lasted: a child has not fully recovered until he catches up on any weight loss suffered.

Left *If your baby starts to play rather than feed, it may mean that he is ready to start being weaned.*
Right *This toddler is able to feed herself quite efficiently, though she may need help if she loses interest.*

Family meals

Babies like joining the family for meals, and particularly enjoy the company of other children. And even if at first they don't actually take in much food at the family table, shared mealtimes provide a good opportunity for them to get used to the idea of eating with other people – and imitating the way they eat.

Underweight babies

The ideal pattern of weight gain illustrated on pages 96–7 shows a continuous upward curve. Of course, in real life, no baby's growth pattern is quite so regular. If your baby is being weighed weekly you will almost certainly find that there are weeks when there is no weight gain, or even a slight loss. Usually there is a straightforward explanation. It may be that the baby has been weighed at a different time of day, or has eaten less at the most recent meal. A baby who has any illness, even a slight cold, will often lose weight rapidly, only to put it on again just as fast once he has recovered.

However, if a baby fails to gain weight over a period of a few weeks, this is cause for concern, and you should consult your doctor about it. The failure to grow may be an indication of a physical problem which has so far gone undetected. Or it could mean that the baby is simply not getting enough of the right kind of food – which can also be a serious matter.

There are many possible reasons why a child may not be adequately fed. We all think we know what a good diet is, but, nevertheless, we may not be aware of the precise needs of a young child. If your baby is underweight it may be that the food you are offering him is insufficient or inappropriate. Sometimes, parents are so anxious that their children should not become overweight that, with the best of intentions but in ignorance of babies' real needs, they restrict their food intake. (This may happen in a family where the mother is, perhaps, rather over-concerned about her own weight.) For some general guidance on the nutritional requirements of children, see pages 496–7. Your doctor or a dietician will be able to give you more specific advice on what your child needs.

Sometimes parents' feeling about the situation is that they offer their child food, but he refuses to eat it. If this is your view, you may need to look more closely at your relationship with the baby. Some babies are temperamentally difficult to feed, and some parents are less easygoing than others. If you find it difficult to tolerate a baby who throws food around, or makes a fuss over eating, you may be inclined to remove uneaten meals rather too briskly, and fail to respond adequately to signals of hunger.

Recent research suggests that, even where there are no such obvious problems, persistent underweight can be an indication that there is something amiss in the interaction between a baby and the person who is responsible for feeding him, usually his mother. Sometimes, a mother seems unable to recognize when and how her baby needs feeding – perhaps because she just doesn't know how to read the baby's signals, perhaps because she is herself unwell or depressed. As a result, the baby does not take in the food he is offered.

It is sometimes suggested that children can fail to grow for emotional reasons alone: that children who are not loved do not thrive, even if they are fed adequately and eat enough food to enable them to develop normally. It is certainly true that babies need love and affection, perhaps as much as they need food. Babies who are suddenly separated from their parents, or who are in a family where the mother is depressed and unable to function properly, often fail to put on weight. Overall, however, the connection between emotional deprivation and failure to grow is far from straightforward, for it is difficult to be sure that the emotional problems, or the surrounding circumstances, do not lead to a reduction in the amount of food taken in by the children. What does seem to happen is that when parents fail to respond to their baby, then the baby becomes unresponsive too. In an extreme case, if a baby is regularly left to cry, and not fed, changed or otherwise given attention when he needs it, he may give up, stop crying and become apathetic and sickly, failing to show any sign of healthy responsiveness or appetite.

If you feel that emotional problems between you and your baby may be contributing to feeding difficulties, then, for his sake and your own, you need to seek help. Dealing with this problem is nothing like so easy as arranging a physical examination, but, again, your first call could be on the family doctor, who should be able to advise you. Support can do a lot to relieve tensions, and when help is given to a family even babies who have been persistently underweight can usually catch up and begin to grow along a more normal curve.

Failure to thrive

If, for no evident physical reason, a baby or child is significantly underweight and remains so, failing to gain or perhaps even losing weight over a considerable period of time, doctors may speak of 'non-organic failure to thrive'. Usually, when babies who have been diagnosed as 'failing to thrive' are taken into hospital, fed regularly and given affection and stimulation, they start growing. If, when they return home, their rate of growth again slows down, there are clear signs of where the problem lies. It is evident that, if the baby is to continue to thrive, the family as a whole needs ongoing help. However, so long as the problem is recognized and children and families receive the treatment they need, most of these children go on to develop normally.

Overweight babies

Only a few generations ago, fat babies were the fashion. Now, many parents are inclined to worry if their baby shows signs of becoming overweight. They are concerned that excess weight may not be healthy, and they may also fear that if they allow their baby to become overweight they will set a pattern that could persist into adult life.

There is usually no reason at all to become concerned just because a baby is a bit plump. The proportion of body fat increases markedly in the first year and most of the babies who look fat at nine to twelve months will be a lot slimmer by the time they are two or three.

However, there are some babies who, instead of beginning to slim down, continue to gain body fat at a rapid rate and become grossly overweight, or obese. The excess weight carried by an obese baby may slow down his progress towards mobility, and, generally, make him less inclined to be active. This can be the start of a vicious spiral: obese children are likely to be teased by other children, and may then eat more to comfort themselves.

If you are concerned that your baby may be too heavy for his own good, you should consult your doctor about it. Broadly speaking, obesity is determined by weight for height, and usually a baby (like an adult) is considered obese if he is 20 per cent above the weight expected for his height or length. However, skinfold measurements – the thickness of the skin when held in a pinch-like grip – are also relevant, and it takes experience, and a special instrument, to do accurate skinfold measurements, especially on a baby.

If a baby is found to be obese, the doctor may recommend that he should be offered slightly smaller amounts of food at somewhat less frequent intervals, and that water should be given to satisfy a small part of the daily fluid requirement. None of this should be attempted without medical advice and careful monitoring: if you reduce a baby's food intake you run the risk of restricting his growth and development. Even with an obese baby, the goal of treatment is not that a baby should lose weight. What you want him to do is to maintain his weight at the same level until the length catches up. Height and weight increase can then resume a normal pattern.

Equally important in treating an obese baby is that the whole family's attitude to food may need to change. If a baby is obese, usually at least one parent is obese as well. It does seem that a tendency to fatness can be inherited (adopted children reared by obese parents are less likely to be overweight). However, the family's eating patterns are at least equally significant. It may be that the whole family is overeating, or eating the wrong foods, and they may all need to be given nutritional help and guidelines.

Emotional attitudes to food are also relevant. Some parents respond to all expressions of distress by offering food, even when a child is really looking for attention, a cuddle, or reassurance in some other form. This can set up a pattern whereby the child, in turn, learns to equate food with love and comfort. The parents may need help to learn to respond to their baby's signals of distress more appropriately.

Bone development

During the first years of a child's life the bones increase in number, as well as in size and weight. The wrist bones, for example, are not present at birth, but by the time a baby reaches twelve months he has three. (This is one of

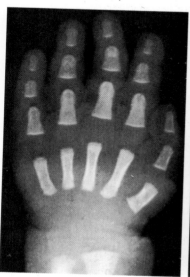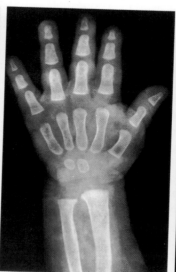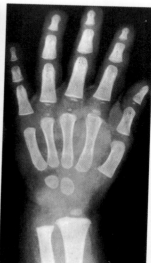

The bones in the baby's hand at birth, twelve months and eighteen months.

the physical developments that needs to take place before a baby can hold things securely.) Six more wrist bones develop during childhood and adolescence, making a total of nine in the adult.

Another important development is the hardening of the bones. The bones of a newborn baby are soft, which is one of the reasons why he is floppy (and why, a little later, he is supple enough to perform surprising tricks such as putting his foot in his mouth). Bones become harder through childhood and adolescence. Before the end of a baby's first year, his bones are hard enough to support him as he stands – although, as usual, the story of progress is not a simple one: before a child becomes upright, his muscles also need to develop, and his brain has to mature.

In the newborn baby, the skull is made up of several bones, with spaces (known as fontanelles) between them. During the process of birth the bones slide over each other, allowing an easier passage into the world. By the time children are around two years old these bones have fused together.

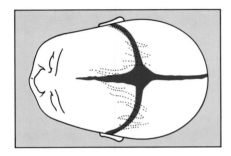

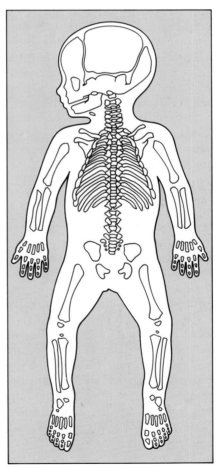

Right *The newborn baby's skeleton is composed of soft bones which will continue to grow and harden through childhood and adolescence.*
Above *The newborn's skull has spaces (called fontanelles) between the bones. By the time the child is two the skull will have fused together.*
Opposite *During the first years of life the child's bones actually increase in number. A baby is born with no wrist bones but by the time he is twelve months old he will have three and by adulthood he will have nine. As the bones develop he acquires greater control of his hand and wrist movements and becomes able to hold things more securely.*

105

Muscle development

Muscles grow rapidly during infancy: in the first eighteen months the muscle mass increases twice as fast as the mass of bones. The number of muscle fibres does not increase – a baby has the same number of muscle fibres at birth as he will have as an adult – but the fibres become longer and thicker.

The muscles develop from the inside out and the head down, following the proximodistal and the cephalocaudal laws of growth (see page 92). In early infancy, most of a child's muscle power is required for breathing and the diaphragm is the most hard-working muscle. The respiratory muscles of a young baby are twice the size of the muscles in the arms, which is why babies' arms are so small in proportion to their chests. As the limbs become more active the muscles of the arms and legs grow faster. The earliest sign of controlled muscle movement, as opposed to automatic reflex movement, is the control of the neck muscles which lift the head. Your baby may be able to support his head briefly by the time he is three weeks old; at six weeks he may lift it slightly. By three months his neck and back muscles are strong enough for him to raise his head and chest. By around six months he will probably be able to sit alone momentarily, and by eight months he will be strong enough to sit unsupported, with a straight back, for quite a while. Soon, the muscles of his legs will have developed sufficiently for him to be able to stand, and then to walk.

Some muscles take a long time to gain strength and size and to be brought under control. For example, it is usually not practical to try to toilet train a baby much under eighteen months – the muscles of the bowel and bladder are just not strong enough.

Teeth

There is wide variation in the ages at which babies cut their teeth, though they usually come through in the same order. Early teething does not indicate that a child is advanced, nor does late teething mean that a child is backward. Children simply respond to a hereditary teething pattern.

Generally the first teeth, usually the lower central incisors (the cutting teeth), come through at about six months, followed by the upper central incisors between six and eight months. The four lateral incisors then appear on either side of the central incisors, at around nine months. These are followed by the four front molars (the flat grinding teeth), usually between ten and fourteen months. The canines (the pointed eye teeth) come in to fill the gap between the lateral incisors and the front molars between sixteen and eighteen months. The back molars do not appear until around the end of the second year. By two and a half, most children have all twenty of their baby teeth.

The amount of discomfort suffered as the teeth come through also varies

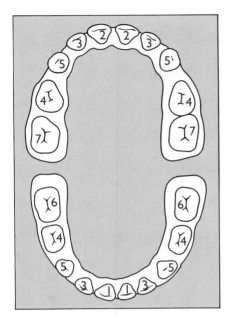

The illustration indicates the order of appearance of the primary teeth and the average age when they erupt. But the age when teeth come in can vary considerably.

1 – 6 months
2 – 6–8 months
3 – 9 months
4 – 10–14 months
5 – 16–18 months
6 – 20 months
7 – 24 months

from child to child (and even from tooth to tooth), but it can be quite severe. You should suspect teething problems if your baby's gums are red and sore and one cheek is flushed. Teething is also often accompanied by an increase in dribbling. If he is in pain he may well be fretful. His general behaviour may be affected too – children often regress, demanding to be picked up and carried when they have been walking for some time, or refusing to use a spoon or drink from a cup. Do not worry that a new achievement has slipped away: once the pain has subsided your baby will soon be practising his skills again, and making new progress.

You should be careful, however, to avoid the temptation to attribute all problems around this stage to 'teething troubles'. If you do this, you will risk missing the signs of illness. A baby who has diarrhoea, or a slightly raised temperature, for more than twenty–four hours should always be seen by a doctor. If a baby's temperature suddenly shoots up, medical advice should be sought at once.

The development of the brain

At birth the brain is approximately 33 per cent of its adult size but only 25 per cent of its eventual weight. By one year it has reached 66 per cent of its adult weight and by five years the figure is 90 per cent. The brain continues to increase in weight for the next twenty years or so; but the rapid growth over the first few years shows how much is happening in this period.

The anatomy of the brain is remarkably complete when the baby is born.

Carrying messages

Messages travel from one cell to another via axons, which are fibres going out from the cells, and dendrites, which are extensions of the cells themselves. The all–important junctions between axons and cells are called synapses: a synapse can occur between an axon and a dendrite or between an axon and the actual cell body. The complexity and the efficiency of the brain is a question not simply of the number of cells, but also of the number of connections that are available to enable message transmission.

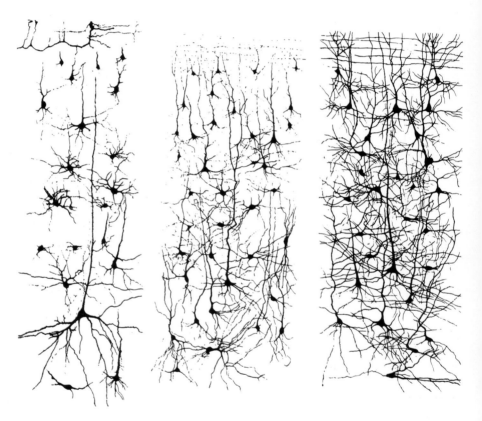

The developing system of nerve fibres in the visual cortex of a baby's brain. During the first two years of life the number of connections increases dramatically, allowing ever more complex messages to be transmitted within the brain.

All of the neurones, or nerve cells, are present, a million million of them. However, this does not mean that the newborn's brain is able to function fully. What is largely missing is the complex system of nerve fibres which transmits messages to and from the brain and between the brain cells (see the section on 'Carrying messages', above). There is a rapid proliferation in this system during the first two years of life.

Another critical feature of brain development is the formation of protective sheaths, of a fatty material called myelin, around the nerve cells. The insulation provided by the myelin sheaths allows messages to be transmitted more rapidly and with greater efficiency. Myelination is incomplete at birth and develops in different parts of the brain at different times. It is almost complete by the time a child is two, but continues to develop into adolescence.

The development of the brain progresses according to an orchestrated sequence. At birth, the cortex – the grey matter that forms the outer surface of the brain and regulates all complex thinking – is barely able to function. Only the parts of the brain that lie below the cortex are effective, and they cannot do much more than command the use of reflexes. As, over the following months and years, the connections of the cortex form and myelination proceeds, the child's brain becomes capable of increasingly complex operations.

So the brain is programmed to develop in a certain sequence. However, the way the brain develops is also greatly influenced by what happens to it: the way it is nourished, stimulated and protected. The genes provide a recipe, not an unalterable blueprint.

First, there are certain influences from which you would certainly wish to protect your child. Accidents involving head injuries are an obvious potential source of damage to the brain. Because the brain continues to develop through childhood, there is some degree of plasticity: that is, if a child's brain suffers injury it is possible that other parts of the brain will take over to a certain extent from those that have been damaged. The younger the child the less specialized, and therefore the more adaptable, the brain. We should not exaggerate this plasticity, though. Not every part of the brain can be replaced: for example, if the whole of the visual area of the brain is destroyed it is not conceivable that changes will occur to enable the child to see; and the older the child becomes the less likely it is that adaptation will occur.

Some pollutants can damage the brain. There have been tragic incidents where children who have chewed objects painted with a lead-based paint have incurred fatal brain damage. In some places lead is found in drinking water – not enough to kill anyone, but quite sufficient to cause a reduction of some points in measured intelligence. The precise effect of lead from petrol fumes is still uncertain; no one, however, could reasonably argue that it does children anything but harm.

On the positive side, you can help your child, in this as in so many areas, by ensuring that his nutrition is adequate (see pages 496–7). For the brain to develop to its full potential, a child needs a healthy diet throughout childhood and adolescence.

There is also evidence to indicate that the physical development of the brain is influenced by the richness or poverty of the environment. For obvious reasons, experiments cannot be carried out on children's brains. However, studies of rats have offered startling demonstrations of the effect of stimulation on the brain. Young rats brought up in cages with food, water and 'toys' (ladders to climb, boxes to explore, and so on) were compared to rats brought up with food and water but no toys. When the animals were tested, those raised in the enriched environment showed evidence of a greater aptitude to learn, and better problem-solving abilities. When the brains of the rats who had been stimulated were examined, it was found that they had heavier cortices and more extensive connections between the neurones, and there were also other biochemical differences. The indications are that the environment in which the rats were raised played a significant part in the physical development of their brains.

You can help your baby enormously by offering him varied toys to play with and by being there to encourage him and share his experiences.

On the Move

Skills involving movement – sometimes referred to under the general heading of motor skills – include such diverse activities as turning over, walking, picking things up and dropping them, and manipulating implements such as spoons. Large movements, such as walking, are referred to as 'gross motor' skills. 'Fine motor' refers to smaller movements: most of these are hand movements, such as those involved in drawing and writing.

If you know something about development of the brain and of the large and small muscles that control movements, it will help you to know what to expect from your child at what age. You will then be in a better position to match activities with the child's abilities. An understanding of typical timetables will tell you when to expect milestones in your child's development and help you to identify any problems he might have.

It is equally if not more important to appreciate the sequences of development. Learning to move and coordinate the body is a predictable, orderly process: you cannot run before you can walk. Each child's development has unique characteristics, but your child is likely to turn over before sitting and to crawl before walking. Some children do not crawl in the conventional way, and some do not spend much time crawling; but nearly all children will try some crawl-like form of movement before they walk.

Motor development follows the cephalocaudal and proximodistal laws (see page 92), proceeding from the head downwards and the inside out. Babies lift their heads before they can turn over, and are able to kick before they can voluntarily wiggle their toes.

The two major skills gradually acquired during the first eighteen months are the ability to move from place to place and the ability to reach and grasp objects. These skills are achieved in small steps with many milestones along the way, and they develop alongside each other. The toddler who can stagger from one parent to another, or put one brick on top of another, is giving a virtuoso performance.

Large body movements

Lifting the head

It is awe-inspiring to think of all the stages a baby has to go through before he can accomplish the feat of sitting up unsupported. First, he has to learn to control his head while being held. A newborn baby's head is floppy, and needs constant support; but by about three weeks of age most babies can begin to support their heads for short periods of time.

The next stage is for the baby to lift his great, cumbersome head, the largest part of his body. Imagine yourself picking up a large weight with your head while lying on the floor – that will give you some idea of what a baby has to accomplish. The muscles in the neck need to mature before the baby can control them sufficiently to manage this feat. Your baby will be able to raise his head very slightly (just enough to turn it from side to side) when he is about six weeks old, but he will probably be three months

By about four and a half months a baby can use the weight of his head to roll over on to his back.

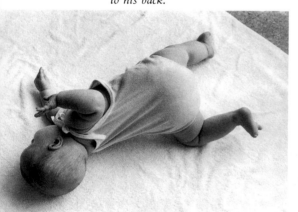
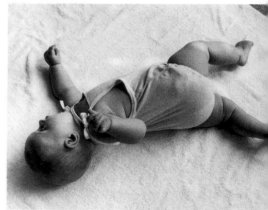

before he can lift it right up, while lying on his tummy. Once the baby has learned to lift his head he will be able to satisfy his curiosity about the world by looking around; he can turn towards sounds, and turn away from something he does not want to look at.

Turning over

By around four and a half months, a baby has usually discovered that he can use the weight of his head to propel him over on to his back. This is a major milestone, but it often happens accidentally, taking the baby (and his

This baby has discovered how to roll over from his back to his front, which is more difficult. Now he is in a position to learn to crawl.

parents) by surprise. Sometimes it comes as such a shock to the baby that it provokes an outburst of tears.

Turning over in the other direction, back to front, is even more difficult, and usually comes a little later. Again, the first occurrence is often accidental. Once a baby can roll over it is quite possible that he may roll off any surface on which he is placed. As the first roll may be accidental, it is difficult to predict when it might be coming; so you need to increase your vigilance from the time your baby can first raise his head.

Sitting up

As your baby's muscles have been growing stronger, exercises such as lifting his head and rolling over have been helping him to increase control over his body. Moreover, usually, once a baby has enough control to support his head, his parents start to pull him up to a sitting position – and so he gets a general idea of what is expected. Sometimes as early as five months, usually by the time he is about six months old, the baby's back is strong enough, and sufficiently under his control, to enable him to sit up unsupported for a moment. By eight months he can sit unsupported for longer, and by nine months he will be able to sit alone on the floor for ten to fifteen minutes.

Once a baby can sit up his world changes dramatically. It is now much easier for him to look around and find out what is happening – particularly what people are doing. He can reach for things, pick them up and manipulate them much more easily than he can when lying down, so he can do a lot more with his toys, which gain a new interest. By this time he is better able to balance, and his concentration span is increasing markedly.

Babies develop different styles of getting about. This one is experimenting with the straight-legged 'bear-walk' – it obviously works for him!

All these developments mean that the baby can keep himself occupied and entertained for longer periods of time.

By about ten months the baby can usually control the sitting position and turn to one side; a few weeks later, he can move from a lying position to sitting, and back again.

Crawling

Just as there are stages in sitting, so there are in crawling. First the baby has to bear weight on his arms: he pushes up from his tummy on to his forearms, then to his hands. Next he has to extend his arms fully. Then his knees come up under his body; and then he crawls.

Most babies crawl; if they don't crawl, it is usually just that they have adopted some other method of getting around – bottom-shuffling, perhaps, or doing a 'commando crawl' (lying flat, using their arms to pull them along) or 'walking like a bear' (a sort of straight-legged crawl, which looks extremely uncomfortable). But a few babies are simply not allowed the opportunity to crawl. There are still some people who think that early walking is a sign that a child is generally advanced, and parents who hold this mistaken belief sometimes force their babies into walking positions, so that they are discouraged from crawling. This is an opportunity lost: crawling is good exercise, and an efficient way of getting around – and, evidently, babies enjoy it.

Standing

If you hold your newborn infant up, providing support under the arms, he will not be able to hold his head up, but he will make instinctive stepping movements. This stepping reflex is beginning to disappear by the time the baby is two months old. At about four months a baby supported under the

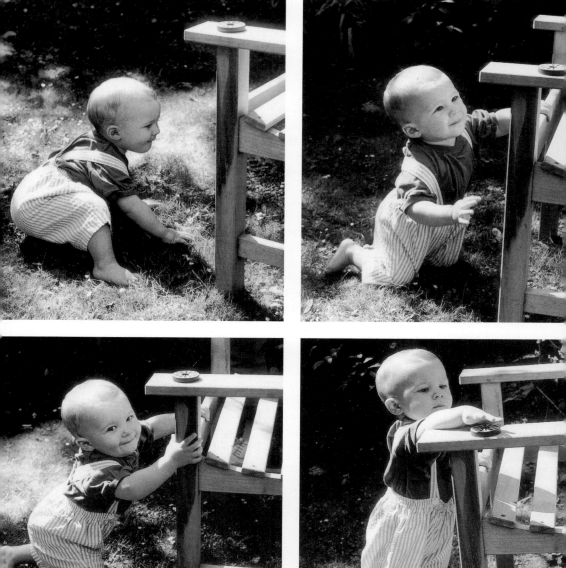

By about ten months most babies can pull themselves up into a standing position, so long as they have something stable to hold on to for support.

arms will hold his head up, but his legs will dangle. If held like this two months later he may be able to stand, but probably only for a few minutes.

Before a baby can stand unsupported, he needs to be able to stretch out his hips and knees, and he must also have considerable muscle power and the ability to balance. By the time they are about ten months old most babies are able to pull themselves up from the knees into a standing position, holding on to something for support – only to discover, quite often, that then they cannot sit down again. A baby will sometimes stand for quite a long time, holding on to the side of his cot, perhaps, until he gets frightened and starts screaming. Of course, as soon as he is helped down he stands up again, and the process starts once more. Sometimes it is possible to distract the baby to some other activity, but generally you will just have to be patient. Soon – usually by his first birthday – he will discover how to sit down. By then the baby will probably also be able to hold up one foot, supporting his weight on the other, while holding on.

Most babies learn to stand up by themselves at round about twelve months. They can still only manage it, though, by placing their feet wide apart to help them balance. By about a year and a half most babies have good balance. They can sit down without any difficulty, and the distance between their feet is smaller. They can walk forwards, sideways and backwards. Standing still is difficult, though, requiring more concentration and effort than most babies believe it is worth.

Your baby may not stand until well after his first birthday. This is not uncommon, and so long as the child is healthy and developing in other respects, it need not give cause for concern. However, if the baby is still not standing by sixteen months, it is worth mentioning to your doctor.

Walking

Parents await with great anticipation the day that their baby begins to walk, and most try to help things along by encouraging the baby to walk holding on to a hand. Most babies can walk without support before they are fifteen months old, but there is a great variation in starting ages. Some babies begin to walk unsupported as early as nine months; other children do not walk until eighteen months or even two years.

If your baby is not walking on his own by about eighteen months you should ask your doctor to check that there is nothing wrong, but late walking is not in itself usually indicative of problems. The child may have inherited a tendency to late development of the spinal cord – late walking may run in the family. A bad fall or an illness around the time when a baby would normally be beginning to walk can hold things up, as he may need a long time to recover his strength, confidence and interest in new activities. Or the baby may not have had sufficient space or time to practise walking. Then again, a really efficient crawler may simply not find it worthwhile to walk until he is old enough, and strong enough, for walking to be relatively little effort.

Going up and down stairs

If your baby has access to steps or stairs, you will probably worry that he could fall down them, and you will naturally want him to be able to manage them safely as soon as possible. Parents sometimes try to train their babies to climb stairs by holding them on the stairs and coaxing them to go up and down, but there is no evidence that this helps much. The best practice for stair-climbing is crawling. It strengthens the muscles and gets the legs and arms ready to support the body as the baby pulls himself up from step to step.

When climbing begins, babies often become quite obsessively attracted to stairs. Up they go – and can't get down again. Fortunately, there is usually a parent close behind to help. After a few dozen repeats of this game, most parents will buy a stair-guard so that they can relax their constant supervision; but do remember that the baby needs to practise his newly discovered skill, and give him the opportunity to climb as often as you can.

It takes a long time to master going downstairs. Most children first discover that they can get down on their bottoms. This works so well that it may be quite a while before a child tries another way. Then he may crawl down backwards – often a frightening manoeuvre for a parent to watch.

By eighteen months or so your toddler will probably be able to walk upstairs and may also manage to walk down – in both cases holding on to a rail or the wall, and putting both feet on each step.

Stair-climbing is an activity that parents need to supervise constantly, until they feel quite confident that the child can manage it safely. If a fall occurs, it can cause serious injury; even a fall that results in no physical damage can bring about a loss of confidence, and put the child off trying again for quite a while.

Small body movements

At the same time as a baby is mastering large body movements such as rolling over and sitting, he is also learning to make finer movements, particularly to use his hands.

Babies learn about the world primarily through hands-on experiences. It is through their sense of touch that they find out about the size and shape of objects; there is nothing like getting the feel of something new to help a baby explore and understand his environment.

Using the hands

If you touch a newborn baby on the palm of the hand, he will curl his fingers around yours. This is an automatic response, the grasp reflex. By three or four months the involuntary element has disappeared, and the reflex has been integrated into a grasping movement which is under the baby's control.

Before he can grasp anything purposefully and hold on to it, the baby has to have the ability to focus his eyes on the object, to turn his head to follow it, and to control his arm movements sufficiently to keep the arms steady and adjust their speed. He needs much the same degree of control of his neck and head muscles as he needs to be able to turn over, and babies generally learn to grasp at about the same time as they first roll over. The two skills do not develop in isolation.

Newborn babies usually lie with their arms at their sides and their hands closed, with the thumbs tucked underneath the fingers – until they start to cry, and then they flap around wildly. During the next couple of months they gradually gain more control of their arms, their fists open and their fingers stretch out.

By eight or ten weeks the baby's hands are open, and he is beginning to watch them as they move. This is an important advance in his progress towards hand-eye coordination – the process by which the eye informs the brain, the brain tells the muscles, and the muscles respond. At this age your baby cannot yet reach objects for himself, but if you hand him something he will hold it, for a minute or two at least.

By three months the baby will be able to bring his hands together and play with his fingers. Babies of this age love watching their hands as they clasp and unclasp them and press the palms against each other in a clap-like gesture. Your baby will be able to swipe at things now, too: he will not catch them, but he is heading in the right direction. You may see him lifting his arm and bringing it part-way to something – perhaps a toy hung over his cot. The hand opens, moves towards the toy, and then closes again. The baby can make grasping movements, but he cannot yet coordinate his actions so that he can catch the toy.

Between three and four months he will begin to grope for things using his whole hand – from time to time he may actually catch what he is after. It will help him to get the experience he needs if you sometimes deliberately place toys so that he needs to grope for them. If things are handed to him all the time he will have no opportunity to try to reach them for himself.

By the time they are about six months old babies are able to reach for and grab things with both hands: one hand moves slightly before the other, and both close on the object. At around this age babies begin to extend their exploration with their hands, using them to touch, stroke and pat. You may notice that your baby becomes increasingly interested in how things feel, and spends a lot of time patting the carpet, and stroking his blanket, or your clothes.

By about seven months a baby can grasp with more control, using his thumbs in opposition to his fingers in a mitten-like grip. He can hold an object in each hand – and will bang together two toy bricks, for instance, with evident enjoyment. Between seven and nine months he will also learn to move things from one hand to the other. However, at this age he cannot yet release things: he will put what he is holding into the other hand before the fingers of the first hand let go.

During these months, too, a baby is learning to move his hand from the wrist: by eight or nine months your baby will probably be able to wave goodbye with a gesture from the wrist only.

By nine months a baby has such fine control over the separate fingers that he can use his index finger to point, and he can grasp things between the thumb and the index finger. He may also make his first attempts at scribbling, if you give him a thick crayon.

By about ten months most babies can release things easily; they then immediately put in a lot of practice, dropping food and toys from pram or high chair – and demanding with delighted squeals that they be picked up, so that they can drop them again. The endless repetition of this game can become exasperating. However, you may find it easier to maintain your patience and good humour if you realize that, although your baby may not exactly be learning about gravity through this exercise, he is finding out about a sequence of cause and effect, and discovering a lot about space.

Over the months that follow, as his muscle control improves and he practises his new skills, he will become increasingly adept. He will learn to build towers out of blocks, to hammer pegs into holes, and to fit shapes into appropriate openings. He will also learn to feed himself.

Feeding

Eating without help is a refined motor skill, involving complex hand-eye coordination and the ability to control muscles, which it takes a long time, and a lot of practice, to develop.

By seven months (opposite left) the baby can hold objects in a mitten grip. By ten months (above) he has far greater control over each finger and is able to pick up small objects in a pincer grip. Later (opposite right) he will be capable of fitting shapes into a simple sorting box.

Once a baby can sit up and hold an object in both hands, usually when he is about six months old, he may try to hold a bottle or a cup with a lid and a spout, but he will probably drop it quite quickly.

By seven months your baby may be able to use his mitten grip to grab a biscuit and eat it without help. He may also try to catch the spoon while you are feeding him.

Between nine and twelve months most babies learn to hold their bottles or lid cups with both hands, and by twelve months your baby will probably be able to hold on to the spoon. He will need help getting the food into his mouth, though. You will have to go on feeding him for some time yet. He may spend a few minutes feeding himself with great enthusiasm, but the amount of food he actually takes in will certainly not be sufficient.

With practice, by the time he is about fifteen months old, the baby, still employing the mitten grip, will be using a spoon quite efficiently, and getting a good deal more of the food into his mouth, though you will still need to keep an eye on him to make sure he is actually taking in enough. He can hold on to a cup for a few minutes and drink from it, but he still needs someone there to hand it to him, and to take it back.

By eighteen months the baby will be getting the food into his mouth fairly safely, but not neatly, or with elegant table manners. Often, the spoon will turn over in his mouth, tipping the food out again. He will be able to lift a cup to his mouth and hand it back when the drink is finished – usually. He's not reliable yet, though, and sometimes he will just let go.

Right or left-handed?

Handedness is a characteristic peculiar to humans. Although some species of animals show preferences, they are less consistent than humans. Animal preferences are also more or less equally divided between right and left. Humans, of whatever race or culture, are mainly right-handed, and remain so from an early age.

Almost equally universal has been the myth that the right side of the body is associated with the pure and the good, the left with evil. (Only the Chinese provide an exception.)

The development of a consistent hand preference has been related to the two hemispheres of the brain. There is some evidence to suggest that in right-handed people the left side of the brain has more widespread connections to the right side of the body, making voluntary control of the right hand easier.

Some preference for using one hand rather than the other can often be observed in a baby as young as six months old, and handedness is usually established by the time a child is two. However, some children remain ambidextrous until they are four or five, and they may change their preference as late as six.

It is not at all a good idea to try to change a child who shows an inclination to use the left hand rather than the right. You will not alter the child's natural preference, but you may well make him feel confused and frustrated. However, your baby is more likely to develop some ability, strength and control in both hands and arms if he varies the hand he uses – so you might try placing a spoon, for instance, sometimes in one hand, sometimes in the other.

Can parents help with skill development?

As a general rule, a normally healthy baby, given adequate opportunities and encouragement, will learn to sit up, to walk and run, to reach and grasp for objects with no special help from adults. There is some evidence that, given encouragement from an early age, a baby may develop a skill such as walking slightly earlier than would otherwise be the case. Whether this achievement is worth all the effort involved, however, is another question.

She explores the world as far and as fast as her legs will carry her.

What a child does need is the opportunity to practise a skill once it has emerged. Here the influence of parents can be highly significant. This becomes especially evident when they choose to emphasize a particular skill. Some parents spend hours encouraging a toddler to kick a ball, others are constantly handing their child shapes to post in a sorting box, or jigsaw pieces to fit into a simple puzzle. Not surprisingly, the children's skills tend to develop along corresponding lines – although parents who think they can produce a star footballer simply by providing a lot of practice and praise are, more often than not, in for a disappointment. The key is to give every encouragement to the development of skills for which the child shows a preference. In other words, take your cue from your baby: don't try to mould him into the person *you* want him to be – or the person you wish you had been.

When skill development is slow

Parents are usually the first to notice (and to worry about) a delay in any aspect of their child's development. They are, after all, the people most familiar with the child – and those who care about him most.

What parents may not be aware of is the wide range of ages at which it is normal to develop certain skills. For example, tables of development generally note that the 'average' child walks holding on to furniture at about ten months. They are often less clear about the fact that around 25 per cent of children can be expected to walk holding on before they are seven months; and about 10 per cent do not achieve this milestone until they are over thirteen months. So a child who walks holding on at seven months is not unusually advanced; and a child who doesn't manage to walk until he is thirteen months is not out of the ordinary either. Again, although the average age at which children learn to sit without support is five and a half months, about 10 per cent of children are still not sitting up by the time they are eight months. And while thirteen months is the average age at which children walk unsupported, 10 per cent of children are still not walking alone at between fourteen and fifteen months.

A slight delay in development of a particular skill is not in itself a sign of backwardness. There are peaks and plateaux in skill development as there are in physical growth, and often a child who has seemed slow to develop a skill will have a spurt and quickly become as adept as his contemporaries.

However, it is true that if development over a range of skills in a particular area is consistently slow, you can anticipate that this is probably not going to be a sphere in which your child will excel. If a child is slow to crawl and then to walk, and does not walk upstairs alone until he is well over two, it is unlikely that he will turn out to be a champion athlete. He may have

Helping a blind baby to become mobile

The motor development of blind and sight-restricted babies presents a special challenge, since it is hard for children who cannot see to develop the confidence to crawl and walk and explore independently.

Blind babies need to feel secure about where they are and where they are moving to. It helps if they can feel firmly anchored to the ground, or some other fixed object, and for this reason blind babies often bottom-shuffle rather than crawl. You can help a blind baby to walk by encouraging him to side-step alongside a couch, so that his body remains in contact with the couch the whole time.

Generally, in teaching a blind baby, sound and touch have to be substituted for sight. If your baby is blind, you will help him best by talking to him as much as you can, whenever possible touching him at the same time, to let him know that you are there and what you are doing. If you can make the baby understand what is going on around him, he will be able to locate himself, and other people and objects, in space, as he needs to do before he can feel confident enough to begin to move.

difficulty in learning to ride a bike, he may not be good at games.

An awareness that a child is not naturally adept at certain skills can be of positive value to parents. If you notice that your child's development of physical skills is rather slow, although he is developing normally in other ways, you can help him by encouraging him to join in physical activities, and by making vigorous play fun for him. At the same time, be sensitive to his reactions and don't push things too far if he is timorous or hesitant. Encourage, too, the less active forms of play that may come more naturally to him, and make sure you don't give him the message that physical adroitness is all-important.

When there are problems with skill development

Although a mild delay in development is not usually cause for concern, it is more worrying when the delay becomes marked. Sadly, in some cases, seriously delayed development can be an indication of a disability.

Again, it has to be emphasized that most often parents are the first to notice that something is wrong. They may become concerned, for instance, that their child does not seem to be moving around as much as other children of his age, or that he never reaches out for things as other children do.

Well-intentioned friends often advise parents to wait a bit longer, in the hope that their fears will prove to be unfounded. This attitude is misguided: if all is well, then the sooner the parents have their minds set at rest, the better for them and their child. If there is a problem, the earlier it is diagnosed the more the child can be helped. For their children's sake and their own, parents need to trust their instincts. If you are concerned about your baby you should not hesitate to seek medical advice – and, if you are then still not satisfied with initial reactions from the medical profession, to persist. It may be necessary to carry out a series of tests on the baby to find out what, if anything, is the matter. If there is found to be a disability, your child will receive professional help, and you will also be taught how you can help him to become mobile.

A word of warning here, though. While it is often possible gently to nudge delayed developmental stages by means of carefully planned stimulation, parents need to be aware that any approach to the training of children with poor movement control has limitations. Every so often a new training programme hits the headlines: rarely, if ever, have these wonder cures been rigorously tested. Some children may indeed benefit, and you may feel that you are willing to try anything that could help your child. But try to keep your expectations realistic.

Responding to your baby's development

We do not always appreciate how much a baby's physical development transforms his experiences. For instance, when a baby is able to sit up he sees things from a new viewpoint. Once he gets on the move, his world is vastly enriched. Try to imagine how things must seem from the perspective of a crawling baby. Objects such as shoes, or dirt on the floor, are fascinating because they are so close – much closer, usually, than people's faces. Crawling babies are also quick to learn one of the most important lessons in life – that they can exert some control over what they do. To a casual onlooker the baby who crawls up to a fragile table and knocks it over is clumsy; an ignorant onlooker may even think the baby is being 'naughty'. Someone who is more thoughtful, and who knows a little about how babies develop, will realize that the baby is learning about cause and effect and about mastery over his environment.

You will want to give your baby every chance to explore this strange new world, but you must also be vigilant as you adapt to his growing independence. A baby who can roll over may suddenly fall off a high bed or changing table, a crawling baby can get into places where it is dangerous for him to be. He has no idea of the risk represented by the unguarded electric socket, the protruding saucepan handle, the cleaning fluid in the bag of shopping. To him they are merely enticing objects. It is up to you to make sure his environment is as safe as possible.

When the baby becomes a toddler, his world again magically expands – and so does the range of hazards to which he is susceptible. At this stage children have developed sufficient physical strength and skill to run straight into danger, while they have not yet acquired the sense and experience that will later alert them to potential risks. Toddlers need almost constant supervision and even then any toddler is bound to take a few tumbles. It is reassuring to know that, in some ways, a toddler's body is well equipped to survive minor falls. An accident which could result in a broken bone for an older child may be less serious for him, as his soft bones tend to bend rather than break. In the head, the last and largest fontanelle does not close until the child is about two years old, which means that the skull can give a little when it is bumped. None the less, any bad fall, in particular any fall which results in a child's becoming stunned or unconscious, must, of course, be taken seriously. If a child who has had a fall shows any of the symptoms listed below you must make sure he is seen immediately by a doctor:

- if he is unconscious, even for a moment
- if there is a visible head wound
- if there is any bleeding from nose, mouth or ears
- if he vomits
- if he remains pale, or in an unusual mood
- if he goes to sleep, especially if he then either breathes noisily or cannot be woken

Even if none of these symptoms is present, you should seek medical help if you are worried or in doubt.

toy they are after from a box of similar toys. They will also pick out the products they see on television in the supermarket, and find the hidden chocolate bar in the cupboard.

Since, obviously, young babies cannot tell us what they understand, we have to make some assumptions about how they classify objects and people and give meaning to their experiences. It has been observed that with babies as young as two months mothers change their voice patterns depending on whether they are warning, soothing, promising, commanding or just burbling on to the baby. The assumption is that even at this early age babies respond appropriately – otherwise, mothers would hardly be so consistent in making the changes. Experiments with infants three to four months old have shown that they can discriminate between different facial expressions. One cannot be sure that they ascribe meaning to expressions in the way we do, but the fact that they look at happy faces longer than at sad ones suggests that perhaps they might. Babies as young as three months appear to become happier when looking at a happy face, and sadder when looking at a miserable face, so long as the face is accompanied by an appropriate voice.

The development of perception is a process which takes place so naturally that most of us do not even notice it. However, it does not happen automatically. A baby may be endowed with clear vision, good hearing and sensitive touch, but he needs many opportunities to experiment with those senses before he can learn to interpret the world around him. Moreover, he needs his parents' help to organize his impressions. Every time you point something out to your baby ('There's our ginger cat in the garden', 'That man's looking cross'), you are helping him to develop perception.

Visual perception

It is not easy to obtain any precise measurement of what a baby sees – indeed, it is not until children are about four years old that they can reliably cooperate in tests in which they identify shapes or letters. Before that we have to rely on observing their behaviour – which gives only a crude measure – and on electrophysiological tests (there is one that traces messages from the brain to the retina, for example). However, on both these measures it is clear that a baby's powers of vision improve rapidly during the early months, as the visual cortex develops. By about three months babies can usually coordinate their eyes so that they work together and their vision is generally sharper. By six months their range of focus has widened and they can see in much greater detail; by a year their visual powers are generally well developed.

What do babies see?

At around two months, there is a marked shift in visual perception. While the newborn baby uses his limited vision mainly to locate people and things

How visual perception develops: birth to eighteen months
As with all tables mentioning ages, this should be seen as a rough developmental guide.

Newborn

Can tell bright from dark tones
Some colour perception
Pupils react to light
Closes eyes to sudden bright light
Turns head towards light
Opens eyes when held upright
Blinks in response to sound, movement or when surface of eye is touched
Follows a moving target 20–25 cm/8–10 inches away through an angle of 45 degrees

One Month

Blinks defensively when something comes towards him
Watches mother's face with increasing alertness
Can see a face from a distance of 15 cm/6 inches
Can follow in range of 90 degrees

Two Months

Looks at faces more often and scans them more broadly, looking at details of the face
Cannot focus both eyes on the same point
Eyes follow a moving person
Eyes follow dangling toy from side to a point beyond the middle of his chest

Three Months

Fascinated by faces
Able to focus both eyes on the same point
Moves head deliberately to gaze around him
Looks promptly at objects placed at midline of body
Follows dangling toy from side to side (through 180 degrees)
Colour vision may be fully functioning
Recognizes photograph of mother and begins to recognize other faces

Four Months

Can tell the difference between happy, surprised and angry faces
Looks at dangling objects immediately

Five Months

Perception of depth improves
Will reach for objects perceived to be in reaching distance

Six Months

Adjusts his position to see objects
Visually very alert
Looks at 'attractive' faces longer than 'unattractive' ones

Eight Months

Can judge size of an object up to 60 cm/2 feet away

Twelve Months

Eyes follow rapidly moving objects

Eighteen Months

Identifies small details in pictures

(see page 69), now the baby seems more interested in identifying what he sees. His gaze moves back and forth within the contours of an object, rather than staying on the edges. He is now able to perceive things in more detail, and is much better able to differentiate patterns. This ability increases over the following months. Though in the first two or three months a baby will clearly discriminate his mother from other people when she is present – and, therefore, he is getting cues not only from her appearance but also from her voice, touch and smell – he will probably not recognize a photograph of her face, in isolation, until he is at least three months old. Even then, most babies only recognize the face in front view; they are confused if it is posed differently – in profile, for instance. By five or six months babies can recognize a familiar face in any pose.

Seeing in colour

By the time babies are three months old they appear to have full perception of colours, with all their hues and variations. A baby of this age can, for example, see that a toy is painted in several different colours.

The perception of distance

Even an apparently simple act such as reaching for an object and grasping it involves considerable skill, not only of the muscles but of the eyes and brain. Before a baby can get hold of a toy, for example, he has to be able to judge where in space the toy is. In other words, he has to perceive the distance in space between himself and the toy.

Distance perception is also in operation when we look at a picture and can 'see' that a house is 'nearer' to us than a tree in the back garden. The image that the eye receives is, of course, flat, but we learn to interpret the way things are represented.

In an ingenious experiment to test babies' distance perception, the American researchers Eleanor Gibson and Richard Walk devised an apparatus which they called 'a visual cliff'. This is a platform consisting of a large glass sheet placed over a piece of material patterned with checks. On one side of the platform the patterned material is immediately under the glass, while on the other it is some way below, giving the impression that half-way across there is a sheer drop. When babies aged six months and older were placed on the platform, only a few were willing to crawl across the 'visual cliff'. Even when coaxed by their mothers from the other side, most of the babies, although evidently distressed at not being with their mothers, crawled away from them on to the shallow side. Clearly, these babies perceived (and feared) the apparent drop.

The same apparatus was later used by other researchers to test distance perception in younger babies, who were not yet able to crawl. Babies were set on both the 'cliff' and the 'non-cliff' sides of the platform, and their heart-rates were measured to see if they responded differently. In babies as young as two months there was evidence, from changes in heart-rate, that

Left *Babies of three to four months can already discriminate between facial expressions.*
Right *Grabbing her mother's lip, she demonstrates her growing ability to judge distance and coordinate hand and eye movements.*

there was perception of danger when they were placed on the 'cliff' side. One month old babies, though, did not show any difference in their reaction to the two sides.

The perception of size and shape

Think for a moment of a car. If you look at it close up, the image that falls on your retina is large (if you are really close, you cannot see anything else). If you then look at the same car from further away you will have a much smaller image on your retina – yet your brain will know that the car is the same size as it was when it was close to. We take it for granted that an object will stay the same size, no matter how near or far away it is; but this is a big thing for a small child to learn. Similarly, it takes time for a baby to realize that an object's shape remains the same – that a plate, for example, stays plate-shaped, even if it is tilted.

Newborn babies have no concept of constancy in size or shape, but both develop during the first year. Babies start to develop the ability to judge size at about six months. By eight months they can judge the size of an object at up to about 60 cm/2 feet away. An eight month old baby will recognize that a ball this distance away will get larger as it rolls towards him, and he may open his arms to accommodate it.

The perception of sound

It is even more difficult to find out precisely what babies can hear than it is to investigate what they can see. The simplest way is to watch a baby while various sounds are made. If the baby moves his head towards a sound, this may indicate that he can hear it. Another method, based on evidence that babies change their rate of sucking when they hear a new sound, is to give a baby a dummy, and measure his sucking as sounds are played to him.

A recent discovery, made by timing the rate of sucking, is that babies as young as one to six months can distinguish between sounds of speech. What is more, when they are very young they seem to discriminate between the sounds of different languages equally well. Unfortunately for those learning a foreign language later on, this ability narrows down very early: when babies start making their first sounds in their own language they begin to lose their ability to discriminate sounds in languages to which they are not exposed. For example, Japanese babies can perceive the difference between 'l' and 'r', two phonemes which are not used in Japanese speech. Japanese adults and older children find it much harder to make this distinction.

One group of researchers tested the children of Hindi, Salish and English-speaking mothers in an English community. At between six and eight months, the babies were about equal in their ability to distinguish Hindi sounds from Salish sounds. By the time they were a year old, the English babies could no longer distinguish between Salish and Hindi.

However, during the latter part of the first year a baby's ability to discriminate sounds in his own language improves. Babies also become better at working out where sounds are coming from.

Touch

During the early months babies make increasing use of touch as a tool of exploration. As a baby moves his mouth or hands over something, the receptor cells in his skin are activated, so that he experiences the object's shape and texture. Touching is good exercise for him, too. As his fingers and hands, or lips and tongue, go over and over an object, taking its qualities in, muscles, tendons and joints are brought into action.

Taste

At birth babies distinguish between sweet and sour tastes – and much prefer sweet things (see page 71). As, over the first years of life, the receptor cells of the tastebuds mature, they develop the ability to make more subtle distinctions between tastes.

As babies taste their first foods, parents may wonder at the preferences they display. Genetic influences play a part: babies can inherit a greater ability to distinguish bitter flavours, for example. There are also such considerations as the way a baby may be feeling on a particular day. A cold can make food taste different – and so can feeling cross. And as we all know (but do not always take into account when preparing babies' meals), the taste of a food can be affected by the taste of whatever came before.

As a baby grows older, experience exerts an influence. For example, American children, who have more experience of spicy foods than Japanese children, tend to like spicy foods much more than Japanese children do. Particular foods also collect associations. By his own first birthday, a baby may already be enjoying birthday cake not only because of the sweet taste, but also because it is connected in his mind with happy occasions. On the other hand, he may have learned to associate certain tastes with being ill.

Quite simple things, like pouring water, give your child the chance to develop his perceptual skills.

Combining the senses

We do not know whether babies are born with an ability to bring together the information they receive from their different senses. However, it is certain that they are able to do this from an early age.

Very young babies turn their heads towards familiar sounds, as if to see where the sound is coming from. And at three to four months, when a baby hears the voice of his mother or father on a tape-recorder he will look at the appropriate parent: evidently, babies of this age are already accustomed to using sound and sight together, and are beginning to understand that people have a characteristic appearance and sound. By four to six months a baby will recognize the squeak his teddy bear makes and look towards the teddy when he hears it, and when he hears a dog bark he will know the noise comes from the dog and not the cat. It will be another year or so before he can form the sound 'woof-woof' to describe the dog, but the image of a dog who makes a sound like that is already beginning to grow in his mind.

How parents can help
You can help your baby develop his perceptual skills by introducing him to a variety of experiences. These need not be elaborately orchestrated: your daily life will be new and fascinating to him. You can prop a young baby up in his pram to give him a view of his surroundings. He will enjoy watching you working in the house or garden, or doing the shopping. Similarly, babies and toddlers love exploring handbags and kitchen cupboards, which are always full of interesting objects. When possible, take unhurried walks, carrying the baby or, later, holding your toddler by the hand, stopping to investigate anything that interests him. Give him the time and opportunity to explore different surfaces and textures: the sand at the beach, the puddles after a rainstorm, squashy playdough.

Memory

It is possible to cope with everyday living without sight or hearing – even, in extreme cases, without either. A person with no ability to remember could hardly live at all, in any real sense. He could learn nothing and make no progress but would be, as in infancy, totally dependent on others. What, though, are we really talking about, when we speak of memory?

Memory is the process by which people retain information and then retrieve it for use at a later time. The word 'memory' actually refers to two processes and a thing. The processes are learning something in the first place and then remembering; the thing is the assumed change that takes place in the brain when we learn.

Despite years of experiments and of studying both the structure of the brain and behaviour in humans and animals, this change remains a mystery:

we still do not know what happens inside a person when memory traces are laid down or when an event is remembered. However, we do know a certain amount about the processes of learning and remembering. We know, for example, that repetition helps people to remember. We also know that there is a distinction between recognition and recall. Recognition (remembering something when we see, hear, touch, smell or taste it) is invariably easier than recall (remembering in the absence of any physical stimulus).

The development of memory

When do babies begin to develop memory? It is evident that very young babies have powers of recognition. Experiments have shown that babies less than a week old can recognize their mothers' voices, and the smell of their breastmilk (see pages 70–1). Studies of slightly older babies show that by two months babies have developed considerable ability to remember what they have learned, and that by three months they can remember for a lot longer.

In one study of babies aged from two to four months, a mobile was strung across each baby's cot and a ribbon tied from the mobile to one of the baby's feet. Even the youngest of the children soon learned that if he kicked the mobile moved.

The mobile was then taken away. When, after a short interval, it was fixed on the cot again, observers watched to see if the baby kicked in a way that would indicate that he recognized the mobile and remembered what to do to make it move. They discovered that at two months babies could remember for up to three days, and by three months they remembered for over a week.

The researchers involved went on to conduct another experiment, with results that were even more challenging to received ideas of babies' capabilities. Babies of two months, having learned the kicking action, were given an eighteen-day break, then reintroduced to the mobiles. At first they did not react at all, but when the mobiles were moved to remind them of the previous response, they began kicking vigorously after a few moments. The memories were there, but the babies needed a reminder before they could retrieve them.

Parents have provided many examples of behaviour on the part of their babies that seems to indicate a remembrance of past events. Not surprisingly, babies seem to have richer memories in the context of their homes than they can demonstrate in the laboratory. Babies between seven and eleven months old remember their mealtime, bath and sleep routines, their favourite stories, and games such as peekaboo and pat-a-cake. As young as eight months a baby may show some remembrance of an object he can neither see nor touch – for example, he may look for a lost toy in a place where it is usually kept. At nine months he may show unmistakable signs of remembering that when the babysitter comes his parents leave, or that something painful happened the last time he was in the doctor's surgery.

Where has it gone?

Try this experiment: take a toy or any other favourite object belonging to your baby and, in the baby's full view, hide it under a piece of cloth that is within his reach.

Watch to see if the child searches under the cloth for the toy. A four month old is unlikely to show any inclination to look – even if you hide the toy so that a little bit is sticking out, and it seems to you that he should be able to recognize it. Between four and eight months he will begin to look for a partially hidden object. He probably won't look for something that is totally hidden, however, until he is between eight months and a year.

According to some psychologists, this shows that younger babies cannot imagine that an object exists if it is out of sight. An alternative explanation, which seems more consistent with what we know of babies' memories, is that they do know objects continue to exist, but they have not yet grasped the idea that one thing can hide another – they think, perhaps, that the cloth has replaced the toy.

From the time they are about five months old, babies hugely enjoy 'hiding' games. For instance, try holding up a towel in front of a toy. If the baby takes a swipe at it, move it closer so that he can knock it down: the baby will be rewarded by finding the toy, and he will feel a sense of achievement at having knocked the towel down without help.

Peekaboo, where you hide your face behind a cloth or your hands, then peep out, is a game most babies find endlessly entertaining. A toddler or even an advanced crawler can play hide and seek: older brothers and sisters hide and the little one will come looking for them.

What helps babies remember

Of course, in most babies leading a normal life, the faculty of memory develops without the need for any particular parental strategies. You may be interested, though, to notice what kinds of remembering your baby is doing, and what helps him to remember.

One of the things that helps babies remember is repetition. They hear their names over and over again and learn to recognize them.

It is easier for babies to remember anything if they make active contact with it, rather than passively observe it. And an object or experience that is available to more than one sense at a time is easier to remember than one to which a child has access by one sense only; thus babies are more likely to remember what they can both touch and see than something they can only see, and if they can hear it as well (as they can, for example, a ball that tinkles as it rolls), they will be even more likely to remember it.

Babies and toddlers also find it easier to remember when they can make a mental map in which a fact or action can be located. Within the familiar routine of the house, they will remember their bath or their cot, together with the toys and actions that accompany bathtime or bedtime.

To summarize: for babies as for adults, memory cannot be studied in isolation from other faculties. There is an interaction between what happened, what the child understood and what he found meaningful and interesting.

Attention

The ability to attend, or concentrate, at will develops throughout childhood. Even during his earliest days a baby's attention may be caught by a face, or a certain shape, pattern or colour; he will then gaze at it for a few seconds, or minutes, until something else diverts him. By about two months babies have more control of their attention, and they tend to look longer at something if they haven't seen it before.

This increase in control comes about in part because the brain is now more mature. However, to some extent, it is a skill that has been acquired by practice. Think of the interaction that has been taking place between mother and baby. She approaches, perhaps making cooing noises; her baby gazes at her and smiles; she smiles back; the baby wriggles, his gaze still on her. Both are rewarded. As these interactions are repeated, gradually the baby's attention span increases. The best way for parents to help their baby develop his ability to attend is, simply, to spend time interacting with him.

However, playing with objects helps too. If you watch your baby carefully, you will see which things capture his attention. You can then give him more experience with what he enjoys most – you might perhaps like to incorporate a favourite toy into some of the games you play together. Again, if you want to extend his attention to something he doesn't seem particularly interested in, you could incorporate that into a game he enjoys.

Social and Emotional Development

So much attention is paid to babies' growth, and their acquisition of skills in sitting, walking and talking, that it is easy to overlook the importance of social and emotional development – or to feel that development in these directions will just happen, with no help from parents. Yet most people would acknowledge that the development of the ability to relate successfully to other people is essential to a happy and fully human life. One could argue, indeed (some psychologists do), that this is both the basis and the aim of every type of development.

While what happens in early childhood is far from being the sole determinant of adult character, there can be no doubt that secure and happy childhood relationships provide a strong foundation for later life, and that unhappy early experiences can have devastating long-term effects. It is also true, of course, that many parents with little intellectual knowledge of child psychology seem naturally able to give their children the emotional nourishment they need – while other, perhaps more knowledgeable parents may, because of their own limitations, do much less well in this direction. None the less, if parents have some understanding of how children develop socially and emotionally, they should be better able to provide for their children's social and emotional needs.

Attachment

In ordinary conversation we may use the word attachment in describing any close relationship. In the theory of child development, it is defined in a way that is both more limited and more significant, for it refers to the process by which a lasting, loving bond is formed between a baby and the key person, or persons, in his life.

A child's primary attachment, which develops over the first few months of life, is most often to his mother, but it may be to his father or to another caregiver. This is the person the child seeks out, for care and, especially, for comfort when he is distressed (think how frequently a toddler who has fallen over can be comforted only by his mother). He protests when she, or

A baby's gentle exploration of his father's face helps strengthen the bond between them. A responsive parent will allow the baby a turn when they play together.

he, leaves him, and may show great anxiety if the separation lasts for longer than a few moments. This is especially the case when a child is very young. As they grow older, children usually grow attached to one, two or even more other people, in addition to the first attachment figure.

Of all the concepts employed in the study of child development, attachment is the one with the most important implications for parents; a knowledge of the way children and older people become attached to each other is central to an understanding of child behaviour.

The reasons for attachment

There are basic biological reasons why a baby should attach himself to an adult, and a failure in the process of attachment can lead to significant emotional damage.

Quite simply, babies, like the young of any species (but for longer than most), are vulnerable and need protection. The baby will instinctively seek out someone to protect him, will become attached to that person and will try to ensure close contact, especially in times of distress. This closeness may be physical or it may be maintained by sound, or by sight. Its power comes not from the number of times the child and the adult make contact, but from the intensity of the contact.

The baby's seeking for attachment is half the story; the other half is the biological need in adults to look after their young. Think how most adults feel impelled to behave towards a baby who shows signs of distress: the urge to cuddle, to comfort and to keep the baby safe is very strong.

Although your toddler is growing in independence, you are still the secure base to which she returns.

Sadly, though, this is true only of most adults, not all. Some find great difficulty in forming an emotional bond with a baby.

The development of attachment

If all goes well, a baby's primary attachment develops over the first six months or so of his life. The classic theory of attachment, as described by the psychiatrist John Bowlby, does not prescribe stages through which children have to pass, but, rightly, places the emphasis on developmental pathways which begin in infancy and continue through childhood to adolescence, adulthood and old age. The newborn baby has an array of potential pathways available: which one will be followed depends on the interaction between the individual and the environment. It is possible, however, to perceive some stage-like patterns in the development of babies' first attachments.

From birth, or soon after, a baby will cling, cuddle in, make eye contact and respond to an adult's efforts to soothe him when he cries – a pattern of behaviour that is well adapted to encourage attachment in a caregiver. From early on most babies respond most readily to their mothers, but during the first few weeks they will cling to anyone, make eye contact with anyone, and, a little later, smile at anyone.

One of the most exciting discoveries in the whole field of child development has been the finding that babies just a few days old can form rudimentary but nevertheless real social relationships with adults. These tiny babies are already able to take turns in simple 'conversations' with their parents and others. The hallmark of the responsive parent is the ability to tune in to a baby's communication patterns – to allow the baby a turn.

By the time your baby is about three months old, he will clearly be smiling more at you and other familiar people than he does at strangers. However, most babies at this stage show a warm acceptance of new people, and a relative they have never seen before will probably be treated to a delighted smile too.

By six or seven months the baby will almost certainly be showing a firm attachment to one particular person. At the same time a wariness of strangers is likely to become evident. The chosen person is nearly always the baby's primary caregiver – usually his mother. But although a baby will probably become attached to his mother first, he is likely soon also to show attachment to other people who care for him: his father, an older brother or sister, perhaps a grandparent or a nanny or childminder.

By the time they are a year old, most babies are attached to their fathers, as well as their mothers. In one American study researchers found that, at the approach of a stranger when both parents were present, babies of a year old would go to their fathers as often as to their mothers. When in distress, however, babies of this age will still usually turn to their mothers first.

Patterns of attachment

Three basic patterns of attachment have been defined by Mary Ainsworth, an American researcher who worked closely with Bowlby.

In a *secure attachment* a child welcomes contact with a parent or parent figure and uses this relationship as a secure base from which he can take off and explore the world.

An *anxious/resistant attachment* is characterized by uncertainty. Children are unsure whether their parents will be available when needed; therefore they tend to be clinging and anxious about venturing out into the world. In this pattern of behaviour the key emotion is conflict, created by parents who are inconsistent: here and helpful one day, gone the next.

Babies with an *anxious/avoidant attachment* make little protest at separation from any particular person. Sadly, some children – for example, those brought up in institutions where there are frequent changes of staff – have no one to become attached to. These children may tend to ignore or avoid caregivers, or they may go to anyone and form what seem to be close relationships effortlessly. This may be perceived as an easy friendliness, but can be a sign of a tendency to form only superficial relationships.

Patterns of attachment tend to persist. One reason is that parents usually go on treating children in a particular way; another is that a pattern once established is likely to be self-perpetuating. So a child who gets off to a good start will tend to behave in a way that maintains both his own security and his parents' confidence and responsiveness.

There is, however, a shift in what has been described as the ownership of the attachment pattern. At first the pattern of attachment is the property of the relationship: that is, the way it develops is determined by the way parent and child behave to each other. As the child grows older the pattern becomes, in Bowlby's words, 'increasingly a property of the child himself, which means that he tends to impose it, or some derivative of it, upon new relationships such as with a teacher [or] a foster mother'.

Forming a secure attachment

It is important to realize that a child does not become securely attached to a person just because that person gives him food and physical care and spends a lot of time with him. What seems to be crucial is the quality of the interactions between baby and adult.

A baby is more likely to become securely attached to someone who loves him, and who habitually treats him warmly and affectionately and takes pleasure in his company. This does not mean that a relationship is doomed if the parent is occasionally angry or irritated with the child. It is the general pattern that counts. The odd spurt of anger that occurs within a normally loving relationship is unlikely to be seriously damaging; however, parents who are often angry, rejecting or neglectful tend to have anxious and insecure children.

Love, though, is not quite enough; an attentive responsiveness to the baby's signals is also important. Parents who, loving their baby, respond appropriately to his expressions of need provide the ground for attachments of the most positive kind.

What seems to be the problem, and how can her mother help? Interpreting a small child's wishes can be difficult and takes patience and sensitivity.

Tuning in to your baby

Problems arise when parents fail to respond appropriately to their baby's signals. It sometimes happens that babies give confusing messages. Difficulties can occur, for example, with blind babies. While a sighted child will wave arms and legs in all directions at the approach of a loved one, a blind baby tends to become still, waiting for a sound. If the parents of a blind child are not aware that the stilling response is one of welcome they can misconstrue it, and feel rejected.

Or it may be that the baby's signals are normal, but the parents are not tuned in to them. It can happen, for example, that parents, instead of entering into a responsive dialogue with a tiny baby, overwhelm him with a barrage of stimulation. The baby, quite naturally, may tend to withdraw in self-defence.

Parents who respond inappropriately may merely have an intellectual misunderstanding of what is needed. The parents who assail the baby with constant chatter, face-pulling and other attention-getting tricks may have a general idea that stimulation is a good thing, and fail to realize the importance of taking cues from the baby, and giving him his turn.

With other parents who behave inappropriately, the problem goes deeper. Parents who are under stress, particularly if they are depressed, can find it difficult to respond to a child's needs. Some parents simply do not know how to form an attachment; not having been securely attached to their own parents, they have never learned.

Parents who have difficulty in relating to their babies can be helped. For example, the parents of blind babies find it much easier to respond once they realize what their children's signals mean. The parent who overstimulates a baby because of an intellectual misunderstanding of what babies need will also benefit from simply acquiring more accurate information. Depressed parents, and even those who never had a secure relationship with their own parents, can often be helped by psychiatric treatment or counselling. But of course, to seek help with a problem, you first need to recognize that the problem exists.

And you need to recognize the problem in time. Although there is no evidence that a failure to form a close relationship in the first year sets an irreversible pattern, it does seem to be the case that the older a child becomes without an attachment the less likely it is that one will be formed. Institutionalized children who are adopted by the age of four usually become attached to their new parents, but it takes them a long time to develop the feeling that they have a secure base, from which they can go out to develop other friendships and attachments.

Attachment and later life

Attachment is more than just a matter for babies, it is, as Bowlby said, 'a principal key to the mental health of the next generation'.

Follow-up studies to see what happens to children whose early attachment patterns were recorded have come in for some criticism, partly because a precise measure of attachment is not easy to make. Results have not always been consistent, but certain trends can be perceived.

Secure, closely attached preschool children have been found to get on better with other children and with unfamiliar adults than those who are less secure. Their make-believe play is more complex and more sustained than that of anxious children, and they show a greater interest in exploring their environment.

Anxious children have been found to have rather more psychological problems as they grow up, but it must be emphasized that no one can make the simple prediction that an insecure two year old will have psychological problems; in any child's life, there are many factors at work.

Separation anxiety and fear of strangers

At around the time that children show their first close attachment, usually six or seven months, most (though not all) begin to display both anxiety at separation from their parent or parent figure, and a wariness of strangers. In many cases this wariness is strong enough to be recognized as fear. During the following months this pattern of apprehension tends to become more marked. Both separation anxiety and fear of strange adults peak at around twelve to sixteen months (though, interestingly, some researchers have found that at about twenty months many children seem particularly agitated when they encounter strange children). Thereafter most children become less fearful, but some remain quite timid, and nearly all will revert to being somewhat shy and clinging when they are under stress.

It seems fairly certain that both fears are biological in origin, for they have been observed in a wide variety of cultures throughout the world (and, interestingly, baby monkeys show similar reactions). A rather surprising finding is that babies who are cared for at day nurseries, or for some other reason are looked after by several people and are therefore familiar with a wide group, show fear of strangers at the same stage, and in much the same ways, as babies brought up within a more limited circle.

Parents are sometimes alarmed that their sunny, friendly baby has become fearful, but, far from being cause for worry, these fears should be regarded as signs of developing awareness. Separation anxiety is a clear indication that a child has formed an attachment. Having recognized and attached himself to a protector, the baby wants to stay near the chosen person. Equally naturally, as his awareness develops, he becomes wary of those who are unfamiliar. How does he know that they are not going to harm him? Indeed, how many of us would be happy with the thought that our children would go cheerfully with anyone who made advances to them?

What parents can do

On the whole, all you can do about fear of strangers is to accept it as an aspect of this stage of your baby's life. You can, however, act to avoid reinforcing or prolonging fearfulness. Although it is absolutely normal to show fear, there is considerable variation in the degree of fear displayed by individual children. A partial explanation for this probably lies in inborn temperamental differences: identical twins show more similar reactions than non-identical twins. But some learning is also involved. Babies tend to look towards one of their parents (usually the mother) when something out of the ordinary happens, and to pick up the parent's emotional state. If your baby perceives that you are nervous when meeting someone his shyness will be intensified. If you can remain calm, he will learn, gradually, to recognize whom he can trust.

Separation anxiety may present a rather knottier problem. Leaving a baby while he is in this clinging and fearful phase can be upsetting for all concerned – indeed, you may wonder if it will be best never to leave your baby at all until he has grown out of some of his fear.

A distinction has to be made here between separations lasting a few minutes or hours and those involving days and nights. Almost inevitably there will be some brief separations; moreover, even if you could contrive always to be with your baby, this would probably not be a good idea – for him or for you. An ultimate goal of bringing up children is to help them become more independent of you; and an early part of that process is a gentle managing of this period when your child is fearful of losing your support.

On the other hand, your baby is probably going to be upset at being without you, even for a short time; so do not subject him to additional strain by leaving him in the care of a stranger. If you are fortunate, you may be able to leave him with someone who is already familiar to him – a grandparent perhaps, or a neighbour he sees regularly. But if you have to introduce your baby to an unfamiliar babysitter, make sure you do it well in advance. Though it may take a little planning, it should not be too difficult to have the babysitter come round to tea or to play a couple of times, so that the baby can get used to him or her.

Lengthy separations are another matter entirely. At this stage any separation of more than a few hours is likely to be extremely painful for the baby, and should as far as possible be avoided. If protracted separation is inevitable (if, for example, you have to go into hospital), you should make sure the baby is cared for by a loving, familiar person, preferably someone to whom he already has some attachment, and who can give him a lot of time and attention.

Relating to brothers and sisters

Older children

If your baby has older brothers and sisters, he will soon be aware of them. They are around a lot of the time, so they quickly become familiar figures; they have the active faces and high voices he finds particularly attractive;

Older children often make good companions for babies and toddlers but the relationship cannot be forced. Let them find their own moments of harmony.

they may help take care of him, hold him, sing and talk to him and play with him. He is unaware of the complex emotions older children in the family may feel, their jealousy or their potential for aggression. It seems reasonable to assume that babies are likely to become attached to their brothers and sisters within their first year.

In order to test the theory that babies form multiple attachments, psychologists Rudolph Schaffer and Peggy Emerson, working in Glasgow, asked mothers to describe their babies' reactions when separated from their parents, their grandparents and their brothers and sisters. By the time they were eighteen months old, babies showed signs of being upset not only by being separated from their mothers and fathers, but sometimes also when separated from grandparents, and very often when parted from siblings.

149

Toddlers tend to be more confident when a brother or sister is near. In laboratory studies, toddlers as young as sixteen months have been observed to explore over a wider area, straying further from their mothers, when a brother or sister is also in the room. Again, if a child's mother is not there when a stranger comes in, he will go to a brother or sister for reassurance. Evidently, brothers and sisters can form part of a child's secure home base.

Judy Dunn, a British psychologist, studied small children in a Cambridge nursery. She found that almost invariably a toddler would settle more easily if his older brother or sister were there, and if the older child were absent the toddler clearly missed him or her. In this nursery children as young as fourteen months went to their older brothers and sisters for comfort, and, even more interestingly, these babies would comfort the older children if they were in distress.

A new baby

Many children acquire a younger brother or sister when they themselves are only twelve to eighteen months old, a time when their need for a close, secure attachment is still intense. Manifestly, it is not easy for a child of this age to adjust to the arrival of someone who is going to take up a great deal of his mother's time and attention. Indeed most children, no matter what their age, give some signs of upset following the birth of a new baby.

In the Cambridge study mentioned above, 93 per cent of the toddlers who acquired a new sibling showed an increase in attention-seeking behaviour, and many had sleeping problems. On the other hand, toddlers also show a lot of interest in, and affection for, a new baby. They comment on the baby, and will entertain and try to take care of him or her. As young as eighteen months they will try to join in bathing, feeding and dressing.

What parents can do

Having two babies in the family is rarely an easy situation, and it is certainly one that requires thought and forward planning. You may want to change your toddler's routines: to stop breastfeeding, change sleeping arrangements, put him in a different room, get him into a toddler group, even move to a new house. If you possibly can, make any changes of this kind at least six months before the birth of the baby, or put them off until six months after. It will take your child some time to adjust to these incidental changes, as well as to the new baby. Do not ask him to cope with everything at once. Try, too, to avoid giving him the impression that the baby's birth has changed everything for him.

What should you do to prepare your toddler for the baby's arrival? Long-term preparations don't mean a lot to a child of this age. Telling your child a new baby is coming, showing him picture books, introducing him to other new babies, will probably not make much impression. Nevertheless, preparations of this kind do serve to introduce the subject. If nothing else, telling your toddler a story about the new baby will familiarize him with the concepts and language surrounding the event – even though he will probably only have a vague notion of what is going to happen, and no idea at all of the impact the event may have on his life.

Most toddlers are attached to several people by the time they reach eighteen months; and the time around the birth of a new baby is going to be much less difficult for a child if people he is close to are there to give him lots of time and special attention. If it has happened that your child does not have an attachment to anyone other than his mother, the months of pregnancy should be used to guide him gently towards affectionate relationships with some other people – above all, with his father. A father who, so far, has perhaps felt excluded from the intense mother-child relationship can really come into his own now.

Just before the birth, give some indication of when it will be, and, in the case of a hospital birth, of how long you, his mother, will be away from home. At the same time, reassure your child about the arrangements that have been made to look after him. If he is to be away from home, go with him to where he will stay.

If you are going into hospital, when the time comes to leave you should say goodbye even if this means waking the child up: far better this than that he should wake to find you gone.

If you are having your baby at home, make sure there is someone there whose sole job is to take care of the toddler. He will want to come in and out of the room where you are as he wishes, but he may be more involved in his own play than the birth.

You should be aware that, when you see your child again, after the baby is born, he may not be as interested in the baby as you would like: indeed, he may give both of you a cool reception. It will take him time to adjust to these dramatic changes.

You should not be too surprised, either, if he regresses: he may, for example, stop saying his few words, or even ask to be breast- or bottle-fed like the new baby. If this happens, the worst possible approach is to scold him or tell him to be big. Let him too be a bit babyish for a while, it will do no harm.

You may find that your toddler becomes extremely troublesome when you are caring for the new baby. The more deeply involved you are in feeding or bathing the baby, the more likely he is to start exploring the electric socket, tip out the baby's bathwater or empty your cupboard. It helps to have your strategy prepared – though you may have to accept that even the best-laid plans will not work perfectly, or every time. If you have ready a drink or snack and/or some special toys or a favourite activity, the toddler may keep himself occupied while you are feeding or changing the baby. Even better, try to think ahead and plan jobs he can do to help you. And when he does help in any way, be sure to give him lots of praise. He needs to feel that he is valued by you for himself and also *because* he is older and helpful. Build on this, subtly emphasizing the advantages of being older. One father invented the Saturday Morning Club for people who could help him go shopping: only the older child qualified for membership.

Most babies can find comfort in something to suck, whether it is a thumb, a toy or a ragged piece of blanket.

Your toddler is going through a wide range of emotions. He needs you to acknowledge his feelings of jealousy, but do not make too much of them, and certainly do not punish him for having them. Emphasize instead his positive feelings: his interest in the baby, his love for you, his pleasure in being helpful, and in his own activities. Make the most of the times when the baby seems to show a liking for the older child – smiling and gurgling at him, perhaps. Point out that babies smile and gurgle at people they love and feel are important.

Although a toddler up to eighteen months is more likely to lash out at you than at the baby, don't put temptation in the way of even the least jealous child: make sure there is no possibility for damage, whether it be deliberate or accidental.

Comfort objects

A baby sucking his thumb, or holding on to a raggedy blanket edge as he drifts into sleep, a toddler caressing his cheek with a tattered scrap of fabric – these are poignant images with which almost all parents are familiar. Most children between the ages of four months and a year find some way of comforting themselves: a baby may suck his thumb or twiddle his ear, or he may become inseparably attached to a 'comfort object' – a toy or a piece of material which he will carry with him everywhere. Parents quickly become aware of its importance, and make sure that it is always packed when they go away from home, and that it never ends up in the washing machine at bedtime.

A baby's comfort object is his, and his alone. No one, brother, sister or friend, would dare to appropriate it. The recipient of large doses of active affection, it will often be grubby, and almost inevitably end up mutilated; but it can never be changed, unless the baby decides to change it. However, the comfort object is not necessarily always treated with affection: on occasion, particularly if it is a toy such as a doll or a teddy bear, it may be on the receiving end of an angry or frustrated outburst.

Whatever form it takes, the comfort object assumes a life of its own. Comfort objects serve an important purpose in helping babies make the transition to toddlerhood. (For this reason they are also called 'transitional objects'.) Although you continue to provide a secure base for him, your growing child will inevitably confront times of frustration and anxiety as you recognize and encourage his increasing independence. In the anxious moments when you are not there, or cannot attend to his wants immediately, he clings to the comforting security of the well-loved object. As he comes to realize and accept that your absence is only temporary, and gains confidence in his own ability to survive until you come back, so his attachment to the comfort object diminishes. It has served its function.

Substitute care

A high proportion of mothers with children under school age work outside their homes, full- or part-time (in Britain over 25 per cent, in the United States and Australia more than 50 per cent). Sometimes the father is able to take over the care of the children in the mother's absence; but this is still not common. There is, in addition, a small proportion of parents who belong to the social class where it is normal to employ a nanny. One way or another, a lot of babies are looked after, for substantial amounts of time, by someone other than a parent.

Substitute care comes in many forms, including relatives, nannies, au pairs, childminders, neighbours, crèches and nurseries. The various types of care can be divided into three broad groups: care from an individual in the child's home, care from one person in someone else's home, and group care. For the baby there is a great deal of difference between being in his own familiar home and going out to someone else's home. And being in someone else's house, even if the caregiver has other children to look after, is different again from being in a nursery or crèche with a group of children and, possibly, several carers.

The need for continuity

When you arrange substitute care for your child, it is important to keep in mind his need for security and continuity. You should try to ensure that the caregiver you choose has a style of caring that is broadly similar to your own. Your baby will not be happy (and nor will you) if the person looking after him has very different ideas about how children should be treated. Think what it must be like for a baby who has become used to a great deal of attention to be left alone in his pram for much of the day; or for a toddler who has been encouraged to make his preferences known to find himself in a situation where children are expected to be seen and not heard.

You need to feel comfortable with your child's caregiver, too. Any unease between you is likely to communicate itself to the child. On a practical level, it is essential to your child's well-being that you feel able to tell the caregiver about anything that concerns him. You need to make sure, to start with, that the person who is going to mind him knows as much as possible about him, his routines, habits and preferences, and any special words and expressions that he uses, or that are used to him. But it doesn't stop there: you will need to go on telling the caregiver about anything that happens that affects the child – and that can range from a restless night to a family break-up. On the other side, you must of course be able to trust the caregiver to tell you anything you need to know about your child.

Finally, having chosen a suitable substitute caregiver, you should do your utmost to ensure that this person will stay with your child for a good long time – in fact, the longer the better. A child needs to establish an attachment to the person who is looking after him; and when a nanny or childminder leaves a child who has become attached to her (or him), the child can become insecure, anxious and unhappy.

Introducing a substitute caregiver

Any child needs time to adjust to an important new person; when you are bringing a new caregiver into your child's life, do it gradually. If you have arranged for care at home, you should stay with the child and the caregiver for the first few days, while, by degrees, you play a more passive role in your child's care, allowing the person who is to substitute to take over. This is more difficult to arrange if the child is to be cared for outside the home, at a childminder's or a nursery, but you should do your best to make the transition as gentle as possible.

The period between six months and around a year, when your child's primary attachment is at its most intense, is the time when he is likely to be most distressed by the introduction of a new caregiver. If you are careful to make a smooth transition you might manage, without too much upset, to introduce a nanny or other help to look after him in his own home. But it is really better not to ask him to adapt to care outside the home, at a childminder's or a nursery, during this period, or, indeed, until after the most intense phase of his fear of strangers is over. It is much easier for a child to adjust if care outside the home is either begun during the first three or four months, or put off till he is at least eighteen months old.

A further factor to consider when introducing children to group care is the finding that fear of strange children can peak at around twenty months. Again, if children have to go to a nursery or crèche at this age, a gradual introduction is called for.

How does substitute care affect attachment?

Many parents fear that if someone else takes care of their child for much of the time, he may fail to form an attachment to them. This can happen, but whether it does or not is up to the parents.

For example, a baby who has been looked after by a nanny for the major part of his waking hours since he was very young is certainly likely to form a close attachment to the nanny – indeed, it would be worrying if he did not. But this does not mean he cannot become attached to his parents as well. Although the amount of time parents spend with their baby has significance, it is far from being the most important factor. As in the formation of any attachment, what matters is that the relationship between baby and parent should be sufficiently warm and loving, and that the parent should respond appropriately to the baby's signals (see page 145).

A sense of self

The self-concept, the sense each of us has of himself as a unique individual, begins to develop in earliest childhood. For the baby, the first step towards a self-concept comes as he forms the idea that he is a separate person – separate, that is, from his mother. The newborn baby can hardly differentiate himself from his mother: the two seem joined as one, in a symbiotic relationship. The emergence of a baby's sense of himself as a separate individual takes place gradually, over many months, as he comes to realize that he can have an effect on other people: he cries and his mother picks him up; he smiles and his father smiles back; later, he drops a rattle and someone returns it to him. Through this process the baby's sense of a difference between self and other slowly develops.

In one intriguing set of studies, designed to establish just when babies come to see themselves as individuals, babies were first simply put down in front of large mirrors; observers then watched to see how they behaved. Usually a baby between nine and twelve months old would pat the image in the mirror or otherwise try to interact with it, as if he perceived the reflection as another child. Then the experimenters, under the pretence of wiping the baby's face with a cloth, put a spot of rouge on his nose, again showed him his reflection in the mirror, and watched to see whether he would touch the spot on his own nose, or the nose in the mirror. None of

A nine month old perceives the face in the mirror as another baby. By twenty-one months he will probably have realized that it is his own reflection.

the babies under a year old touched their own noses, but 25 per cent of fifteen month old children did; and when the experiment was tried on children twenty-one months old, 75 per cent of them touched their noses. They had acquired the idea that the face in the mirror was a reflection of their own.

In another set of studies, children were shown photographs of themselves, and asked to name the child in the picture. A few children were able to do this at fifteen months; most could do it by twenty-one months.

So it seems that by the latter part of the second year most children have acquired, not only a sense of themselves as individuals, but also some image of their own appearance – quite a remarkable achievement.

Even at this early age it is possible to see the foundations being laid of a crucially important by-product of this sense of self, that is, a sense of self-esteem, which is discussed more fully in later chapters. All development builds on what has gone before, and it is never too early for parents to start to convey to a child the message that he is valued.

A sense of achievement

For babies and young children, developing is largely about learning to control their surroundings. A baby who smiles at his mother and gets a smile back can already feel in control of a brief social exchange. He has a sense of achievement: his action has caused a reaction. A baby who can grasp a bottle or hold a spoon is beginning to control his own feeding routines. When babies are trying, but failing, to control a situation they often become frustrated and tearful – as, indeed, do parents, when they feel they cannot control their children.

Here I am! It is very important to recognize your toddler's achievements.

No one, baby or adult, can win all the time. The aim (easy to write about, less easy to attain) is to help children develop an appropriate amount of self-control, and a fulfilling sense of achievement. In the attempt to reach this goal, conflicts are inevitable. For example, difficulties often arise because a child attempts a task he is unable to manage: a baby trying to get down the stairs for the first time may have to be stopped for safety reasons. But sometimes, even at a young age, the problem is conflict of will. A parent wants a baby to sleep, for instance, when he is just not tired. These conflicts can bring out the worst in parents. It is at the crisis point that parents – perhaps reminded too forcibly of their own mothers or fathers – may find themselves resorting to tactics they vowed they would never use.

Some parents seem always to be pushing their babies to eat more, sleep longer, play on a higher level and behave better than they are able. Having reasonably high expectations, and encouraging your baby to live up to them some of the time, will stretch the baby. But when expectations are constantly too high, whatever is achieved there are going to be frustrations.

Some parents are rushers. 'Let's hurry up and clear that away so you can have dinner'; 'Hurry up with your dinner so we can go out' – a steady stream of 'hurry up' conversation goes on and babies, it is safe to say, though they may not understand the words, do understand the attitude. This pattern is particularly counter-productive at the toddler stage. Toddlers, if constantly rushed through everything, never have the time to practise their newly learned skills: the toddler who is learning to walk, or to climb, or to feed himself, and is always being hurried will feel very frustrated. On the other hand, parents have rights too, and their own lives to lead. No parent can walk at toddler speed everywhere. There has to be a balance, so that parents can support their toddler's need to learn control and to feel achievement, and yet not totally abdicate from their own needs.

Play

Play is an essential part of being a child, from earliest babyhood onwards. Indeed, the ability to play is a joyful quality that most people, luckily, can take with them into adulthood. But though adults usually feel they know when a baby is playing – and though they themselves generally tend to approach babies in a playful way – it is not easy to define exactly what play consists of, or what purpose it serves.

Babies are clearly not playing when they are sleeping, feeding or crying, or when they are in a wakeful but passive and reflective state. Again, if a child does something not as an end in itself but for some other purpose (for example, to gain approval or acceptance), the playful quality of an activity seems to be submerged, and it turns into something more like work. Nor does it seem quite like playing if a child is not free to choose whether or not to do something. No one would say that a child who persists in an activity that gives him no pleasure is truly playing; nor is the child who is passively watching someone else doing something, even if that 'something' is playing.

So what is play? Perhaps all we can say is that when a baby is playing, he is actively doing something that gives him pleasure and satisfaction, which he has freely undertaken to do for no other reason than that he wants to.

The role of play

Play, then, is something that babies – and others – do because they like it. The baby is aware of no other reason for playing than the pleasure and satisfaction it gives him. But much thought has been given to the role of play in the development of the individual and the species; and some of the theories about the purpose of play have produced useful insights and contributed valuable strategies for enriching children's opportunities in play.

One concept of play postulates that the stimulus for playing behaviour is an inborn biological need for new experiences. This view, first put forward in the nineteenth century by German psychologists, again came into favour in the 1960s and 1970s. The contention, made on the basis of child observation and animal experiments, is that humans (and other species) need new experiences if they are to develop in a healthy way – and, indeed, if they are to survive. The curiosity that children display is seen as an indication of their need for stimulation. However, while there is much to support these ideas – certainly deprivation of appropriate new stimuli is impoverishing – it is worth pointing out that uncritical extrapolation from them has its dangers. An enthusiastic heaping up of over-rich experiences can provide a harassing environment for young children. They need new experiences, but they also need peace to digest what they experience.

The nineteenth-century educationalist Friedrich Froebel regarded play as a way of learning: he thought parents should provide experiences and materials which would help children to find out about the world and about themselves. A similar approach was taken by Maria Montessori, who is especially associated with early learning, and remembered for the educational play equipment she developed. In her view play is a means of experimenting, solving problems and creating. Children enjoy play because it gives them a sense of competence that contributes to their well-being. Montessori had a deep belief in structured experiences which help children use their senses to discriminate sounds, colour and taste. She felt that children should be given plenty of time to explore water, mud, sand, flowers, and find out about the physical world at their own pace. This is perhaps her greatest contribution to attitudes among present-day parents: we can now accept that toddlers who appreciate splashing in water, pouring sand or investigating a daffodil taken from a vase, far from being destructive, are engaged in the important task of discovering how the constituent parts of their world behave.

Montessori also emphasized the importance of parents' taking cues from their children, following the child's interests as he explores and plays. At the same time she stressed the need for adult involvement, and the role of adults in teaching children about their surroundings, by providing experiences that are attractive enough to hold children's interest, and focus on one learning point at a time.

Freud, too, had theories about play. For him, play was a way of expressing emotions and learning to come to terms with unconscious fantasies and fears. Play was designed to master the environment symbolically, in an attempt to reduce the sense of threat that children experience in a frightening and uncontrollable world. In play they can feel they are bringing their environment under their own control. Fantasy play in particular enables the child to transform the world into something less frightening, re-creating reality in a more acceptable form.

One of the fullest expositions of play comes from the Swiss psychologist Jean Piaget, who believed that play contributes to the process of forming intelligence. He argued that for babies between birth and two years, who are using their physical senses to explore the world, play takes the form of repeating the same explorations over and over again – touching, tasting, smelling, looking and listening until they have mastered each new piece of material; then, once they have gained control of an object, or an experience, they are spurred on to play with it even more, because of the positive pleasure they derive from the sense of mastery.

Piaget took the view that fantasy play, which usually starts to appear when a child is between twelve and fifteen months old, is no different from any other play, except that children do not use it as a way of learning something but only in order to deal with what they know already. They do not learn to drink from a cup by pretending to drink from an empty cup; when they play at drinking they are practising the skill they have acquired, gaining confidence and taking pleasure in their sense of mastery.

Although because of Piaget's emphasis on the connection between play and learning he has become firmly identified with the early-learning aspects of play, perhaps his most important contribution for the parents of young children has been in encouraging them to provide opportunities for children to practise and consolidate their new skills happily.

So, as Froebel said, 'play is never trivial, but serious and deeply significant.' When we consider its value to a child in learning to master the world, we can see why it is often said that 'play is the work of a child.' Nevertheless, though certainly play is worthy of study at the highest level, parents will be missing the point if they concentrate too much on its meaning and purpose. Far better to focus on the enjoyment involved: children play because they love playing. If we keep that in mind, the rest will follow.

How play develops

As a baby develops from stage to stage, physically, perceptually, emotionally and socially, so his play changes; as his abilities evolve, different activities become possible and different forms of play become appropriate and satisfying to him. So, too, do different playthings (see pages 166–7).

A newborn baby shows little interest in inanimate objects, but even at two weeks his interest is caught by randomly moving things that he can see at close quarters; he can hear well and turn his eyes to seek the source of a sound; the pattern he most likes to look at is that of the human face; when in the more or less upright position that seems necessary for him to become

Looking at faces is the most exciting, captivating form of play a baby can have.

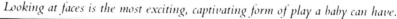

alert, he needs complete support. All this adds up neatly to the fact that the perfect plaything at this age is a grown-up person, whose animated and responsive face, interestingly intermittent vocal sounds and safely supporting arm combine all the features that seem to please him most.

During his first few months, watching and listening are a baby's most vital activities. As he is held in arms or on a lap, gazing into his mother's face, listening to her voice, exchanging eye contact and coos, being gently jiggled and bobbed, he is laying the foundations of many of a human being's most important capacities: he begins to absorb the turn-taking of exchanges between people which will later blossom into communication by speech; he learns that his wishes and needs can elicit a response from another person; he starts to develop a sense of his own body, its boundaries and sensations.

About two months from birth, a milestone is passed when the baby's hands, gradually losing the grasping reflex that has kept them curled into soft fists, become able to hold an object that has been put into them. Even before hand-eye coordination has developed to the point where the baby can successfully reach for an object himself, he finds it absorbing to hold something, and later to wave it about.

By three months the baby's early grasping movements have developed into something more purposeful. Over the succeeding months, as he masters the skill of grasping, his interest in objects increases. This process receives a boost when, at around six or seven months, he learns to sit

When he can sit up, he starts to explore those faces in a rather more immediate way!

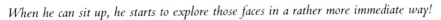

unsupported: now he is able to look around more widely and easily and, with both hands freed from the need to hold on to support himself, he takes great pleasure in reaching for things, grasping them, investigating them. Everything he grabs is explored, at first by his mouth and later – when the early sucking reflex has lost its primacy – by his fingers, pulling, prodding, squeezing. Everything is new to him and everything is of interest.

At the same time, he is learning to move about. Whether he starts by crawling, shuffling or some other method, being able to move independently must mean to him an amazing freedom. When he begins to walk, probably some time between ten and sixteen months, there is another critical advance in his sense of liberty and mastery. He gets enormous satisfaction from moving around, at once improving his physical control and investigating his surroundings from his new perspective.

And he is investigating all the time. When, by about ten months, he is able easily to let go of objects, he will make a game of that too, dropping and later throwing food and toys for you to pick up, and learning, by the way, about space, about cause and effect, and about how things go and come back. Soon he will be able to put things into other things, or arrange them beside, on top of or under each other. As he does so he will be beginning to develop a realization of the relations and comparisons between things on which the whole structure of human conceptual thought depends.

Most babies love putting things on top of each other and then knocking them over, but it takes a great deal of coordination to pile bricks or beakers into a tower. It is helpful to remember that knocking down comes before building in the normal sequence of development, so a baby needs many opportunities to destroy someone else's tower before he can build one of his own. If everyone perseveres, your baby will probably be able to stack

Babies begin by knocking things down rather than building them up.

three blocks one on top of another by the time he is about eighteen months.

Making a drawing is well beyond the scope of babies at this stage, but from as early as about nine months a baby may get a mitten grip on a crayon and swipe at a piece of paper. These random marks made during the scribbling stage are very exciting to most babies. Scribbles are among the first ways a baby can make his original marks on his surroundings, and, with luck, this is the spirit in which drawing and writing will develop over the next years – as a creative discovery.

This toddler, building an interesting construction,
demonstrates powers of concentration and coordination.

In the baby's second year, a dawning understanding of the functions of objects and the intentions of people will lead him to try pretend play of a simple kind, as he starts to explore the uses of things and the roles of people in his life. Objects and activities come to have meanings, instead of simply physical properties to be experienced. A toddler who knows about eating from a spoon, or having his face wiped with a flannel, will try pretending to use the real spoon or flannel to feed himself or wipe his face, practising the real activity in a repetitious game.

Later on, probably after the age of two, children will extend their pretend play to include another person, playing at feeding or manipulating a family member, animal or toy. As they grow older the scope of pretending continues to increase, coming to involve the creation of imaginary cars out of chairs, houses out of boxes, horses out of sweeping brushes, and then role-playing games of mummies and daddies, nurses and doctors, cops and robbers, and so on. But these belong to later chapters.

Playing with your child

Some parents find that playing with their children comes naturally. But for others – perhaps the majority – amusing a young child for long stretches can be quite burdensome. Often a parent finds that one stage of a child's development somehow fits in easily with his or her own nature, but that it is hard to feel interested in another stage. A mother who effortlessly coos and babbles with a young baby may become irritable under the pressure of her toddler's constant demands that she should be the passenger in the bus he is driving; a father who is ready to build elaborate brick bridges for a two year old may find it boring and unrewarding to keep up a dialogue with a tiny baby.

Realizing the scale and importance of the ground your baby is busy covering can help you find interest and satisfaction in his achievements during these months. Similarly, some understanding of the developmental stage that the child has reached will help you to find appropriate and satisfying things for him to do, since you will more easily realize what skills he is keen to practise. Even small babies give cues for the kind of interactions they find pleasing – imitating facial expressions, playing peekaboo games, dropping something for you to pick up. Even if you don't enjoy picking up a rattle ten times in five minutes, you will be able to respect the fact that your baby is learning to communicate and to understand.

Often, parents who have found it quite easy to play with their baby in

Stimulation

Playing with babies, and offering them varied and interesting playthings, helps them to advance more rapidly both in muscle control and in the development of concepts.

Several studies of babies between the ages of five months and two years clearly indicate that they learn to reach and grasp more readily, and show more active interest in new objects and experiences, when their parents respond to their need to investigate the world around them. In relation to babies and toddlers, this means, quite simply, offering them a variety of play materials (including common household objects) and allowing them the freedom to explore them not only visually but also with their mouths and hands.

It is important to note, though, that the parents in the studies offered stimulation in response to the babies' signals. Parents need to be sensitive here, and aware of the risk of overwhelming a young child with too many toys and experiences. A baby who is overstimulated can become exhausted, confused and irritated – and quite as miserable as a baby who is bored because he has nothing to do.

early infancy, running more or less on instinctive reaction, find themselves at a loss at the crawling stage, when babies want to extend their activities but their repertoire is still limited. It is worth remembering that play can be very simple – as simple as passing a toy back and forth between you and the baby, or putting a woolly hat on his (or your) head, and taking it off again. Even small variations (hand a different object, put the hat on back to front) can renew the interest for the baby, if not for you. To help you find such artless activities rewarding, you can remind yourself that participation in the baby's play – whether by you, another adult or an older brother or sister – is never wasted. From the earliest days most play is social, in the sense that babies are social beings who cannot exist in isolation, and many of the skills they have to practise are concerned with relating to other people. The kind of give and take and turn-taking that occurs at this age between the baby and older people is of great benefit as the basis for the child's ability to relate to other people throughout his life.

Toys

So people come first. But children also benefit from having objects to help them play. Many children have grown up successfully with a minimum of commercial toys, making creative use of everyday things that they find around the house – an old saucepan and a spoon, for example. But nowadays parents tend to feel that they are expected to buy toys of some kind, and there is no doubt that some of these toys enrich children's play.

For parents, the chief virtue of a toy may lie in the hope that it will keep the baby amused long enough to let them start on their own neglected tasks. More positively, toys may help parents relate comfortably with their children, and increase their interest in play. There are many toys that promise amazing educational results, and some of them work well. These may be of special value to those parents who feel happier in the role of teacher than that of playmate. But try to bear in mind that when the advertising surrounding such toys encourages parents to have unrealistic expectations, the danger is that they may come to feel frustrated and disappointed, not only in the toy but in their child.

The choice of toys is no easy matter. Parents can often be seen dragging home an inappropriate purchase that has entranced them, but that their infant will not fully enjoy for several years (by which time it may well have disappeared, or, worse, shed vital bits). Everyone is bound to make such mistakes once in a while, and they do no great harm so long as the toy is safe, and does not lead to lost tempers, or end up making children feel inadequate. And if, 'unsuitable' though it may be, it extends the interaction between parent and child, then the money was well spent.

Clearly, though, some understanding of a baby's likely developmental needs at each stage will help in choosing toys that enhance a child's experience and help to practise new abilities. The chart on pages 166–7 has been designed to give some general guidance.

How babies play

This chart is to help you select toys and activities which will aid your child's development.

	What your baby is doing	Toys and activities to try
Newborn	Enjoys faces	Paint a face on a paper plate and let your baby follow it with his eyes, at a distance of 20–25 cm/8–10 inches
	Likes to look at patterns and shapes	Hang mobiles at a distance of 20–25 cm/8–10 inches
	Loves new sights	Change his point of view by letting him look over your shoulder
	Sensitive to textures	Change the pattern and texture of his cot cover
		Give him a soft, furry surface to lie on
	Attracted by sounds	Provide musical cot toys
	Eyes follow a moving object	Hold a rattle above baby's face and move it slowly from one side to about the middle of his chest
One Month	Wants to be with you	Use a baby sling
	Likes to see things move towards him	Attach a piece of elastic to a small stuffed animal and bounce it towards him
	Likes to listen to sounds	Tape-record familiar sounds
		Play a radio for him
	Enjoys being touched	Use baby oil and massage him all over his body
	Kicks his legs	String soft balls and foam bricks or rattles across cot to encourage kicking
Two Months	Likes to change perspective	Put him in a bouncing chair
	Interested in unexpected noises	Offer squeaky toys
	Kicks mobiles	Hang kicking objects at different lengths – let his feet reach the mobile
	Notices his own hands	Play gentle clapping games
Three Months	Focuses eyes	Play with hand or finger puppets
	Can play with fingers – likes swiping	Put rattles or toys on a string he can swipe at
	Likes to see himself	Provide a baby mirror
	Likes to listen to sounds coming from different places	Use a bell, squeaky toy or rattle to attract baby's attention
	Exercises legs	Hold an inflated beach ball over baby so he can kick it
	Attracted to your voice	Talk to him on a toy telephone
	Likes rhythms	Place a clock which ticks nearby
		Play music for him
Four Months	Wants to reach and exercise	Put a cradle gym in the cot
		Play 'bicycles' with his legs
	Learning about cause and effect	Roll wheeled toys down a sloping surface
	Tracking – follows moving objects with eyes	Blow soap bubbles
	Experiences new textures	Give him a textured ball or different pieces of cloth

	What your baby is doing	Toys and activities to try
Five Months	Likes to do things with you	Involve baby by putting him in a baby bouncer, chair or on your back in a sling or carrier
	Turns over	Play roly-poly games
	Learns to manipulate with hands	Provide a toy 'activity centre'
Six to Nine Months	Can grab things	Provide rattles and toys which can be hung over cot for baby to grab
	Sits with support	Give him toys he can reach for and explore (with his mouth first)
	Repeats activities	Give him a variety of toys which can be manipulated
	Starting to eat food at the table	Suction toys work well on table tops
	Imitates what he hears	Show him pictures of familiar people, animals and objects and name them
	Likes the sound of your voice	Sing nursery rhymes, lullabies
Nine to Twelve Months	Likes toys on which he has an impact	Offer xylophones and simple musical instruments
	Learning about sinking and floating	Provide bath toys (funnels, sponges, containers)
	Coordination improves: holds and releases things	Give him nesting beakers and a toy box for filling and emptying
	Hand-eye coordination progressing	Introduce a simple posting box
	Recognizes familiar pictures	Provide books with clear, colourful pictures
Twelve to Fifteen Months	Learning to walk	Pull-along toys and baby walkers are popular
	Interested in mobility	Introduce first large ride-on toys
	Hand-eye coordination improving	Provide puzzles and jigsaws with simple shapes
	Understands words	Provide a variety of picture books
	Ideas of size and shape develop	Offer sorting and stacking toys
Fifteen to Eighteen Months	Begins to climb	He might enjoy a low climbing frame
	Starts to pretend	Provide dressing up clothes; 'shops' equipment; playhouses, etc
	Likes new sensory experiences	Provide materials for sand and water play; playdough and clay
	Hand movements becoming more skilled	Give him plastic containers with lids which can be taken on and off; finger paints and wax crayons
	Can follow stories and loves repetition	Read story books or make up stories
		Sing action rhymes with him

Managing play

A small amount of initial planning and organization can go a long way towards facilitating a child's play, while, at the same time, saving parents a good deal of time and effort.

Parents can decide the amount of space in the house which can be used by the children, and the freedom with which they will be allowed to use the space. Some parents are willing to turn over the whole house to children. Others allow only a portion of each room, or sanction the free use of one room. A clearly defined system, whatever the details, can be a relief to everyone – so long as you don't make a playroom and then expect your toddler to play in it on his own for long stretches of time: at this age, 'under your feet' is precisely where he wants, and needs, to be.

Similarly, a well thought out storage system for toys and playthings, if adhered to without undue anxiety, can save a lot of work and keep toys readily available for spontaneous play.

Parents also manage the relationships that young children have outside the home. The best plaything you can offer a child is another child, and it is entirely in the control of adults whether children get a chance to have friends over, or go to toddler groups, playgrounds or parks. In the early stages, usually until their third year, they will play alongside each other, without much interaction, but after that they will begin to join together, at first perhaps in games such as chasing or imitating each other, later in co-operative play with the same toys. Slightly older brothers and sisters can be ideal playmates – though it is worth noting that if toddlers always play with older children, they can become passive, forever waiting for the bigger ones to take command.

The messages in play

In every daily interaction – caring, feeding, teaching – parents impart information about their own attitudes, opinions and responses, and the way they view their children. These messages are delivered for the most part quite unconsciously; nor do the children realize that they are taking them in. None the less, they are being absorbed.

Play activities are often loaded with such messages. When rolling a ball for a toddler to kick, one parent may let the child know that if he misses it there is plenty of time to get much better. Another, disappointed at the child's first clumsy attempts, may make him feel a failure. Parents who do not appreciate that knocking down towers of bricks is a valuable step on the way to understanding how to build them may feel that they have produced a destructive toddler – and can communicate their fears to the child.

Fortunately, most parents are delighted by the achievements of their babies and toddlers, and the positive messages they give in response to their efforts help the children to have a sense of themselves as competent and successful.

Sleep

Sleeping is an important activity for babies – as, indeed, it is for all of us. A third of most people's lives is spent in sleep. Yet its nature is not fully understood: while we can recognize it as, in the definition given in *The Oxford Companion to the Mind*, 'a healthy state of inertia and unresponsiveness', we cannot fully explain the mechanisms that bring it about.

However, we do know something of what sleep seems to do.

Sleep assists in growth and restoration of the body: growth hormone is released in humans during sleep, and the growth of new cells is faster during sleep. Babies, of course, are growing at a tremendous rate – so this is one clue to the importance of sleep in their lives.

Sleep seems to assist in memory: we – and babies – perhaps need a period of sleep for memory traces to be strengthened.

During sleep we dream, and there is some evidence to suggest that we need our dreams if we are to remain mentally healthy. We know nothing, however, of babies' dreams.

There are two types of sleep and four levels. The first type is orthodox, or regular, sleep and the second is paradoxical sleep, during which it is possible to observe the sleeper's eyes moving rapidly, though they remain closed. During paradoxical or rapid eye movement (REM) sleep, brain waves show patterns closer to those of wakefulness than those of orthodox sleep. At birth babies spend about half their sleeping time in each state. By six months the proportion of REM sleep has dropped to 30 per cent, and in most adults it is about 20 per cent. Neither state of sleep is deeper than the other, and mental activity continues during both. If adults are woken during orthodox sleep they are likely to report that they have been thinking about something, while if they are woken during REM sleep they will report dreams. However, we cannot be certain that babies dream during REM sleep. They usually go into this type of sleep more quickly than adults. If their REM sleep differs from the adult kind in this way, it may also fulfil a different function.

The four stages are related to the depth of sleep, stage one being the lightest. Several cycles of sleep occur during each sleeping period, with movement from one stage to another and back again. Most people wake or reach a near wakeful state several times during each night: the 'good' sleeper drifts back again to a deeper stage without being aware of waking.

Developing acceptable sleep patterns

By the standards of most human societies babies come into the world with their internal clocks poorly set. At birth they tend to sleep most during the day. Gradually a night sleep pattern emerges, and by three months about 70 per cent of babies take their major sleep during the night.

Most parents want their children to establish a sleep pattern that fits in

Newborn babies tend to sleep most during the day, but by about three months the pattern has changed and most babies take their longest sleep during the night.

with family habits; and children can be encouraged to adopt acceptable patterns from an early age.

Even the way parents deal with a baby's night feeds sets up expectations. Usually, parents want the night feeds to end reasonably soon, so that they can have an unbroken night's sleep. At the same time, parents often find that night feeds are calmer and less pressured than feeds during the day, and once they are awake, they are tempted to prolong the feeding time, cuddling the baby or walking around with him. The tiredness they feel in the morning is counterbalanced by the satisfaction of the caring time spent with the baby in the night. However, if your baby finds night-time feeding sessions particularly enjoyable, he is likely to go on waking, for the pleasure of the contact with you, long after his need for physical nourishment during the night has ceased. You may find, indeed, that instead of diminishing, the night-time wakings become more frequent, and the baby stays awake for longer periods. You should consider whether it would not be better to encourage him to sleep at night, by seeing to his night needs quietly, taking the least possible time and paying him the minimum of attention. Don't worry – you will be able to give him the love, warmth and attention he needs during the day. Indeed, you will be much better able to do this if you are not dropping with tiredness from lack of sleep.

Another crucial issue is how parents deal with bedtime. The transition from waking to sleep, which should be simple and matter-of-fact, can be tiring and complicated for both parent and child. There should be clear, predictable routines surrounding the time of going to sleep.

Families develop their own bedtime rituals, but a typical routine for a baby or toddler might include a bath or wash, putting on the child's night clothes, perhaps a last drink, tucking him up in his cot or bed, a story or song, a goodnight kiss – and, then, goodnight. However, some families adopt sleep rituals that lead to stimulation and, if anything, keep the child awake for longer: you might enjoy a vigorous romp with your toddler when he is in his pyjamas – but you should not then be surprised if he shows some reluctance to settle down quietly! Sometimes routines that seem quite simple at first escalate into elaborate complications – another drink, four or five stories, just one more song – until parents can feel as if they are being put through the ropes. If you are content to stay with your child, rocking, patting, reading or singing until he falls asleep, that's fine. But if you find you are becoming frustrated and resentful, perhaps you need to realize that you don't have to respond to all your child's demands. You too have needs, and wants, and it is reasonable to set limits.

As night sleep gets longer, daytime naps diminish. By one year most babies have a nap in the morning and another in the afternoon or early evening. Usually the morning nap goes next; it is not uncommon for children to take an afternoon nap until they are four or five.

As the time of napping comes to a close you may find that you have to make a choice: you can encourage your child to go on taking his daytime nap, and have him invigorated and lively at what is supposed to be bedtime; or he, and you, can endure a miserable, whining period during the day in return for an early night and sound sleep. There is no perfect answer, choose whichever way you think preferable; but once you have decided, do try to stick to your chosen course.

Sleep difficulties

In a way, it is nonsense to talk about sleep difficulties: it would be more accurate to say parental difficulties with sleep patterns, since a problem to one family is normal behaviour to another. There is no universally right or wrong sleep pattern: whatever suits the individual and the family is the correct solution. For example, in our culture there tends to be something of a taboo against the idea of children sleeping in their parents' bed. In many others, people are shocked at the notion of a young child being put to sleep alone: it is customary for babies and toddlers to sleep with their parents, and older children, at least of the same sex, will share a bed. Again, in Britain perhaps the majority of parents at least hope that young children will be asleep by early evening, so that they can have the evening to themselves. Americans are often more easygoing about this and may just let children stay up until they seem tired – which can be very late at night. Then, some parents seem to have endless patience with their small children; others find that unless they have babies asleep early and efficiently, they themselves become worn out and frustrated, and the whole family suffers.

Having made the point about each family having its own perception of what a problem is, there is no doubt that sleep problems are common in cultures where children are expected to sleep alone. In Britain one preschool child in five will present parents with a major and persistent difficulty. One New York study found that around 30 per cent of children under three woke once or more every night. This suggests the possibility that the origin of many sleeping difficulties may be a fear of separation.

So it is easy to understand why children should want to sleep with their parents. Nevertheless, parents' needs and expectations have also to be considered. If you and your partner are happy to have your child in bed with you, there is no problem. However, many parents find that somehow they have got into the habit of having the child in their bed, for all or part of the night, and that this is creating real difficulties for them. They do not want to have to cope with disturbed sleep and an interrupted sex life; they want the child to sleep in his own bed.

Altering established sleeping patterns is never easy, and can be painful for both child and parents. Parents need to be firm and consistent in their intention, while making sure that their child does not feel rejected – and this, often, at a time of night when all they want to do is go to sleep. However, staff at Great Ormond Street Children's Hospital have devised some procedures which have proved helpful to many families with sleep problems. Recognizing that leaving a child to 'cry it out' can be too upsetting for everyone involved, their advice is that, having set your goal, you should consider approaching it in small steps, rather than adopting an all-or-nothing attitude.

For instance, if your child needs you to stay with him until he is asleep, you can try a gradual approach to leaving. At first you might sit beside the cot or bed, holding his hand or stroking him gently. After a time – it may be a few nights, it may be many – you can stop touching, while still sitting close. The next step is to move your chair a short distance away; then, over time you can position it nearer and nearer to the door. (It is a good idea, early on in this process, gradually to stop talking or singing to him, to make no or only monosyllabic responses to questions and to avoid eye contact – having a book to read can be helpful.) Finally, you can move the chair outside the door, staying ready to be called back in – for the briefest of visits – if necessary. If your child is used to going to sleep in your arms you can start by trying a similarly gradual approach to putting him down in his cot, involving leaning over, cuddling, stroking and soothing, and so on.

Again, if your child sleeps in your bed and the business of leaving him alone in his own room proves too painful, in prospect or reality, you could,

I need you, even though it's the middle of the night! It takes time to get used to sleeping in your own cot.

as an initial stage, make up a separate bed for him in your room. Later, when he is used to sleeping in a bed on his own, you can take the further step of moving him into another room.

It all takes time; but a habit that has been established for the best part of a child's life is not going to be changed overnight. And, however gradual the process, it also takes firmness of purpose. If, for instance, your toddler has been accustomed to coming into your bed when he wakes in the night, but you want him to stay in his own bed, you are going to have to take him back every time he comes in to you. Having decided to do that, you must not waver. If you let him in sometimes, because he is too upset, or you are too tired, or for whatever reason, he will get the message that his efforts can succeed – and go on trying.

173

Communication

The ability to communicate in words is the single most important skill that a child acquires. Once language has developed it forms the basis for almost all subsequent learning and is the medium through which most relationships are conducted.

Early communication

Long before a baby can say any words, conversations take place between parent and child. Think of what happens when a parent dresses, changes or baths a baby. As the hand is pulled through the sleeve the parent bends to kiss the palm and the baby smiles; as the nappy is being changed the baby squirms to show his annoyance and the parent pulls a face to distract him; the baby splashes, the parent dodges, and the baby crows with delight.

Both parents and babies are active participants in these early conversations. If the early gazing is returned with a smile, if the first kisses are delighted in and fussed over, if the coos and gurgles are noticed and imitated, then an atmosphere is established in which the baby can develop a language of words. If – for whatever reason – the baby's overtures meet with no response, and these first exchanges are not made, the development of verbal communication will be hindered.

The language of crying

Crying is an important means of communication for a baby – a powerful way of alerting his carers to his needs.

There are three main points to bear in mind when considering babies' crying. First, they do a lot of it – or, at any rate, most of them do. Research indicates that in their first three months 70 per cent of babies cry for an average of two and a half hours a day. By twelve months the average is down to one hour.

Secondly, the amount of crying does vary greatly from one baby to another. Some babies cry a good deal less than the average quoted above; others, unfortunately, cry more. If you become skilled at forestalling or calming your baby's cries, you may be able to reduce the time he spends

Smiles and laughter

Most babies begin to smile properly (that is, as an expression of pleasure) at about four to six weeks. Smiles may be elicited by various sights and sounds, but they come most readily in response to the human face, the human gaze, the human voice. By about three months babies smile more at familiar faces.

As children grow older they will smile not only at people, but also in recognition of an achievement.

Evidently, smiling has a biological basis, for blind babies begin to smile at about the same time as those who can see; the difference is that sighted babies smile more as they grow older, while blind babies smile less.

By about four months most babies are able to laugh. Laughter, like smiling, almost always comes as the result of interacting with people – making a marvellous reward, and encouragement, for parents.

crying. Don't count on this, though! The amount a baby cries does seem to depend, to quite a large extent, on his own constitution and temperament. The individual crying pattern of a particular child also alters as he gets older. For the first nine months babies' crying patterns tend to be erratic; they settle down to greater consistency by twelve to eighteen months.

The final point is that, worrying though crying can be, it is not all bad. A baby who never cries can miss out on attention. A 'good' baby, who never seems to need to communicate by crying, is one to watch carefully.

Identifying cries

Mothers may learn to identify some different kinds of cry: hunger, pain, tiredness. In practical terms, however, comforting a baby is often a question of going through a mental check-list of possible causes.

Hunger

Hunger is the first thing most people think of when a baby starts to cry, and it is, indeed, the most common cause of crying in young babies. Research confirms what every mother knows, that most babies cry less after they are fed, and almost all of them cry if the breast or bottle is taken away before they are full.

Discomfort

When a baby cries after a feed the cause is often discomfort from wind: his stomach is distended by air he has sucked in with his milk. If you hold your baby upright against your shoulder and rub his back he will usually burp the air out within a couple of minutes. If he is uncomfortable because of undigested food in his stomach or intestine he will settle down once he has passed a bowel movement.

Too cold or too hot?

Babies are happiest at a uniformly warm temperature, and they will cry if they feel cold. This is probably why they frequently cry when they are undressed: the sudden drop in body temperature is uncomfortable for them. Usually, a baby won't cry just because his nappy is wet, but he may well cry if it is not only wet but cold too.

Worrying that their babies may get cold, parents are often inclined to wrap them up too warmly – which the babies don't like either. A baby who is dressed in several layers of clothes, with a blanket on top, in a warm room, is highly likely to become fretful.

Crying for companionship

If your baby is fed and you can find no obvious reason why he should be uncomfortable, it may be that he is crying for companionship: he wants to be played with or cuddled. Warm contact with your body, or the sound of your voice, will quickly comfort him.

By twelve months he realizes that crying brings him attention, so he will cry with the intention of getting someone to play with him.

Fatigue

On the other hand, babies also cry because they are tired – fatigue is a common cause of crying in babies. If this is the problem, the baby is likely to become even more miserable and irritable if you pick him up and play with him. However, gentle rocking or patting may help him get to sleep.

When young babies begin to cry they kick and wave their arms – which stimulates them to cry more. Eventually, a baby may work himself up into quite a frenzy. Swaddling the baby loosely in blankets, so that his movements are restricted, may calm him down.

Crying out in pain

Continuous crying can mean that a baby is physically ill or in pain. If your baby's crying seems to you excessive, or if he cannot be soothed, you should consult your doctor, who can help diagnose a physical problem if there is one.

Anticipating pain

Between nine and twelve months, as their ability to remember past experiences develops, babies will begin to cry in anticipation of a frightening or painful event. Babies of this age often cry when they see a doctor's needle, or even as they cross the surgery threshold – presumably because they remember that last painful injection.

When you don't know why

Various reasons have been suggested for persistent crying that has no obvious cause: for example, it may be that a baby who cries a lot has a difficult temperament; or perhaps his nervous or digestive system may be slow to mature. At around two weeks, about one in five infants develops colic, which is characterized by a pattern of intense crying for as long as three or more hours every day. There are many theories about why colic occurs, none of them proven.

If you feel that your baby cries more than others, you should get your doctor to check that there is no medical reason. You can also try the various soothing methods suggested below. Beyond that, there is not much to be done. Try to take comfort from the knowledge that most babies stop their inexplicable crying by the time they are between ten and sixteen weeks old. Possibly this is because their nervous and digestive systems have caught up; it may also be relevant that now they are beginning to interact and play more they have other activities to keep them occupied. Meanwhile, you will be best able to help your baby through this difficult period if you can manage to remain affectionate but unflustered during his bouts of crying.

Comforting your baby

Once your baby has begun to cry in earnest, it may be difficult to comfort him. Just as some babies cry more than others, so babies also differ in their readiness to be soothed. Boy babies as a rule tend to be more difficult to soothe than girls, and there are some noticeable differences between cultures. For example, Chinese, Japanese and Navajo babies seem to be considerably easier to soothe than European or American babies.

All the following methods have been found to help, in some circumstances. They often work best in combination: evidently two methods of comforting are better than one, and three are often better yet – a crying baby may need swaddling, rocking and the radio on before he calms down.

Contact

A crying baby will often begin to calm down if you hold him closely to you: holding your baby against your shoulder, in time-honoured fashion, is always worth a try. Sometimes just pressing the soles of a baby's feet can help, as can touching his face lightly. A gentle massage can be very soothing. And some children can be comforted simply by being placed on something soft and furry.

Gentle rhythms

Young babies – especially babies of two weeks old or less – can be soothed

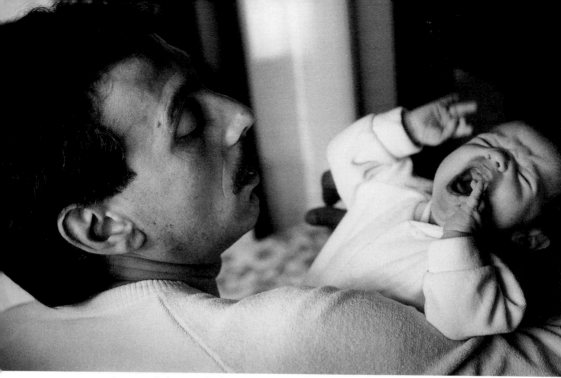

A crying baby may be hungry, tired or uncomfortable. Sometimes, though, he just needs a cuddle and some attention – the feel of your body and the sound of your voice. Hold him closely and sing or talk to him softly.

by rhythmic motion, such as rocking or patting. Walking up and down with the baby against your shoulder often does the trick – although there are babies who seem to respond only to the motion of a car, and reduce parents to driving aimlessly around the streets in an effort to get them to sleep!

From time immemorial parents have soothed their babies by singing lullabies. If your voice or your patience gives out, you could try sometimes substituting a record or tape, or putting the radio on low. Some parents swear by tape-recordings of heart beats, or of womb sounds. Others find that any gentle, rhythmical music, or even the steady purr of a vacuum cleaner or fan heater, works equally well.

Swaddling
Swaddling loosely in a shawl or a blanket can help a very young baby – especially if you then walk around carrying him upright on your shoulder.

Sucking
Sucking is a natural way for a baby to find comfort. The sucking reflex comes while babies are still in the womb, and some babies suck their fingers or thumbs even before they are born.

If you think your baby might be comforted by sucking, but he has not yet discovered that he can suck his own hands, you can try helping his hand to his mouth a few times, to see if he would like to suck it. Though a dummy will do no harm, the baby's own thumb is preferable. As part of his own body it is under his control as an extraneous object can never be, and, moreover, it is sensitive: the baby can explore his mouth with his thumb.

Coping with crying

Some babies have particularly piercing cries which are agitating to listen to, and some parents have a low threshold of tolerance. It is well established (scientifically as well as informally) that crying not only rouses people to action, it can also irritate and anger them. Spending all day with a crying baby is lonely and frustrating. Parents can come to feel depressed and discouraged, sometimes angry – or even violent. If you feel this way, it is important to ask for help and support. Professional counselling, or the support of a group of parents with similar problems, can be extremely helpful.

Sometimes contact with other human beings is the most important need. Try taking your baby – and yourself – out of the house. Just seeing other people and watching their activities – in a neighbour's home perhaps, or a playground, community centre or shops – may be enough to take the baby's mind, and yours, off crying.

The parents of crying babies are subjected to quantities of good advice. Often what they need most is not advice, but some time off. It is good practice to let your baby be cared for by someone else for brief periods of time: short but regular breaks should be on every parent's list of coping strategies.

Towards a language of words

Cooing and vocal play

When they are about two months old, babies start to produce coos – delicious sounds which are the first a baby makes out of happiness.

Coos, which contain vowel sounds and a very few consonants, first emerge as single sounds (like words) and then come in series (like sentences); but they differ from words in that they lack timing and meaning. Sadly, cooing is short-lived: it has almost disappeared by about twenty weeks.

By four or five months babies' vocal cords are sufficiently developed for them to start experimenting with pitch, voice and breath to produce different sounds. These sounds, which may include growls, bubbling noises and trills, are distinctive for each child and are a primitive form of communication. When babies make them they expect a response, and they usually get one, for who could resist?

Babbling

Babbling, which usually begins at around six months, but can appear as early as four months, includes a full range of consonants and vowel sounds. All babies, whatever their culture and whatever their parents' native tongue, seem to use the same kinds of sounds. Babies produce sounds which are not heard in their native language, and even deaf babies babble. There is no general agreement on the relationship between babbling and subsequent language development, although it seems likely that the exercise provided by babbling is a necessary preliminary to gaining full control of the tongue, lips and palate.

By six months babies are able to control the sounds they make to the point where they can repeat them. They often seem to become fascinated by a particular syllable and will echo themselves, producing a sound such as 'bababababa' or 'dadadadada'. Some parents feel that they detect the baby's first word at this stage. While the 'word' is more likely to be only a form of babbling, the mistake can serve a useful purpose if it encourages parents to spend time imitating their baby's sounds, so that he can imitate them back – a game which babies adore, and which is a great help to them in this vital stage of speech development.

At around nine months, babies begin to use babbling in a more conversational way. It is at this stage that their ability to distinguish phonemes in foreign languages (see page 135) begins to diminish, and they start limiting the range of sounds they make to those that are made in their language environment. At this stage, too, they begin to make a few sounds that may seem like their earlier babbling, but these are used to communicate or to express feelings – a baby may have one particular sound that he makes when he points, for example.

At three months a baby enjoys exchanging coos and gurgles, and will smile in response to your words.

Patterned speech

Between ten and twelve months, babies begin to string sounds together in a way that seems very like speech, using all the intonations and stresses of the language they will be speaking. Some babies are very good at making themselves understood: they can use their babbling to convey exactly what they want, and by the time they speak their first word they have already been communicating for a long time. Other babies go through this stage more quickly, never become particularly adept at making themselves understood through babbling, but may speak their first words earlier.

Understanding language

Babies are on the receiving end of language from the moment of birth, perhaps even before. Small babies react to speech more than to any other sound: some show a degree of synchronization with an adult voice when they are less than twenty-four hours old. By his second month your baby may smile directly at you if you speak to him. At three months he will turn towards you when he hears you speak.

He is already learning that language is a means of communication, that words have meaning and that voice inflections convey messages. By the time he is five months old your baby may respond to his own name, and at six months he will probably recognize some other frequently repeated words, and the gestures that accompany them: words such as 'bye-bye' (waving), 'up' (with open arms) and 'come' (hand held out). Babies of this age already have a good idea of what language and speech are about. They know, for example, that if someone can be heard talking there is probably a person around, even if that person cannot be seen. Moreover, a baby can react to what people say even when they are not speaking directly to him – for instance, he may get upset if his mother speaks to an older brother or sister in a cross voice. At this stage babies can often be soothed by the sound of someone talking on the radio.

By eleven months babies may respond to simple questions ('where is the dog/your teddy?') by looking or pointing (their language of gestures matures alongside their understanding). By fifteen months they recognize the names of various parts of their body; and by eighteen months they can identify pictures of familiar objects when they are named.

In these early months of learning your baby will often show signs of understanding words and phrases well before he speaks them. The process is the same when an older person is learning a foreign language: it is always easier to recognize what is being said than it is to recall words in order to say them.

Acquiring words

Children learn words by gathering together the available clues. Every routine activity, every play session in a baby's life, is surrounded by a circle of words created by his parents. It is out of this that the baby decodes a language.

For example, mother says 'juice' every time she pours out the juice. It tastes different from anything else on offer and if a similar sound is uttered by the child, with hands outstretched – a drink appears. The word is learned because it is often repeated in association with juice and reinforced because when the child wants juice he finds that saying the word is the best way to get it.

Words like 'woof-woof' or 'car' are more difficult for a child to work out. For example, when someone says 'woof-woof' to a baby there is generally a dog around, and the baby soon learns that this word seems to have

---

Early words
One of the children studied by Elizabeth Bates, a researcher in early childhood language, was a little girl named Carlotta. Her account of Carlotta's language development presents a picture which may be taken as fairly typical.

Between nine and thirteen months Carlotta began to name. She used the word 'nana' for all requests. She used 'bam' for knocking over towers and 'brr' for moving vehicles along. She had another word, 'woowoo', which was her response to the question 'how does the doggy go?' while looking at a picture of a dog in a book. By thirteen months 'woowoo' was a word which meant dog – both in real life and in pictures. Animal names, along with names for items of food and drink, appear frequently in the lists of first words collected by researchers.

The child who is slow to speak
Parents naturally may become anxious if their child seems slow in beginning to speak; however, it is important to realize that the boundaries of normal speech development are quite wide.

The average age at which a child turns towards the sound of a voice is five and a half months, but one child in four does not do this until he is seven months, and one in ten has still not been observed to do it at eight months. The first recognizable word is an eagerly awaited milestone that is reached at an average age of ten months; but 10 per cent of children thirteen month old still have not said a word that can be understood by anyone else.

If your child's speech is developing at the rate of this slowest 10 per cent group, you should ask two questions: is there any evidence of hearing loss and does he seem able to understand what you say to him? If you have any doubt on either of these counts, seek medical advice. If you are satisfied that he is hearing and understanding well, there is probably no cause for concern about slow speech during this first eighteen months. The likelihood is that, given time, your baby's speech will develop normally.

something to do with the dog – but exactly what remains to be discovered by trial and error. At first a baby may use 'woof-woof' to mean every animal, perhaps even every part of every animal, including the food they eat. If the baby is told repeatedly 'that is the cat', he gradually learns that 'woof-woof' should be confined to dogs. Little by little, increasing accuracy is acquired.

The first words

Most researchers into early language define a word, in this context, as a sound which is used regularly to refer to the same object, action or person. An early word often does not relate in any obvious way to the adult word for the same thing but to be considered a proper word it needs to be understood by another person. By the end of their first year most babies have one or two words or sounds which are used consistently and intentionally to refer to particular objects, people or events. This is the emergence of true speech.

It is usual for a baby's first words to be intelligible only to those who know him well, and who are familiar with the routines of his life and the words that accompany the routines – in short, those people, generally the parents, who have written the script.

These early words are often holophrases, one word or sound that is used to express something an adult would use a sentence for, or one word which is over-generalized to apply to many things. They are personal words, usually, at this stage, poorly articulated, and cannot be understood unless you are in tune with what is happening.

After the first few words have emerged, there may be something of a plateau. Typically, it takes three or four months for a child's vocabulary to

How language develops: birth to eighteen months

As with all tables mentioning ages, the months given below should be seen as a rough developmental guide.

	Understands	Expresses
Newborn	Responds to high-pitched voices Words engage his attention and may comfort him Synchronizes actions with the sound of an adult voice	Several different cries Loud noise evokes startle reflex
One Month	Responds to mother's comforting sounds Stops moving and listens to sounds Is startled by sudden noise Stops blubbering (not crying) when hears a familiar voice Can differentiate between a friendly and an angry voice Takes turns with mother; gestures or makes noises when she has finished talking	Small throaty noises Most sounds made to communicate discomfort, distress and excitement
Two Months	Listens to person speaking	Coos, making some vowel sounds May smile at speaker
Three Months	Shows pleasure in social contact Attends to sound of rattle if it is 15–30 cm/6–12 inches away at ear level Looks at person speaking	Coos when happy and when alone; gurgles Makes more vowel sounds Exchanges coos with familiar person Smiles in response to speech
Four Months	Attends to rhythm and pitch of language rather than words Heart-rate goes down when hears a familiar sound Changes expression when displeased	Laughs out loud Experiments with different sounds and produces some consonants
Five Months	Responds to own name	Imitates sounds
Six Months	Knows 'bye-bye', 'mama', 'dada' Turns immediately when hears mother's voice at a distance Shows some understanding of emotional state of mother's voice	Babbles spontaneously Uses monosyllables, then double syllables Combines vowels and consonants Protests vocally Talks to himself in tuneful sing-song voice Squeals with delight
Seven Months	Starts to understand content of speech	Likes to talk to himself
Eight Months	Awareness of speech content develops	Imitates babbling sounds
Nine Months	Stops when hears 'no'	Babbles are inflected, with rising and falling intonations Imitates adult sounds like a cough or 'brr' noise Shouts to attract attention, waits for response and tries again Enjoys communicating with sounds

	Understands	Expresses
Ten Months	Uses gestures to indicate some objects	Imitates pitch May says first words, usually 'mama' and 'dada'
Eleven Months	Points to things May respond to simple questions by looking or pointing	Produces sounds which echo last words said to him
Twelve Months	Understands names of family members, car, dinner, bath, walk, cat, dog and some other objects Turns when hears his name Responds to simple instructions, like 'wave bye-bye', 'clap hands', 'where are your shoes?'	Babbles continuously, sounding like conversation Uses most vowels and many consonants in babble May speak one or more words besides 'mama' and 'dada' Imitates sounds and words enthusiastically
Thirteen Months	Will hand toy over on request Looks in their direction when person or familiar object is mentioned Will come when called Responds to gestures Acknowledges the names of people and pets Listens for a few minutes to stories, rhymes	May speak three or four words May have a sound or word for thank you Often attempts new words
Fourteen Months	Points to coat to indicate he wants to go out	Puts all kinds of sounds together Speaks three to five words Uses gestures and sounds instead of crying for what he wants Repeats sounds of words
Fifteen Months	Understands names of various parts of the body Understands 'no', 'come', 'show me', 'look' Identifies pictures of a few named objects	Speaks four to six words plus names May say 'there', 'bye-bye'
Sixteen Months	Might watch children's television	Uses six to eight words clearly plus names Uses one word to express when he wants to be picked up
Seventeen Months	Brings toys or objects from another room if asked	Adds new words every few days
Eighteen Months	Identifies pictures of familiar objects when they are named Understands simple questions	Can speak about forty or fifty words including names Uses two-word 'telegraphic' phrases Favourite words frequently include 'all gone', 'thank you', 'bye', meaning that task or event is completed Word most often used is 'no' Refers to himself by name Tries to sing Replaces gestures with words

By eighteen months your child's vocabulary will be in the region of forty to fifty words – and conversation starts to sparkle!

reach ten words. However, during all this time children are learning more and more concepts, and their comprehension is increasing rapidly. Once the first nine or ten words have been mastered there usually follows a dramatic expansion in vocabulary. At eighteen months, the average child has a vocabulary of forty to fifty words and by the time he is two this will have increased to nearly three hundred words.

The first sentences

By the time they are about eighteen months old, many children are beginning to combine words to make two-word sentences such as 'more juice' or 'daddy gone'. Or, rather, it would be more accurate to say that they begin to combine ideas: 'bye-bye' may sound like two words, but it only covers one idea, whereas 'daddy gone' is a combination of daddy and an action.

Speech at this stage has been aptly characterized as 'telegraphic', because, typically, these early sentences contain only those words that are vital to the message – that is, generally, nouns, verbs and adjectives. Prepositions, articles, inflexions such as the plural 's', and so on, are omitted. The ubiquitous 'more' is not an exception. This word may be categorized as a comparative in adult speech: most toddlers use it as a command – 'give me more . . . !'

186

Conversations

Some of a baby's earliest verbal conversations are responses to having people or objects pointed out: 'who's that over there?' – 'dadad'. Parents give the lead and babies answer with a single word. By about eighteen months children can participate in slightly longer dialogues.

Language and the hard-of-hearing child

Just as few children who are called blind can see nothing at all, so there are degrees of hearing loss. There are several ways of classifying people who are hard of hearing, one of them being based on the loudness of sounds that cannot be heard. A mild loss is found when someone cannot hear a whisper, a moderate loss is when there is difficulty in interpreting a normal voice at a distance of about 90 cm/3 feet. A severe loss is the inability to respond to the human voice at all, and in profound deafness there is little or no response to any sound.

Another way of measuring loss is by reference to the range of sound frequencies which can be heard. The most common deficiency is in the higher ranges. A child with a high tone loss will not be able to hear the high ranges of the voice and will have problems with certain sounds.

Deafness was described by Samuel Johnson as 'one of the worst of human calamities'. An undetected hearing loss is certainly a calamity for a child, who can feel desperately bewildered and cut off from the world. Parents, and later teachers, can come to think of him as stupid, as naughty, as a daydreamer, and he can be led to see himself as inferior. If the problem is detected early, not only will the child receive help with his physical problems, but these social problems can be avoided.

A severe hearing loss will probably be picked up when a baby is very young, as it will quickly become apparent that he shows little or no reaction to sounds. A mild or moderate hearing loss can often go unnoticed in a young child: parents should take note if a toddler does not respond when called, or does not turn round when there is a knock or ring at the door. Often, however, the earliest indication of a moderate hearing loss is delayed speech. If you have any suspicion that your child is not hearing well, you should make sure that he has a reliable hearing test.

The problem is that not all hearing tests are reliable. Testing a child's hearing requires special equipment, and considerable skill in interpreting the findings. One of the difficulties is that hearing loss can fluctuate, perhaps coming and going with ear infections or colds. So it is possible to go to a doctor one day and be told, correctly, that there is no hearing loss, yet find a week later that the child does appear to have problems in hearing. The only real answer, with any suspected hearing loss, is a discussion with a specialist and, if it is thought necessary, a full hearing test.

Treatment of hearing loss depends on the cause of the problem: some children will be helped by having grommets (little tubes) inserted into their ears, others will benefit from surgery. Hearing aids can help some children.

The effect of hearing loss on language development depends partly on how soon the loss is picked up, partly on how severe it is, partly on how much help is available and partly on the characteristics of the child. Once the extent and nature of any loss have been established, parents will be given guidance, probably by a speech therapist, in how best to help the child's speech develop in a way that is as close to the normal pattern as possible. If the loss is mild it may be enough to be aware of the need to take care over certain sounds and to make sure that the speaker's face is in a good light, so that children can make maximum use of lip-reading and other cues. With a severe loss, more specialist help may be needed. A general rule is that you should not talk to deaf children in any special, shortened sentences; be natural and speak just as you would to any other child.

Language development in deaf children

Studying children who do not hear speech clearly helps resolve to some extent the issue of how much language development is innate and how much is due to the experience of being surrounded by language. Researchers study deaf children not only to help them, but to learn about hearing children as well.

An important area of study is language development in the first two or three years, the time when language is most easily acquired by hearing children. What do children with extremely poor hearing do at this time?

The answer is that nature seems to find a way to help them communicate: children who cannot hear use signs instead of words. They start to make signs at much the same age as a hearing child would begin to say words (rather earlier, if anything), and they develop them in much the same sequence as hearing children acquire words. If nobody teaches them signs they will just make up their own. It appears that there is an innate drive to learn a language of some kind.

It is illuminating in this context to note that the 10 per cent or so of deaf children who are born to deaf parents generally fare better than those born to hearing parents, mainly, it seems, because they are immediately in an environment where the communication system is geared to their needs.

The use of sign language

There is still some controversy over whether deaf children should use signs or whether it is better to use oral language only.

One school of thought argues that children should be discouraged from using signs, even forbidden to do so, since if they use signs they may be less motivated to learn to lip-read and to speak. Others say that while children should be encouraged to learn to lip-read, their powers of expression will be impoverished if they are compelled to rely on oral language alone. Much of the detail of speech is lost to a lip-reader: sign, on the other hand, is a rich, precise and flexible language, and deaf people seem to find it a more natural means of communication than the spoken word.

Deaf children instinctively communicate through signs, which can be developed into a rich and flexible language. This little girl began to sign when she was about nine months old, and her baby sister, a hearing child, also signs.

To some extent this is a topic for the more specialized literature, but we should make two observations.

The first is that in the event children use signs whatever their teachers say. They might as well learn to use them properly.

The second is of interest also to those studying language development in hearing children: even if signs are used, it is a help to the deaf child if the person communicating speaks aloud as well. It might help you see why if you try listening to someone speaking with their back turned to you. You will notice how disconcerting this is: we pick up a great deal from the facial expressions of a person speaking, as well as from his lip movements.

How parents can help

The best way to help your child's language development is to set an early pattern of enjoyable communication. If you attend to your baby's facial expressions and imitate them, smiling and frowning with him, if you pick him up when he reaches out to you, if you play with his kicking feet or give him your finger to grasp, it will help him to realize that he can communicate with you, and that communication is rewarding.

Most parents naturally murmur words ('there, there', 'oh, that's a good baby', 'don't worry, sweetheart') as they pat their babies' backs, or jig them up and down in their arms. The babies may not understand the words, but they find the sound soothing, and it seems to help them associate communication with words. It certainly helps babies learn words if their parents talk during routine activities such as bathing, dressing and nappy changing ('now, where's your sleepsuit . . . oh, there it is!'). Words associated with familiar routines are commonly among the first children say when they begin to speak.

Young babies tend to gaze at objects that interest them. Later, they will often spend a lot of time pointing at things. If parents extend this interest by picking an object up, playing with it or looking closely at it, while talking about it, the baby will learn that words can be associated with interesting objects. Carry your baby around the house, or walk around holding your toddler's hand, and when something attracts his attention, stop and talk about it. We take everyday things for granted. They are new and fascinating to a young child, and he needs to learn about them, and what they are called – surprisingly often, children starting preschool don't know the names of simple things like their coats and hats, not to mention curtains and cutlery.

You can also use pictures to teach a toddler the names of things and help you respond to his questions. Books with simple, realistic pictures are useful; and a parent who takes the time to collect pictures of everyday objects for a homemade book will find it can be used over and over again.

Little children enjoy nursery rhymes, and the rhythm helps them to remember the words. If you sing or recite rhymes often to your baby you will find that when he begins to speak, even while his vocabulary is still very limited, he will be able to fill in key words. At first you will have to wait a while and encourage him to respond, but once they have learned this

---

Bilingual children

Parents may wish their children to learn to speak two languages from an early age – perhaps because the family has more than one native tongue, or because the children will need to speak a different language at school from the one normally spoken at home. They are often concerned, though, that this is asking too much of a young child, and particularly, that the child could become confused between the two languages.

In fact, young children seem to cope well with learning to speak two different languages. Their early language development is usually a bit slower but they soon catch up, and the experience of familiarity with two languages not only provides them with a useful extra tool of communication, but often enriches their overall intellectual development.

It does help children to discriminate if the two languages are consistently spoken by different people – if granny always speaks French and mum and dad speak English, for example, or if Urdu is spoken at home and English at the day nursery. But you need not worry that if you speak two languages to your child he will never be able to sort them out. It will just take him a little longer.

skill most children seem never to tire of practising it.

It will help a toddler develop his telegraphic speech, so that he can describe with greater subtlety how objects connect, if you make sure you explain those connections to him: 'we are going *upstairs*'; 'teddy is *under* the table'; 'look, Tom, you are sitting *between* Jane and me.'

Baby talk

Adults instinctively talk to young babies in short sentences, using simple language, and usually pitching their voices rather higher than normal. As a baby makes more sounds, and later begins to speak, most parents, delighting in their child, will imitate him – which is a positive and encouraging response to the baby. So parents will naturally, at least sometimes, talk in 'baby talk'.

As a child gets older parents usually adjust their language so that it stays slightly ahead of the child's speech development (although often an early word or two, perhaps an endearingly adapted name for another child or a family pet, is fondly retained and passes into the family's private language). Starting with what the toddler says and expanding on it is a good way of extending the child.

'More bicky.'

'Would you like another biscuit?'

'Up.'

'OK, let's pick you up. Up, up, up we go.'

Prompting is another useful technique.

'What is this?' (pointing to a picture of a lion).

No answer.

'We saw one at the zoo.'

No answer.

'It roared.'

No answer.

'It's a lion.'

'A lion.'

'Yes, it's a lion like the one we saw at the zoo. It roars like this, grrrrrr.'

'Grrrrrr.'

We began this chapter by saying that the changes that occur in these eighteen months seem miraculous. Certainly if you compare your eighteen month old child to his newborn self, it might seem as if the two are different beings. Yet it is possible to trace patterns of development, to see how one thing leads to another, how you have contributed and how much you, too, have learned. In the following pages these patterns of development will be traced throughout childhood. But in this extraordinary eighteen month period the foundations of your child's life have been laid.

Physical Skills

Physical growth and development is necessary but not sufficient for the emergence of physical skills. For skills to flower, children need opportunities to observe others and encouragement to try for themselves.

Gross motor skills

By eighteen months most babies have turned into toddlers. Many of them will have been walking for several months.

In the months that follow they start to acquire other skills – learning to run, to jump, perhaps beginning to pedal a tricycle, to kick, throw or catch a ball. A child of two can stand from a sitting position and return to sitting without any difficulty. She can climb up and down stairs (though she will probably still place the same foot first on each step). Suddenly, too, everything seems to be within the toddler's grasp – she can climb on to furniture, open drawers, haul herself up on to window sills, reach across tables and grab things. The newly acquired skills can be rather alarming for parents, who find they need to be constantly alert.

Walking

An eighteen month old child who has been walking for a while now takes longer steps than she did when first learning to walk. She points her feet straight ahead, does not lift them so high off the ground, and puts them down closer together. She still tends to hold her arms high when walking, but over the next year she will gradually lower them, and her gait will become more rhythmic and regular. Already at eighteen months she may experiment with turning backwards and sideways, but she cannot yet gracefully pivot around a sharp corner – instead she will walk around it in a half-circle.

By two the toddler's mobility has increased considerably; longer legs and stronger muscles mean that the two year old can walk and move much more quickly. By two and a half the child is less top-heavy and her balance is more stable. She begins to lean forward as she walks. She also starts to flex her feet, putting her heel down first and then her toes, instead of putting the whole sole of the foot down at once, and this means that she can

Children are eager to try out their newly discovered balancing skills. Swinging on a frame is an adventure for this three year old, though her mother may be nearby.

walk faster. As walking becomes more automatic, she can turn her head as she goes to look at all the interesting distractions.

Balance

When babies first learn to walk their feet are wide apart to help them balance. Between eighteen months and two their balance gets better, and they can walk with their feet closer together. They are now able to stop and bend to pick things up while walking along, and may drag a toy behind them while they run.

Balance improves continuously during the second and third years as the child's centre of gravity alters, her vision stabilizes and her ability to focus improves. A child who has trouble in focusing the eyes may also have problems with any task related to balance. There is, too, a marked development over this period in the mechanism of the inner ear, which integrates visual and motor information and maintains equilibrium.

When a toddler has developed a better sense of balance she can pick herself up from a fall and keep going. Between eighteen months and two she may learn to manage a little car or simple riding toy, beginning by pushing the feet along the ground and learning to steer to avoid obstacles. Many children start to ride a tricycle by two, pushing it along with their feet. Towards three, with better coordination and balance and stronger legs, they learn to pedal properly.

Running and jumping

The great physical accomplishment that comes between two and three and a half is learning to run. In true running both feet are off the ground at the same time – something which requires strong leg muscles, good balance and fast, accurate timing. First attempts at running are usually more like quick walking or scurrying, and most children can't really run until they are at least two and a half. Many don't manage it until they are three and a half.

As you might expect, children who are given opportunities to run and explore physical movement – especially if they also have the encouragement of brothers and sisters – become more skilful at both walking and running. As a result, they will probably also be more adventurous in attempting other physical activities such as jumping, balancing and climbing.

At around the age of two and a half a toddler will attempt her first jump. She will initially try it from a standing position, but may soon also try jumping from a low step, keeping both feet together on take-off and landing. Her first jumps will be all legs and no arm movements, but with practice she will start to use her arms, automatically lifting them above and behind the body to help gather momentum.

Kicking, throwing and catching

In Britain and Australia, and in other countries where football is popular, children are often encouraged to kick as soon as they can stand unsupported. At around eighteen months children will usually step up to the ball, often bumping into it or falling over it; by two, or perhaps even earlier, they can kick it. Between two and a half and three, as children gain better balance, their kicking improves all the time.

In the United States, where the national sport is baseball, and throwing and catching skills are emphasized, parents tend to spend more time encouraging their children to throw. Toddlers' first attempts at throwing and catching may be made at two and a half or even before, often from a sitting position. When, a little later, they begin to catch from standing, they often find it easier to move sideways rather than backwards or forwards. By the time they are three they may be able to throw without losing their balance, and to catch a large ball with their arms stiffly extended.

Like other physical activities, kicking, throwing and catching skills develop and improve through practice and encouragement. American toddlers tend to learn to throw before they can kick, while with British and Australian children kicking usually comes first, not because they have different innate skills, but because they are given opportunities and prac-

199

tice in different areas. Practice is not all it takes, though: to benefit from practice, the child must be physically and neurologically ready to learn. Occasionally parents make unrealistic demands of their children, expecting them to perform far better than they possibly can, which is discouraging for the children, and counter-productive in its effect. What matters most at this stage – as, indeed, at every stage – is that children should feel competent and positive about their abilities.

How parents can help
It takes a lot of practice to learn to throw, catch, balance, pedal, run and climb, and when children start these activities they generally develop their own particular way of doing things. At this stage how skilful they are depends largely on their body build and leg strength. Parents should not try to make a child concentrate on any one activity until she can do it 'properly'. It is far more fun and a lot more beneficial to let her have a go and enjoy herself, encouraging her to be as active as possible.

Children of this age can gain a lot from using playground equipment, such as climbing frames, swings, slides and balancing beams, provided it is safe and properly supervised. But all they really need is opportunity – when they are ready they will learn new skills and repeat them over and over again.

I'll conquer that football! Children of this age group are often very determined and practise new skills repeatedly. But if they are not yet physically mature enough to cope with certain skills they may get frustrated – time for a parent to lead them back to activities they can accomplish competently.

Fine motor skills

While a toddler is making progress with walking, running, balancing and climbing, her fine motor skills are improving at a tremendous rate. As she matures her brain sends messages of increasing complexity – and her muscles now have the capacity to respond. By eighteen months a child is no longer limited to grabbing and picking up: she is capable of developing an activity, doing things with the objects she has acquired. For example, she can retrieve a small object from a bottle with her finger, and will also think to turn the bottle upside down to get the object out.

At eighteen months the toddler is able to make a tower of three bricks; at two she has progressed to stacking six. By three some children can thread large wooden beads on a shoelace. In doing this they are, of course, not only learning to thread, but simultaneously polishing and refining the skills needed to control a spoon and fork or a pencil.

Skills like fitting, posting, stacking and threading are not easily acquired without help. Left to her own devices the toddler may learn to do these things by trial and error, but she will find it much easier if a parent or older brother or sister gives repeated demonstrations which she can imitate. She then needs lots of opportunity to practise. As long as they have company and encouragement, most toddlers are happy to spend long stretches of time playing with bricks, sorting boxes and simple jigsaws. All of these toys are enormously helpful in developing hand-eye coordination and control of the small muscles.

Fitting jigsaw puzzles together, creating marks on paper; your toddler will enjoy his growing ability to control and coordinate his hands.

Scribbling and drawing

Most toddlers love getting hold of a paintbrush, crayon or marker and 'drawing' with it. They do not need to be taught or asked to draw something specific, all they need is the opportunity. Toddlers of eighteen months to two love the feeling of the brush or pencil on paper, and are endlessly fascinated by the texture and the fact that they can make a mark. Some of them do not even mind if there is only a wet mark on the paper, because colour is secondary.

Children of this age cannot say what they are drawing, for the simple reason that they are not necessarily trying to draw anything, but these marks and patterns are not purely random; they consist of definite lines made by simple movements. One can look on these drawings as, among other things, exercises for strengthening the small muscles. The child clutches the brush or pencil tightly with her wrist held stiff, and her whole arm extends, swinging back and forth, its movement determining the length of the lines. The drawing arm curves towards the body and marks go up and down. She repeats this several times and that is the picture. She may work carefully, watching closely all the time, enjoying her marks but not expecting to control them; or she may hardly look at her work at all, but be drawing while she looks away in a different direction. The brush leaves the paper at the end of a sweep and suddenly the work is finished.

Between two and two and a half toddlers begin to pay more attention to the marks they make, and colour also becomes important. A two year old may still grip the pencil or brush like a hammer, or she may hold it between her fingers, as an adult would. She will slowly learn to use her free hand to hold the paper. As her fingers and wrist gradually become more flexible she will cover smaller areas of paper and may combine a vertical scribble with a horizontal one, or with several other vertical marks; but at two and a half children can still only concentrate for short bursts of time, and they will often spend less than a minute on a drawing.

By the time she is three, a child may spend two minutes or more on a picture. By now she is probably holding a pencil in the adult way. Her images are no longer the product of a single sweeping movement: she pushes and pulls her hand across the paper in quite a controlled way, and makes a larger, more complex variety of marks. Her eyes are fixed on her work. She wants to see the scribble forming and there is now no doubt in her mind that she has some control over it.

At this stage children can combine several scribble marks, frequently covering the whole page. They are learning to make enclosed shapes and discover that a line can help represent an edge which helps make a shape. The pictures become experiments in trying to control marks and, eventually, to make them represent something.

Gradually, the work is becoming more pictorial, but the idea of 'drawing a picture' is not uppermost in the minds of most three year olds; their art is still more to do with what they feel than what they see, and they draw from memory, not observation. Quite commonly, a three year old will fail to recognize as her own a picture she drew the day before.

Most people see very little difference between a scribbling made by a two year old and one by a child of three. They do not consider them important, either – the very word 'scribble' is, in itself, dismissive. But if we stop to reflect on the skills involved we can see that what seems to an untutored observer to be no more than aimless doodling is, in fact, the end result of a whole series of developments in muscle control, in understanding of the relationship between pencil, or brush, and paper, and, perhaps most important of all, in the dawning idea that a mark can represent something in real life.

Scribbling continues to be the primary art form until the age of four. Children who have ample opportunities to scribble as toddlers tend to have more advanced drawing styles when they reach school age. This is not to say that scribblers are necessarily artists in the making, but it is an indication of how scribbling contributes to muscle control.

Towards autonomy

Of all the abilities the child develops during this period, perhaps learning to feed herself and to control her bladder and bowels have the most significance for her personal freedom. As she acquires these skills, she begins to take responsibility for her own body.

Feeding

One way to understand feeding is to see it as a developing process, marked by transitions. In the previous chapter we looked at how the baby is weaned from the breast or bottle and introduced to solid food. The toddler continues this process, adapting to new foods and modifications in her diet. At the same time her eating habits gradually evolve into a rhythm of three meals a day – though with several snacks in between – and as she takes more part in family meals, she begins to learn the patterns of social eating. While toddlers are better able to adapt to changes in their feeding schedules than they were as babies, they eat with greater enthusiasm when their natural rhythm is not interrupted. A toddler who misses breakfast will be restless and temperamental by lunch. She will be very hungry, but may also be so upset and tired she will not be able to eat.

A marked difference between infancy and toddlerhood lies in the variety of foods the toddler is offered. If parents remember how slowly and deliberately they introduced changes in the baby's diet, it may help them to appreciate that the toddler too is more likely to accept unfamiliar foods if they are introduced gradually. Offer new foods in a matter-of-fact way, but take your child's mood into account. There were times when your baby would not eat cereal and needed her bottle. Toddlers, too, are sometimes just not in the mood for new foods, and need the soothing familiarity of an old favourite. Temperament also plays a part in feeding. If your child is

Your toddler may now be quite adept at feeding herself, and can be a pleasant companion at mealtimes.

generally rather fearful of new experiences, she may be timid about trying new foods. If she is impatient, she may find sitting through family meals more than she can manage, and become very fidgety. Children have their own tempo, and some seem to dawdle endlessly over their food. If your child is a slow eater – which is a healthy thing to be, in fact – she should be given more time to finish her meal.

If you are thoughtful enough, you can usually find a way of overcoming aversions to particular foods. Vegetables, for example, are often rejected by children in this age group. Forcing a child to eat something she doesn't want is never a good plan – but you shouldn't think that the only alternative is to take vegetables off the menu entirely. They can be reintroduced in small quantities and different forms – raw, perhaps, or as purées, or juices; a child who rejects steamed spinach may well enjoy spinach when it comes creamed. It is always worth considering whether it may be the texture that the child dislikes. Although by two or two and a half toddlers are able to chew well, many of them still dislike chewing and refuse food which they find difficult to chew. Others develop the habit of keeping food in their cheeks like squirrels, and chewing it gradually – which can be disconcerting for parents!

Parents sometimes worry that their child is simply not eating enough to grow properly. In fact, most studies indicate that, provided they are offered a variety of nutritious foods, most toddlers will, over a period of time, eat an adequate diet. (For details of toddlers' nutritional requirements, see the chart on pages 496–7.) They eat in spurts. They may eat a lot one day and very little the next, or eat nothing but cereal for a week, then have three days of fish fingers. But, over time, it tends to work out. If there is a shortage it is likely to be in iron – so if you are concerned about your child's diet it might be a good idea to reintroduce iron-enriched baby cereals. You also need to control your child's consumption of junk foods: many toddlers regularly eat quite substantial quantities of foods that are high in fat, sugar or salt, which is not a good idea. Again, if children are allowed to fill themselves up on foods that are low in nutritional value, they may miss out on essential nutrients.

However tactful a parent tries to be, there are times when feeding a toddler can become a battle of wills, with the kitchen as a war zone, and food dropped, thrown and smeared all over the place. Often, the battle is not so much concerned with food as with the striving for independence that at this age can override all other considerations – sometimes, even the desire to eat. To defuse tension, it may well be worth giving the toddler a measure of self-determination, so that she is allowed some choice about what and how much she eats, and can decide for herself when she has finished. Having said that, however, it has to be recognized that at this age there are still often times when parents need to help a child finish a meal – when a toddler would eat more, but is too tired, or bored, or whatever, to make the effort of feeding herself. On any particular occasion you will have to use your judgment about whether or not to intervene.

Toilet training

Before children can understand and cooperate with toilet training they need to mature in various ways. They have to be physically mature enough both to control the muscles surrounding the bladder and the anus, and to understand messages that they are about to pass urine or empty their bowels. This means receiving messages before, not during, the event. Most toddlers will look around and be interested in noting a puddle that they are making; what is important is an awareness that the puddle is about to come – which demands the ability to make a connection between a feeling and what follows.

Again, toddlers have to be able to understand what is required of them. It's clear to you that you want your child to get rid of her waste products in a certain place and a certain way; she has to be at quite a sophisticated level of understanding before she can grasp this.

Once a child has reached an appropriate stage of maturity, training will usually go quite smoothly if she can feel satisfaction in the process. There are two significant emotional characteristics of toddlers that parents can build on here. First, children of this age generally very much want to please the people who are important to them – and, of course, parents are the most important of all. At the same time (this is the paradox of toddlerhood – and of growing up) they feel a strong drive towards independence. If you can convey to your toddler the two ideas that *you* are pleased that she is becoming clean and dry, and that gaining control over her bladder and bowels is an achievement for *her*, a move towards independence, she will have double satisfaction. The best way to do this is to offer praise at every success, certainly, but in a fairly matter-of-fact way, to get across the message that while you feel pleasure at what is being achieved, it is, after all, only natural that she should be able to do it. You also need to be able to accept mistakes without any fuss. By all means clean them up in front of the child, but do not suggest that she has done something wrong. Any pressure is likely to be counter-productive.

The course of training

The time to start toilet training is when a child appears ready, not at some specific, dictated age. The external controls exerted by parents will not be effective until the toddler's internal mechanisms are ready to function. Though it can be quite a good idea to start getting a child used to the idea of a pot from an early age – having one around and encouraging her to sit on it occasionally – there is hardly any point in beginning to train her until she is able to indicate a need to empty her bowels or bladder. At some point in her second or third year your child will start to recognize that certain sensations are associated with bladder or bowel fullness; by then she will probably be able to express the need to excrete with some sound or word, or gesture. It may be a sound or gesture peculiar to her, but this doesn't matter, provided she can get the idea across. At this point, she should be given the opportu-

Children may by now be quite capable of removing an uncomfortably wet nappy, and are very interested in investigating what their bodies produce.

nity to use the pot, or a lavatory. If she is resistant or fearful, it is usually best to wait for a short period, then try again. Let your child set the pace of her toilet training, following her signals and interests as you would if she were learning to ride a tricycle.

Though problems can occur (see pages 208–9), bowel training is usually not too difficult, partly because most toddlers need to empty their bowels only once or twice a day, partly because there is generally a reasonable time interval between receiving a message and anything happening. Bladder training can take quite a lot longer. It tends to take boys rather longer than girls. This is almost certainly due basically to the slower maturing of boys' nervous systems, but may also be influenced by the fact that it is usually mothers who do most of the training, and they may well be less knowledgeable, and less secure, about training a child of the opposite sex.

At first it is parents who are being trained, for they have to learn to read the signals and catch the toddler at the right moment. The faster and more consistently you can respond to the signals, the more successful the training will be. This may involve some luck, and some parents take a while to get the hang of it. It often helps to develop a routine of putting the child on the pot after meals or drinks. If, after a few days, this isn't working, it is best to leave it and try again after a short break. If things are going well, you may consider letting your toddler go without nappies. It is easier if you can begin training in warm weather, when you don't have to bundle the child up in a lot of clothes. Choose skirts rather than jeans for girls, and avoid one-piece outfits for either sex.

At the next stage, toddlers can tell you when they want to go to the lavatory, but the words and actions come very close together. This can be something of a problem when you are out with your child. Some parents continue to use nappies when going out even after they have been discarded at home. This saves embarrassment, but it may hold up training. It might be a good idea to negotiate with your child: some prefer to be in nappies when they go out, others hate the idea.

The next stage is when toddlers have enough control to wait while you find a lavatory, or some other suitable place. It can take a couple of months to get to this point, as the strengthening of the muscles is a gradual process. Even after a child normally has a measure of control, accidents will still happen from time to time, usually because the child is too engrossed in some activity to pay any attention to the warning signals.

Once the basics have been established you can teach your child what she should do when she wants to go to the lavatory away from home, when you are not there – at a friend's house or in a toddler group, for instance. (Be sure to tell anyone who is caring for her the words she uses for letting you know she needs to use the lavatory – however commonplace they seem to you, they may not be readily understood by someone outside the family.) You can also begin gradually to introduce the principles of hygiene. Don't try to teach too much at once. Children need to be quite confident about using the lavatory before they can reasonably be expected to wipe their bottoms efficiently, and remember to wash their hands.

Like any skill, learning to go to the lavatory is a step-by-step process: children need lots of experiences and opportunities to practise in a variety of situations before they can really master it.

Staying dry at night
Most children still need a nappy at night for some time after they have learned daytime control – though, oddly enough, some have fewer problems staying dry at night than they do during the day.

Some children become dry at night on their own. They wake up with dry nappies, or refuse to wear nappies at night any more. Others need to be reminded before they go to bed, or their parents may need to lift them before they go to sleep themselves. Many parents restrict drinks around bedtime. This can help children to stay dry throughout the night, but does not train them to be aware of the signals of a full bladder.

Training problems
While most toddlers will deposit their bowel movements in a pot or lavatory without any problem, some are resistant. They may demand to have

their nappies back on, or simply refuse to perform. Particularly, they may resist the idea that their stools should be flushed away or thrown out.

Toddlers don't regard their bowel movements as waste products. Why should they? A bowel movement is another part of the body, and as such fascinating and important. They want to know what it feels like and are curious about what it represents to their parents. They may want to play with their faeces, or smear them. This can start as a sensory exploration, like playing with food, or a discovery of a part of the body, like playing with their hands. Parents should try not to feel, and certainly be careful not to show, any horror or disgust: if a child feels her actions have had this effect, she is likely to become extremely upset, or to take up making a mess with faeces as a weapon – or both. Usually, if you simply clean up in front of the child, with a word to the effect that it would be more grown-up to put it in the pot next time, this sort of messing won't become habitual. But if it happens all the time, or continues much beyond three, it can be a sign of an emotional problem and warrants discussion with a doctor.

Children are also very quick to get the idea that they control their bowel movements. If too much pressure is put on them to do too many things they may resist in this area, which is evidently so important to their parents. If they are adjusting to a new brother or sister, a new caregiver or a change of schedule they may react by keeping their stools to themselves, and become constipated. This is one place where the toddler is in control and can win a small battle. You need to stay calm yourself, give your toddler time and space to relax, and take a look at her life generally. Is there some other problem which could be manifesting itself in this way? For example, does she have the opportunity to give her opinion, to make some choices for herself, and, most important of all, to express her emotions even if they are angry or aggressive? But whether the constipation has its origin in a physical difficulty outside the child's control or in a deliberate withholding of faeces, medical attention will certainly be required if it continues for any length of time, or recurs frequently.

While most children who are developmentally normal in other ways have learned to control their bowels by the time they are four, a significant number are still wetting the bed well after that. The most usual reason for bedwetting is a delayed maturing of the part of the cortex that allows control of urination. Genetic traits play a part here – bedwetting tends to run in families. There is usually no reason to look for outside help with bedwetting until a child is at or around her fifth birthday – though, of course, if this is just one among several developmental problems, you should certainly seek advice well before that. Any child who is still wetting the bed at five should have a urine test, to check whether there is a bladder infection, and may need to be examined to make sure there is no neurological or spinal abnormality.

Daytime wetting needs to be taken seriously rather earlier, since by five almost all children are dry during the day. A child who is still regularly wetting by day at four should have a urine test and a medical examination.

Thinking and Understanding

Children's ability to think is almost always underestimated. Recent research shows that, given a context and language with which they are familiar, children of two or three can think in ways that, only a few years ago, were deemed to be quite beyond them.

Increasing perception

Children's sight and hearing continue to improve over this period. It is difficult to obtain any precise measurement of visual acuity in this age group but the indications are that by three a child's vision is approaching adult levels. Hearing also improves rapidly over the first two years. A two year old's sensitivity to high-frequency sounds is as acute as an adult's. Low-frequency hearing, in which there was a marked deficit at birth, has improved to the point where it is almost, but not quite, at adult level – hearing in the low ranges continues to improve, gradually, up to the age of ten.

During the early days of life, a baby's innate physiological reactions to sensory experiences have not yet been influenced by any preconceptions. By the time the baby becomes a toddler, her experiences incorporate what she has learned. Her innate attraction to sweet things, for example, has already been conditioned by what she sees and hears around her, in the family, from friends and – as she gets older – probably also from television.

As their experience increases, children gradually develop a set of rules which help them understand what they perceive. For example, by the time they are a year old, children already have a well-developed understanding of constancy in size and shape (see page 134). During the months and years that follow, this comprehension becomes increasingly sophisticated. By three children can use complex clues to help them determine relative distance, or depth of field – taking into consideration the shadows cast in a picture, for instance.

Again, by eighteen months children are good at reading facial expressions – something they have learned, largely, from watching the way their parents react to events and emotions.

How children think

The ways that children reason, the strategies they use and the limitations to their powers of thought, have long been a preoccupation of psychologists and educators. For decades there has been a concentrated search for a conceptual framework that will help explain why children think as they do.

Much of our understanding of how children think has been shaped by the ideas of the Swiss psychologist Jean Piaget. By training a biologist, Piaget was interested in how living things adapt to their environment. He began to study children in the 1920s, a time when education was largely equated with instruction: children were to be taught. Piaget changed all this by his perception that children are not just vessels to be filled with knowledge: on the contrary, they are active, experimenting and learning from their experience. This recognition of the fact that children learn best by active exploration of their environment revolutionized the approach of many nurseries and schools, and is directly responsible for much that is best in the education of young children today.

In other areas there has been, over the last twenty years, a shift in the understanding of children's thinking, and many Piagetian views have been modified. Nevertheless, there is much still to be learned from a study of some of the concepts he brought to light.

Stages of development

Piaget developed many of his ideas within the structure of a theory that outlined developmental stages. As he perceived it, children move through several stages of development which, though not rigidly separated, are none the less more or less distinct. Each stage is characterized by an underlying set of competencies which determine what can and cannot be understood.

Piaget saw the age of two or thereabouts as marking a significant move from one stage to another, one of the outstanding acquisitions of the new stage being the ability to use symbols – words, mental images or actions that are perceived as standing for something else. The toddler's use of symbols is most readily observed in play – when a child of eighteen months puts a cup on her head to represent a cap, when a two year old 'drives' a chair as though it were a car, when a three year old feeds a doll. It is significant that the explosion of language takes place at this age, for language is essentially a form of symbolism.

An offshoot of symbolic thought is fantasy and fantasy play. Providing a rich field for children, fantasy can lead to difficulties, at this and later ages, for it is easy to move from reality to fantasy without fully realizing what one is doing. A three year old can put on a cape and be superwoman. If her imagination stops there no harm will come – but if she really believes that she can fly, and jumps confidently from a high wall . . .

Piaget wrote positively about toddlers' ability to use symbols, but in

Above *The ability to concentrate and observe increases steadily between the ages of one and three. This three year old is fascinated by the snails' progress.*
Opposite *More natural history – the furry caterpillar is quite as intriguing as the snails.*

other areas of thought he saw children of this age as significantly limited. The typical two to three year old is, for him, animistic and egocentric, unable to reason except in the most primitive way, incapable of perceiving the way groups of objects are similar. In the last twenty years or so many of these ideas have been challenged, along with the very notion of skills being acquired only as a new stage is reached. It has been realized that Piaget underestimated children's ability because of his tendency to overestimate their comprehension of language. Much of the time, it seems, toddlers simply do not understand Piaget-style questions. When requests are rephrased and tasks set in more age-appropriate ways, children can often, though not always, demonstrate far greater abilities than they have been credited with. Alongside this realization has come a recognition that many abilities develop gradually over time, in a piecemeal fashion.

Animism – the tendency to attribute life and life-like intentions to inanimate objects – provides an illustration of both points. There is no doubt that children in the age group we are discussing do display this tendency. Consider the example of a two year old girl who wandered away from home one night: when she was found walking down a lane near her home, she explained to her anxious mother that there was no need to worry, she had gone for a walk with the moon, who was looking after her. On the other hand, there is equally no doubt that three year olds are capable of discriminating between animate and inanimate objects when asked to do so.

212

What seems to be critical is not so much the child's concept of living or dead as her understanding of the subject-matter being discussed. Perhaps our typical two to three year old is animistic in certain situations but not others, the shift from this form of thinking happening gradually.

Egocentricity, the tendency to see the world only from one's own perspective, was seen by Piaget as the most striking limitation in the reasoning of children of this age. It was originally demonstrated by means of a test in which children were shown a model of a mountain scene and asked to describe what they saw. They were then shown a model of a man which was put on the other side of the mountain and they were asked to describe what the man could see. Children under the age of four reported that the man saw the same view as they did.

The current view, however, is that children even as young as two do not necessarily always see things from an egocentric viewpoint. The more they understand about a situation the less egocentric they are. (This is also, of course, true of most adults.) When three year olds took part in an experiment that involved pictures of dogs and cats rather than of mountains, they showed, without exception, that they were able to assume a different perspective.

The growth of empathy provides another argument against a completely egocentric view. Children are naturally social beings and even as young as two they may have learned a lot about other people's feelings from family experiences. They respond to the distress of others and may try to comfort another child or an adult who is upset.

There are other signs that two and three year olds are gradually widening their perspectives. For example, they tend to use shorter sentences and a higher tone of voice when speaking to a newborn baby. They are also able to share with other children, and sometimes even share spontaneously without being asked. We see here the beginnings of altruism – although we must not expect to find it in all children at all times. Small children are just as likely to ignore, or laugh at, a crying brother or sister as to be sympathetic. And expecting toddlers to share all the time would be to overestimate and overstrain their budding generosity.

Piaget drew many of his examples from observations of his own children, and a remark of one of his daughters was used to illustrate the young child's primitive reasoning. She commented, one afternoon, that it could not be afternoon because she had not had her after-lunch nap. She had reasoned from one particular event to another in a way which seemed to indicate a belief in a causal link where none existed.

There can be no doubt that children do sometimes tend to assume that if two things happen at the same time one has caused the other. This characteristic has far-reaching implications, and should be taken into account by anyone caring for young children, especially in a time of crisis. For example, children whose parents divorce may think that their mother or father

It's not easy to get a cat to do just as you want – pets have feelings and intentions of their own.

has left because of something they said or did. Children who are seriously ill may imagine that their illness came on because of some quite unrelated event which took place close to the time of diagnosis.

However, again, we now recognize that children are not so limited to this way of thinking as was once thought. In an experiment carried out in 1980, children were shown simple pictures to see if they could associate one with another using causal reasoning. Three year olds were well able to do this, adding explanations which indicated that they were aware of the logical chains implied.

We have more chance of discovering what a child is really capable of if we can cue into the child's world, the child's vocabulary. Piaget originally assessed children's ability to classify, that is to assign things to groups, sets or types, by presenting children with cut-out representations of people or animals, and asking them to put together those that went together. In these studies two to three year olds simply made patterns with the pictures. However, other observations of children at play have shown that even two year olds will sort toy cars or farm animals, for example, in a way that indicates some understanding of classification.

Children are now starting to find ways of sharing toys and are learning to show consideration for each other.

A different approach: information processing

In recent years a new approach to an understanding of children's thinking has been derived from a consideration of certain similarities between the human brain and the computer. Of course, there are also vast differences between the two: the most significant being that humans, unlike computers, can monitor their own mental activity, deciding what to attend to and what problems to tackle. None the less, examination of certain aspects of the computer and its function may help clarify some processes of human thought.

Computers work with hardware and software. Humans too have hardware (the brain) and software (mental programs, made up of rules and plans in relation to which information is registered, interpreted and retrieved). Computers become steadily more sophisticated; but new computers are not devised from scratch, they are developed from previous models. Similarly, computer programs become more complex; improvements come from one version to the next, allowing a wider range of operations to be carried out more efficiently.

The parallel with human development is seen in the way our nervous system (the hardware) matures and in the way we learn improved strategies of attention and memory (the software).

This model departs from the relatively simple emphasis on overall structures that was followed by Piaget and looks instead at the various components that make up the system. There is value in looking at attention and memory, for example, as separate issues.

When we look at cognitive development within this framework we see a gradual increase in complexity and sophistication rather than sudden jumps from one stage to another. At the same time, we acknowledge that just as the computer of today, although descended from the computer of 1950, is far more sophisticated, human powers of thinking at fifteen, although developed from those of the newborn, are very different in power.

One of the findings about the way children think that was never explained by Piaget was the fact that a child may be presented with apparently similar tasks, say of memory or reasoning, and perform differently according to the content. Looking at components rather than the overall structure of the thinking process helps to explain this, since it reveals that a knowledge of specific topics directly influences performance.

There are still some grey areas within this theory. We know, for example, that the ability to remember digits improves with age, from two to adulthood. Is the increasing capacity a result of improved hardware, or is it due to greater exposure to numbers and improved strategies of memory? Perhaps the two interact?

The information processing approach is a useful one. It fits neatly with recent observations that children are potentially much more capable than even Piaget imagined. It tallies, too, with the gradual increase in complexity and sophistication which we observe in children's powers of thinking –

something rather different from the transitions between stages described by Piaget. With this in mind we look not for what children cannot do but what they are capable of, we seek not for signs of readiness to move to another stage, rather we try to find ways of explaining concepts to children at their level.

We must not, however, forget the lessons of Piaget. The process of development may be continuous, but the child of ten is still very different from her two year old self. Above all, we should remember Piaget's insistence that children be active. At this and every other age, the more we can encourage them to be involved with their environment, the more sure their progress will be.

Memory and attention

The analogy of the computer can perhaps help us to understand something of how memory works: for the memory too is a store which holds information embodied in a code.

A distinction is often made between short-term and long-term memory, both of which are involved in learning. Information is held in the short-term memory for seconds or minutes; if this information is perceived as valuable, it may be transferred to the long-term memory, where it will be available for recall months or even years later. There is a steady improvement in both long-term and short-term memory between eighteen months and three. By two children can recall interesting events that happened several months earlier, and they are assiduous in remembering what is in their interest – which shop has sweets at toddler level, for instance.

A study to examine the development of short-term memory involved children watching while food was placed under one of several identical cups. The cups were then briefly screened from view and, when the screen was removed again, the children were asked to locate the correct cup. At

The idea of time
By and large, toddlers live in the present. They have a memory for certain discrete events in the past and their behaviour is determined in part by what they have experienced, but they have little idea of the passing of time or of the future. 'We'll be late' means nothing to a dawdling toddler. And a three year old who has enjoyed a birthday may ask for another one the next day.

In developing an understanding of time, as with other concepts, they start by grasping certain particular points and gradually come to put them together to make a coherent theory. In this case they learn first the difference between before and after: 'after tea', 'before bedtime' are ideas that many children can cope with at eighteen months. 'Today' appears in children's vocabularies at about two, 'tomorrow' around two and a half and 'yesterday' at about three. By the time they are three they can begin to learn the days of the week.

A toddler's attention can easily be caught, and held, by something that has lots of little details to talk about. If you show an interest, she will be interested too.

one year the best performance the children could muster was a correct choice among four cups after a one-second delay. At eighteen months they could choose correctly after a five-second delay, and by two they could choose among eight cups after a ten-second delay. Improvements were noted up to the age of three.

The underpinning of the increase in memory seems to be an improving ability to concentrate on what is to hand. Examination of the length of time children spend looking at pictures of familiar and unfamiliar people and places indicates that between one and three there are steady increases.

A sense of humour

According to one definition, humour lies in the dislocation between the expected and what actually happens. We draw on our memories, of events or words, to anticipate a certain outcome; when the outcome is different (so long as the difference is not threatening to us), we find it funny.

As their memories improve and they develop expectations, children begin to be highly amused by such divergences from the expected. Children of eighteen months to two find it funny when, for example, one object is substituted for another in play. Response to verbal jokes appears between two and three. You can make a toddler of just two laugh uproariously by calling the family cat a cow, or an eye an ear. Before she is three, she may be making you laugh with similar jokes.

Language

Between the ages of eighteen months and three years, speech flowers: the child is transformed from an infant with a few words into a prattling member of her language community. At eighteen months children are usually still relying on intimate adults to interpret their attempts to signal their immediate needs; by three most have the ability to communicate quite complex ideas to any other person who shares their native language.

During this period the child's vocabulary, both understood and spoken, grows with astonishing rapidity. But the most significant change is that she moves on from using single words for naming and labelling objects to combining words – first just two, then more and more – into statements, questions, answers, comments, expressing her own thoughts and meanings. This creative flexibility is the essential feature of speech, which sets the human race apart from all other species.

These developments emerge spontaneously, building upon and expanding all the varied forms of communication that have been going on ever since the child was born. From their baby's birth parents responded to her signals, her crying and cooing; then, listening eagerly, they learned to recognize her first words; now they anticipate the first simple questions and conversations that their toddler puts together for herself. Children have a strong inborn drive to learn to speak; all that parents need to do to aid the process is to provide unlimited opportunities for a free flow of conversation to take place, at whatever level is comfortable for the child. The more parents respond to their toddler's talk, the more the toddler feels rewarded and encouraged to speak.

When children begin to express ideas verbally they become more stimulating companions for adults; their new ability to exchange ideas gives satisfaction and pleasure both to themselves and to their parents. They take great delight in being understood and in turn love to hear people's voices responding directly to them. One toddler, when asked if she would not stop chattering for just a second or two, responded, 'But talking is lovely!' The development of speech cannot be treated in isolation from other areas of a child's growth. The different aspects of her development interweave constantly – and it is fascinating to observe how they are all mirrored in her language. Her gradual learning to separate from her mother and her growing ability to recognize other people as individuals manifests itself in her use of pronouns – 'me', 'mine', 'you', 'yours'.

The development of complex thinking is reflected in her ability to ask 'how' and 'why' questions. The subtle differences between a two year old's conversations with adults and the way she talks to her friends when she is playing show that she is becoming aware of distinctions between one social environment and another. We cannot describe language development separately from a child's increasing ability to relate to others, to affect them by her behaviour and to be affected by them, to understand the world and learn to cope with it.

How language develops

Human language is a complex tool, and before she can use it effectively a child has to acquire skill and precision in many different areas. She must be able to listen, so as to disentangle and analyze the sounds made by others; to articulate, so as to achieve the same effects in speech; to grasp the concepts of time and space; to sort out the logic of cause and effect, question and answer; to recognize and acquire the forms used to signal such subtleties as plurals, possessives, past and future tenses; and much else besides. It is an impressive achievement that all ordinary children – not just the clever ones – complete in a very short time. They begin by making simplified attempts at speech which, though childish and incomplete to start with, give them

The toddler's growing ability to exchange ideas and express feelings is very rewarding for both of you.

the satisfaction of engaging in rewarding interaction with other people. Gradually they refine and elaborate their pronunciation and grammar, along with their conceptual grasp of the world they live in, until they become fully skilled speakers.

Language acquisition usually proceeds along a fairly predictable path. Children do not all acquire the same features of language at exactly the same age, but (as in so many fields of development) they usually acquire them in roughly the same order.

Vocabulary

The growth in vocabulary during the toddler months is phenomenal. At eighteen months the average toddler has a spoken vocabulary of about fifty words and understands perhaps four times that number. By her second birthday she will probably be able to speak over two hundred words and may understand as many as a thousand. After about two it becomes difficult to count the number of words children learn because they are accumulating them so rapidly.

Little children naturally talk about the here and now; abstractions and concepts such as past and future do not become real to them until two and a half or three, so words for these ideas are not needed in the early stages. Usually, about three-quarters of a small child's words have to do with

It is interesting to notice the differences between the way your child talks when playing with her friends, and the conversations she has with adults.

objects (including people), or with actions which can be directly observed. Children can refer to actions and ask for an event or action to take place: 'bye-bye', 'night-night', 'up', 'down', 'all gone' are common expressions for everyday happenings.

Children of this age talk a lot about people, particularly their mothers and fathers and the immediate family. They learn the names of familiar foods and clothes as part of their everyday routines. Animals and methods of transport are popular – with the extra appeal that they can be given sound-names, like 'brrm-brrrm' for car, or 'bow-wow' for dog.

As children become more aware of themselves in relation to other people they begin to find words to identify themselves. A toddler may refer to herself as 'baby'; she may begin to use pronouns – 'me' and 'you' – but it takes experience to understand that she is supposed to call herself 'me' while other people address her as 'you'. By two to two and a half most toddlers can use these words correctly and many are beginning to manage 'I', as well. Third-person pronouns do not present the same problem, but children still need time and practice to sort out when to say 'him' or 'her' and when 'he' or 'she'.

The child's growing self-awareness is also reflected in her ability to iden- tify the parts of her own body. By eighteen months she will when asked point to several parts of her body (usually eyes, nose, mouth and ears), and between nineteen and twenty-six months she may start to produce words that refer to her body (or that of a teddy or doll): she may, for instance, say 'wash hands' or 'foot hurt'. By twenty months most children have used one or more of the words 'bad', 'good', 'hard', 'dirty' or 'nice', all of which describe familiar conditions. The words 'pooh' and 'wee' (or their equiva- lents) are added about this time.

Sometimes it is difficult to tell whether a toddler 'really' knows a specific word or not, since most of her use of language is tied to a particular event or situation. She may understand the word for pyjamas when it is used around bedtime, but look blank if she is asked to find the pyjamas in a shop, in the absence of the usual cues for the bedtime routine. Meanings are first learned in a particular situation. A child has to have a great deal of experi- ence in a variety of different situations before she becomes capable of generalizing her understanding of a word to the level that an adult con- siders complete.

On the other hand, a toddler's earliest words are often overgeneralized: for example, 'dada' might be used at first to refer to all men, not just the child's father. But as children approach the age of two they begin to sort out categories and become more specific in their use of words. They can tell you what an object is, where it is situated and who it belongs to. They may not get it quite right at first, but most two year olds use their vocabularies well enough to get the people around them to help them or to give them the attention they want; through a combination of words, gestures and actions, they make known their feelings and their needs.

Children in this age group understand far more than they can say. They don't need to know each individual word before they can understand what is said – they rely on the context and the tone of voice to help them interpret what is being said, and become skilled at picking up key words.

Pronunciation

One of the most noticeable features of small children's speech (and, for some reason, one of the most endearing – at least to their own parents and grandparents) is the many oddities of pronunciation that gradually get ironed out as they grow older and more experienced.

The physical task of producing sounds to match those that the child hears from other people is an intricate one, which requires much experiment and practice. This practice has of course been going on for most of the baby's lifetime, first with cooing and then with babbling of increasingly complex form. Babies in their first year are already making sounds like 'dada'and 'babu', using the stopped consonants *b* and *d* combined with the vowels *a* and *u*. By eighteen months the toddler has a wider range of consonants available to use at the beginning of words: *p, k, n, f, g, m, h* have been added to *b* and *d*. Only a few consonants are used at the end of words to start with: *b, p, k, n, f*.

By the time they are two toddlers can generally use most of the vowel sounds, but there is often a continued preference for consonants made in the front of the mouth rather than the back – as in 'trotodile' for 'crocodile', or 'tutumber' for 'cucumber'. The fact that a child cannot make a distinction in her own articulation between (say) *r* and *w*, or between a hard *c* and *t* does not mean that she cannot hear the difference in other people's speech. A child who pronounces the words 'train' and 'crane' identically as 'twain' may get very cross with a grown-up who misunderstands which of the two words she is trying to say.

Children up to two and a half often omit final consonants, which can make them difficult to understand: 'bus' becomes 'bu', 'coat' become 'coa'. When a consonant is difficult for a child to say she may substitute one which she finds easier – for example, 'fish' may become 'bish'.

Many children have difficulties with consonant clusters: they grow out of this eventually, but it can take time. Meanwhile they find a simplified form – 'poon' for 'spoon', perhaps – which is adequate for comprehension. It is also quite normal for toddlers to reverse sounds, producing, for example, 'goddy' for 'doggy'.

Between the ages of eighteen months and three, some children can still only be understood by people who are thoroughly familiar with their special ways of saying things. This usually indicates that with time other people will be able to understand them. But if by the time she is three a child is still incomprehensible outside the immediate family circle, it is time for her to have a professional assessment by a psychologist or speech therapist. You can start by consulting your family doctor, who should be able to make a referral.

223

Putting words together

When children come to make the giant step of adding words together to say something (usually at about the age of eighteen months), they start with the shortest possible combination (two words) and work up by stages to longer and more flexible structures. At about two they can use three-word sentences; by three they will be putting five words together and using 'and' to link sentences in a string, opening the way to an infinite elaboration of what they may want to say.

At the early stages, speech has a telegraphic quality (see page 186). These telegraphic utterances – 'daddy car', 'no shoe' and so on – are heavily dependent upon the physical context in which they are uttered, to reveal their meaning. 'Daddy car' may mean 'daddy has gone away in his car', 'there's daddy's car outside' or 'I want to get into daddy's car'; 'no shoe' may mean she doesn't want to put her shoes on, she can't find her shoe, or the dog has got her shoe. But then a child's early experiences of conversational exchanges almost all take place in just such a context, shared with the person she is talking to. Circumstances are usually sufficient to clear up ambiguities and give both participants the experience of comprehension and communication. Stimulated by success, the child is ready and able to go on elaborating her utterances.

Turn-taking of a subtle and sensitive sort is already part of parents' and babies' first non-verbal conversations (see page 174), and at eighteen months or so this starts to take on a more mature pattern. Just as adults unconsciously do, toddlers look at a person who is talking to them and then look away as if waiting to reply, then look at the speaker again in readiness for their turn to speak. When talking themselves they will glance away, signalling that they are going to stop talking, and look back again as if to say they would like a reply. All this happens very quickly: an entire exchange may take only a few seconds.

The elaboration of utterances follows a generally predictable pattern. In English, the first three-word sentences are usually formed by adding a second noun to the end of a two-word phrase: 'baby want juice', for example. At this stage speech still has a markedly telegraphic quality. But as toddlers want more and more to be understood, they become more explicit, starting to impose order on their sentences and using more words to fill in details – adjectives, prepositions, definite and indefinite articles, and so on. The order in which they introduce new features usually depends on the frequency of their occurrence in adult speech and hence the amount of evidence the child has to go on in grasping how to use them. First they add 'ing' to verbs – 'cat drinking', for example. This gives them the ability to describe ongoing events. Then they add prepositions such as 'on', 'in', which make it possible for them to specify location – 'cat in basket', for instance. They add 's' for plurals and for possession. By three they are using five-word sentences and expressing more involved thoughts.

An additional feature may not be mastered all at once. The notion that

Fingers are the subject of endless counting games and songs – and, conveniently, they travel everywhere with you.

plurals, possessives and past tenses have to be used all the time may be hard for a child to understand; she may use these forms sometimes and not other times, or in one part of a sentence and not in another. It often takes toddlers a long time to grasp the past tense, particularly – perhaps because toddlers live in the present, rarely reflecting on past experience.

The fact that it takes time to consolidate learning may affect the acquisition of other types of words too: for example, even at three many children continue to believe that 'when' means 'where', so that if they are asked 'when will you go to sleep?' they may answer 'in my bed'.

At the same time as they are piecing together their knowledge of grammatical forms and the meanings of words, toddlers are learning to adjust their style to suit the companion they are talking to. Even two year olds change their speech when talking to younger brothers and sisters, using more repetitions and attention-eliciting words than they do when talking to their mothers. However egocentric and oblivious toddlers may seem to be at this stage, they are already starting to respond appropriately to different conversational partners.

How do children acquire language?

Language-learning is obviously a very complex phenomenon, and no simple description has yet been given of how it takes place. There is much debate in scientific journals about whether grammatical speech is innate in children, or simply learned from the experience of hearing language used around them. In practical terms, both aspects are important.

There is a strong evidence of an innate predisposition towards language learning. No matter how much language a child hears around her, she still has to make sense of it and find patterns in it that enable her to produce not just sentences that repeat ones she has heard and memorized, but original sentences of her own that express new ideas.

Deaf children who do not hear language at all will, without any teaching, begin to sign with gestures that indicate first objects and people, then actions. They seem spontaneously to use signs in a systematic order that helps to clarify meaning and is analogous to the grammatical order of words.

As the linguistic theorist Noam Chomsky showed, the way children use telegraphic language, which differs from any form they could hear in regular use, seems to point to the existence of an innate capacity to formulate rules underlying the language they hear – as also does their invention of erroneous but logical forms such as 'goed', 'mouses' (see page 319).

But language does not develop successfully through innate mechanisms only. Experience of hearing language is essential if a child is to develop the ability to speak. Those who have had no verbal stimulation do not learn language, and deaf children who do not hear language at all do not spontaneously go on to learn such embellishing words as prepositions, past tense forms and adjectives – these have to be taught. The word 'on' provides an example. A hearing child will learn the word from listening to such sentences as 'put it on the table.' A deaf child who relies on lip-reading may not realize that there is a word 'on' in such a sentence, because there is often no associated change in lip movements; and she will not learn the word unless it is deliberately taught. (The language conveyed by lip-reading is much attenuated; this is one of the reasons that many people concerned with the hearing-impaired advocate the use of a grammatically based sign system.) There is a wealth of research to show that language is more advanced in those children whose parents talk to them a lot and give them a stimulating environment, with much to do and discuss.

What parents can do

Most parents, although they are not aware of doing any special teaching, spontaneously include in their behaviour much that is ideally suited to help their toddlers learn to talk.

Parents play word games with babies even before the children say their first words. A valuable early game is pointing to specific objects and naming them, and then encouraging the baby to repeat the name. This can be done in quite an unforced way, whenever an opportunity arises. For example, the natural time to tell your toddler the words for clothes is when you are dressing her; while you are unpacking the shopping together you can tell her the words for groceries. Names need to be offered immediately, while you are showing the object: even a ten-second delay can mean that a toddler forgets what is being named.

As children go through their regular routines they repeatedly hear, and soon become familiar with, the language surrounding the events of the day. All the words around getting dressed, for example, or taking a bath, are

Sharing tasks is an excellent way of getting conversation to flow – there is so much to discuss when you're working together.

repeated over and over, and soon a toddler understands them and can use them appropriately. Parents can help even more by telling children what they are doing and asking them to participate: 'Here is your shoe. Help me put your foot into it.'

Most parents naturally adjust their speech to match their children's level of comprehension. For example, with young toddlers, parents automatically give directions that keep to the simplest form, usually involving only one step: 'Put your toys away', 'Say bye-bye', or, more gently, 'Will you put the toys away, please?' By the time children are two and a half or three, their parents will issue more complicated instructions, often including a reason: 'Put the toys away, or someone might trip over them.'

Listening is crucial: children have to learn to listen and we have to listen to them. Most parents find themselves naturally giving an instant response, in words or actions, to what their toddler says. This shows the child that she has been understood, and makes her feel that it is worth talking to people. 'More juice' might get another cup of juice or a 'no more'; the first response might be more popular, but either is immediate and easy for the child to understand.

Exploring toes is the classic way of teaching a child the numbers up to ten; toes feel ticklish and wiggly and are much more fun to count than fingers.

Most mothers (and other people), when speaking to young children, find themselves adopting a particular style sometimes described as 'motherese'. 'Motherese' involves speaking slowly, using short sentences, enunciating clearly, exaggerating intonation patterns, taking clear pauses between utterances, and generally using language in a more well-formed and intelligible way than people usually do when speaking to other adults. This style of speech helps children learn, because they can both separate out individual words easily and hear the correct pronunciations.

In conversation with their young children, parents generally talk about things which are related to events going on now, or to objects or people that are present. The words they use are simple and unambiguous – 'chair', 'shoe', 'cat', and the like. Again, this is helpful to the children. Toddlers do not like to talk about things which are not immediately available to touch, see or hear, and they will not attend for long if the conversation revolves around a visit they are going to make next week, or a grandfather they have never met – though they will stay focused for longer if you can show them a photograph of grandfather while you are talking about him.

Children speak only when they can understand what they say (we may not understand them, but that is not the point). You will be most helpful to your child if you take your cues from her, supporting and amplifying the kind of things she is able to say, rather than trying to teach new things that may still be beyond her scope. It is unlikely that a child of two will understand a concept such as 'on' or 'under', or be able to interpret a double command such as 'Put the apple in the basket and sit in the chair.' She may just sit in the chair.

Expanding your child's sentences is a way of telling her that you have listened to her, while at the same time you help her increase her vocabulary.

'Doggie eat,' says the child.

'Yes, I'll get the dog food and feed him.'

'Doggie eat food.'

'Yes, Rover likes dog food.'

Similarly, recasting questions helps improve children's vocabulary. If a toddler asks, 'Where's daddy?', a good response could be 'Is daddy in the garden?'

Expanding does not involve correcting children's language or grammar; you just repeat some of the words and make a few additions. It is not wise constantly to correct children. Toddlers whose speech is often corrected tend to have smaller vocabularies at three than children who are allowed to say what they want without fear of correction.

It will help a child get on terms with more abstract concepts, such as 'big' and 'heavy', if parents can use such words in many different situations, perhaps encouraging children to repeat them: 'Ouf! This is a big, heavy box . . . what a big bus . . .' – trying to match your behaviour with the meaning of the word. The same applies to relational ideas such as 'in', 'on', 'beside', 'behind', and so on.

Some words, such as the names of colours and shapes, may have to be deliberately taught, because children do not easily pick them up from incidental conversations. There are various toys made for just this purpose: but beware, for some try to teach too many things at once. Children struggling to learn colour words may be confused if they are confronted with colours, shapes, fitting and posting all at once. They will learn faster if their attention can be focused on colour, and preferably on one colour at a time.

Parents can also make use of the fact that children understand more than they can say. A game of 'find the . . .' can be fun and help in building vocabulary – 'find the sock, find the spoon, find the red sock, find the green sock . . .'. So much learning depends on practice, and this kind of game provides an ideal way to help.

229

Keep a toddler busy and involved in the story,
pointing and talking about what's going on.

For toddlers, learning is doing, not sitting down and being passively taught. They are so busy flitting from one activity to another that their learning is normally accomplished on the run. They associate words directly with actions and learn more easily if they can take an active part in what is going on. Playing with them is a way to stretch their attention span and help them learn vocabulary. Take a bowl of fruit, for example: toddlers will learn the names of fruits if they can handle them and play with them at the same time. The shapes and colours will attract their attention and make a strong connection with the words used.

There are many other games which actively engage children and teach as well. Games such as hide and seek or oranges and lemons help them learn to hear, follow instructions and understand simple concepts.

If you want to communicate with an active toddler it will help if you put yourself on her level so that you make eye-to-eye contact. Being in touch physically, perhaps putting your hands on hers or sitting her on your knee, also helps. It is rewarding to a child to feel close to her parents and be talked with or read to in a loving and direct way. Much family conversation takes place literally and figuratively over a toddler's head, and it is more enjoyable for everyone if she can often be singled out for a chat or an explanation.

Learning language, or anything else, is an active process and the more children can be encouraged to respond to questions the better. Once again we can think of the parallel with learning to speak a foreign language: it is only when you have to contribute to a conversation that you really begin to make progress.

Using books and pictures

Picture books are wonderfully useful in helping children learn language. The first book – usually, indeed, called something like 'Baby's First Book' – might consist of a series of simple, realistic pictures of everyday objects, one object to a picture and one picture to a page. You can encourage the child to look at the pictures and say what is there.

Later on, choose a book with slightly more complicated pictures, perhaps showing more than one object within a simple context. Say there is one of a train in a station. The first question can simply be 'where is the train?' Once the child can point to the train, she can move on to responding when parents say, 'what is that?' Soon she will be able to incorporate the station, and perhaps the people on the platform.

Some books provide opportunities for children to practise sounds, or the names of familiar objects – 'what does the dog say?' Some encourage them to respond with actions '. . . all fall down!'

After the first picture books children can move on to simple stories. Do not be surprised if your toddler wants to hear the same story over and over again. You may find it unbelievably boring to read a story for what seems like the four-hundredth time. For the child, this repetition is building a foundation on which subsequent learning will be based.

Language difficulties

Because the period from one and a half to three is the stage when language is progressing most rapidly, it is also the time when any hold-ups in linguistic development are likely first to become evident. When a child is eighteen months old, parents can still feel there is plenty of time for a late developer to catch up, but by the time their child is three they will begin to worry if her language is falling noticeably behind the expected rate of progress. The milestones of development sketched above will help parents to reassure themselves that their child is progressing in the ordinary way, but for those who feel anxious, some more precise indications are given here to show when to seek help.

Professional advice should be sought for children who:

By eighteen months
Do not understand simple commands such as 'give it to me'
Do not point to familiar objects or people when they are named
Show no interest in communicating by any method
Do not try to imitate or to say words
Use less than ten words

By two years
Do not relate two nouns in the same request – 'put the cup on the table'
Have a vocabulary of less than fifty words
Still echo most of what is said to them
Do not use simple two-word phrases – 'shoe gone'
Do not use consonants in speech (especially if they don't say *b,d,p,m,n,t*)

By three years
Cannot select pictures by verb only – 'who's eating?'
Do not understand simple prepositions: 'in', 'on', 'under', 'behind'
Do not use three- or four-word sentences with some past tenses and plurals
Do not ask questions using 'who', 'where' or 'what'
Have speech that is unintelligible to strangers more than 80 per cent of the time

Identifying language problems

The classification of speech and language problems is no simple matter. Various contrasts are invoked to help in the task of differentiating a disorder from others with which it might be confused.

One of the first distinctions to come to mind is that between receptive and expressive disorders: is the problem one of input or output, of receptive or expressive language? (In practice the two may overlap: a deaf child will have primary receptive problems but will also find it hard to speak as clearly as others.)

Another basic criterion is the distinction between organic and functional disorders. Under the former heading come conditions clearly related to established anatomical or neurological causes, while the latter encompasses those where there is no known organic cause. Functional disorders may result from emotional or intellectual neglect or acute anxiety.

The problem here is that it is often impossible to classify a particular case simply as one or the other. For example, a child with an organic disorder may develop secondary behaviour problems which themselves interfere

---

The autistic child
An autistic child is unable to communicate with his parents or other people, although he may be of average intelligence. Such children seem to live in a world of their own, not connecting with anything or anyone. There is no universally accepted explanation of what causes the condition, but it is generally agreed that the symptoms include:
• a profound failure to develop social relationships
• retarded language, including problems with comprehension and peculiar speech patterns; some autistic children do not develop language at all
• strong resistance to changes in routine or surroundings
• ritualistic repetitive behaviour is common in autistic children, as is a short attention span, but these symptoms may not always be found.

with language acquisition. Then again, there are conditions, such as autism – which can bring a dramatic distortion or loss of language – that are classified by some authorities as organic, but by others as functional.

Children suffering from learning difficulties provide another example of the pitfalls of distinguishing absolutely between organic and non-organic factors. Where the difficulties are severe, the primary cause of both the learning problems and the associated language delay is likely to be organic. The milder the degree of disability, however, the more likely it is that environmental factors (such as the way the child is treated by her immediate family) play an important part.

Again, there are undoubtedly children who have language disorders which are not apparently related to organic factors or learning difficulties, or anything to do with their environment. Classically they receive a diagnosis by exclusion: if it is not this, that or the other, they are given the diagnosis of developmental disorder.

Another distinction often made is that between language deviance and language delay, together with an associated contrast between normal and abnormal development. Once again problems abound, this time chiefly semantic. 'Deviant' can be applied to any pathology: it means no more than 'abnormal', and is more of a description than a diagnosis. But in everyday practice the word is used to signify that a child's use of structures, pronunciation, vocabulary, and so on, are outside the normal pattern of the culture to which she belongs. The contrasting concept of 'delay' is invoked if every aspect of a child's language is normal apart from the age at which acquisition occurs. Delay can appear in all areas at once, or there can be an immaturity of just one or two aspects of language.

Certain problems specifically affect the process of speech production. These include disorders of fluency, which affect the ease and rapidity of speaking. Stuttering is an example of lack of fluency, but once again there are problems of definition, for hardly any two stutterers are alike.

Voice disorders include stridor, a noise produced by unusual friction when breathing; variations in the efficiency of the vocal cord vibrations, leading among other features to 'breathy' voice; 'hyponasality', which produces sounds similar to those made by speaking with a blocked-up nose; and 'hypernasality', where the noises produced sound as if too much air is escaping down the nose.

Disorders of articulation range from complete unintelligibility at one extreme to mild problems with single sounds at the other – saying *w* for *r*, for instance. Disorders of phonology (the sound system) arise when a child has difficulty in discriminating and using the different features of consonants – for example, *f* may be pronounced as *b* or *s* as *d*, and final consonants may be omitted from words. At this age many apparent 'errors' of articulation or phonology are in fact part of a normal pattern of development. Many three year olds say 'poon' for 'spoon' or 'tips' for 'chips', for instance.

A condition which has been identified only recently is the semantic-pragmatic disorder. The conversation of children with this problem shows persistent features that are not normal at any age – that is, there is more to it than immaturity. The prevailing characteristic of the language used by children with this problem is that it is inappropriate: conversation fails to flow smoothly because the children express themselves in an odd way and seem unaware of the conversational needs of others. This can be most puzzling to parents, for the children seem to have nothing wrong with them; they appear to have the ability for both understanding and producing language, but progress in social spheres is painfully and embarrassingly slow. Relatively little is understood about what causes this pattern, and it is hard to treat.

The child who loses the language capacity she has already developed is always a cause for grave concern. Although such loss is a rare occurrence, the third year is one in which it is likely to happen if it is going to. If it is noticed that a child is actually retreating from the level of language that has been attained (not simply pausing for a temporary lull in development), medical advice should be sought at once.

Speech and language therapy

The best person to help a child or family grappling with language problems is the speech and language therapist (called in some countries a speech and language pathologist). These therapists have been trained in the study of human communication and they specialize in the diagnosis and treatment of speech and language problems.

The first task of the therapist is to establish just what the child can and cannot do. This will involve a mixture of observation and formal testing. Much of the information gleaned from an interview comes from listening to children in free play or everyday conversation. For young children, the tests are given as games. A child who is familiar with games of the 'show me your nose/ears' pattern, as most are at this age, will not find it very different when the therapist puts out a row of small objects and asks her to point to them in turn. She will not notice that the therapist is using carefully chosen forms of words that will reveal as much as possible about the linguistic structures that the child can or cannot handle.

A wide range of skills will be assessed, including the child's level of attention, listening skills, powers of auditory discrimination, fluency and vocabulary. There will be questions for the parents to answer about the child's development in other areas, since language ability must be put in its context as part of the child's overall development. If you have a baby book or any record of walking and other milestones in the child's life, it will be useful to take it to the first session. It will also be useful to put your child in the context of her family: if there have been others with slow or deviant language development the therapist should be told about them, and how they turned out in the end.

Once the preliminary information has been obtained, it will be possible

Going to a speech therapist can be an enjoyable experience, especially when the sessions are full of games. Children may be seen in a group or individually, and parents are often involved in back-up work at home.

to formulate some hypotheses, which may then need testing. If, for example, all other areas of development are normal, a hearing loss may be suspected. Even if the reason for a speech problem seems obvious, there may be a need to explore further. A child born with a cleft palate, for example, is more likely than not to have some difficulties with speech, but may also have a mild hearing loss which could go undetected.

The therapist must systematically differentiate the disorder from others with which it might be confused. Differentiating between organic and functional disorders can bring wide-ranging implications both for treatment and for the way in which parents view the problem.

When speech therapists are working with young children, much, if not all, of the therapeutic work is in the form of games and everyday activities which can be fitted into the child's usual routine. Use is made of toys and pictures, and parents are almost always involved, to back up the work done by the therapist. Some children are seen individually, some in groups. Individual sessions usually last about thirty minutes, though the initial assessment takes longer.

It is not possible to generalize about the length of treatment, since so much depends on the nature of the problem. The outlook for all children depends in part on the extent and nature of their difficulty, in part on how often they can see a therapist (there is a chronic shortage in many parts of the world) and in part on the support that the family is able to give them.

The majority of children seen by therapists are suffering from a delay in the development of expressive language, and if this is an isolated problem which is not associated with general developmental difficulties, the outlook is good. A three year old can be expected to make noticeable progress in three months, with continuing general improvement predicted during the next twelve months. Children with associated learning difficulties are

235

not expected to be able to develop their language at a rate faster than their general progress. Children with severe language problems make slow progress; there is often particular difficulty in developing two- and three-word phrases and in using parts of grammar correctly.

What parents can do

Support and encouragement from the family is perhaps the most important factor in helping a child with a language difficulty. It is vital to keep on communicating with the child, without becoming discouraged or allowing a non-communicating child to slip into isolation. The following guidelines are based on a leaflet entitled 'Teaching Your Child to Talk', published by the College of Speech Therapists, London. They are not intended to replace speech therapy, but to encourage and aid parents to provide special attention at a comfortable and appropriate level for a child with little or no speech.

• Use short, simple sentences and speak slowly.

• Name the objects your child has or uses, and encourage her to imitate you, but do not be discouraged if she does not copy you at once or all the time. Do not expect perfect imitations: 'milk' may come out as 'mi'.

• If the child's first words do not emerge naturally, they will have to be taught directly. Choose words with sounds that are easy to reproduce, for example those with *m*, *p*, *b* and *w*, where it is easy to link the movements of the speaker's lips with the sound made. Show her the object as she tries to say its name.

• Build up a basic vocabulary of meaningful words related to objects, people and activities within her experience. Keep repeating words within the context of appropriate regular activities: for example, teach her the word 'water' while she is having her bath. Introduce new words gradually.

• Encourage her to carry out instructions when she can understand the words used, *before* you expect her to repeat the words herself.

• Do not try to correct the child's errors with individual sounds; it is better for you to repeat the whole word correctly.

• Gradually build towards using two- and three-word sentences.

• As her vocabulary grows, encourage her to express her needs in words.

• Do not be dismayed by a child's repetition of words: 'Please daddy daddy, can I can I go to the shop shop with you?' This is not stammering, it is a stage in the development of fluency.

• Finally, do not expect a child who does not begin to talk intelligibly until the age of four to be as fluent a speaker by the age of six as one who was speaking clearly at two. She will need time to establish her speech skills.

Emotional Development

When children can walk and run they will, almost without exception, explore their immediate surroundings. When they can think and use language they explore the world of ideas – including ideas about themselves: most significantly the very idea of the self, to which are linked notions about sex and sex roles. What is more, during the period from eighteen months to three, as the sense of the self deepens, they also begin to experience the danger of threat to the self: they encounter fear.

The idea of self

During this period children become increasingly aware of themselves as individuals. By about two a child can recognize her own photograph, and may be referring to herself by her own name and as 'me'. By two and a half she will be beginning to have some notion of body image – whether she is tall or short, fat or thin – will probably know her sex and age, and may be using 'I' and 'mine'.

The essence of the notion of self is that one is differentiated from others but also in some respects similar to certain people. The pattern of perceiving oneself in relation to others, for good or ill, persists throughout childhood into adult life.

Here parents have a great responsibility, for to a large extent the child builds her image of herself on the basis of the way she interprets the behaviour of people who are significant to her; and her parents are the most important of all. Children are no different from adults in needing to be valued, but they need more frequent reassurance that this is so, and have fewer resources for dealing with rejection. It is up to parents to help build their self-esteem by recognizing and acknowledging their worth. Sticking a two year old's drawings on the kitchen pin-board may seem a trivial act; but it will give your child the assurance that her work is prized. Much time is spent on discussion of the value or evils of various forms of punishment, and it is appropriate that this topic be considered. But the real power is vested not in punishment but in praise. Parents who indicate, by whatever means, that their child brings them pleasure build a secure foundation for her present and future life. Parents who indicate, by whatever means, that a child is not worth bothering with, sow seeds of destruction.

can take. Like thumbsucking or rocking, masturbation appears to provide comfort to children – with the bonus, presumably, of more pleasurable sensations than thumbs can offer. A boy may rub his penis to help him get to sleep, and many toddlers fondle themselves when they are anxious.

Even during the first year of life, babies enjoy touching and playing with their genitals, just as they like exploring other parts of the body. Toilet training draws attention to the sex organs and intensifies interest in them, and children often begin to masturbate actively at this stage. This is perfectly natural and understandable, but some parents can get quite upset about it – particularly if the child masturbates in public. It is neither helpful nor feasible to try to stop masturbation altogether, as the child will probably just carry on in secret, perhaps guiltily. But a child can reasonably be asked not to do it in public – it is not too early to learn that there is a time and a place for everything.

A few toddlers masturbate very frequently. This may be an indication that they are tense, and need the activity to relieve the tension. In this case forbidding masturbation certainly isn't going to help, as it will just increase the stress on the child. Instead, parents might look for the cause of the tension and try to make life generally less stressful for their toddler – which may indirectly lessen the need to find comfort in masturbation. Of course, it is quite as likely, if children masturbate a lot, that they are doing it because they like the feeling! If parents really find it too much, their best course is probably to distract the child with new activities.

However, as it involves the genitals, it is something adults tend to focus on. Parents who calmly accept, or even scarcely notice, thumbsucking or rocking in a child of this age can get quite upset about masturbation.

The vocabulary of sex

One of the earliest language games that toddlers and parents play together is the naming game – show me your nose, show me your ears, where are your toes? Parents do not use baby names for these organs. But when it comes to naming a genital organ, children are often told that it is their 'wee-wee' or 'pee-pee', or some other name suggesting that parents are embarrassed by using the adult words for the genitals, or are only prepared to acknowledge their toilet function.

There are other ways of dealing with the question which may be more helpful to children. Some parents simply use the adult terms, others adopt a euphemism that is in fairly common use among the child's peer group, and many resort to a mixture of the two. Even if you do feel more comfortable using euphemisms on a day-to-day basis, it is advisable at least to tell children what the adult term is, so that they are properly informed.

Because they are not able to see their genitals and they are close together, girls sometimes think that they have one opening for everything. It will help them to be clear about this if they are taught that they have an anus, a vagina and a bladder opening. Naming these separately is useful here.

Fears

As all parents know, toddlers and little children can often be troubled by fears, sometimes mild and sometimes extremely intense, sometimes understandable and indeed useful, but sometimes quite startling and irrational. We may see a fear of deep water, or of fierce dogs, for example, as a sensible reaction – but why should a child suddenly develop a fear of a ticking clock or a previously trusted friend? During the period from eighteen months to three years, as their physical and intellectual capacities develop and they have increasing contact with the outside world, children go through considerable changes in the way they experience and express the emotion of fear. But to the concerned parent it can seem that new fears are springing up everywhere – just as you have helped the child get over one fear another takes its place.

It is biologically and psychologically normal for toddlers to be fearful of certain situations, events, objects and ideas. (It is more common than not, for example, for children to fear monsters and the dark at some time.) However, there are wide variations among children in the degree to which they experience fear and the ways they express it. While some may be dangerously bold, others become so acutely fearful that their timorousness interferes with their well-being and development. There is no doubt that some toddlers suffer from what may be seen as an overdose of natural fear; the parents of such a child may wonder whether this excessive fearfulness is due to the child's nature, her experiences, or a combination of both. They may wonder if they themselves are in some way responsible for her fears, and will want to know how they can best help her.

The nature of fear

Fear is a universal protective response, which is essential to survival since it alerts us to danger and prepares us to deal with it. It has two components: psychological discomfort (the subjective feeling of fear) and physical arousal (for example, increased heart-rate). Fear at all ages always involves the perception of a threat to the self – either to physical well-being and safety, or to self-esteem and psychological well-being.

The physical maturation of the nervous system underpins the physiological response to fear. Nerves and brain need to have reached a certain stage of development to enable the full range of bodily sensations associated with fear (increased heart-rate, 'butterflies in the tummy', and so on) to occur.

A certain level of mental development is also necessary to feel fear. Before a toddler can feel threatened she must be able to perceive and discriminate between persons and objects and between the familiar and the unfamiliar in her environment. She must also possess sufficient cognitive maturity to appreciate that certain persons or situations can threaten her safety and happiness. Clearly, threats cannot be referred to the self until a working notion of identity exists. The development of fantasy – the ability to imagine things – lays the way open for a whole range of childhood fears.

Timetable of typical fears

Hence, different fears are typical of different ages, depending on the child's physical and mental maturity – and, of course, on the changing nature of her own experience of the world, which will directly affect the form her fears take as she grows older.

The fearful responses of a very young baby who has not yet formed an idea of the outside world can be construed as primitive reactions: they are most commonly elicited by unexpected loud noises and by rapid or abrupt displacement in space (a fear of falling). By eighteen months these reactions are beginning to decrease, but they are usually still noticeable in children up to two years old (and to some extent right through life).

The fear of strangers and separation anxiety that are such a marked feature of toddlerhood have already been mentioned, and will be dealt with more fully below (see pages 245–7). They usually manifest themselves at around six or seven months old, along with a child's first attachment to a close parental figure, and are related to her developing ability to distinguish familiar people from strangers. They are at their most intense in the early months of the second year, but they persist throughout the period dealt with in this chapter, usually fading by about three or four years old.

As toddlers mature and their knowledge of the world widens, their fears of such things as noises and sudden movements decrease: they are learning by experience that many apparently frightening objects and events are not really threatening. As they begin to use their imagination and memory, and acquire more understanding of language, through which they learn of things that are not part of their own direct experience, fears begin to centre more on certain stereotypes – such as wolves or lions, burglars, witches, monsters or ghosts – and on non-physical ideas like the dark or being alone, death or abandonment. Fears of specific animals and/or the dark often appear in two year olds and may continue until they are five or more. Fears

---

Fear, phobias and anxiety

Fear General non-specific term, used informally both for the emotion of fear and for the objects and situations that arouse it.

Phobia Clinical term for a persistent and pathologically intense fear, often apparently irrational, of something specific, leading to a compulsive need to avoid that thing or event. In everyday use can be applied to a fear which has a rational origin, if the fear reaches an extreme pitch. A child who has been bitten by a dog is justified in feeling fear of dogs, but if the fear becomes obsessive it can be characterized as phobic.

Anxiety Feeling of uneasiness or apprehension (which can be quite intense, even if vague), often with an obscure or unidentifiable source, or linked to a situation or pattern of events rather than a specific object.

of monsters and imaginary creatures are common around three. An example of toddler imagination is the fairly common fear of being sucked down the plughole with the bath water as it runs away, or of being flushed down the lavatory. Cause and effect have begun to play a part in their reasoning, but they are not yet able to put realistic limits to what they believe possible.

In three year old children the early stages of fear of not being able to achieve may become evident, as may the first signs of fearing ridicule.

How fears arise

Both genetic inheritance and personal history probably play an important part in each individual child's experience of fear. Genetic factors seem to help determine a child's general degree of responsiveness to all emotions, including fear, and may even make some contribution to the content of some apparently universal fears, but in tracing the origins of a child's selection of specific objects for her fearful feelings, her own experiences are evidently central.

It was fun playing hide and seek in this tree trunk a minute ago, but now where has everyone gone? For toddlers the worst fear is abandonment, a feeling that can come upon them quite suddenly.

Learning fears

We all know that fears can be learned by experience – 'the burnt child dreads the fire.' There are innumerable examples of children who have been put off the idea of dentists for ever by an unhappy early experience, or who are frightened of dogs after a nip from a puppy. Fears of this kind need no explanation: an emotion that motivates us to avoid repetition of what we register as a dangerous event can easily be understood as having its origins in the urge for survival. But what about the child who is terrified of lightning or spiders or – as in a case reported by Edward Sarafino in his book on childhood fears – red doors?

Fear is contagious, and children learn fears from observing the behaviour of other people, especially their parents. This again has a clear survival value, for a young child is in no position to judge for herself which features of the complex world will or will not prove a threat the first time she meets them. Even as adults, when faced with the unfamiliar we look for clues which will help us understand what is going on. We ask 'is this dangerous or can we relax?' In such a situation children tend to look first to their parents' faces, where they may read involuntary signs of tension – eyes wide, eyebrows raised and drawn together. It is all too easy for parents to communicate non-verbally fears which they would not wish to pass on to their child – fears of a new group situation, perhaps, or swimming, or mice.

We can see many examples of the transmission of fear when we look at the history of specific fears in families. There is often a case of a child, parent and grandparent all having the same fear – sometimes approaching a phobia – of (for example) snakes, spiders or thunder.

Children often learn fears from their contemporaries, too. The psychologist J.B. Watson observed Vincent, a toddler who showed no fear of rabbits until, one day, he was taken to meet a rabbit with a little girl of his own age called Rosie. She cried at the sight of the rabbit and Vincent 'caught' her fear. He continued to be afraid for some time, although he did not see Rosie again.

Many childhood fears which are at first hard to unravel may be accounted for by the mechanism known as conditioning, whereby an incidental feature encountered at a time of heightened emotion – in this case, fear – becomes permanently associated with that feeling. In the Sarafino case mentioned above, the child who feared red doors turned out to have been conditioned by an unpleasant experience in a doctor's surgery which was entered through a red door.

Irrational fears

Many people believe that children's development may lay them open to apparently irrational and imaginary fears, as they come to terms with their own aggressive feelings and unconscious conflicts. Two and three year olds may be frightened by everyday objects on which they project their own angry feelings. The monsters, crocodiles, vampires, and so on, that almost all children seem ready to conjure up in their imaginations may be a representation of a vague sense of threat and potential danger that the child cannot locate firmly either inside or outside herself, as she struggles to make sense of her perceptions of anger and aggression in herself and others.

The biology of fear

Unravelling the reason why a certain child has fixed on a specific object for her fear does not help to explain the fact that some children are very much more fearful than others. A genetic factor is presumed by many researchers to play an important part. The explanation is based on the idea that some children are born with a high level of emotionalism as part of their temperament. They have a predisposition to be more fearful than others and they are likely to be more susceptible to the whole range of experiences that involve fear.

It may help parents to feel more relaxed and accepting of their children if they can recognize that some differences between children may be genetic in origin. If a toddler is very shy of new people, for instance, though her brother at the same age was outgoing, parents sometimes feel that they must have treated one quite differently from the other; in reality, it may be that the children have innate differences of temperament. Having said this, we should point out that an acceptance of genetic factors in the formation of children's fears does not imply that such fears are fixed for ever. Genetic differences are significantly modified by experiences throughout life. A fearful toddler who has generally reassuring experiences will not necessarily carry her timorous temperament into adulthood; a naturally hardy child who is exposed to much insecurity may become fearful.

Support for a biological theory of fears comes from the observation that some fears – of the dark, of strangers – seem to arise in cultures all over the world, irrespective of children's experiences. It is likely that this type of fear is in some way genetically determined, and that children are programmed to experience them because they have a protective survival value. Fear of strangers and separation anxiety are the central examples.

Separation anxiety and attachment theory

Some of the most influential work ever carried out in the field of developmental psychology took separation anxiety as its focus. These studies, by James and Joyce Robertson, involved close observation of children in hospital, which revealed that children who are separated from their mothers, especially at a stressful time, suffer enormously. This realization led to a dramatic change of hospital practice: as a result, in all hospitals that have any sensitivity to their patients' needs, parents are now encouraged to spend as much time as possible with their children.

The observations of children who were separated at times of stress showed that there is usually a clear sequence of behaviour. First there is a determined protest, with children crying and screaming for their mothers. Next comes a quieter period, of detachment, and then, in extreme cases, comes despair, when they are quiet, seeming to be 'good'. This last phase

It isn't easy for you to leave each other, but you have to learn to be apart sometimes. Take it gently and show her that you are confident she can cope.

led to tragic misunderstandings, giving rise to the myth that children in hospital are better off without their parents. Sadly, the observers who made this judgment mistook the absence of protest for contentment. It was only after the children were returned to their parents that the true state of affairs was revealed. Instead of a welcoming child, greeting parents with hugs and kisses, there was a child who was angry and sullen, who ignored her parents as though they were strangers, and took a long time to recover her previous trust in them. Children who went through many long and lasting separations showed longer-lasting reactions, with the effects sometimes still evident in adulthood.

If we accept the theories of John Bowlby, separation anxiety is explicable to a large extent (although, by this age, not entirely) by the theory of attachment. This theory has already been discussed at some length (see pages 141–8). To recap the salient points here: children have a biological need for an attachment figure (in practice usually the mother), who is a source of protection. If that highly significant figure disappears when the child is too young to understand that the separation is temporary, a high level of anxiety will be produced, leading in extreme cases to a sense of des-

246

pair. It seems that the vulnerable period for separation anxiety is roughly between six months and four years.

Bowlby argues that many of the fears we have been discussing in this chapter stem from an original anxiety about separation from the mother or other loved one. This fundamental fear becomes unconsciously transferred to other things, like snakes or the dark. This explains why toddlers generally feel less frightened of their particular bogies when their parents are near them. It is not only that they trust their parents to protect them from danger, but also that if the general underlying fear has not been aroused by parental absence, the specific form that fear usually assumes will seem less threatening to the child.

Stranger anxiety and fear of the unexpected

The theory that fears stem from a basic anxiety over the loss of a parent does not automatically throw light on other very general experiences, such as fear of strangers, or fears of animals. Another explanation suggests that children's fear of strangers is a particular case of a much more general instinctual fear of the unexpected or surprising.

Observation of both adults and children lends some support to this theory. We are all to some extent disturbed when the unexpected happens; the less we feel able to predict what is going to happen the more insecure we are likely to be. This explains why some children (and some adults) do not like going to sleep in strange places. At the age of two children cannot tell us exactly what they think is going to happen and so we do not have the opportunity to correct misguided anticipations and save them from frightening surprises. Sometimes, when parents have arranged what they are sure will be a treat, they are astonished and disappointed to find that their child responds with panic to the new experience. Clearly, the more parents can prepare toddlers in advance for anything new, the better the outcome is likely to be.

Managing fears

Pointing out dangers

Sometimes we have to teach children a reasonable degree of fear. For example, most parents want their children to be wary of strangers and to be careful in traffic, and will try to make them aware of the dangers involved. A major obstacle to this kind of teaching is children's inability to anticipate the future and to understand rules of long-term cause and effect. It is no good telling a toddler that eating sweets will give her toothache because in the child's own experience that is not true: eating sweets and getting toothache are separated by months, possibly years. If parents warn their toddler who is about to go up a climbing frame that she may fall, the chances are that the child will continue to climb, for the hypothetical danger is quite unreal to her. If, however, this is a child who has experienced the reality of a fall from a height, there is some point in giving a reminder.

Helping children cope with fear

A self-confident child is far less likely to be plagued by fears than one with a poor image of herself. The first step in preventing fears is, then, to help the toddler towards a self-respecting sense of ability to master the environment. Realistic praise for achievements, along with an implicit message that the toddler can be trusted to venture into new realms, while being safely restricted against danger, will help to this end.

It is equally important to give children confidence to tell you when they are afraid. It does no good at all to respond contemptuously to expressions of fear with remarks like 'Only babies are scared of that.'

Most children have to experience some fearful situations in the natural course of their lives. And if parents were to try to spare their children all anxiety, all separations and all changes (supposing that were possible), the children would find it very hard to cope with the world when they had to leave their parents' protection. It is through the gradual, supportive introduction of new people, objects and experiences that children learn to overcome fear.

If your child is facing a potentially frightening experience, you can help by preparing her for what is to happen. Perhaps she has to make a visit to the dentist, and you know that a painful procedure may be involved. If you tell her categorically that it will not hurt, you run the risk not only of setting up a lasting fear of dentists but also of shaking her confidence in you. It is far better to be honest with her, and to say that the dentist may have to do something that will hurt her, but the pain will soon pass. You should explain to her, too, that the dentist doesn't want to hurt her, but her tooth has to be filled (or whatever) because otherwise it might fall out. A young child won't necessarily grasp all the details, but she will find it much more possible to cope with the pain if it doesn't come as a complete shock, and if she has some understanding, however vague, that it isn't inflicted from malice, but for her benefit.

Preparing for separations

The best preparation for separation is separations. Parents who never leave their children, ever, make it very difficult for them to cope when some separation becomes inevitable. But separation is not in itself an adequate preparation; early experiences have to be carefully planned. The key aspects to remember are: that separations should at first be only brief, gradually increasing to several hours or even a day or so; that your toddler should be looked after during the time she is away from you by someone with whom she is already familiar; and that you must yourself feel confident in leaving your child. If you are anxious fear will be communicated, making matters worse.

The same principles can be applied to the introduction of children to a nursery or preschool playgroup. For the transition to be smoothly effected, both you and your child must be comfortable with brief separations. It will help if you are accustomed to spending short periods of time apart; it will

This little girl is happy to let her mother go for a while, so long as she has her grandfather to play with.

help too, if you are confident that your child can cope. And it is important that the child should have already met the teacher or group leader, so that the person who is to look after her is familiar to her on her first day.

Overcoming phobias

Specific fears are much easier for a family or a therapist to cope with than more general states of anxiety. A standard way to help is to introduce the child gradually to the feared object, while she is supported by someone in whom she feels confident. If, in addition, the child can herself determine how quickly she approaches the feared situation or thing, the treatment will be more effective. So, to help Vincent overcome his newly acquired fear of rabbits, we could bring a rabbit in a cage into a room where he was sitting comfortably, perhaps on his mother's lap. Then the rabbit would be moved nearer to him at a pace he dictated. This approach will usually eliminate a mild fear in two or three sessions; a deeply ingrained phobia will take longer.

Helping an anxious child

Some children are what might be described as pervasively anxious: their lives seem to be clouded by free-floating worries. An anxiety state, to use the technical term for this diffuse condition, can develop in an otherwise stable child as a result of an exceptionally anxiety-provoking experience such as a road accident or the death of a member of the family or a friend. Usually it arises as an accentuation of a pre-existing tendency to react with undue anxiety to normal stresses. Chronically anxious parents can both pass on their emotional tendencies to their children and also, by their anxiety, introduce greater stress into family life.

Parents will best help an anxious child by themselves being reliable and available – and not anxious. So they may well need to deal with their own anxiety first. This is not always an easy task, and for their child's sake and their own they may wish to seek psychological help. Usually, it is only when anxiety is causing marked interference in daily life that direct professional help is required for the child.

Overcoming more resistant fears

Although most fears of childhood pass within a year or so of their own accord, some are resistant to change. Children who are exposed to the extremes of fearful situations – those who live through wars, tornadoes or other man-made or natural catastrophes, for example – are likely to remain very fearful. If they suffer from post-traumatic shock disorder, they may refuse to have anything to do with any person or object associated with the experience. They may constantly relive what has happened through nightmares, in their conversation or in their drawings and play. Or they may steel themselves and become outwardly completely unemotional. But even children who have undergone the most traumatic experiences can be helped to overcome their fears and anxieties, though such help may have to come from skilled hands and can be a long time in taking effect.

Nightmares and night terrors

Experiences of fear that take place while the child is asleep present a special case. Nightmares, like other dreams, usually happen during the lightest stage of sleep when the brain is more or less alert. It is not certain at what age children begin to dream. They may start before they have the capacity to tell us what is going on in their heads. It seems likely that they begin some time in the second year at the latest.

Nightmares are so common that they cannot in themselves be seen as a sign of emotional disturbance. Children wake easily from them, and generally all they need is comfort. As their command of language improves, they can be encouraged to describe the dream; parents should then give a sympathetic but matter-of-fact response. We do not know for sure why children have nightmares, but many psychologists believe that one function of dreams is to process thoughts that have not been fully dealt with during waking hours. If this is so, then the contents of the nightmare may give some clues about what aspects of life are requiring more thought from the child. One toddler who had cut his leg badly dreamed the next night that the sky was raining blood: he needed reassuring that his wound was being properly looked after. Often, though, nightmares – like other dreams – defy this kind of direct analysis, both because children of toddler age cannot describe their thoughts fully enough and because the connections between a child's experience of her life, her imagination and the dream-content may be too complex or idiosyncratic for anyone else to understand.

If a child has frequent or recurring nightmares there may be cause for concern, and it is worth having a look at what has been happening during the day, or wondering whether there might be something going on in the home which the child could be picking up and only partially understanding. If the problem seems acute, advice should be sought from a child psychiatrist or psychologist.

Night terrors are different from nightmares. They occur in the deepest period of sleep, and are certainly frightening for the parents who witness them. Children undergoing them look as if they are having the most terrible experience imaginable: they cry out, and sit up and stare into space with a terrified expression. Worst of all, they may call out, shouting things like 'No, no, go away, take it away, no, no.' Because they are in such a deep sleep they are hard to wake, and eventually they slump back into bed, still fast asleep. The next morning they are usually unperturbed, with no memory of the event; they cannot understand what you are talking about.

Fewer than 5 per cent of children experience these terrors, about which little is understood. They occur more often in boys than girls. Though they tend to happen more at times when toddlers are under stress, there is no evidence that they are any indication of significant emotional disturbance.

A cure for night terrors

While night terrors do not indicate that there is anything wrong with a child, nevertheless they can be very worrying for parents, particularly if the child has them four or five times a night. If they are this frequent a drug can be prescribed which decreases the amount of time spent in deep sleep. However, it is better to avoid drugs if possible. A preferable method, devised by the London child psychiatrist Bryan Lask, is either to note the times at which the terrors occur (they usually happen at the same time each night) or to sit with the child for a night or two to observe whether she manifests restlessness, heavy breathing, sweating, or some other change just before the terror; on subsequent nights the child should be fully woken for five minutes, either about fifteen minutes before a terror attack is due, or at the first appearance of the warning signs. If this process is repeated for half a dozen nights running the terrors usually cease.

Sleepwalking

During the periods of deepest sleep the part of the brain that controls movement is alert while the rest is inactive. As with night terrors, children do not seem to be aware of what they are doing when they sleepwalk. They show no sign of emotional disturbance. However, sleepwalkers can hurt themselves, so if a child shows signs of sleepwalking it is advisable to ensure that doors and windows are securely closed, and take any other precautions you may think necessary. Sleepwalkers are difficult to wake, and it is best just to lead them quietly back to bed.

The cure advised for night terrors can be helpful for sleepwalkers.

Growing Independence

Children learn to walk, to run, to talk, to think, to wonder about themselves. If all these abilities and attributes are put together they point in one direction: towards growing independence.

The child's striving for psychological separation from the parents is the outstanding, and sometimes most maddening, characteristic of this age group. (It is *psychological* separation – the need to stay physically close is still strong.)

This phase is a psychological birth, a mirror to the physical birth that occurred earlier. Toddlers are seeking a sense that they can be in control, an acknowledgement that they are autonomous individuals. This need can be summed up in the phrase 'me do it'. (Someone once said that toddlers have a sign on their foreheads which says 'Help me to do it myself.') Unfortunately, the range of options open to them to achieve these ends is limited. At this age toddlers cannot express their psychological needs in words, they have to rely on behaviour.

The child psychologist Judy Dunn noted, in her extensive observations of toddlers, that the number of conflicts between children and their mothers (when children protested, resisted or repeated prohibited behaviour) doubled between eighteen and twenty-four months. When engaged in these conflicts most children showed tremendous emotion, its expression ranging from angry expressions and loud shouting to tantrums and self-injury. She also observed that they often delighted in upsetting their mothers, and reacted to their mothers' anger by smiling.

It sometimes helps, when faced with what seems an impossible task, to reinterpret the situation. The next time you find yourself faced with a screaming two year old, try seeing what is going on, not so much as a battle between you and your child, but rather as a battle within the child. She is grappling with the need to be psychologically independent while remaining physically dependent. Because she is so inexperienced, because she is learning as she goes, she has no other recourse than to swing to extremes, seeming to want to be totally autonomous, inappropriate though that may be. As the American psychologist Jerome Kagan put it in *The Nature of the Child*, 'Nature intended the child to be neither too humble nor too aggressive, just civilized.' Reaching a happy, civilized medium that allows a sense of individuality within a harmonious family relationship is something that children, with their parents' help, have to achieve for themselves.

The child who can amuse herself when she wakes is gaining a new maturity.

The need for discipline

Rules, regulations, discipline – all these words conjure up a picture of the stereotype Victorian father, dominating a cowed, miserable child with unthinking cruelty. But it need not be like that. Rules and discipline can be the vehicle by which children learn how to control themselves, within the context of a family code of conduct.

Children need to make sense of their world, to develop an understanding of what they experience so that it fits a predictable and understandable pattern. Related to this need for a predictable world is the need for security, especially when children are reaching out into independence, experimenting, trying to reach that civilized equilibrium that we all hope for. Parents also have their needs: if they are exhausted, distraught, defeated by their children, they cannot function properly.

The keys to meeting these needs are found within the family system. The ideal is a framework which is clear, predictable, logical and understandable, within which all family members operate, which manages at the same time to be sufficiently flexible to cater for individual needs. Children thrive within families where the implicit message is that the parents are ultimately in control, but they exert their control in a way that fosters their children's development. Discipline is the means by which order is brought to this system.

Structure and consistency

There is much value for children (and most adults) in having a basic structure to daily life. This does not mean that parents should be rigid in imposing a routine: there must be flexibility here as in other areas. But children feel more secure if their lives have some rhythm and order, so that they can predict what is going to happen and when. The bedtime routine is especially important to many children, perhaps because it signals that all is well with their world despite the impending temporary separation. Most families develop some variation on the bath-story-goodnight kiss routine, which occurs at about the same point every day – though there will, of course be special occasions when children stay up a little later, or have an extra story.

If life is to have a predictable structure there must be consistency. Children are more comfortable when they know where they are. This is another of those obvious statements – everyone agrees that it is better to be consistent, the difficult bit is maintaining consistency. It bears saying, though, for many behaviour problems fade away when children meet with consistency. Parental use of the word 'no' provides a clear example. Life is simpler, for children as well as parents, if 'no' is used to mean 'no'. It doesn't help anyone if a child is given to understand that 'no means no sometimes, but quite often it will get to mean yes if I just go on long enough.'

Setting limits

Setting limits is akin to establishing routines, a positive aspect of discipline that helps bring the world under control for the toddler, as well as allowing parents their own living space. For example, you may decide that your two year old can watch television, but for no longer than half an hour a day, and only programmes made for children (you may add that you would like to be there, so that you can watch together and talk about programmes – which is the best way to learn from them). Or you may decide that your toddler can play in the sitting room so long as she doesn't stand on the furniture or take things of yours from the shelves.

Toddlers can cope with limits so long as they are consistently enforced, not too many and not too difficult. They do have to be realistic: at two children can probably help put toys away, but can't reasonably be expected to tidy up on their own. They might sit in a restaurant for a short time, but probably will not behave throughout a whole meal without games or toys to keep them occupied. It is also unrealistic to try to work on every area at once. If a toddler is having to cope with toilet training she may not be able to take many limits in the way of tidiness or table manners. If you are trying to sort out a major problem with night waking or tantrums, it may be better to ease up on other areas for the time being.

Limits must also take account of children's nature and their need to grow and learn. A child's natural curiosity, for example, can lead to trouble – but the exercise of curiosity is essential to mental growth. It is far better to tolerate some apparent naughtiness than run the risk of stifling a child's sense of inquiry.

Toddlers at the younger end of this age group do not pay attention to lengthy exposition of a parental viewpoint but they can learn to respond to a code word or phrase. One of the advantages of clearly set limits, adhered to consistently, is that a reminder can be given in a few words. So if there is a shopkeeper who tends to be grumpy with young children you might have a rule of 'Quiet in Mr So-and-So's shop'. The whole business of keeping to the limits can become a sort of game, and children can be praised for being so grown up that they are able to keep rules.

As children grow a little older, you can expect more of them. The capacity to recall information develops steadily over this period, as does the ability to generalize from one situation to another. If you stop your child taking things off shelves during a visit to a supermarket she might remember not to on the next visit; she might even, of her own accord, apply the same rule in a department store. However, she may equally well take something off the shelves and say 'no' at the same time, reminding herself that this behaviour is not acceptable. She may also rehearse situations with a favourite teddy or doll – perhaps shaking a finger and saying 'no'. She is learning to give herself reminders.

Discipline with care

If a child has done something wrong, and you both know that it is wrong, she will expect some consequences. You must keep to your side of the bargain by disciplining her in a way that both of you see is fair. What you do is up to you, but remember that it is as well to get it over as quickly as possible. If you go on complaining or sulking about the action for the rest of the day, you will be providing a model of behaviour that she will almost certainly copy. It might also help to remember that toddlers love attention; sadly, some get it only if they have done something wrong.

Freedom of choice

When children are allowed no choice in any area of their lives, their urge to assert their independence will be thwarted. Confrontation is the almost inevitable consequence. However, there is a problem of balance here, for if

child's way of protecting herself. Self-assertion is better than passivity, and an angry response may be healthier than one of acquiescence.

Coping with tantrums

If you apply the following guidelines in dealing with tantrums, you can help reduce their intensity and number.

• Do not lose your temper. It may not be easy to control your own mounting rage and frustration, but remember that the tantrum is frightening enough to the toddler; if she feels that her mother or father is out of control too she will be terrified. (If you do lose control, apologize afterwards. The apology will help show the child that losing one's temper is not acceptable behaviour, for anyone; and it may help her, also, to begin to learn the important lesson that parents, too, are imperfect – and can admit it.)

• Keep a written note about what triggered each tantrum: you may discern a pattern. It may be that tantrums tend to occur when your child is hungry, or overtired, or overstimulated, and you will know to be especially careful not to let these circumstances arise. Or it may be that there is a tantrum every time you go to the supermarket. For the time being, you might limit shopping trips and try to get in and out quickly.

• Do not give in to a tantrum, even if you feel guilty, foolish, petty or mean for holding out.

• Choose a course of action for dealing with tantrums, and stick to it – you may need to keep to it consistently for a month or more before you see any positive results. The following methods have proved effective.

Ignoring the tantrum. Starve the tantrum of attention. Simply make sure that your child is safe and then turn your attention away. Occupy yourself with something else, and try, as far as possible, not even to look at the child (although you will have to sneak the odd glance to make sure she is safe). Of course, it is difficult not to pay attention to a screaming toddler – especially in public. If your child has a tantrum while you are out, carry her to a quiet place where there is no one but you to hear while she winds down.

Holding your child. This means just what it says: holding the child firmly, but not so firmly that it hurts. Within your containing arms (and possibly legs) your child is able to express her emotions verbally until she and they are exhausted. You stay in control, the child can let rip in safety.

• Do not argue or try to explain your actions to a toddler in the middle of a tantrum. While she is upset she cannot listen to you and she will not be able to understand.

• Do not reward a tantrum. Rewards can come in subtle forms. For a toddler, a reward might be hearing you describe the tantrum to the other parent, or to grandparents, especially if you smile or laugh as you give the account. Some time after the episode you may want, for both your sakes, to give

Tantrums may be the child's way of asserting herself when she is frustrated or angry – but parents can be amazed by the force of feeling displayed.

your child some extra attention – to read her a story, perhaps, or have a cuddle. But leave long enough for the child not to see a direct link.

• Avoid using drugs. When children have persistent tantrums, particularly at bedtime, it can seem that medication is the only solution. But children must learn to have control over their emotions and if they are drugged to calm down they receive a negative message: that when there is something wrong they cannot do anything about it. Anyway, the tantrums will probably resume once you stop the drugs, and children of five or six who are having tantrums are even harder to deal with.

Parents have their limits too. Sometimes parents get so overwrought by tantrums that they feel they have to get away from their children or they might harm them. It can be safer to put your child into a room on her own (and, of course, check her periodically) than it would be to keep her with you. Some parents arrange with a neighbour to take over for a few minutes at a moment's notice. This may be helpful at the time, but it is not without its dangers. Leaving your child by herself for a while in her own home is one thing; taking her to someone else's house, and putting her in someone else's care, when she is in a highly emotional state, may signal to her a far deeper rejection than you mean.

If your toddler has had a tantrum and you have coped with it, even by sitting in a room ignoring it, when it is over you will probably be in need of some time off for yourself. As soon as you can, give yourself some time to relax, calm down, and come to terms with your own frustration and anger. A five-minute walk or even a few deep breaths can make you feel different.

If this all sounds too difficult, remember that this independence-seeking stage is not all thunder and lightning. Not every child goes through it in a blaze; some manage it relatively quietly. And almost all swing frequently back into dependence, coming back to be cuddled in times of crisis.

Play

For the toddler as for the baby, play is a self-motivated activity that is its own reward: if it is not fun it is not play. As the growing child develops new capacities and skills, the scope of her play widens constantly, providing endless interest as she practises new abilities and takes pleasure in increasing mastery over her own body and environment.

Parents can do a great deal to enable children to play at this age, but the key word is 'enable'. It is all too common for parents who recognize the importance of play to organize it so highly that it becomes work for them and boredom for the child. As a parent, your role is essentially to offer the opportunities – the materials, environment, example and encouragement – for happy and productive play and then leave your child free to get on with it. The actual playing can only be done by the child. Even when you play with her, you should try, so far as possible, to follow her lead.

It is worth remembering, too, that no matter how rich or satisfying the play situation, young children do not generally persist in one activity for long. In America Jerome Kagan has found that for toddlers of twenty-seven months episodes of play last an average of about twelve minutes (at seventeen months they are sometimes as short as ten to fifteen seconds). However much you may yearn for your child to be happily and independently occupied, during the toddler years she won't concentrate for long enough to give you time to cook the dinner without interruption, or to finish a chapter in your book.

Learning through play

As Piaget showed us (see page 211), it is through exploration of the world around them that children learn. Much of children's play is essentially exploration and experiment. Freedom to play gives the child a chance to discover her own strategies for coping with everyday problems. A toddler tries to scribble on a piece of paper, imitating something she has seen mum and dad do. Nothing happens. Eventually it dawns on her that the pencil has two ends, only one of which will make a mark. When she has been through this process on her own, the toddler has started to learn, not only how to use a pencil, but also an even more fundamental lesson: that when one approach fails, you try a different strategy.

260

Play helps toddlers to confirm advances they have made, not only in physical mobility and dexterity, but also in conceptual thinking. For example, a toddler will learn quite a lot about shape and size from playing with a simple posting box; as she hammers pegs into a hole in a board, she is not only improving her coordination, but will also learn some elementary facts about the effects of force exerted on objects.

Through play, children can also begin to build a feeling of confidence and self-reliance, free from the risk of failure. They are under no pressure to reach goals or to succeed in meeting other people's expectations. If they do not manage to achieve what they are attempting, it does not matter – no one is watching to point out their mistakes and correct them.

The way children play with language provides a special example of the general process of acquiring competence through play. Often, before toddlers incorporate new behaviour into their everyday lives, they will rehearse the words and practise the script. They can be heard mumbling things they have heard – including (and perhaps especially) instructions and scolding. It is almost as if they are trying to tell themselves how to behave.

Early play experiences also provide the setting for children's first attempts to get along with other people. The rudiments of cooperation are explored by degrees as toddlers encounter each other.

Play has a special value in helping children work out stressful experiences. Most parents, fortunately, know nothing at first hand of children traumatized by war, whose reactions to terrible experiences have led psychologists towards the realization of the therapeutic value of play. But any observant parent may notice how children can use play to help them regain their composure after a disturbing experience. Thus a child who has felt anxious on a visit to hospital may play at hospitals, a child who has seen a road accident may recapitulate it in play, in an effort to gain a sense of control over the alarming events.

Some parents feel they should try to stop this kind of play on the grounds that it just reminds the child of something best forgotten. This is a mistake: worries that a child is prevented from expressing in play will not disappear, they will go underground, perhaps to surface in other ways more difficult for child and parent to deal with. This is not to say that parents should intervene to try to get their children to play out their emotions. What is needed is the recognition that a child may sometimes need the opportunity to play out worries at her own pace.

The role of imitation

An important way of learning at any stage of life is through imitation; and imitation requires practice. Play provides the toddler with the necessary opportunities. Toddlers are not able to bake cakes, write letters or drive cars, for example, but by the age of three many toddlers can accurately imitate the actions involved in all these. They have learned to match their own actions to the complicated behaviour of adults and to understand something of the purposes that motivate behaviour.

Toddlers also imitate each other. An informal tutoring takes place between children as they play. If you watch children playing with bricks or in a sand pit you will notice that when one toddler initiates an activity other children are soon doing the same thing. Around the age of two, when children are walking more confidently, a favourite game is for an adult or an older brother or sister to pretend to run away and, when the little one begins to chase after, to turn around and chase in return. This kind of imitative swapping of roles involves turn-taking and the ability to read another person's signals – skills it is essential for the toddler to learn. Toddlers don't grasp them in one go: they will often mix up the person who is hiding with the one who is seeking and be unable to work out who is chasing whom. But this is a beginning for all sorts of learning that will come later.

The ability to imitate is an invaluable tool for learning precise skills. Copying a parent who is demonstrating a skill – threading beads on a lace, perhaps – opens the door to much satisfying play as the child repeats the achievement many times, always improving her control and accuracy.

Physical play

Given the opportunity young children naturally build strength and endurance during their play sessions. Any healthy child can become fitter by playing vigorously, putting just the right amount of stress on heart and lungs with self-regulated bursts of running and chasing – although even at this age, as parents will notice, some children are stronger, have greater endurance and quicker reactions than others; for there is a lot of variation in heart-rate, oxygen intake, biochemical efficiency and type of muscle fibre from one child to another. Children are very good at finding the level that suits them. The grown-ups' job is simply to make sure that the child's life includes enough inviting opportunities for active play, and to leave it to the child to make use of them.

Rough and tumble

With any kind of play there will always be some children who love it and some who don't seem to take any interest in it. After all, children are individuals from the start, with their own capacities and aptitudes. Rough and tumble play provides a particularly noticeable example: there are some children who just love to chase and will get into rough and tumble play any time they can, while others are systematically happier playing in a quieter or more sedentary way.

Free and spontaneous rough and tumble play is different from climbing, swinging and other active equipment-based play. Children who like rough play may not necessarily be keen on, or adept at, using swings, slides and climbing frames.

During the toddler years at least, the difference between rough play and hostile play is fairly obvious (as children get older it can become harder to tell). Rough play among toddlers is accompanied by laughs or smiles; running, wrestling and laughing all come together within a short period. Frowns, pouts and crying belong to real fights, which usually result from a grab-and-take situation that has no part in rough and tumble.

None the less, studies (and daily life!) reveal that many mothers tend not to like this rough free play, often see no reason for it and are likely to intervene to stop it. Mothers often give active rough and tumble play as a reason for taking a toddler out of a particular group of children or play situation. Fathers, on the other hand, are usually quite comfortable with rough and tumble – in fact, the earliest play of this kind is usually initiated by fathers playing with their babies.

There is a danger that in the modern world rough and tumble play may be squeezed out of children's lives by lack of space, dislike of behaviour that seems aggressive, and an increasingly organized attitude to physical exercise. It is not easy to produce a foolproof demonstration of the value or necessity of rough play. Nevertheless, it would seem intuitively wrong to try to suppress something which is spontaneous, evidently represents a strong drive in many children, and does not do any particular harm to those children who don't want to join in, since they easily develop strategies for avoiding it. It is sometimes right for parents to forget about analyzing everything and be ready to say, 'My child seems to need to play in this way – look at the pleasure she gets out of it! That's enough for me.'

Rough and tumble among toddlers can look aggressive, but for many children it is a spontaneous form of play, a way of letting off steam.

Exploration and discovery

Exploration and discovery account for many of the play activities most enjoyed by toddlers, who are busily continuing the process – begun in babyhood – of experiencing the physical world they live in. They need frequent opportunities to experience all kinds of substances as they put together the concepts of everyday life: wet, dry, full, empty, sinking – and many more besides.

Water – whether in a water table, a paddling pool, a bath or just a bucket – provides perhaps the most exhilarating play of all. Just swishing hands about in water can be a soothing and absorbing activity for a toddler. It can be varied by providing soap bubbles, filling a balloon with water, adding a jug and a couple of beakers, or a floating duck. Don't put in too many toys: some toddler water tables are so full of playthings that the children can't get to the water. You can control the mess by covering the floor with plastic and allowing only small quantities of water. Outside, in the summer, water is one of the happiest ways to amuse several toddlers together: they may not seem to interact very much but they certainly enjoy each other's company as they sit and splash.

Sand, wet or dry, comes a close second to water. Its clean grittiness is satisfying to touch; children can dig in it, feel it, pat it and shape it. Wet sand is easily controlled and built up. If children can add their own water it

Getting the feel of sand and pebbles between your fingers, digging into earth – two of childhood's great sensory pleasures.

becomes even more fun, and the differences between wet and dry are memorably brought home. A full watering can is plenty for several children at a sand tray. Buckets and spades are hardly necessary – although a wooden spoon to push in and out can be welcome.

Any number of other materials – mud, clay, flour, dough, finger paints, for instance – are fun for children to explore. Each has its own nature, new to the child, and its physical properties need repeated investigation before it becomes a known quantity. A child thoughtfully squeezing, rolling and patting a pliable lump of playdough, dividing it into balls, clumping them together and beginning all over again is learning a lot about physics, as well as exercising the sort of pleasurable control that may in time lead on to a richly creative expression of her sense of form.

Although some skills have to be explicitly taught, toddlers also need the opportunity to experiment and to use objects in 'wrong' ways. For instance, most children, when they are learning to use a spoon, will 'mess around with it', throwing it about, turning it over and seeing if it works that way too – doing anything they can think of. This kind of experimentation helps children create a variety of possibilities with one object. If they just used the spoon to eat properly, think what they would miss: the opportunity of finding out about gravity, balance and the effects of throwing. Children need to be given opportunities like this to develop their creative thinking processes, doing something experimentally rather than always following

Most small children love cutting shapes out of playdough, or moulding clay. And as they play they are learning a lot about the world.

the rules, and never finding out what happens if you don't.

Toddlers inevitably make something of a mess, whatever they are doing, simply because their control is not sufficiently well developed for them to handle things tidily. But, quite apart from that, many children seem to get real satisfaction from messy play – with water, paint, earth, whatever comes to hand. Here again, if we stick with our definition of play, the fact that children seem to enjoy making a mess should be sufficient reason for allowing them to do it. Damage can be limited and anxiety and inconvenience minimized by sensible precautions (newspaper on the floor, comfortable overalls on the child).

Make-believe

The dawning ability to think in symbolic terms, which occupies such a central place in the development of language over these years, adds a whole new dimension to play for the toddler. Once a child has reached the stage where she can make one thing stand for (symbolize) another – whether it is a word standing for the thing it refers to, or a doll being treated as if it were a baby, or a circle and two strokes on a paper representing a person – the rich world of fantasy and pretend play is open to her. Ideas, behaviour and relationships can be explored and played with in symbolic terms, much as objects can be physically played with, and for a similar purpose: to understand and gain mastery over the complicated world which the toddler is constantly encountering.

The development of fantasy play closely parallels the development of language. Children who are using single words to refer to objects can make the simple substitution of pretending that an empty cup is full and 'drinking' from it. At about the same time as they begin to put two or three words together to make simple sentences, they start to elaborate their fantasy play, so that it involves two or three actions. For example, a two year old may make an empty cup into a full one by pretending to pour milk into it, drinking the milk and saying 'all gone'. From being able to pretend actions by themselves with simple implements (comb, spoon, cup), they progress to being able to make another person the subject of the action (combing father's hair, feeding teddy from a cup). This happens at around the same time as they begin to use sentences involving a subject, a verb and an object. Between two and three they begin to pretend with a new freedom, using substitute objects to stand for the real one: combing with a ruler, feeding a brick to a doll, making a chair into a car.

Playmates

Between the ages of one and two children change enormously in their response to other children. While infants may be interested in watching each other at a distance, toddlers are usually enthusiastic about playing near, if not with, other children. They may not play cooperatively for very long, but they give lots of signals that they are trying to get along.

You can help by encouraging two year olds to play with others of their own age, but until they are approaching three their attempts to play together are likely to seem a hit-or-miss affair. Parents can go to great extremes to arrange play sessions for little children, only to find that one toddler sits at one end of the sand pit while the other plays at the other. You might think that neither knew the other was there, but if you watch for a while you may notice that they are playing in almost exactly the same way. One piles the sand into a hill, and so does the other; one makes a hole in the sand and the other does too. This 'parallel play', which usually emerges between eighteen months and two, sometimes earlier, consists of two children doing the same thing at the same time, but independently.

The next stage is playing together. This usually starts during the third year, but for some children, particularly those who have had a lot of experience with a group of other children, or one special friend, it comes much earlier. Playing together, children can help each other learn new skills. Children in pairs often spark each other off: they will suddenly come up with creative ideas, a spontaneous solution to a problem or new words that they have not spoken before.

Although these children look so absorbed in their own play, they will none the less be watching and imitating what the others do. This is one of the ways toddlers learn to play cooperatively.

However, when children of this age are playing together a good deal of their play (about half, according to one research study) ends in quarrels, usually over a toy or other possession. Even when two identical toys are available, children can squabble over just one of them. In fact, it is valuable for them to go through these disagreements. They may not learn to share immediately, but they do start to get an idea of bargaining and negotiating, and will eventually manage to share, at least some of the time. What is more, through such conflicts toddlers begin to learn the difficult lesson that we are all different, and we have differing opinions.

Toys and play materials

Toys and play materials are a central part of most children's lives at this age. They are important not only for the satisfaction the child gets from playing with them, but also for the way they lead on to social relationships. One study found that during the first stages of friendship toddlers played with toys about 90 per cent of the time. The toys acted as bait, attracting other children, and were at the centre of most disputes between toddlers. Ultimately, when children learn to bargain, they become more aware of the person they are negotiating with, and the other toddler becomes more important than the toy.

Bricks and constructional toys

Bricks – whether old-fashioned wooden ones or modern plastic ones that fit together – are popular with most children, and they can learn a lot from them. (As with so many objects and activities, however, parents should be warned that a minority of children show no interest in them at all.)

At this age children can't build anything very elaborate, but they do enjoy making their low towers and tracks, and putting a few pieces of a simple construction set together can make a satisfying play session. It is important to avoid the temptation just to take over. Toddlers know when they cannot live up to parents' expectations, and if they see parents building complex structures that are quite beyond them, they may lose interest.

Sorting and grouping toys

The ability to cope with the sorting and grouping of objects is fundamental to thinking, and play can make a big contribution to the way children learn these skills. Toddlers will readily hand out biscuits, 'one for you and one for me'. Matching one object to one person or putting round pegs into round holes helps them to notice the distribution of similarities and differences. Toys like posting boxes, puzzles and collections of small animals provide the opportunity for practice in sorting.

The kind of toy that encourages children's participation in problem-solving often holds their interest longest: rings to be stacked, shapes to be pushed through slots, containers to be filled and emptied have a lasting attraction. By three, a toddler may be sufficiently well coordinated to

A teddy can be a good friend – he is always there, and never has anything else to do in the kitchen. A favourite toy can be a great support to a child, helping her through difficult experiences.

string large beads on a lace; she may also recognize a few colours and shapes, and know when she is stringing all the red ones or all the round ones together.

Dolls and teddy bears

Children of this age are often strongly attached to dolls or teddies – and if it so happens that a child has fixed on a soft toy as a comfort object (see page 153), it will have in addition a special kind of symbolic meaning and value. The toy may have a hard life, since most of what happens to the child will happen to it too. If the child has to have an injection, the toy gets one first – and a dozen more afterwards, if it has been a nasty experience for the child. Similarly, a toddler who is afraid of the dark may put her doll or teddy to sleep in a darkened room, as part of an attempt to conquer her own fear. At the same time, the seeds of empathy with other people may be found in the child's assumption of the role of caretaker or parent to the doll.

Toys for fantasy play

Toddlers like to have props that stimulate their imaginations. Without any help, they can begin to incorporate objects they find into their make-believe. If they come across a pair of discarded high-heeled shoes they put them on and pretend to be mummy; if they find a lipstick, they know what to do with that too – though they may try it out on the wall first. A box can become a garage, be lived in or driven around, a broom handle can become a horse. A box full of old clothes which are easy to take on and off, an old handbag, a fireman's hat, all help children to become someone else.

Children get a lot of social experience from carrying out a different person's role. This kind of imaginary play allows a toddler to go through motions and solve problems of everyday life in make-believe. Don't be too preoccupied with whether your child gets the details right all the time. If she puts on a fireman's hat to make an arrest, there is no need to tell her

Two mothers taking their babies to the park. One wants to stop and feed her baby while the other wants to get on. It's all very close to children's own experiences.

where she has gone wrong. She will learn about the details in time: for now it is more important that she has the confidence to keep on fantasizing.

Play with everyday objects

Exploring the home takes up a lot of time in the toddler years. When your child was a baby she noticed a lot of what was around her, but her ability to hold and manipulate was rudimentary. Now, with her growing mobility and dexterity, she can get her hands on objects and play with them, explore them and make something happen – even if it is a crash.

Toddlers find many everyday objects just as fascinating as toys. Pots and pans, boxes of different sizes, shapes and materials, jars with or without tops, the Aladdin's cave inside a handbag – the possibilities are endless.

It is up to parents to decide which household objects and materials can and cannot be treated as playthings. Every child has to learn eventually that some things are not for playing with, because they are too dangerous, too precious or too messy, but it is not reasonable to expect children of this age to be consistent about remembering what they should avoid. It is the parents' job to make it clear what things are not to be played with – and then effectively to prevent the children from getting hold of them.

Drawing and painting materials

Drawing and painting have already been discussed, in relation to the toddler's developing ability to manipulate a pencil or paintbrush (see pages 202–3). The symbolic aspects of painting, which later come to have such rich creative content, begin to appear in rudimentary form only towards the end of the toddler stage, when the child is about three; however, most little children of eighteen months seem to get great satisfaction from episodes of scribbling with a crayon or slapping on brushfuls of paint, and it is well worth providing plenty of these play materials. Children of this age do not come across drawing and painting by chance; they need the help of adults to set up the situation and to supply and control the materials. A baby can play with a crayon simply as an object, but more interesting and constructive activity will come much quicker if she is given encouragement and opportunities to imitate.

The role of parents

For toddlers as much as for babies, parents hold the key to play and playmates. They decide on the neighbourhood where they will live and they must take the initiative in making social arrangements. Indeed, as many parents would testify, their own social lives can come to revolve largely around the arrangements they make for their children.

We have already discussed the way parents are imitated by children in everything they do: this includes the way they make friends. Toddlers watch the way their parents approach other people, then turn round and approach their own friends in the same way. It is hardly surprising that a sociable parent is likely to have a friendly youngster, and an isolated parent to have a toddler who does not interact easily.

Of course, children and parents can profitably play together – at this age, often more successfully than two children. It is often the adult who begins by introducing a game or toy. A word or gesture can extend a toddler's interest, lengthening the attention span. Parents also contribute when they intervene at a crucial time to help children get along better, suggesting strategies and extending a game, renewing or reorganizing materials that have got into a muddle. Two children fighting over a toy can be helped if the parent comes into the argument and suggests that they sort out a way to share. All the same, parents must be wary of taking too much control over play, for children can then lose interest. While a toddler is at play she can be in charge: it is the toddler's world even when it imitates that of the adult.

Some parents find it a struggle to cope with their toddler's increasing need to be assertive and independent and respond by restricting their children. The parent who feels it necessary to have a strict routine, who finds it hard to allow children much independence, can consciously balance this tendency by allowing a toddler blocks of time when she can play in a leisurely way. There should be plenty of time to imagine, to play out fantasies, and to practise newly learned skills. It is a shame if this is jeopardized in the rush to various groups, gym sessions and other activities.

A place of her own
A toddler needs a place where she can keep her clothes and another place where she can keep toys and favourite objects. It will help her to have a sense of order if she can reach these places, open the drawers for herself, and, as she gets older, start to participate in tidying up. The more readily children can find places for things and help keep themselves organized, even at the toddler stage, the more competent and in charge they feel.

If at all possible, try to provide a private place for your toddler – a space, however small, where she can get away from family activities, avoid brothers and sisters, and be able to look at pictures or just play alone. Ideally, it should be equipped with a toddler-sized table and chair. No one feels comfortable for long with feet dangling in the air and no back support. The table will be used for paint and clay, so it need not be in perfect condition. If parents get too concerned about the state of children's furniture, it defeats its own purpose.

It is sometimes possible to provide a special place for children to look at books and be read to. A few cushions in a corner of a room with a box for books makes a start; it is even better if you can include a large comfortable chair for a grown-up to sit in to read to children.

Some space to run about
Parents can become concerned about how they are to provide sufficient opportunities for active play – especially if they have the kind of toddler who loves rough and tumble (see page 262). While a quiet child may thrive

This is my place, these are my books, my clothes, my toys. In here I have things just the way I like.

on a daily walk or trip to a playground to play on equipment, a more active toddler needs a lot of time and space to run about. Indoor spaces are seldom really appropriate. Outdoor space needs to be open and not cluttered. If you are the parent of an active toddler, and you don't have a garden or a readily available park or stretch of countryside, you may find that you spend a lot of your time, first searching out suitable play spaces for your child, and then getting her there. If you do have an outdoor area you can give over to children, you need to keep the plan simple and safe. You don't need much equipment – an active toddler may, indeed, find apparatus frustrating in a small garden or yard, because it gets in the way.

The period from eighteen months to three is a dynamic time, encompassing a succession of developmental explosions. It may sometimes have been a daunting experience; it will certainly have been an exciting one. Generally, the third birthday heralds a rather quieter stage, of developmental broadening and deepening, as the child moves out into new worlds.

Physical Growth

During the years from three to seven, chubby, pot-bellied toddlers grow into slimmer, straighter children, whose stronger muscles, harder bones and more developed brains enable them to enter a whole world of new achievements.

Physique

In most developed countries, we expect a gain in height of around 6–7.5 cm/2½–3 inches a year between three and seven. By six, most children have reached about 70 per cent of their adult height. The rate of growth in developing countries is more variable, reflecting differences in levels of nutrition and health care.

During the fourth, fifth and sixth years, again where nutrition and care are adequate, children usually add about 2.25–2.7 kg/5–6 lb a year to their weight. This increases to about 3 kg/7 lb in the year between six and seven.

Children become leaner. The thickness of the subcutaneous 'baby fat' decreases by about half between the latter part of the first year and the end of the seventh (the decrease is less in girls than in boys). The tummy that was so protuberant in the toddler years gradually reduces, as the child's muscles and spine grow stronger and internal organs move down into the pelvis.

Nutrition
Nutritional needs change somewhat during this time, because children's requirements relative to body weight are less than in infancy. So, despite their increased size and activity, children's appetites generally decline a little. What counts is the content of their intake, not sheer quantity. But even after paying attention to providing a well-balanced diet (see pages 496–7), parents sometimes worry that because their growing child seems to be eating less than before he is not eating enough. If your child is energetic and active, with bright eyes and glossy hair, and full of pep after a good night's sleep, then the likelihood is that he is well nourished. However, if you are concerned that he is under or overweight for his height, it is certainly worth asking your doctor to check him over.

At three this little boy still has something of his baby tummy. By seven he will have lost all his baby fat and become slender and long-limbed like his sister.

Bones, muscles and teeth

Children of this age become sturdier too. The number of bones in the hand, wrist, ankle and foot continues to increase until adolescence. All the bones of the body gradually harden and grow in size. The skull, which grew very rapidly in the first years, increases more slowly now. Between the ages of five and twelve it grows only about 3 cm/1⅛ inches. A seven year old's skull is usually about 49 cm/19½ inches in circumference, and the average adult head is only 5–6 cm/2–2½ inches bigger.

Muscle size increases steadily in proportion to body weight until the age of five or so, and then there is a spurt for about a year, followed by a slowing down until puberty. In both sexes an increase in the capacity of the circulatory and respiratory systems leads to increased stamina.

Usually, all the milk teeth have come through by about two and a half. Between three and five the face tends to grow proportionately more than the skull and the jaw widens ready for the permanent teeth to come through. A spurt of growth in the jaw between five and seven brings about a

The chubby fullness of the younger child's face contrasts vividly with the changing proportions of his older sister's face.

noticeable change from the baby face to a more mature look.

The first permanent teeth are the first molars. They usually erupt when a child is about six, but there is wide individual variation in the timing. Once the molars are in place, the milk teeth begin to be shed, in roughly the same order as they first appeared. In most children the shedding of the milk teeth and the eruption of the permanent ones take place at about the same time, but sometimes a child will have a gap for a while, and sometimes new teeth appear before the baby teeth have left a space for them.

Problems of overcrowding or crooked teeth may start to become apparent at about this time. Orthodontic intervention is not usually undertaken before the age of eight or nine (see page 372), but there is no need to wait until then before seeking advice. If you are worried that your child's teeth may not be growing properly, you should certainly consult his dentist.

The brain

The brain and spinal cord, like the eyes and ears, all of which achieved 60 per cent of their adult size in the first two years of life, are growing more slowly now; but by seven they have become nearly adult in size. Myelination of the cortex (see page 109) is almost completed during this period, and the complexity of brain activity advances, with an accompanying shift in brainwave patterns so that they are much closer to those of an adult. It might seem tempting to claim that it is these changes in the brain that lead to the skills that show such marked development over this period – reading and writing, throwing and catching, and many others. But we need to remind ourselves that all we can observe is an associated change; it is equally possible that children's increased activities actually help to bring about the greater complexity of the brain. Science is constantly encountering similar difficulties in establishing the operations of cause and effect between separate changes that are observed to occur together. In this case, as often, the most probable explanation lies in an interaction between the two. The changes in children's activities may stimulate more complexity in the brain and the changes in the brain lead to more complexity and skill in the child's behaviour.

Sight

A child's ability to observe details – his visual acuity – improves slightly during this time, partly as a result of physical maturation, mostly because of his increased experience. There are also some marked changes in the way children use their eyes. Between three and five children look most at the internal details of a figure, with only an occasional eye movement around the outside. By six and seven they are beginning to search systematically from top to bottom, with occasional eye movements into the centre.

Checking sight

Although extreme disabilities in vision are usually detected much earlier than this, more minor difficulties may not become evident until this stage. When children who were able to cope at home cannot manage the extra demands of nursery or school, parents or teachers may wonder about their ability to see clearly. If children frequently screw up their eyes, hold objects very close to their faces or seem unable to recognize shapes at a distance, it is worth taking advice, if only for reassurance that nothing is seriously wrong. Testing eyesight is a normal part of a routine developmental examination at clinic or school, but these tests are usually fairly cursory, involving little more than checking that children can match shapes (or letters, if they are old enough to recognize them). This screening procedure assesses only the middle field of vision. If a problem is suspected, then more elaborate tests should be carried out to assess near vision and the ability to coordinate both eyes.

In fact the number of children with significant visual problems is small. Estimates vary from country to country and from study to study, but in the United States it appears that about 15 per cent of school-age children have some defect. This figure may indeed sound alarmingly high, until one realizes that, in the vast majority of these cases, wearing glasses provides perfectly adequate correction: only about 0.1 per cent of the American school population has a visual condition that is handicapping.

Hearing

There are only relatively small physical modifications in hearing during this period. However, it is a time when parents need to be aware of their child's hearing, for increasing demands on children's comprehension and participation can reveal impairments which have so far passed unnoticed. Parents and teachers should be on the alert for any signs of difficulty.

Checking hearing

Hearing loss is more difficult to detect than visual problems, largely because there is greater day-to-day fluctuation in the degree of loss. Parents should be alerted to the possibility of a problem if children complain about their ears for any reason; if there are frequent infections of the ear, nose or throat; if language is slow to develop or speech is indistinct; or if the child is always asking for remarks to be repeated. As with visual tests, the routine methods of assessment used in developmental tests may not be very searching, and should be seen as no more than a starting point. If a hearing loss is suspected, expert help should be sought as soon as possible.

Approximately 0.18 per cent of American school-age children are thought to have some form of hearing impairment: of them about 6 per cent are profoundly deaf; the rest suffer from degrees of hearing loss varying from mild to severe (see page 187).

Physical Skills

A child's development during these years involves constant interaction between the growth of his body and the use that he learns to make of it. Physical growth in body and brain has to take place before a child can develop certain abilities. But growth alone is not enough: practice is essential if the physical potential is to be realized. So the skills that children show depend partly on the level of their physical development and partly on what practice they are encouraged and allowed to take. In turn the amount of practice will be determined partly by the children's own nature and partly by their parents' attitudes.

As children grow, so individual differences are more apparent, and age-related tables become suspect. From now on, the age at which skills are achieved is increasingly dependent on children's own inclinations and their family's lifestyle. For example, if children have parents or older brothers and sisters who enjoy active games themselves and are ready to join in with them in the playground, they will tend to be more enthusiastic about such activities, and may achieve physical milestones earlier. So all the ages given in these sections are to be seen as a rough average guide only.

Gross motor skills

Between three and seven a child's physical abilities and behaviour undergo a steady, progressive transformation. By three a child is walking with a longer step than he had in earlier years, and running with more confidence. The four year old walks with swinging steps, almost like an adult's, and he seems to take great pleasure in stunts – whirling and leaping. The five year old has become more poised and controlled: he may seem to be less active because he is not in constant restless motion but maintains a position for longer. In fact he is more active, achieving more with greater economy of effort and movement. Six year olds enjoy climbing, dancing – they are all arms and legs. By seven there is increasing evidence of personality differences: some children become less active, some become more cautious.

Practically everything that active children do gives them exercise and practice in the use of their bodies and the exploration of new potentialities of their developing physique. Children invent their own exercises when they climb, run and engage in games – exercises which stretch them more

Children vary in their daring. Exploring the equipment in the playground gives a satisfying sense of achievement and helps the child to learn her own limits.

gently and in a more interesting way than most formal classes. As their lives come to include longer periods of concentration on mental activities that keep them physically passive (especially at school, where random activity may be discouraged in the classroom), it is important to realize that they need periods of energetic play to let off steam.

However, children between three and seven are developing socially and psychologically, as well as physically. They are starting to be aware of the skills and achievements that are admired and enjoyed by adults and older children, and this awareness influences their physical activities and goals – and the attitudes and aspirations of their parents. While spontaneous play of an unstructured kind provides a child with plenty of opportunity for exercise, fun and increasing competence, as he grows older more emphasis is put on acquiring and improving specific skills in areas such as throwing and catching, roller skating or riding a bicycle, in which strength, coordination, balance and timing are all harnessed into a complex whole that has meaning for the child and his friends.

Balance

The ability to balance is dependent on the quality of vision and focusing powers, on the efficiency of the mechanisms of the inner ear that integrate visual and motor information, on a child's ability to fix his attention. By three children can often stand on one foot for a few seconds; by four they can do it for up to eight seconds. Much depends thereafter on the child's innate ability – and on his personality. When faced with a climbing frame or a bicycle without stabilizers, children vary in their daring.

Running

Many three year olds run better than they can walk, although it is usually not until they are five that children are able to run lightly on their toes. During this period they learn to turn corners at a run, to accelerate and

decelerate and to come to a sudden stop. Now that they have a dependable competence in walking and running, they like to experiment with hopping, skipping, jumping, moving sideways and backwards and so on. After five or six children run like adults, and their speed depends largely on strength and body size, which determines length of stride.

Jumping, hopping and skipping

Children of this age seem to love jumping. They can get both feet off the ground at three or four, and even as young as three may be able to jump 30 cm/12 inches off the ground.

Children can hop on one foot a little at three to four; by five they can hop for a distance of more than 4.5 metres/15 feet. Skipping is quite a tricky skill to acquire, demanding as it does both balance and a sense of timing, but most children can skip by the time they are five. By six they can skip in time to music.

Climbing

Though most two year olds can get up and down stairs alone, it is usually not until children are four that they can take the steps smoothly, using alternate feet coming down as well as going up. By five they may begin to climb trees and some six year olds can even use climbing ropes (though some children – and adults – never manage to climb a rope). They can now hang by their arms, swing by their knees and turn somersaults around branches and climbing frames. At seven, even as their climbing skills continue to improve, they may be more aware of heights and become more cautious.

Kicking, throwing and catching

Some children are kicking balls by the time they are two, but they rarely gain much control before five. Many five year olds can kick a ball to a distance of 3.5 metres/12 feet.

Throwing with aim begins to develop at any time between three and seven. At three many children can catch a large ball with arms extended and can throw without losing their balance. By four they can flex their arms at

These six year olds are clearly relishing the warm-up for their judo session – an enjoyable way of improving balance and coordination.

the elbow and may be able to move about in response to the direction of a ball's flight. By five they take a more adult sideways stance in throwing and can throw with a clear aim. As they get older, children develop a more mature technique involving maximum arm and trunk rotation; they learn to follow the flight of the ball and to wait for it with hands and arms well controlled and fingers relaxed.

Swimming

Becoming at home in the water and learning to swim is not only important for safety reasons, it is great fun for children as well. Swimming also provides gentle exercise for many different muscle groups. Differences in temperament mean that some children will be bold in their approach to water, others cautious: let them choose their own pace. First swimming lessons should be playful and full of games; learning to float and kick in the water comes first, leave the strokes till later. All children need supervision all the time they are in the water, since difficulties can develop very suddenly.

Riding a bicycle

Children can often pedal at three, and are usually adept on their tricycles by five. The transition to a two-wheeler depends partly on the child's aptitude in balancing and partly on the encouragement given. Many children see riding a bicycle as a mark of maturity and independence. Six to seven year olds usually learn without undue difficulty – although again it must be acknowledged that some children never learn.

Dancing and gymnastics

The rhythmic properties of music appeal strongly to most young children, who love to throw themselves around expressively. Most will have more understanding and enjoyment of dance if they are allowed to move in response to music with relatively light direction, but ballet and tap-dancing classes, provided formal activities are not introduced too early, can be great fun. More serious training usually begins about seven or eight, though the very talented child may benefit from formal training earlier than this.

Children can enjoy gymnastics from an early age, and many sports centres organize toddler gym sessions, in which children can tumble about under supervision, trying out their capacities. However, training in formal gymnastics – handstands, cartwheels and so on – indeed any classes in which the teacher's intentions take precedence over the child's self-limiting preferences, should not begin until four at the earliest.

Team games

Team games don't really come into their own until later age groups. But three to seven year olds need other children to play with, and they will cooperate in team games even though these are slightly beyond their physical ability and concentration. Provided that the game is seen as a vehicle for enjoyment and exercise, rather than a desperate struggle for victory, it can be a really good experience.

Whatever the game being played, careful supervision is of great importance – without the facilitating control of an adult, it can all degenerate into an unrewarding muddle. The supervising adult will help most by providing firm but gentle guidance plus lots of praise and encouragement. It is perfectly possible to conduct such a game with no criticism of the players' ability. Sadly, one sometimes sees a grown man heaping abuse on a six year old who lacks skills: this is appalling behaviour on the part of the adult, terrifying for the child and any other children who are involved. Such an approach can do nothing but harm.

Seven year olds will enjoy taking part in team games, and can learn a lot from playing with older children.

Fine motor skills

Different cultures prize different skills: the form taken by a child's developing dexterity and hand-eye coordination will be strongly influenced by the particular skills which are valued by the society into which he is born.

The differences in children's ability to use eating implements provide an everyday example of the effect of cultural influences. In countries where knives and forks are commonly used it is rare that both are employed skilfully before the age of five; give these children chopsticks and they would be lost. Yet in China the average age at which chopsticks are used effectively is two and a half. There is no evidence that Chinese children have greater innate dexterity; it is simply that from an early age they are given a great deal of practice and encouragement in using chopsticks.

Drawing and writing, which occupy such an important position in literate societies, call for precise muscular control allied with increasingly complicated forms of intention and understanding. Quite young children often like to try copying tasks, which help improve hand-eye coordination. It is important to remember, though, that a child's ability to copy, like his ability to draw, improves with age, and it is no use trying to rush the process. A three year old's copying will improve with practice, but no amount of practice will make him copy as accurately as a five year old, because the nervous system cannot be pushed into premature development. Between five and seven, most children reach a stage where they can make a good attempt at producing a recognizable copy of an image which they perceive. Teachers appropriately take advantage of this development in teaching children to write.

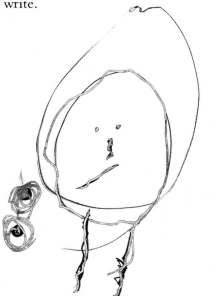 

Drawing

As babies and toddlers, children have a perception of the way specific things and people look, but they do not yet have the muscular control to express their perceptions in their drawing. By three they are beginning to bring together their perceptions and their ability to make representations. There is still a long way to go. For example, many three year olds clearly have a perception of the differences between a square, a triangle and a rectangle; they can copy the shapes using matchsticks. But they still lack the skill to draw them on paper.

Still, by three, most children who have been given an opportunity to scribble will be able to make an approximately circular mark on a piece of paper. At this age it will only rarely be more than a vague round and round movement. But by the time he is four or five a child will be able to produce a well-proportioned circle using a single line.

Most four year olds can draw a crude cross, and by four some children are also beginning to draw squares, though others won't be able to manage a good square until they are five or more. Diagonal lines are much harder to copy than horizontal or vertical ones, and children usually find triangles rather difficult. They can sometimes draw a crude triangle at five, but won't achieve an accurate one for a couple of years more. Similarly, a five year old can attempt a diamond shape, but we should not expect precision under the age of seven or eight.

By three, children's drawings are beginning to include recognizable representations of people and things. Their drawings of people follow a more or less predictable pattern. First they will draw just the head; soon they will add a few squiggles inside the head to represent a face; then legs which come straight from the head. Arms come next, usually sticking out of the head as well. It is not until children are about four that they draw a body to

The three year old's drawing (opposite left) *shows a head with legs sticking out; between four and five children add bodies, hands and fingers* (opposite right). *Later the faces become more expressive and the figures are given hair and clothes* (below).

287

A five year old's drawing of a house (above) *makes use of the geometrical shapes he has learned about. The six year old's drawing* (opposite) *shows an attempt to represent two sides of the house, and the branches of the tree.*

go with the arms and legs, and details like hair and ears come later. No one quite knows why children leave the body out in the way they do; a child can point to his own tummy, for example, long before he can draw it. It is sometimes suggested that children don't draw bodies because when they look down at themselves they can see their arms and legs, but the trunk is not so clear. This is not really convincing when one reflects that children are perfectly capable of observing someone else.

Drawings of houses and outdoor scenes follow a pattern as well. Early pictures, done before the child is five, seem at first to contain unrelated marks which float all over the page but on a second look an attempt to balance the picture may become evident. By the time the child is five and a half these marks begin to show up as houses, people and other parts of a whole picture. Circles, triangles and squares make up a large part; the sun is a circle and the square becomes home. Various triangular shapes may represent people, windows, animals, clouds and other features. Between five and seven they will begin to show in their drawings that they have a notion of the inside of an object, and an understanding that a thing has a front, back and sides.

Despite observable similarities, there is a great deal of individual variation in children's styles of drawing. Some like to splash colour all over the page, others prefer small, neat shapes in the bottom part of the sheet only. They can be highly original.

288

Writing

Discovering that writing is different from drawing is a lengthy process for children, and they need to encounter many examples of writing in use before they can really grasp the idea. Eleanor Gibson, an American psychologist, has said that children need to learn that:

- writing is not making pictures

- writing is linear (horizontal or vertical) and directional

- each letter is different

- writing is composed of more than one letter

- the letters may be joined together

- the same shapes come up again and again, since the number of letters is limited

Often, in its earliest stages, writing grows out of children's drawing. In the course of experimenting they find themselves making curly loops which become a way of travelling across the paper. The connecting loops grow into a spiral, becoming smaller as control is refined.

Most children begin to write letters and numbers between four and six, sometimes earlier. At first they tend to spread them all over the page and may enjoy them as patterns rather than anything meaningful. A child may be able to write his first name by five, or it may take him another year to manage this. At this stage letters usually range from 12 mm/½ inch to 5 cm/ 2 inches in height and are rarely all the same size.

289

In early writing (above) the letters are large and tend to spread over the page. A year or so later (right) the letters are much smaller and more uniform.

on sunday I went to my kung fu lessons I gave my friend paul a kung fu kick I said sorry but he said thats all right you where only practicing that was in the morning. In the afternoon me and peter went out

At six or seven letters and numbers are aligned horizontally, and have got smaller – they will probably now be about 6 mm/¼ inch. Between six and seven most children learn to write their last name, as well as the first, and may perhaps begin to write very simple stories.

What parents can do

Writing is a complex phenomenon, and learning to write takes a long time. As parents you can help prepare your child for writing, in various ways, from very early on.

You are helping him when you encourage him in activities such as fitting, sorting, painting, doing puzzles, which may seem to have nothing to do with writing, but which all help to develop the muscle control that is essential.

At the same time, you can make sure he has plenty of opportunities to become familiar with all kinds of writing. You can help him to an awareness of letters and writing by providing lots of examples of things written for different purposes: shopping lists, notes to people, letters, recipes, are all opportunities to share writing with children. Provide plenty of stimulation for writing – writing about pictures he has painted, making greetings cards, writing letters or lists. To start with, you can write down what he dictates, demonstrating, by reading them back, that his own words have somehow been stored on the page.

If you want to teach your child to write, rather than just preparing him for writing, you should make sure that, from the start, you show him how to form the letters properly. Otherwise he may have to go back and re-learn later – a much more difficult task than learning from scratch. There are various books available which show how the letters are formed. If you feel unsure in this area, though, it will probably be better to leave actual writing until he goes to school.

When he does begin to write, allow him to use whatever grip is comfortable for him. The most common grip, with the pencil held between thumb and first finger and supported by the other fingers, is fine for most people, but individuality should be respected here. It is even more important that you should not force or even encourage him to use one hand rather than the other to write: let him choose. In most children it will be clear which hand is preferred long before writing becomes an activity in its own right (see page 122). If your child is left-handed you can encourage him to tilt the page so that the left-hand top corner is higher than the right; he will then be able to write without covering up what he has just done.

The clumsy child

All children are clumsy at some time in their lives. Even a ballerina had to learn to walk once, and must have fallen over in the process, like everyone else. But while most children, with practice, achieve coordination, some just seem to go on being awkward. They have persistent difficulty in catching a ball, doing up shoelaces, riding a bike, controlling a pencil. Poorly coordinated children often come in for a lot of criticism from impatient adults: 'butter fingers', 'always tripping over your own feet', 'lazy', and so on. They often learn that the only way of avoiding their difficulties is to get out of attempting such tasks at all.

In this context we are not discussing children with a diagnosed disability, rather we refer to one end of a continuum, with well-coordinated children at the other end. Some authorities prefer not to use the word 'clumsy', arguing that it is too vague to have any scientific meaning. They would rather talk of children with perceptual-motor problems, or coordination problems, or to describe children in terms of difficulties in certain specific areas – using a knife and fork, for example. We use 'clumsy' in this section because it is readily understood: in this instance (as is quite frequently the case) the more scientifically acceptable terms do not convey the meaning so clearly.

Clumsy children easily get to feel inferior – and their peers tend to see them as inferior, too. They cannot hide their problem; everyone knows about it. And the older children get, the more they are asked to be neat and skilful. When they go to school, they may be intimidated by the very idea of attempting writing and drawing; they may even have trouble walking around a classroom without knocking things over. It is desperately frustrating for a child to feel that he is not able to carry out what he is asked to do, and is not living up to expectations.

What parents can do

The best cure for clumsiness is a great deal of practice, but this is just what clumsy children shun, because they are so bad at the tasks they have to repeat. Helping a clumsy child involves psychological care as well as attention to physical control: if your child is inclined to be clumsy it will take all your sensitivity as a parent, plus, probably, a certain amount of ingenuity, to persuade him to do the practising he needs. The more you can present activities as a game the better. And the more they are carried out in an atmosphere of success the more likely he is to succeed – so it is equally important to build his self-confidence generally, for example by often asking for something that is known to be well within his capacity.

But just practising is not enough: the practice has to be of the right sort. Motor skills are complex wholes involving many components, and it is often difficult to determine just what a child is doing wrong. Catching a ball, for example, involves positioning the body, tracking visually, moving arms and cupping hands, then varying the position of the hands and the pressure of the fingers once the ball has arrived. Mindless general practice – practice, in fact, in doing something the wrong way – will only make matters worse. If you are keen to help it is best to seek advice from an occupational therapist or from someone else who is qualified to analyze your child's movements, and who can make specific suggestions about what is needed. Your doctor should be able to refer you for this kind of advice. If expert help is not available, try yourself to work out in detail what is needed, so that you can teach strategies to overcome specific problems. If your child has difficulty in dressing himself, for example, try to detect just what it is that is so difficult, by analyzing the components of the process.

Once you feel you have a clear picture, you can help by giving practice at the appropriate level, always trying to ensure that you and your child are partners in the enterprise. Break down complex tasks into small steps that seem manageable, and keep training and practice sessions really short – just a few minutes on each task. Don't hurry the child, let him find his own speed. Praise him when he gets things right, but don't go over the top, or he might feel irritated, or humiliated, at having praise lavished on him for something other children seem to do easily. It is better to keep it all fairly matter-of-fact, as if success in this area is just what you expect of him.

Thinking and Understanding

Four year olds love to sort shapes and sizes and through this hands-on experience they begin to learn basic mathematical concepts.

During the years from three to seven a child's powers of thought are developing rapidly. His perceptions become more acute, his attention, his memory and his imagination come increasingly under his control, his reasoning capacity expands. All this opens up new horizons for learning, for personal and social development and for creativity.

Throughout this age group children continue to learn best by doing. For example, it is usually through hands-on experience – by taking things in play and adding them together, separating them, sorting them into groups

Is he hyperactive?

Each generation has its fashions, in child psychology as much as in every-thing else. A preoccupation in some countries in the last few years has been the study of a group of children who are spoken of colloquially as fidgets, always on the go, all over the place, and in psychological language may be described as hyperactive, overactive, or suffering from attention deficit disorder.

The three components of hyperactivity, or attention deficit disorder, as generally defined, are:

- a high activity level

- an extremely limited attention span

- impulsiveness

It can be difficult for parents to determine whether a child is simply of an active temperament, but with an activity level that falls within the normal range, or has an activity/attention problem. Expectations play a part here. If the first child in a family was particularly quiet, for example, parents may be so shocked by the impact of a normally active second child that they decide he must be hyperactive. By way of contrast, families who are active, outgoing and boisterous may find a hyperactive child blends in with family life, and the problem may go unrecognized until the child starts school.

However, if a child, at four or over, exhibits many of the following char-acteristics, the likelihood is that his attention span is short, that he is rather difficult to manage, and that you and he could probably do with some help. It might be worth consulting your doctor if you find that your child:

- flits rapidly from one activity to another

- often finds it difficult to listen to a story for even two or three minutes

- rarely manages to sit through a meal

- tends to run about and climb on things excessively

- fidgets much of the time

- moves about excessively during sleep

One of the most confusing aspects of hyperactivity is that it can be situation specific – that is, a child may be hyperactive in one situation but not in another. This can be puzzling, and annoying, for parents, who may think that if a child can be still in one place at one time then he could be still all the time if he wanted to. To argue in this way, though, is to misunderstand the condition. Few if any children are driven to be hyperactive all the time – any more than a smoker, no matter how addicted to nicotine, smokes con-tinuously. Hyperactivity is a name for a characteristic behaviour pattern, not an all-or-nothing condition.

This six year old remembered his holiday so well that he was able to draw the ferry he travelled on, and include the correct number of decks and funnels.

are a few which are simple enough for six and seven year olds – some are used by children even younger.

A form of rehearsing, that is repeating a word or phrase over and over, has been observed in children as young as two – for example, when they have hidden an object, and want to remember the hiding place. They seem to be doing just what adults do when they want to remember something – a name or a list, for instance. In experimental conditions, those children who talked to themselves about where they had hidden an object were able to remember the hiding place more easily, even after a distraction such as playing with something else. It seems that their memories were reinforced by the rehearsing. The best way to encourage your child to use this strategy is to demonstrate it yourself, so that he has your example to follow.

Clustering objects into categories begins at this age and is a good example of the way a knowledge base helps memory. Children who have knowledge of categories ('fruit', as opposed to 'vegetables', for example), will automatically arrange lists of objects that they are asked to remember in clusters which they are familiar with. The more of these categories a child can draw on with ease, the better his memory will be able to function.

Short-term memory and learning

Assessment of short-term memory is usually carried out by asking children to repeat a string of numbers, or words, or word-like sounds. It has been found that at three children can often remember three digits, at four to five they can manage four, and by seven many can remember five.

This gradually increasing power of the short-term memory is of the

utmost importance. Parents as well as professionals have long been aware of the significance of the short-term memory in providing some of the building blocks of language development; a recent piece of research indicates that in some areas (particularly the acquisition of vocabulary and the mastering of a crucial stage of reading), it is even more important than had previously been thought.

As part of this research, children's memory for speech sounds (their phonological memory) was tested by having them repeat non-words, that is, sound combinations of varying length and phonological complexity which resembled words but which were not actually part of the English vocabulary. The children tested were aged four, and none had yet learned to read.

In almost every case there was a direct association between a child's short-term phonological memory and his vocabulary. The most likely explanation seems to be that a key to building vocabulary is the ability to construct a representation of the sound of a word which will remain stable long enough for it to be transferred to the long-term store.

In follow-up work it was found that the efficiency of children's short-term phonological memory was a remarkably accurate predictor of the ease, or otherwise, with which they later learned to read. This aspect of the memory was particularly important in mastery of letter-sound associations (the idea that certain shapes make certain sounds). Children have to learn to link letters with sounds at an early stage of reading. If they fail to acquire this ability, they encounter great difficulties in learning further reading skills.

Powerful confirmation of the importance of short-term phonological memory came from another study, this time of children aged between six and eight, of average ability in non-verbal areas, but suffering from language disorders sufficiently severe to restrict their skills in this area to a level normally found among children eighteen to twenty-four months younger. These children had what the investigators described as dramatic memory deficits: their short-term memories were at a level of development approximately four years younger than their chronological age.

Imagination

At three and four children are beginning to imagine and fantasize in a more controlled way than hitherto. They can be in one place and visualize another, they can live again something that happened in the past, and fantasize about the future. A four year old staring into space, conjuring up the image of his favourite television character, has taken a great leap forward. As a toddler he could put bricks into a box – now he can imagine himself doing it.

Investigative play is an important part of young children's imaginative and conceptual growth. Playing alone can be just as satisfying as playing with others.

Throughout this age group, the power of imagination continues to deepen, expand and become richer. By seven the child will be much more flexible in his thinking, and have a far greater awareness of what is around him, than would have seemed possible a few years earlier. Separating reality from fantasy is a necessary step towards creating a valid picture of the world.

Fantasy

Fantasy or make-believe play is the first sign of imagination at work – and we can see the glimmerings of this as early as a child's second year (see page 163). From two onwards children's make-believe play develops rapidly, and by four it may be quite creative and involve several elements – dressing up and going out to a pretend tea party, perhaps, or building an airport and making planes for it. If children can imagine something, they can play it, transforming their surroundings through the power of their minds: a stone can become a poisoned cake, a piece of rag a sumptuous cloak. A garden shed can be transmuted into a magic castle, a tree house can turn into a ship, the space under the stairs become a witch's den.

When children reach school age fantasy play becomes more complex and sustained. Boxes of clothes and props are transformed into costumes for family dramas that make soap operas look tame by comparison. Their shops are intricate establishments with cash registers, advertisements and customers, music is played by bands with as many instruments as there are children, ballets are created and danced. Children begin to create marvellous imaginative structures with bricks, construction toys, clay and paint.

From the age of about six onwards, private daydreaming may also come to play an important part in a child's life. Sometimes daydreaming gradually replaces overt make-believe play – or the two may continue, sometimes parallel, sometimes interweaving.

Through fantasy play and daydreaming, children win the freedom of their own imagination: they become more creative in their thinking, and tend to be bolder in attempting to work out solutions to problems on their own. More subtly, fantasy can allow an acting out of emotion by gradual degrees. It seems that if children can play through an experience that has been, or is, emotionally overwhelming, they will be able, gradually, to bring their emotions to a bearable level.

Fantasies and stories

One of the most touching aspects of young children is their gullibility. You may be charmed when your four year old looks up at you with trusting eyes as you tell him about Santa Claus or the Easter Bunny; but he may also readily believe that he was left on a doorstep, or that he will be turned into a frog if he tells a lie. Children can become anything and be anywhere at a moment's notice. To pretend to be a beautiful princess is to be one. To dream about being eaten by a goblin is to be consumed and terrified –

perhaps for several nights. The line between reality and imagination is a thin one and children are constantly deepening their understanding of what exists and what is fantasy.

Children need the adults in their lives to be both honest and sensitive in this area. This can be a tricky business for parents. Some feel uncomfortable about any deviation from the truth: even stories of Santa Claus are avoided. A rule of thumb for parents who feel ambivalent is that it does no harm to maintain a fiction like Santa Claus as long as it affords pleasure to the child, provided that it does not involve responding to his questions with a lie. Once children begin to ask searching questions which indicate that they are suspicious it is wiser gently to tell the truth.

Parents need to be sensitive to the kinds of stories their children like to hear, and those that frighten them. It can be difficult to predict what they are going to find frightening. Sometimes, a child will have a nightmare after what seems to a parent a totally innocuous little fairy tale: there can be a world of difference between the story the parent tells and the form to which it is transmuted by the child's imagination. Children who seem frequently to be disturbed by what they imagine can be helped through discussion. This is one of several reasons why it is a good idea for parents to watch television with children: any potentially worrying aspects of a programme can then be talked through afterwards.

Some children enjoy being frightened, especially when they can frighten

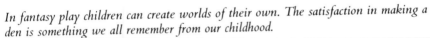
In fantasy play children can create worlds of their own. The satisfaction in making a den is something we all remember from our childhood.

themselves and control the emotions. To this end they will put on masks or costumes or watch scary cartoons and films. This can provide some innocent fun. However, if a mixed group of children is involved, and particularly if some of the children are very young, parents need to be wary. What to some of the children is just a game may be very frightening to others.

A lie or a made-up story?

Parents often find it worrying if their children tell them something that is untrue. They may even imagine that these are the first manifestations of a deceitful nature (parents can exaggerate quite as much as children).

It may be helpful, first of all, to try to distinguish between lies and fantasies. Lying involves deliberately deceiving another person, usually so that the person telling the lie may gain in some way. A fantasy, on the other hand, is essentially within oneself. It may be shared with others, but that is incidental.

There is no reason to be at all concerned if a three or four year old sometimes comes up with stories of a lion in the kitchen or a spaceship on the roof; stories like this, at this age, are a manifestation of a rich and healthy fantasy life. However, if a child always seems to be telling fantastic stories, or if such stories persist beyond the time when everyone has openly acknowledged that they are untrue, it is worth giving some thought to why this should be so. If all the stories are a form of boasting, a warning light may shine. Most children embellish the occasional story, but if a child habitually exaggerates his exploits or his possessions, it can be an indication that his self-esteem is low; this is a way of making himself feel bigger and stronger. It is not unusual for children to start telling a lot of exaggerated stories at about the time they start school – perhaps because they are feeling rather small and uncertain of themselves in the new environment.

If you suspect that your child may be showing off as a cover for feelings of inferiority, it will probably be better if you avoid engaging battle – intervening with the truth as each fiction is embellished; concentrate, rather, on building his self-esteem. Give more attention and approval to his real strengths and abilities, while paying little heed to the fancy stories.

If, however, you know that the child is actually telling a lie, rather than indulging in a comfortable fantasy, you should make it clear to him that you know what he is saying is not true. It is worth bearing in mind that many children of this age believe that their parents know everything that goes on. When they lie to you, they believe that you know the truth, and that they will be caught out. They may find it very disturbing if (apparently or in reality) you believe them after all.

Your best course will be to acknowledge the lie, stating clearly that you know what the truth is, and that you don't like lying. Your child can then feel confident and secure that his parents are aware of reality. When children are trying to sort out fact from fiction, an activity which takes up a large part of childhood, they need to feel that their parents are a constant, reliable source of information.

Constructing a model of the world

Through perceiving, attending, remembering and imagining, the child begins to develop a mental model of the world and the people in it. Communication helps him to refine the concepts that make up this model: he communicates his ideas to other people, who correct, modify or affirm his viewpoint. Parents have an important part to play here, since most young children turn first to their parents for verification of their ideas. The more sensitive they – and others who act as teachers – can be to a child's mood, interest and level of understanding, the more effective these communications will be.

Concepts that are understood in simple terms to begin with go on to develop greater complexity. A child's earliest concept of work may be only whatever his father or mother does for a living, but later it will include an ever-widening range of occupations. In the same way a child's first concept of a car may comprise just four wheels and a body; later it will develop to include an understanding that there is an engine; later still will come increasingly fine discriminations of steering, brakes, and so forth. A child may develop extremely refined concepts, in some areas, at a very early age – some four year olds can identify not only makes but also models of cars. Whether or not a child develops such a sophisticated concept of a car will be influenced by his ability to focus on and pay attention to details, his memory, his interest in cars, his exposure to cars and how effectively he is taught about cars (in this case, probably through informal exchanges with adults or older children).

Children's growing understanding of the complicated topic of money provides one example of the way they develop concepts. A child's earliest notion of money will be a simple extrapolation from what he sees around him; this is then modified by teaching and experience. It is not uncommon for a child of three or four to believe that his daddy has an endless supply of money in his pocket – or that if this runs out he can always find more in his wallet. At this age, few children would exchange a ten pence piece for a pound, as most assume that the larger the coin, the greater the value. At six and seven most children know the values of different coins and are beginning to recognize that some objects have more value than others. However, they tend to believe that shops and banks give out money freely as it is needed. After all, they see money being handed over as change, or in return for pieces of paper – even coming out of a hole in the wall! It is only after many experiences and much discussion that children can begin to understand ideas such as those of profit, budgeting, or, for that matter, saving up for something you want.

Children in this age group do not usually understand complex processes such as how food is distributed or goods are made. They do not realize that food goes from the farmer to the shop or that goods are made in factories – the goods sold in stores have always been there or are made by the

Playing shops is one way of discovering what it is like to be a shopkeeper. Using pretend money is a step on the way to learning about the real thing.

shopkeepers. Egocentricity comes in here too. The goods in shops are there for them; the bus driver who takes them to school does it because they need a lift – even after they have some understanding that people are paid for working, children often cannot conceive of anyone being paid for the type of job that is a direct service to them.

One way children do a lot of learning about life is through their memory of past events, from which they derive scripts, mental notes about what is going to happen and how people are expected to behave (see page 300). Take the experience of going to school each day: a child may remember that he has his breakfast, puts on his coat, remembers his lunch, walks to the bus stop, gets in the bus and goes to school. Knowing this script, he doesn't have to think about every detail and as he grows older he will learn to carry out most of it automatically, leaving his mind free to plan his school day, study for a test or remember his homework. A child who knows the school routine or school script has more time to concentrate on the new information he is learning. By the same token, a child who does not know a script has to spend a lot of time paying close attention to the details of the new experience. (Once a child knows the script, he can find any disruption to his routine very disconcerting. Asking him to eat his breakfast before he gets dressed or to brush his teeth before he combs his hair may cause protests.)

So this is where we get our milk! Visiting a farm can help a young child make the connection between what is in the shops and where it comes from.

Another function of the script is to provide a framework within which children can learn more abstract concepts. The abstract concept of time, for instance, develops out of a child's various scripts – for going to school, celebrating Christmas, having birthdays, and the rest. We can teach a child how to say the days of the week, read a clock, count the days to his birthday; we cannot teach him what it means for his birthday to be twelve months away, until he has experienced several birthdays and the gaps between.

By about three many children begin to see that time continues. There are events that happened in the past which they remember, and events in the future that they can anticipate. Thinking about time as past, present and future is a new and exciting development. They are on their way to understanding the complex concept of time.

But a child may have the script for going to school and coming home, he may know that he will be picked up when the big hand is on 12 and the little hand on 3, and still have very little idea of how long it will be before three o'clock comes. If it is a good day at school three o'clock may surprise a child by coming early. If it is a bad day and all the other children are being picked up, the time from three to two minutes past can be an eternity. We never lose a subjective sense of time entirely; at any age, happy times seem to go by quickly, while unpleasant events take for ever.

Reproduction and birth

Children's views of sex, reproduction and birth stem partly from what they observe or imagine for themselves, partly from what they are directly taught.

At about four, most children have a general idea that a special relationship exists between their mother and their father, but, even at seven, few have much idea that this is a sexual relationship. Researchers have divided the views of this age group on reproduction into four categories. First there is what has been called the geographical view: a baby is inside the mother and simply emerges at an appropriate time.

Then there is the manufacturing idea: the baby is made outside the mother and put into her by non-sexual means.

The agricultural view is that babies are fully formed in miniature in either the sperm or the egg.

Finally, some children are realists: they have a reasonably accurate idea of what actually happens.

It is generally best, when children first ask questions about where babies come from, to give the simplest possible explanation (see page 239). If you can do this in a positive, relaxed way, so that they feel comfortable about coming back to you with further questions, you can put right any misunderstandings, and add details little by little. What sometimes happens is that embarrassed parents find themselves embellishing a story that wasn't true in the first place, which doesn't help anyone.

The seven year old does, though, have far more understanding of the objective passage of time than he had at four or five. He likes to participate in planning his day and will ask in September how long it is till Christmas. He may even think in terms of years – 'how many years till . . . ?' Though at six children often like to think about the past, to hear about what they did as babies and tales of their parents' childhoods, a sense of the sequence of history rarely comes before seven – indeed, many adults never make any discrimination much more subtle than that between the present, the recent past and the more distant past.

Obviously, children need experiences to learn scripts, so the scripts they learn are by their nature culturally determined. Children who grow up in the San Blas Islands will not be adept at distinguishing one kind of car from another. Children who are born and brought up on a farm will have a much clearer understanding of where food comes from than city children who only see food in shops. A child who sees drums made in the community and played in ceremonies will have a concept of 'drum' that is very different from the concept developed by a child who uses a drum in playgroup or nursery school.

The way a child constructs a model of the world is a complex process, involving biological, social and behavioural changes, nature and nurture. No theorist or child psychologist has so far managed to give us a complete picture of how the child does it, and all we have been able to do here is to touch on some of the relevant components. In the pages that follow we describe in rather more detail some aspects of how children build up one particular concept: that of number.

An old person

I know an old person he is 166 years old. people have white hair or grey hair. and old people have lumpy backs. and old pepel have walking sticks and crooked backs. If there were no walking sticks they would fall over

This six year old's writing shows that he is beginning to have a sense of the passage of time – and of what it means to be old!

Learning about numbers

For many years, under the influence of Piaget, the general opinion among teachers was that children below the age of six or seven were incapable of understanding mathematics. Children who learned to count were seen as performing, repeating parrot fashion the names of numbers with no real understanding of the concepts behind the names.

It is true that many children who can count do not necessarily understand the nature of the numbers they are repeating. However, recent studies have shown that some can indeed grasp the nature of number even before the age of five.

Rachel Graham in the United States, and Martin Hughes in Britain, have used games to show that three to five year olds can understand the idea of addition and subtraction, providing that the numbers involved are below four, that the sums are done with material objects such as sweets or bricks, and, most importantly, that everyday language is used rather than the formal language of mathematics. Ask a four year old how many is two bricks and one brick and there is a good probability that you will receive the correct answer. Ask what two and one make and you will probably be given either no response or a wild guess.

Nevertheless, as Martin Hughes points out, at some point children need to bridge the gap between counting what they can touch and see to counting numbers when they are not related to a concrete object, and even, at a further remove, when they are written down. They also need to recognize when mathematical language is being used and interpret it.

311

The language of mathematics

Children often have trouble understanding and applying the language of mathematics. In the earliest stages they need to understand words like more, less, several and some; then come bigger, biggest, taller, heavier, between, and so on. Many children understand these words when they are asked, for instance, to choose the biggest slice of cake, but have understandable difficulty when asked to write a number that is bigger than 6. Asked to find a number that is between 2 and 4 they may, quite logically, put any number in between the two and feel they have got it right.

Some problems arise because mathematical language includes many words that have double meanings for children. For example, the concepts of putting together, taking away and borrowing, which a child understands in terms of everyday events, may be very difficult to grasp in their mathematical sense.

Children need to translate what they know already into the new language of mathematics. While mathematics is not often spoken in the home, parents do help familiarize children with this special language when they play counting games and rhymes, and when they try to involve the children in discussions which include mathematical language. They can also help children make the transition between concrete and abstract by sometimes presenting them with situations where they need to count but do not have the objects to be counted to hand. In these instances children may spontaneously or with prompting count on their fingers. Fingers can be used to represent either concrete objects or abstract numbers, so they provide a useful link between the concrete and the abstract.

Later, children will have to grapple with written symbols. Many five or six year olds will write sums like *5 − 3 = 2* or *5 + 3 = 8* and may produce page after page of them with correct answers. But their comprehension of these signs can be fragile: often children do not realize that they have universal applicability, they think they are only for workbooks. In other words, they have learned + and − as a trick rather than with true understanding. However, by creating a connection between concrete objects and mathematical symbols it is possible to teach children even as young as four what these symbols mean.

Drawings can provide a bridge between concrete and abstract notions of number.

The symbols of mathematics

A useful way to help young children understand mathematical symbols has been demonstrated by the British psychologist Martin Hughes. Working with four year olds, he used imitation sweets and a set of identical tins. The children watched while he put the sweets in the tins and they then cooperated in putting a plastic number on each tin to indicate how many sweets were inside.

Once the children had the idea that in each case the number on the outside corresponded to how many sweets there were in the tin, Hughes added or subtracted one sweet, putting a sign ($+1$ or -1) on the box to show what he had done. He then asked the children how many sweets were in the tin. While not all the children got all the answers right, the proportion of correct answers was high enough to provide convincing evidence that this method of linking symbols with concrete objects had been effective in teaching the meaning of the symbols.

What parents can do

There is a lot parents can do, in the course of everyday life, to provide preschool children, and young schoolchildren, with the experiences they need as a basis for learning mathematics.

• Give your child experience in comparing amounts – both of things which can be counted, like cars and bricks, and things which can't, like sand and water.

• Provide lots of opportunities to count things, giving him a hand, when necessary, to rearrange objects so that they are easier to compare and count. Ask him to bring you numbers of things – two cups, five spoons; this will help to make counting automatic.

• Simple exercises such as setting the table will help a child understand the concept of one to one correspondence. Don't worry if he gets the order of the numbers wrong as long as he gives one number to each object.

• Get him to select a certain number of one category and an equal number in another category and put them together: 'Take out seven forks and seven spoons and give one to each person who is coming for dinner'; 'Choose five friends to invite to your party and get each of them a party hat.'

Children are encouraged to recognize and continue sequences of patterns – an exercise which helps them to understand numbers and grouping.

- He also needs to learn how to create numbers for himself – so ask him, for example, to draw three of something, or five.

- Ask questions which stimulate him to pay attention to differences and similarities. Elephants and cats are animals, for example – but what different animals. Pineapples and bananas may not look much alike, but they are both fruits.

- Find opportunities to sort and match – encouraging your child to match the shapes of biscuits, for example, or to sort his toy cars.

- When you use objects in different ways, discuss that too, pointing out, for example, that a knife remains a knife whether it is being used for cutting or spreading.

- Give children opportunities to find out and investigate things according to their characteristics. See if they can hold two characteristics in their minds at once (difficult for a three year old) – 'Can you point to the round, prickly animal?'

- Children also need to be aware of what *doesn't* belong in a category. Try putting something on the dinner table that doesn't normally belong there, and ask your child if he knows what it is. He needs opportunities, too, to experience 'an empty set', a category which has nothing in it. You can ask him, for example, to put all the two-holed buttons in this dish and the four-holed buttons in this one, and buttons with five holes here – when there are no available five-holed buttons.

- Give your child the opportunity to make comparisons – the baby is smaller than I am, but I am smaller than my older sister.

- Ask him to arrange things in order and describe how he has arranged them.

- Give him the opportunity to fit one ordered set of objects with another – to put lids on jars, for example.

- Ask him to order things according to more abstract concepts – such as sweetness, or preference.

Once your child has started school, you can help by reinforcing what is being taught. For example, the concept of division can be reinforced at home when a cake is cut, or sweets are handed round.

If he has some difficulty in understanding a mathematical problem, you may be able to help by showing him how to break it down in terms of basic concepts. If he understands the components of a problem, he will be better able to think it through. Children often need to be reminded about the knowledge they have already which they can bring to a new problem. You may also need to go back over concepts that have already been learned to make sure that he really understands them. For example, a child may know the same and different, but become confused when he is given an outline picture and asked to colour in three objects which are the same. It may be that he has only had experience of matching concrete objects and is not used to two-dimensional representations.

When he is going through the transition to school mathematics, give him opportunities to symbolize the way things are added together using his own methods of drawing. Ask him how he would make a drawing that shows there is nothing in a box, for example. Find opportunities to get him to explain how he has worked out mathematical problems – asking questions like 'How did you know we needed three more glasses on the table?' or 'How can we find out how much money we will need at the shop?' Being able to tell a mathematical story or give an explanation in mathematical terms will help him understand the kinds of problems he will meet in school and will help him develop confidence. It is not providing an accurate answer that is important in these situations, but being able to give a coherent explanation. Like someone learning a foreign language, the child embarking on the language of mathematics needs to enjoy the opportunity to speak without constantly having his grammar or his vocabulary corrected.

Sorting his toy cars gives this child a chance to compare the differences and similarities between them. He may already be able to distinguish the cars according to make, model and type.

Language

Children's language develops alongside their powers of thought. By the age of three most children have acquired the basics of language: they have a large and ever-growing vocabulary to refer to their experience of life and they take great satisfaction in using the words they know to make statements, questions and demands. But their utterances are usually short and simple in form and factual in content. In the years between three and seven, as their experience of the world increases and their thinking becomes more sophisticated, the content of what they say becomes increasingly complex, coming to encompass ideas of future and past time, logic, probability, might-have-been, and other complexities. At the same time their language becomes capable of more subtlety and variety, constantly approaching closer to the full adult range of pronunciation, grammar, syntax and vocabulary. It is also during these years that written language joins spoken language as a central element in the lives of children in literate societies, as they start to acquire the skills of reading and writing.

Again, at some time during this period, children begin to develop the conscious ability to think about language. They notice and become interested in commenting on similarities and differences between words and ways of saying things – an interest which is often embodied in a delight in verbal jokes, riddles and puns.

How language progresses

If we compare the kind of utterances we expect a voluble three year old to produce and understand with the sort of things that seven year olds can handle, it becomes clear how much progress is made during this period. But we must remember that children are on a developmental timetable. No child acquires the full adult forms of language at once; immature forms and babyish pronunciation and constructions persist for varying lengths of time, disappearing gradually as the child reaches new levels of maturity. For this reason, it is best to take a relaxed attitude to language teaching. Usually, children will eventually outgrow linguistic errors; but every parent needs to be aware that no amount of correction will make children talk in a more grown-up way before they have passed through the necessary preliminary stages.

316

Seizing the opportunity for a conversation, two little girls chat together with enormous expression and vivacity.

Vocabulary

By the time they are three most children are doing as much talking as adults, if not more. They don't even need another person there to talk to, a small child on his own will chat away happily to himself.

Though averages can be as deceptive in this as in other contexts, it is interesting to note that the average three year old has a spoken vocabulary of about 1,000 words, and a five year old has about 5,000. At six, children understand between 8,000 and 14,000 words.

All children in this age group can understand more words than they can say, but the difference between active and passive vocabulary is not always constant from one child to another. Some children can hear the difference between a word as they say it and as it is spoken by an adult, and they may be reluctant to utter something they cannot pronounce correctly. Others burble away merrily, apparently quite oblivious of their mistakes, bringing new words (or approximate forms of them) into their speech without hesitation or self-consciousness.

The development of vocabulary in the years up to seven involves not only a great increase in the sheer quantity of words known to the child, but also an increasing precision in the use of words. For a toddler, 'cup' will do for anything he drinks from; an older child will distinguish between cup, glass, mug, and so on. As they progress, children need to learn innumerable peculiarities of their own language. Why, for example, should the opposite of 'light' be 'heavy' one minute, 'dark' the next?

Pronunciation

At three, pronunciation is usually still a good deal less than perfect. In most languages some consonants are more difficult to articulate than others; in English, for example, the consonant sounds at the beginning of 'this' and 'thin' are often acquired quite late. So are the consonant clusters so plentiful in English, such as *str* in 'strong', *mpt* in 'thumped', and many others. For an English-speaking child the process of mastering all the usual consonant clusters is often a long one, but most children have more or less managed it by about five.

Another aspect of pronunciation which matters to some parents is accent. In most communities, social and local variations exist in the way different groups pronounce the same words. Most parents who have moved from one part of the country to another will have noticed how the local accent becomes quite natural to their children in a short space of time. Some parents may find this troubling, others accept it completely – but whatever their reaction, once children go to school they almost invariably adopt the way words are pronounced by their contemporaries in addition to – or sometimes instead of – the way they are said at home, if there is a difference between the two.

Grammar and syntax

The most significant area of development in the language of three to seven year olds is in their syntax – that is, the way in which they can organize their words into phrases and sentences. Sentences become longer and more complicated in their structure, and the right forms of words are used in the right places more often.

Although there is no one accepted theory of how children acquire an understanding of the grammatical structure of language, the spurt that takes place in these years in children's competence and interest in more complex language fits with the general developmental picture at this age. Between the ages of five and seven children are looking for rules everywhere: in routines at home and at school, in games, in play, they seem to want to search out the rules that explain what's going on. In the same way they spontaneously use the evidence of the language they hear all around them to work out the underlying regularities that make sense of it all, and start to apply them with increasing virtuosity in their own performance.

pleasant way to facilitate a child's language learning (and the way that most parents adopt most of the time, without thinking twice about it) is to engage in responsive talking with their children, confirming correct expressions with a simple unstressed repetition: 'This apple's a brighter red than that one,' hazards the six year old; 'Yes, brighter than that,' agrees the parent, indicating at the same time 'Yes, you said that right.' The parent can supply by a fuller restatement the right way of saying something that the child isn't yet able to manage: 'Dogs are more friendlier than cats, aren't they?' 'Well, most dogs are friendlier than our cat, I suppose, but I've met cats that are even more friendly than a dog' – or any other combination of casual information and evidence for linguistic learning. Children sometimes get completely bogged down in a first attempt at some complicated or unfamiliar expression; if a sympathetic adult responds with an unobtrusive rephrasing they will get the information they need at the time when they are most receptive to it.

Language problems

Any marked problem with language development will probably have emerged before the child is three, during the period when language is first making its appearance (see pages 231–2). But it is sometimes difficult for parents to recognize relatively mild language delays, because they get so used to their own child's style of speech. It may only be when a child goes to nursery school or playgroup and can be compared with a number of others that his parents realize he is falling behind.

Some teachers of young children are astute at picking up language delays, but others may feel that a child is not paying attention, or may even tell him not to talk 'baby talk', as if he could choose to speak in a more mature way. The need to deal properly with language problems was highlighted by a British study published in 1985 by Jim Stevenson and colleagues. They followed up more than five hundred children between the

This little boy is completely absorbed in his work with the speech therapist.

ages of three and eight, and after taking a number of possibilities into consideration concluded that there was a direct association between mild language problems at three and behaviour difficulties at eight.

Parents who are anxious can consult their family doctor for an opinion, or referral to a speech specialist (see page 234). There may be reason to do so if, at four, a child does not seem to be able to follow a story and comment on what is going to happen next, or if he shows signs of not understanding everyday conversation. Every child turns off sometimes, but a blank look a lot of the time warrants further investigation. Other possible indicators of language delay are, at four: failure to use full sentences; usually getting word order wrong; inability to recount what happened in a story or at an event like a birthday party; noticeable non-fluencies in speech; at five, difficulty in following two- or three-part commands ('Put your coat on and give the book to Jane'); an inability to relate events in a simple sequence.

What parents can do
Parents have an active part to play in the catching-up process. You can help by all the means suggested on page 236, and in the following ways.

• Provide opportunities for games and rhymes, which help a child learn turn-taking and conversation skills.

• Repeat catchy phrases like 'we all fall down' or 'hands and shoulders, knees and toes', which help a child learn about sequence.

• Give directions in short sentences, which allow a child time to identify articles or carry out instructions like 'find your shoes' or 'wash your hands'.

• Provide experience in classifying objects: all the zoo animals can be kept together, or all the things that go with brushing teeth.

• Expand the child's own sentences: if he says, 'This is my car', you can reply 'Yes, it's your car, it's blue and the doors can open and close.'

• Keep choices simple: 'Would you like the apple or the orange?'; 'Do you want the green car or the red one?' This will help the child focus on particular words.

• Do not directly correct wrong grammar: most children are doing the best they can, and it is much more encouraging to provide good examples.

• Never use the inducement of holding back food or toys until your child says the right word or names the object; it will make the situation between you more tense, and the child less likely to say the words consistently.

Reading

For an adult who is used to reading, being in a foreign country where you cannot read the signs gives some hint of what it may feel like to be a child, excluded from access to all information presented in written form: signs, lists, notes, advertisements, newspapers, not to mention books. Reading is essential for participation in our society, and for the independence that children want too.

Families provide the stimulus for most childhood learning and reading is no exception. If older people in the family read books, children imitate them. A child who never sees adults reading for pleasure cannot be expected to learn to read easily or happily. At school, his teachers may be able to impart to him the mechanics of reading – but it is a rare teacher who can stimulate a love of books in a child whose family does not value them.

What reading involves

There are many similarities between learning to talk and learning to read. In both processes a child moves gradually from a passive experience of other people's activity towards active participation and finally to complete independence. You begin by reading to your little baby who curls up on your lap and listens, enjoying hearing your voice in comfort and warmth. Then your toddler begins to keep up his end of the reading, pointing to the pictures, answering simple questions and repeating favourite words. When he picks up a book and stares into it, imitating you reading a story, he is beginning to act like a reader – just as, when a baby babbles, he is beginning to act like a speaker. Over time, he begins to take a more positive part, predicting what will happen next, filling in familiar words, picking out words beginning with familiar letters.

When the first words are spoken each word is like a telegram, containing a huge message. Given the opportunity, children can start to read in the same way. Advertisements, shop signs, street signs, telegraph to them a whole idea, giving them the experience of receiving a message from something written. Gradually children realize that print has a special meaning, a meaning different from pictures, which can be translated into spoken words that they understand.

Pre-reading skills

The physical and intellectual processes underlying reading are complex – but so too are those that underlie learning to talk, and the one can happen as easily and naturally as the other, given the right opportunities.

Before they can begin to read, children need to grasp certain concepts about books and print: that print conveys meaning, that (in English) it reads from left to right in a line and from top to bottom of a page. Letting children play with books, showing them how to turn the pages and how to begin at the beginning will all help develop this awareness. Most toddlers can recognize the covers and text of a book which is for them, and see the difference from a closely-printed grown-up book. Soon, they also come to recognize the patterns of words. Early books begin with large letters and a simple vocabulary: 'look', 'wait', 'stop', 'Sally' have their own shapes which children can remember from one page to the next.

One of the advantages that comes to children who have stories read to them is a ready understanding of the idea of a beginning, middle and end. A child who has often heard 'Once upon a time', and all that follows, begins to know the elements of storytelling and relates easily to the narrative form.

Reading strategies

Some children discover reading for themselves, but most need to be introduced to the range of strategies available for learning to decode print. There are three main strategies, all of which play their part in children's successful reading, though some readers may tend to rely more on one than on others.

The phonetic method

Since words are made up of letters and letter combinations, knowing the sound values represented by the letters enables the reader to decode many words – though not all, particularly in English, which is famous for its non-phonetic spelling. This method enables children to sound out a large number of words which they have not read before, though it does not ensure that they will understand the words in context.

Look and say

Fluent readers take in a whole word at a time, recognizing the overall shape and not waiting to sound out the individual part. Plenty of experience can help children to do this from the outset and enable them to take on board a large set of such word-shapes. The set is constantly added to as they become familiar with words that have started out by being decoded phonetically.

Reading for meaning

If a child has a lively sense of written material as coherent and interesting, he will often be able to make an intelligent guess at parts of a text that he cannot at once interpret – analyzing the text not in segments of words or in whole words but in terms of the sentence or longer passage, using the context to provide clues. Such guesses can then be tested phonetically or by recognizing the word-shape.

Reading at school

In practice, most schools use a combination of the strategies described above in teaching children to read, although there may be a greater reliance on one or other of them. The attitude to books may vary from a total adherence to graded readers in a specific programme, through a mixed use of readers and other books, to a free system where children choose their own books from the classroom shelves. Cooperation and understanding between school and home is much more important in making children feel confident and happy about their efforts and their progress than any particular reading programme that may be followed. Most teachers today welcome any interest that parents show in reading at school, and will gladly enlist your participation, provided that you are prepared to follow the general pattern of their teaching methods, to avoid confusing the child.

Helping your child to read

Most parents feel quite happy about helping their child as he learns to speak – and yet often they are diffident about taking any part when it comes to reading, though the two processes are very similar.

The biggest help that you can give is by showing that you enjoy reading yourself, and by being ready to read with your child whenever you can. Create a warm, supportive atmosphere during story time at home, with plenty of talk about the story you are reading. When your child begins to identify words, keep the focus on meaning rather than spelling. Do not correct every mistake, and give lots of praise when he gets words right.

When he is a little more confident, the following approach can help. Let your child choose a book to read to you, without worrying too much about whether it is above or below his reading level. Sit beside him or with him on your knee, so that you can both see the book. If he hesitates over a word, you simply supply it as a matter of course, without any criticism, and quickly enough to forestall loss of interest. Knowing he will get through the story at a reasonable pace and without too much of a struggle is very encouraging for a beginning reader.

Learning to read is a gradual process. Children often enjoy looking at books together, talking about the pictures and the story.

Problems with reading

Some children learn to read easily – some even seem to teach themselves. Others find the process more difficult. Many who seem to progress rather slowly through the beginning stages later catch up, and become perfectly competent readers. But if a child reaches, say, six and a half or seven, and has had a year or eighteen months of people trying to teach him to read, and still cannot make a start, then warning bells should sound. Parents should not be put off by teachers who say that the child will grow out of the problem, or that there is plenty of time. They may be right; but if they are, nothing will be lost by undertaking a few simple investigations. And if there is an identifiable problem, then the sooner the child can be helped the better.

Auditory perception

A child who has even a small hearing loss is likely to have problems in learning to read, and any child with reading problems should have a hearing test. There are also children who have excellent hearing, but who are nevertheless unable to discriminate between similar sounds, rather as people who are tone-deaf cannot distinguish between notes in music. Confusion between the short vowel sounds 'a' and 'u' is particularly common – some children find it impossible to distinguish between the words 'hat' and 'hut', for instance.

Visual perception

Children must be able to see in order to read print and any child having problems learning to read and identify pictures should have his vision tested. But perfect vision is by no means essential for reading: most partially sighted children can learn to read. Children who, even using their visual aid, have as much as 75 per cent sight deficiency can read as accurately as children with normal sight; the only difference is that they read more slowly. Indeed, short-sighted children often learn to read rather before their contemporaries – perhaps because they are more comfortable with print, which can be brought close to, than running around a playground, or trying to play games that demand efficient distance vision.

Children need not only to see, but also to make sense of what they see. Little children have to learn that a car, for instance, may look different when it is viewed from different angles, but it is still a car. Now, as part of the process of learning to read, they have to be able to grasp that *b*, *d*, *p* and *q* are not just the same letter seen from different angles. Confusion between these letters is quite common in five and six year olds, but usually passes around the age of seven. If it persists much beyond seven or eight, some investigation is in order.

Intelligence

Though, as one might expect, children with a high measured intelligence generally learn to read more easily than those whose measured intelligence is lower, there is nothing like a one to one correspondence between measured intelligence and reading: many children who do not do particularly well on intelligence tests can read quite adequately. If there is serious difficulty, though, an intelligence test may be appropriate.

Language development
Speaking, understanding and reading language all go together. The child who brings a rich vocabulary to the printed page will learn faster because he has a wider fund of words to draw on when the guessing starts. Children confident in using complex phrases and tenses will find their way about a text that much more easily.

Emotional problems
Reading, in the early stages, requires much concentration, persistence and determination. Any kind of emotional disturbance can interfere with all three.

Teaching
Sometimes, the problem does not lie with the child at all, but in the way he has been taught. Teaching can be inadequate for various reasons. Sometimes a teacher is just not very good at teaching reading, or is good for some children but not others. Difficulties can arise if a family has moved often, or there has been a high turnover of staff within a school, so that a child has had a range of different teachers, all using slightly different methods.

Spelling and its difficulties
Spelling, like reading, is a complex activity involving attention and memory as well as perception and thinking. It is evident, though, from the number of people who can read well but are poor spellers, that there are differences in the skills required.

In some languages spelling is almost exclusively phonetic: that is, what is written corresponds more or less consistently with what is pronounced. Other languages, of which English is a prime example, have special rules and exceptions to rules attached to their spelling. About half the words in English cannot be spelled correctly using a purely phonetic method.

Some people rely mainly on retaining a picture of words in their memory – for them words look right or wrong. Others make extensive use of rules such as 'i before e except after c'. Most children can read far more words than they can spell correctly, rather as they understand more than they can say. Even if they use a shape-recognition strategy for reading, children generally use a phonetic strategy when they write, composing the words according to the sounds of their letters: 'I had a grate tim at mi arntis', for example. It is quite common for a child who has written a word resourcefully like this to be unable to read it back again later.

Children of six and seven are just learning to spell, and no one expects

Then we went to my cusons and we had sume Fiyarwek's and we had lost and lost of romen candolls and at the vely end we had to cathren Wheeols and the gloden ran was very priy And We had culod Spuclos and the culod spuclos were green and red and then wentwent home And flopt into bed

Young children tend to spell as they hear. This six year old's version of 'fireworks' seems quite logical to her.

them to spell perfectly. Mistakes of the phonetic variety are an indication that the child is learning the value of letters. However, as we discuss below in the section on dyslexia, bizarre spelling is a cause for concern.

Helping children with reading and spelling problems

The first step to take is to ensure that hearing and vision are functioning well. Next comes a careful analysis of the errors the child makes: this should be carried out by a teacher or psychologist who has been trained in this type of analysis. A remedial programme should then be put into action according to what the analysis reveals. If there is still no progress an educational psychologist should be consulted as a next step.

Dyslexia

A minority of children are baffling: no matter who tries to teach them, no matter how hard they try themselves, they make painfully slow progress – at times it even appears that they are going backwards. They may complain that their eyes 'go all funny' when they try to read but, when tested, their vision is intact. They may spell in such a bizarre way that suspicions are raised about their hearing, but tests then reveal that there is no problem there either. In these circumstances, parents and teachers may begin to wonder if the child is dyslexic.

What is dyslexia?

Dyslexia is an extreme difficulty in learning the fundamental skills of reading and/or spelling in an otherwise normally functioning person. It is independent of intelligence in that children can be affected whatever their scores on an intelligence test, and it occurs at all social levels.

This definition may seem clear and uncontroversial, but in the past there have been furious arguments about dyslexia. Some assert that it does not exist and that children with extreme difficulties simply fall at one end of the range, while those who learn easily are at the other. Others jib at the way that dyslexia is defined only by what it is not: if the child has not learned to read, despite the fact that he is not deaf, or short-sighted, or unintelligent, or emotionally disturbed, then he must be dyslexic. Those who fall into this latter group prefer the term 'specific reading retardation', and base conclusions about the child on the discrepancy between obtained reading scores and those predicted from the child's intelligence.

Today these arguments have largely subsided, and most psychologists and teachers accept that there are some children who have specific difficulties. Estimates of how many children are affected vary, but 4 per cent is the most conservative figure, while some put it as high as 10 per cent. Almost all agree that more boys than girls are involved, at a ratio of 3 or 4 to 1.

Indications of dyslexia

There is no one set of symptoms or indicators of dyslexia, partly because it can take several forms: it should perhaps be described as 'the dyslexias', rather than just 'dyslexia'. However, the following features are frequently associated:

• delayed language development

• clumsiness

• problems with learning the difference between right and left

• difficulties with sequences: children who are dyslexic tend to find it difficult to remember sequences like the alphabet, months of the year, or telephone numbers; they may reverse letters in a word, confusing 'on' with 'no', for example, and reverse the letters themselves (*b* for *d* is most common, but *p* and *q* may also be confused, and sometimes the four letters are mixed up together)

• bizarre spelling: this must be distinguished from spelling mistakes which have a certain logic; we can easily see how a child might come to write 'nos' for 'knows', 'doos' for 'does', 'cof' for 'cough'; 'shakn' for 'said', though, can be described as bizarre.

All these indications can also be found in children who subsequently go on to read perfectly well. In basing any judgment on them, the child's age must be taken into account. For example, reversals are normal throughout the age group covered by this chapter; if they continue after seven or eight, though, there are grounds for concern.

Causes of dyslexia

There is no general agreement on the causes of dyslexia. Some believe that it is genetic, others that it is associated with some abnormality of the brain which may or may not be inherited. There is no firm evidence that dyslexia runs in families; but nor is there evidence that it does not.

wutsa PoN+M

a lit l grn fal ban

and hescrud

and rand to

her Muthe

and sand

I f gl

ban and

her nuthe

bup up the

'Once upon a time a little girl fell down and she cried and ran to her mother and said I fell down and her mother jumped up.' Children who are dyslexic often spell in a very bizarre way. Here, for instance, a six year old spells 'girl' as 'grn', 'fell' as 'fgl'.

What can be done?

If you suspect that your child may be dyslexic, the first step is to obtain a thorough assessment. This will involve an examination of the child by teachers and psychologists, and possibly also by speech and/or occupational therapists. This is not a task to be performed in a few minutes: the more severe the problem, the longer the assessment is likely to take; several hours is not uncommon. The first step is to evaluate how severe and specific the reading problem is, which means assessing other skills to give a comparison. That done, it is normal to concentrate on reading and spelling and related areas in order to try to identify the nature of the deficiencies. It might be found, for example, that a primary problem is one of visual perception: the child can see well but cannot make sense of what he sees.

Help for children takes two forms. The first is carefully planned remedial teaching, either in very small groups or on a one to one basis. The most successful method found so far involves a detailed structuring of what is taught, with a systematic approach based on the association of sounds and letters and letter combinations. Some children diagnosed as dyslexic do, eventually, learn to read fluently, others may read but continue to find the process something of a struggle. Much depends on the severity of the problem and the quality of the teaching. The majority of children will make some progress, provided that they are well taught, but, no matter how good the teaching, progress is likely to be slow, and some spelling weakness will probably remain.

The second form of help is primarily the province of the parent, although teachers can also play an important part. Children who are failing in any significant way have a hard battle to maintain their self-esteem. Yet if they come to think of themselves as stupid, lazy or incompetent, not only are they going to find it very difficult to keep up the struggle to overcome the specific problem, the unhappiness, and feeling of failure, can easily come to pervade other areas of their lives. There are three basic ways in which parents can help support a dyslexic child's self-confidence. First, you should ensure that the child knows that everyone has appreciated that there is a problem (in this context the word 'dyslexia' can be useful). Second, you must maintain the child's belief that success can come, albeit slowly. (It is easy to hide behind the label of dyslexia and give up all attempts at reading and spelling correctly; this must be avoided.) Third, you need to provide a lot of support for the child's other activities: being good at swimming will not directly improve his reading, but it will increase his self-confidence – and having confidence will help him in every area.

Parents should be wary of quick or simple cures. In the past it has been suggested that children should learn to sing to learn to read, or take antihistamines, or wear a patch over one eye, or use coloured spectacles, or have their heads massaged. Some of these methods may help some children, but none has been accepted as being of general value, and none is a substitute for good teaching.

Writing

A degree of manual control is of course necessary before a child can write successfully (see page 289), but there is more to writing than being able to manipulate a pencil. As with reading, children generally take most easily to writing if they come upon it as a normal and enjoyable element in their surroundings – that is, if their parents surround them with written materials and print, take the time to write down and read back to them the stories they make up themselves, and encourage them to produce their own writing. Just as with talking, children seem to have a desire to write and to take the initiative. As with learning grammar, they are ready to discover the rules rather than being taught them by being constantly corrected. They may begin their efforts to read by trying to read their own writing.

When children have got a firm grasp of the idea that print carries messages, they will usually begin to write squiggles or letters that stand for whole words, in a way that is comparable to the telegraphic phase of early speech and the single-sign beginnings of reading. It may be extremely difficult to interpret what they are trying to communicate, because the squiggles do not at first have any identifiable relation to what they are meant to represent. Given plenty of opportunities to hear stories and to participate in reading books, they begin to recognize words and start to write with meaning; one squiggle may turn into the first letter of a word.

The process of learning to write properly involves many of the same elements as learning to read, such as a grasp of the conventions of sequence and the phonetic value of letters and their combinations. Schoolchildren must also learn about punctuation, upper and lower case letters and many other details. Later, they will learn that written language differs from spoken language in some respects, such as the stricter constraints on the kind of grammar and vocabulary that are considered correct.

Social and Emotional Development

It is relatively easy to measure children's height and weight and not unduly difficult to gauge their progress in the acquisition of physical and mental skills. Investigating their emotional development is more problematic. However, there are times when, in order to give our children appropriate help and support, we need to have some understanding of how they are developing emotionally.

Self-concept and self-esteem

'Who in the world am I?' asks Alice in Wonderland. 'Ah, that's the great puzzle.'

Some psychologists think that the essential clue to discovering what makes a person tick is an understanding of the way he perceives himself. It is the nature of a person's self-concept, they argue, that determines the choices he makes in life. It is the self-concept that underlies a feeling of well-being on the one hand or depression on the other. Closely related to the notion of self-concept is that of self-esteem – the subjective view of one's own worth. People's ideas about themselves develop in childhood, and although these early ideas may be modified over time they continue to exert an influence throughout their lives.

Children between three and five or six years old tend to describe themselves almost entirely in physical terms. They will talk about themselves as having freckles or red hair, or being big or little, and may mention favourite activities and things they can do. But even at three children begin to make a distinction between the private and the public self. Researchers have noted in children of this age a difference between the speech for self that may accompany a problem-solving activity, which is abbreviated and almost inaudible, and speech for others, which is more clearly articulated and in more complete sentences.

By six or seven a child will start to describe how he feels, and how he sees aspects of his own personality: he may say he is happy, sad, or scared, for example. He may also be able to evaluate his skills – saying, perhaps, that he reads well, or is good at running. Gradually, his ability to reflect on himself increases. He becomes able to compare himself with other people – to look at himself and say 'I am like him or her in that way, different in this way.' His sense of self also begins to develop a certain stability and consistency: he feels he is 'a clever boy', perhaps, or 'a stupid child', and he will still think of himself as clever, or stupid, tomorrow. As these examples indicate, a child's emerging sense of self is greatly influenced by his growing ability to interpret what other people feel about him.

Self-esteem is difficult to measure in children much under seven, because they have only limited ability to express themselves in words. There is no doubt, though, that their self-esteem needs to be nourished from the earliest weeks and months. Temperament plays a part in how a child feels about himself, but mostly because it influences the reactions he gets from other people. Nothing matters more to a child than his perception of how his parents feel about him, and the way you manage your child from day to day will strongly influence his sense of himself. For example, if you overprotect him, he may feel that he needs an adult with him to accomplish anything, that he alone is inadequate. On the other hand, if he is always left entirely to his own devices, he may come to feel that he cannot expect help, or doesn't deserve it. It is not always easy to find the correct balance, and no one gets it right all the time: but you can be certain that one of your most important tasks is to nourish in your child a sense of self-worth strong enough to override occasional feelings of frustration and failure.

An ebullient sense of self starts to emerge in children's drawings and stories.

Perception of others

Between the ages of three and six children are able to differentiate between themselves and other people, but they cannot easily distinguish their own thoughts and feelings from other people's. They tend to assume that everyone feels the same way as they do. At six to eight children become increasingly aware that another person's feelings may be different from their own, although for some time to come this awareness will remain fairly limited.

Young children are rarely capable of seeing the possibility that there may be a distinction between what people say and what they think. For example, they will implicitly believe someone who, having lost her dog, says that she will never have another one. It is usually not until a child is eight or over that he is capable of understanding that there may be a discrepancy between what the person who has lost her dog may say and what she really feels: she may want another dog even if she says she doesn't.

Children under six or seven tend to limit their descriptions of other people to comments on their appearance, or some particular possession. These descriptions often focus on what another person does in relation to the child, and can seem very egocentric – 'Aunt Sue brings me presents', or 'Georgia hits me.' Slightly later, at seven and a half or eight, a child might ascribe psychological characteristics, talk about his aunt as kind, or his cousin as bad-tempered.

Sex roles

We can learn a lot about the way people see themselves from considering their views on certain areas. We all have ideas about our ability, our strength, our popularity and so on. One concept which will affect all of these notions is the role a person assigns to him or herself according to sex.

As we discussed in the last chapter (page 238), differences may often be observed between the play patterns of boys and girls even as young as eighteen months. From four or five onwards children tend increasingly to prefer to play with children of the same sex as themselves. We may wonder why this separation takes place. The American psychologist Eleanor E. Maccoby suggests that one contributory factor may be that girls become wary of the rough and tumble play that boys tend to enjoy, and of boys' generally more competitive, dominating approach to games. Another suggestion is that girls are put off by the fact that they find their requests have little impact on boys. It seems that by four or five girls are already accustomed to using polite suggestions to influence adults and other girls successfully; boys of the same age, however, tend not to respond to polite requests from girls.

There have been various studies which shed some light on the way four and five year old boys and girls interact. In one, boys and girls watched cartoons on a screen. When a boy and a girl were paired to watch together, by themselves, in most cases the boy got more than his fair share of access to the screen. When there were adults in the room, even if they did not intervene, the girl got equal access. It is as if the adult presence inhibited the boys' assertiveness.

In another recent study preschool children were brought to a nursery in groups of four, and an adult was posted at one end of the room. When four girls played together they seemed happy to stay away from the adult, but as soon as boys were introduced into a group (so that it consisted of two boys and two girls), the girls moved closer to the adult; when the adult changed position, the girls also moved to keep close by. Their response was clearly

Even when children have been brought up in a non-sexist way, by the time they reach school age they tend to play in separate groups of boys and girls.

to do with the boys being there, and what that meant to them. This seems to lend some support to the theory that what keeps the sexes apart may be boys' greater tendency towards aggressive play, and their reluctance to accept direction from girls.

Stereotyping the sexes

By the time children reach school age, most have begun to develop stereotyped views on what is acceptable behaviour for male and female. Over the early school years, these stereotypes tend to gain in strength. Studies of children in Britain, Ireland and the United States, published in the mid-1970s, showed that by nine or ten children frequently described women as weak, emotional, sentimental and affectionate. Men were described as strong, robust, aggressive, cruel, coarse and ambitious. However, more recent evidence shows that when fathers take an active role in raising their families the children develop more liberal notions of gender roles and behaviour.

It appears that parents and teachers can influence children's appraisal of sex roles in very subtle ways. For example, in one research study children were asked to imitate how their parents might request them to bring a book. It emerged that girls were generally asked in a polite manner –

'Would you please get me the book?', whereas boys were told what to do, in imperative mode – 'Get me the book.' This brings us back to what we said earlier about boys' reluctance to respond to direction from girls. Could it be that we model polite requesting for girls – but fail to impart to boys the notion that they might respond to polite requests?

Studies also show that at school girls tend to stay physically closer to their teachers and will move around the room with them; by doing this they acquire considerable attention and positive reinforcement from the teacher. This raises the question of whether boys, who are less likely to stay close to their teacher, therefore get less attention. In this area research results are contradictory. Some studies indicate that in the early years of schooling boys are more likely than girls to get negative attention, in the form of scolding or disapproval, from teachers. Overall, though, it seems that teachers do not necessarily give less reinforcement to boys.

Friendships

By the age of three most children have begun to make friends; over the years that follow friendships come to play an increasingly important part in their lives. The skills involved in choosing friends and keeping them are learned over a lifetime, and young children are just beginning to find their way, but from the very beginning the ability to make friends offers rich rewards. We have also to acknowledge that there is a strong link between an inability to make friends as a child and emotional problems in later life.

An increasing awareness of others is the quality which makes it possible for children to form friendships, and it is also fundamental to the development of moral thinking. Friendships sustain and extend a child's moral development and enable him to explore his growing sense of the needs of other people.

Friendships allow children space and time to try out new ideas. Children learn from each other in ways they never can from adults, and friends set standards against which they measure themselves. When children begin to read they do not compare their performance with their parents' reading ability, they look at their friends and see if they are doing as well or better. When they take part in sports they compare themselves with each other all the time, even in groups where non-competitiveness is a leading principle.

Friendship also offers emotional support. It is easy to underestimate the pressures on children; a close friend can be a source of great comfort and reassurance. And, perhaps most important of all, having friends conveys to the child the feeling that he is wanted.

Making friends

By three, most children are playing with other children rather than just around them, and they definitely want to play with certain children more

Cooking is twice the fun when you can share it with your friends!

than others. These first friendships are usually with children like themselves, of much the same age and interests, although at this point friendships may be based on shared playthings as much as on shared views of the world. Indeed, little children may appear to choose friends on the basis of material attributes. If asked 'Why do you like Peter?' a three year old might well reply 'Peter has a bike.' This answer, though, does not indicate that the child is being materialistic, simply that he is less able to think in abstract terms – 'Peter is kind.'

However superficial the reasons for initial attraction, friendships develop as the ability to understand and communicate grows. Children may begin to recognize that their friends' emotional states can differ from their own, although they will not always read these emotions accurately. Even at three children show concern for each other; they may be mutually supportive, and miss each other when they are not together.

By four there is a shift in thinking: children will value what others do and make choices accordingly. 'She likes to go swimming and so do I.' 'I like to play shops but he won't.' If children cannot share activities with each other it is unlikely that they will choose to spend time together, even if they played amicably at an earlier age. Between five and six friendships tend to become more stable, for by this time the reasons for choosing friends are related more to personality and interests.

Although individual friendships between boys and girls can remain firm, by the time they are five or six children tend increasingly to gravitate towards their own sex. Some parents are dismayed by this, fearing it is an indication that their children are developing sexist attitudes. Usually, the best solution is to encourage individual friendships with the opposite sex and let group activities take care of themselves.

Influences on friendships

The increasing ability to communicate in words contributes a lot to a child's capacity to build and maintain a relationship. Memory also plays a part: if

Special friendships start to form when children have begun to develop a clearer idea of their own identity and interests.

there is to be continuity in the friendship, children need to remember the kind of activities they enjoyed together and the ways that other children play; if there were any problems or upsets in previous play sessions, children may have learned, and may now remember, how such problems can be handled.

Most importantly, the concept of having a friend is available to children only when they have become aware of themselves as individuals and can recognize that other people are different. They need to have a sense of self before they can start to show real preferences for other children.

A child's experience of adults has a bearing on how easily he makes friends. In general, children who have a firm attachment to their mother or mother figure are better able to make friends than those who have no such attachment – presumably because they start from a more secure base. Children's social skills are also affected by the examples before them. Their view of other children will be greatly influenced by their parents' attitudes to their own friends. If people outside the family tend to be regarded with suspicion, children will pick this up, and find it hard to break through the emotional barrier. Equally, a child who is constantly criticized, always falling short of parental expectations, will be more likely to expect other children to reject him. We should not, however, assume that all children who have difficulties in making friends come from unhappy homes – temperament plays a big part.

Shy children

Shyness is almost certainly underrated as a source of distress among children. In an American study published in 1982 almost 40 per cent of eleven year olds described themselves as shy and half of these felt that their shyness was enough of a problem to warrant joining a counselling group to help them overcome the difficulty.

What makes a child shy? Studies of adopted children suggest that shyness is a stable, inherent characteristic of temperament: in assessments of whether they are shy or outgoing, and to what degree, children rate scores very similar to those of their biological parents. One study, however, published in 1985, has pointed out that there is also a relationship between the degree of sociability of children and that of their adoptive parents. A plausible hypothesis is that shy parents tend to produce shy children; and then, because of their own shyness, the parents fail to expose the children to situations in which social skills will be learned, and a vicious circle is set up.

Support for this view comes from work by Jerome Kagan, who studied a group of children at twenty-one months and then again six years later. He found that 75 per cent of the children who were shy as toddlers were still timid and quiet in unfamiliar situations at seven; however, 25 per cent of the shy children had become sociable, spontaneous and talkative. Kagan feels that the children who changed did so because their parents encouraged them to meet other children and helped them to find ways of coping with unfamiliar social situations.

I would like to join in, but I don't know how . . .

Helping shy children make friends

There are many ways you can help your child to become more outgoing.

- Encourage your child to think well of himself. Just listening to a child is one of the best ways of reinforcing his self-confidence. Let him know when he says the right thing, praise him when he makes interesting conversation and has good ideas.
- Children with poor social skills often feel that they do not look right, so be sure to tell him positive things about his appearance and behaviour (taking care, however, not to suggest that you are overly concerned about how people look).
- Provide many social opportunities, particularly with your friends and their children, so that your child has a model of people getting along.
- Suggest ideas for play before he goes to someone else's house, or plan an activity that visiting children can do at your house.
- Point out instances when he has solved a problem with the help of a friend or settled a dispute before it ended in a fight.
- Try to be positive about yourself, as well – if you give the impression that you expect people to like you, your child will find it easier to believe that he, too, is likeable.

Developing friendships through play

Observations of the interchanges between close friends during play have revealed some consistent patterns. Children who are already friends, or who are in the process of forming close friendships, communicate clearly, exchange relevant information by asking questions and find out what the other person likes to do. They also give information about themselves, joke, gossip or fantasize together, and when conflicts arise resolve them without difficulty. They are generally aware of each other's needs and interests.

Taking turns

A favourite conversation of children around the age of three or four is 'Yes, no; yes, no; yes, no' (followed by a round of laughter when a turn is missed).

Taking turns is a universal characteristic of children's language and games. It begins with the early rhythms of mother and baby interactions and becomes a more positive part of play as children grow up. Games like peekaboo establish early patterns for taking turns, and many other traditional games are based on ritual turn-taking.

The ability to take turns is one of the most important social skills needed throughout life: think of people you know who dominate conversations or who clam up and offer little to another person. Children force each other (sometimes not so kindly) into situations where they must take turns and where fair play relies on this ability. A child needs to be sufficiently assertive to claim his turn, but not over-dominant. A child who takes a game over completely is regarded as a bully and avoided by the others, but one who is too reticent and shy is ignored. Unfortunately, either reaction tends

Imaginary playmates

Many children, usually between the ages of three and six, create imaginary playmates. For the child, these imaginary people – who are most often the same sex and age as the child – are real. You may find your child moving over to leave a space for his friend in the bed or at the table. Some children turn to an imaginary playmate when they are reprimanded – others use their fantasy friend as a convenient scapegoat for their own misdeeds!

Parents are sometimes concerned that, if a child invents an imaginary playmate, it may be a sign that he is feeling isolated and lonely. Certainly if an imaginary friend remains the centre of a child's play for an extended period, it can be an indication that he needs to have more opportunity to play with real children of his own age. More often, though, it is just that an imaginative child is using a fantasy friend to embellish his life. An imaginary friend can even be of practical help in allowing a child to practise getting on with others. Once a child has polished his social skills with a fantasy playmate, he can try them out in real life.

Most children tend to give up their fantasy playmates when they start school, though some may relinquish them only gradually.

to make the original condition worse: the aggressive child becomes more destructive, the reticent child withdraws.

Parental behaviour can be very influential here. Mothers and fathers who listen to each other and also find time to listen and talk to their children provide them with a supportive and gentle introduction to social skills – much gentler than they are likely to find among their peers or brothers and sisters.

In one sense, many of the courtesies of everyday behaviour are about turn-taking. When children learn to wait for a snack or a chance to talk on the telephone, they are learning to restrain themselves – not an easy task. But they do need to get that turn, or they will stop trying, and if this happens they may well become either aggressive or withdrawn.

Moral development

Guiding children's moral development is not an easy task – and perhaps it presents more of a puzzle to parents today than it did in periods when clearer guidelines were laid down by society. On the one hand we want our children to be free-thinking and confident; on the other, we want them to have concern for other people. We want them to be assertive and in some circumstances even aggressive about having their needs and their wishes met, but we do not want them to be destructive.

The child's moral development is linked with the growth of awareness at several levels. It involves, first, an understanding of the needs and feelings of others; then a feeling of concern for those others; later comes the development of the conscience.

343

Learning how others feel

Even children under the age of three have been seen to show generosity, kindness and care to others (see page 150). However, making judgments about children as young as this is difficult: we can see what they do, but we can never be certain why they do it. Is the apparent kindness really a result of compassion, or is it due to a desire for adult approval, or perhaps a wish to control others?

The key to the development of altruism – the ability to feel concern for other people – is the extent to which children can see the world from someone else's viewpoint. At first babies think egocentrically – the world revolves around them. As toddlers they may understand that others are separate, and realize that people can be sad, happy, angry or pleased. As they have more social experiences their scope broadens, and they can distinguish embarrassment, worry, joy, enthusiasm and sorrow. By seven or eight children can usually see other people's points of view (sometimes, at least), and may even realize how others might regard them.

Some researchers have found that girls tend to be more altruistic than boys. The American psychologist Carol Gilligan, who has worked extensively in this area, argues that this is because girls are taught to nurture and sympathize, to be concerned about the needs of others; for them morality is defined in terms of relationships with other people. By contrast, boys learn that morality has to do with the resolution of conflicts between individuals, by means of laws and other social conventions. By no means all psychologists would agree with Gilligan's finding that there are major differences between boys and girls in the extent of their concern for others, or with her explanation. Her observations are, however, thought-provoking.

The development of the conscience

A person's conscience is what enables him to maintain standards of right and wrong without needing an authority figure to remind him what to do. The conscience is not a structure, developing until maturity, rather an ever-present awareness which changes throughout life. In the young child we see the conscience in an embryonic form.

Many of the major theories of psychology have something to say about the nature and development of conscience.

Freudian theory describes the emergence of the conscience in terms of the child's need to resolve internal conflict. Early in life the child begins to fear that if he gives in to the demands of his instincts he may be rejected by his parents. In order to reduce that anxiety he has to find out what his parents expect of him and incorporate these expectations into his behaviour.

Post-Freudians also look to relationships with parents (in this case particularly the mother), to explain a child's identification with the parents' values, but they see the mainspring of that process to be the love that exists between mother and child rather than anxiety.

Would you help?

As part of an investigation into the development of feeling for others, child psychologist Nancy Eisenberg asked children whether they would stop to help another child who had been hurt – if stopping meant missing the cake and ice-cream at a birthday party. Most preschool children and a minority of young schoolchildren said they wouldn't stop if it meant missing the party. But some preschoolers and most schoolchildren said they would stop: in this instance at least, they felt that helping another child was more important than their own enjoyment.

Working over a five-year period, Eisenberg found a marked trend: purely self-interested responses became less and less common from the age of four on and had practically disappeared by seven; by this age almost all the children questioned were able to take other people's needs into account.

Theorists of the 'social learning' school believe that children begin to learn what is 'wrong' between three and five years of age. Children follow rules when it is in their interest to do so and good is defined as something which brings pleasant results. In general terms, if they are punished, what they did is wrong; if not, it is right. That is not quite all there is to it: what is right is also what is fair or what is interpreted as an equal exchange, a deal or an agreement. 'If you do something for me, I will return the favour.' 'If you go to bed on time, I will read you a story.'

These theorists, too, regard the identification with a parent or other adult as of importance, although the process is simpler than that put forward by Freud: children learn that certain adults are significant in their lives and they feel rewarded by taking on some of their attributes and some of their behaviour.

Piaget saw moral awareness developing in stages, along with other changes in the powers of thought. Young children do not have the same reasoning power as those who are older, and so they cannot be expected to have similar moral values. He described children up to the age of nine or ten as being in a stage of morality where rules are taken to be sacred and unalterable. Children believe that punishment is meted out according to the consequence of the act rather than the intent of the person; the violation of a social rule will invariably lead to punishment. At around nine or ten children's moral development progresses to another stage, when rules are no longer seen as absolute, but can legitimately be violated when circumstances change. Whether a person intended to do harm or not is now critical to the child's judgment.

Here as in other areas, Piaget's perceptions helped open adult minds to an understanding of how children think. For example, the realization that young children do, indeed, very commonly believe in immanent justice helps us to comprehend how children who are ill may think they are being punished for some wrongdoing. However, again, more recent research indicates that in certain respects Piaget both overgeneralized his conclusions and underestimated the ages at which children can develop certain concepts. In some circumstances children as young as three will take intention into account when making a judgment of an action. For example, a three year old will often more readily forgive an accidental knock than a blow which he perceives as deliberately intended to harm.

All the theories described here help us to comprehend some aspects of children's moral development: none, on its own, explains all moral thinking or all behaviour. What is clear is that an ability to see the world from someone else's point of view is a necessary part of moral thought, and a conscience of some kind is essential to moral behaviour. Both of these presuppose a certain level of development in understanding.

Just because children have reached the stage where they can tell the difference between right and wrong, that does not necessarily mean they will act accordingly. They may lie, steal or hurt another person even though they know it is wrong. We must always remember that there may be more powerful pressures than their consciences acting on children. (Nor are children alone in this – how many adults really practise what they preach?)

What parents can do

The most effective means of encouraging your child to behave in a certain way is by behaving that way yourself: if you want your child to develop concern for others you must show him that you care what he feels and what other people feel.

You can also foster your child's awareness, and his conscience, by encouraging him to discuss moral issues. You can start from his own behaviour: for example, if he takes another child's toy, rather than simply announcing that stealing is wrong, you might explain that the other child is sad because of the loss of the toy. As he grows older, you can challenge him with increasingly complex ideas.

Rules

Though young children are not quite such 'moral absolutists' as Piaget thought, it is true that, up to the age of six at least, they have a tendency to believe that rules are fixed in stone. This is so whether the rules apply to morality, social relationships, or games.

There is something very comforting about living in a world where there are definite, unchanging rules and where breaking a rule entails immediate, predictable consequences. It provides the sort of coherent structure that most children seem to crave. Having rules makes them feel more secure, and knowing that infringements will be noticed helps to give a feeling of basic trust in those who are taking care of them.

Who makes the rules?

Parents and other adults impose rules on children, but children also invent rules for themselves. They make rules about their games, their social relationships and how they treat each other. Rules about the necessity of keep-

'One potato, two potato . . . ' Playground games are similar the world over and each has its own definitive rules.

ing a secret, for example, or not telling tales about another child, are commonplaces of children's morality which most have learned by seven – and which may well conflict with adult rules. Underlying this conflict is the increasingly powerful influence of the peer group. For much of the period we are discussing in this chapter children look to their immediate family for standards to follow, but by six or seven other children have also become important as people who should be pleased, imitated and looked up to.

When rules conflict

Children often regard the habits and routines of their household as the norm, and may be confused if things are different in another child's house. For example, if there is a strict rule at home about sitting up straight at table, a child may be shocked that his friend's parents are evidently not disturbed by slouching. Games, too, may present conflicts, as there are

The rules of the game
Traditional rule-based playground and circle games are particularly popular with five and six year olds, and they may also start to get interested in organized sport and want to join in (see page 285). The games they invent for themselves now often have quite complicated rules. When they choose the children they want to play with they give preference to those who know the rules or who want to play by their rules. Sometimes, their play becomes so complicated and rule-bound that it almost seems as if they are anticipating the elaborate rituals of adult committees and agendas.

inevitably times when a friend has learned a different set of rules. An argument on this subject, to adults a trivial matter, may end a friendship or at least interrupt it: 'I don't want Jill to come. She doesn't play hide and seek right.'

This is the time to teach one of those fundamentals of human behaviour: we cannot expect everyone to do as we do. When we go to someone else's house, or indeed to someone else's country, there will be a shift of expectations; children need to learn to appreciate both the obligation to accommodate and ways of doing so.

Ownership and stealing

Knowing what belongs to you and what does not is a subtle matter. Between the ages of three and five children may believe that wishing for something makes it happen. A child who loves another's teddy wants it, is allowed to play with it, and is then upset when it cannot be taken home. In this sort of situation parents need to be able to see trouble coming, so that they can take steps to forestall it. If a child is becoming attached to someone else's property then he should be told early on that it will have to be left behind. At first the child may not believe this, and there may be floods of tears at the door. But once this has happened a couple of times, he should learn: it is hard lesson, but an essential one.

Taking something directly from another person, which is definitely stealing in adult terms, does not always seem like that to a child. Stealing may also be a way of communicating feelings. For example, if a child takes some change out of his mother's purse and hides it away, it is unlikely that he is taking the money for its own sake: the most probable explanation is that he wants something from his mother even if he has to steal it. In other words, he is saying very clearly that he is seeking attention and love. Parents can properly show disapproval of the stealing; but giving more attention to the child, especially when he is playful or engaging in more positive activities, will change the behaviour far more effectively than punishment.

In this area as in others, family styles vary a lot. In some families, there is very little property which is private and little or no space which a family member can call his or her own. In such a household taking something that belongs to a brother or sister can hardly be called stealing; it is more probably a misguided form of sharing. In other families privacy and ownership are extremely important, and children learn at an early age that certain things are other people's property.

Arguments arise when another person's boundaries are not acknowledged; and it is much easier to learn the limits when they are spelled out clearly and adhered to consistently. If the rules change constantly according to the whim of the parents, a child needs to read complex signals to determine whether or not he will be allowed to take something. For example, clear explanations will be needed if a toy which can be shared sometimes but which really belongs to a brother or sister, is not to cause problems.

Some children have a difficult time learning to put back school or playgroup property. Sometimes they may just be forgetful, sometimes they may consciously want to keep it with them. Most schools, sensibly, treat this fairly lightly, but some teachers, and some parents, behave as if it were a capital offence.

Sometimes a child gets into the habit of taking something small home each day – perhaps only a piece of a puzzle or a paper clip. It may be that he does this, not because the object itself has an intrinsic value for him, but because it helps him to make the transition between school and home more easily. Taking work home would fulfil the same need, but at this age the child may not have the opportunity to do this. This is usually only a temporary problem, but one way of getting around it may be to encourage the child, instead, to take something from home to school.

Aggression

Aggression, defined as activity intended to harm, is rarely seen in children before the age of two (before then children may struggle over a toy, but it is the toy they are concentrating on rather than each other). However, some children in the three to seven age group display quite high levels of aggression. The aggressive child is often unable to make friendships with other children or even to enjoy a sustained period of play with others, and this can set up the familiar vicious spiral: the less accepted a child is, the more extreme his behaviour tends to become.

A distinction should be made between the child who has an occasional aggressive outburst and one whose characteristic response to any frustration, fear or anger is to try to harm someone else. There is no clear cut-off point here, for we are dealing with a continuum; but asking yourself how you expect a particular child to react when thwarted will give you a clue to the level of his aggressiveness.

Theories of aggression

Freud saw aggression as being biologically driven: humans, especially males, are programmed to fight over food, territory and the opposite sex. Cross-cultural studies, however, show that even if it be accepted that aggression is biological in origin, environmental factors can modify it. There is a world of difference, for instance, between conduct in the Amish communities of the United States, where cooperation is encouraged, and behaviour in inner city New York.

Differences between the sexes in levels of aggression are acknowledged by both biological theorists and environmentalists, the one group saying that it is all in the genes, the other that social conditioning explains the disparity. What is clear is that sex differences do exist. Data gathered from over a hundred studies carried out all over the world have demonstrated that males are more aggressive physically and verbally than females. Boys are also more likely to be targets of aggression.

Children need to learn to talk about their feelings rather than fight.

The environmentalists' viewpoint is to some extent supported by observations of the families of aggressive children. The archetypal aggression-producing parent is cold and rejecting, uses physical punishment erratically and permits children to behave aggressively. Young children are also more likely to show aggression if they have aggressive older brothers or sisters.

The story is not quite as simple as this. Research indicates that a child's temperament is also an important factor in the development of aggression: in particular, children who have very high activity levels are more likely to be aggressive. However, temperament is still less significant than parental toleration of aggression.

Patterns in aggressive behaviour

The amount of reliable data on the development of aggressive behaviour is relatively scant, almost entirely limited to one country (the United States), and not as up to date as we would like. However, it seems that there are some developmental patterns. Aggressive behaviour first appears at around two and once children reach three there is quite a high likelihood of their striking out in response to an attack or to frustration. Most children are at their most physically aggressive at around four. Physical attacks become less frequent between four and five and from six to seven onwards there is a marked decrease in physical aggression and a corresponding increase in verbal abuse. There is no certainty as to why physical aggression decreases from four (if, indeed, this finding still holds). One argument is that after four there are more adults providing more constraints, another is that as children's skill in using language increases, they learn to get what they want through words rather than actions. Both are probably relevant. Then again, much human behaviour depends on how a person perceives the intentions of others. The three or four year old may not always be able to tell the difference between an accidental knock from another child and a deliberate attack, whereas the six year old is more likely to recognize the distinction, and to realize that an aggressive response is inappropriate.

There appears to be a minority of children who, themselves aggressive, tend always to construe others as hostile. This leads to a circular problem: the child who believes others to be hostile will be more likely to react aggressively, which will in turn provoke attacks. It almost seems as if some children have a reservoir of aggressive feelings which well to the surface as soon as any provocation is experienced or suspected.

Studies of aggression over time indicate that one cannot make predictions based on the behaviour of children under three, but that the children who fight the most at three or four tend to remain the most aggressive. This is not to say that children cannot be taught to control their aggression. For most children, this is quite possible.

What parents can do

Parents cannot be held responsible for all the aggressive acts of their children, but they can help the children learn to control their aggression themselves. If they are to do this they will have to set limits and enforce them as consistently as possible. Making sure a child has adequate space and time for active play can also help limit aggressive behaviour, by providing another outlet for his energy.

Parents may also need to look carefully at their own ability to control their aggressive feelings. If they launch hostile attacks, physical or verbal, against their children (or each other), the children will learn that it is acceptable to behave in this way. This does not mean that parents should not say when they feel angry. Adults and children can learn to express anger without hurting other people. Though this is easier said than done, trying always to distinguish between being angry at a specific event and angry at a person can help. So can trying to explain why one is upset, thus putting the emotion in a more general context rather than targeting a particular person. As is so often the case, children learn much from the models offered by their parents.

How should parents react to specific acts of aggression when they occur? Demanding that a child makes reparation might seem to be the obvious answer, but in practice this becomes difficult, and may lead a parent to respond in precisely the way the child wants. A child may push his sister over and snatch her toy not because he wants the toy but because he knows that doing so will provoke parental attention. A more constructive way of dealing with the problem is to pay as little attention as possible to aggressive behaviour and show lots of approval for cooperative or at least neutral activities.

Taking risks

A lot of the 'naughty' behaviour of children in this age group may best be understood as a form of risk-taking. The risk need not be physical: deliberately naughty play may involve nothing more dramatic than two children going off together, at home or at school, whispering or messing about when they are supposed to be doing something more constructive.

A simple explanation sometimes offered for such behaviour is that children are trying to attract attention, but, as part of the game is not to get caught, this theory doesn't really stand up. Even children who get huge amounts of attention and love like to be naughty sometimes. It seems that they just want to see how far they can go – to take a risk. Children really enjoy getting away with it occasionally. You are unlikely ever to be able to stop this completely, nor is it necessary to do so.

The situation is a bit different, though, if it occurs too frequently, either at home or in school. It can then be a sign that something is amiss in the child's environment: perhaps it is too loosely structured or, conversely, it may be that it is over-controlled and he is using naughtiness as a means of relieving boredom or rebelling against authority. The child who is never naughty, however, is equally likely to be too tightly controlled.

Where physical safety is the issue, the line between caring supervision and overprotection is thin. Children need to be kept safe, but there are times when they have to be allowed to do things on their own. Much progress involves a certain amount of physical risk. A child learning to ride a bicycle, for example, will fall off many times before he masters the skill. Some parents find it difficult to let go of the bike and allow the child to ride off by himself: but if he is to learn, they have to do it.

As children grow older, you will not be able to supervise all their play, although you will be able to establish guidelines as to what activities are acceptable. Between five and seven children do start to recognize what situations may be dangerous, and limit themselves to a certain extent. But there are, of course some risks that children actively have to be warned against. In this situation it is best to give simple, clear directions – long explanations will only make children over-anxious. For example, it is best to tell them quite unequivocally that they must:

- never climb a tree without asking an adult's permission

- never cross a road without an accompanying adult

- buy food or sweets only in shops

- keep strangers at arm's length – at least

- never accept anything offered by a stranger

- never, ever, go anywhere with a stranger

- never go anywhere with anyone, even someone they know, without asking one of their parents or their teacher first.

Going to School

Going to school is a great step in the long process of leaving the small private world of the family and joining society at large. It is likely that from the age of five, or even earlier, until the mid-teens or later, school will be an important force in your child's life. It will provide much of the framework he shares with other children through most of his formative years, as well as preparing him with more or less success for the world that awaits him. For these and other reasons, you are probably going to find yourself thinking a great deal about school and its related topics and anxieties for many years to come.

Education in the sense of acquiring skills and academic knowledge becomes more important as the child grows older and will be dealt with in the next chapters (pages 383–403, 448–460), but the demands made in these later stages cast their shadow before them and influence the expectations and attitudes of parents and teachers as early as nursery school and playgroup.

The education system of any country has an explicit, an implicit and a hidden role. The primary explicit role is to impart skills, to equip children with whatever tools are thought necessary or desirable in their culture. The emphasis given to this role and the teaching methods employed vary, partly according to the country's educational philosophy and partly according to the individual school. In France and Japan, for example, a high priority is given to the imparting of academic knowledge and to formal teaching. In both these countries, parents know more or less what a child will be learning any day because the timetable is so highly standardized. In Britain and the United States there is much greater variation, and a child moving from one school to another may encounter not only different teaching methods but also a different syllabus (though in Britain the National Curriculum is changing this situation).

A secondary explicit role for education in some systems, though by no means all, is to foster children's physical development through such activities as organized games, swimming and formal physical education.

A role that is explicit in preschool provision but later becomes implicit is to provide children with social experience, to allow them to learn something of the rough and tumble of everyday life, some of the skills needed to get on with others. In a healthy system this experience should also help children to develop self-confidence and a sense of justice and morality.

353

Here we come! The school playground is a world of strong, supportive alliances between children.

The 'hidden curriculum' is described as such because much of it is transmitted without conscious awareness on the part of the teachers or education authorities. It is through the hidden curriculum that the school plays its part in passing on to children something of the attitudes of the culture in which they are growing up. They will learn, for example, how their society views people of various social classes or ethnic origins – and the members of one sex and the other.

Schools can also convey to children something of how society regards them. Well-maintained buildings, with good equipment and devoted, reliable teachers give one message; crumbling buildings with insufficient equipment and too few books, staffed by overworked and frequently changing teachers, give another. The message of care, or lack of care, within the school system can have lifelong effects.

Preschool

For many children the first experience of education outside the home comes in a preschool group. Most nursery schools and playgroups expect children to start when they are about three, some take them earlier. The variety of preschools available overall is wide, with marked differences, from group to group, in philosophy, size and mix of children. However, parents may find that in practice they have little choice, once finance, transport and availability of places have been taken into account.

Parents may wonder if the selection of preschool makes a difference, or, indeed, if such young children should be in school at all. There is evidence to show that children who have a good experience of a preschool group tend to be more resilient, more confident and better able to deal with social situations. They are also better able to plan their work independently.

Types of preschool programme

The nature of the preschool programme offered by any particular establishment depends on the view taken of its aim. One perspective sees it as a direct preparation for formal education, so that children are expected to sit quietly when they are being taught, to learn the basic skills of reading, writing and early mathematics. There will always be parents whose chief anxiety is their children's progress over the hurdles of formal education, whatever they may currently be, and to cater for them preschools like this exist all over the world.

Another approach emphasizes physical, social and emotional factors rather than intellectual demands. The prime aim here is that children should learn to be secure in a group of their peers, and the focus is on allowing children to play. In most play-oriented groups the adults present are seen as facilitating rather than instructing. The children initiate activities and the adults support them. In some groups children are guided and helped to structure their play so that they achieve certain learning objectives set by the teacher: for example, a child who is playing with water might be encouraged to try sink and float experiments.

A third approach focuses on how children learn to think and process information as well as on their social and emotional growth. In this type of programme children and teachers plan the curriculum together day by day. The adults' role is to instigate problem-solving activities by providing materials and active learning experiences which enable children to plan their work and set their own goals. A key element in this approach is the balance between the adult's and the child's initiation and contribution.

While most preschool groups concentrate on one or another of these approaches, some schools are more eclectic and attempt to combine two, or all three. There may be periods during the day for formal lessons or structured learning and times when free play reigns. This may seem to offer the best of all worlds, but as a parent you need to be rather wary of schools which promise everything. There is a limit to how much can be fitted in. If teachers devote most of the time to teaching children formally free play may have to be relegated to the sidelines, both in time and physical space. Likewise, in a group where free play is seen as the most important activity, they may not get around to teaching many formal lessons or managing structured learning activities.

Choosing a nursery school or playgroup

The first nursery school or playgroup a child attends is going to influence his attitude to school for a long time – perhaps for the rest of the school

'Two little dickie birds sitting on a wall . . . ' Playgroup or nursery school may provide your child with his first experience of the enjoyment of group activity.

years. Parents naturally want these early days to be a good experience in themselves, and to provide a happy start to their child's school career. When making a choice it is necessary to weigh up all the features you consider important, taking plenty of time and probably several visits to do so.

Physical surroundings

Playgroups and nursery schools differ a lot in their physical settings and facilities. One may be in a small, home-like building, another may be part of a large institutional setting. One may have a pleasant garden, another no outside space at all. Yet another may have access to a large, well-equipped playground – but if at break times it is crowded with older children, this can be frightening to a small child who is not used to large numbers of people. The facilities and the continuity offered by a nursery within a larger school may be very attractive, but at three or four a child may find a home-like setting or a small purpose-built centre easier to manage than a large, complex environment. You will need to think about all these things in relation to your own child's needs and personality.

What happens at school

Preschool days are an important time for the learning and practising of language and communication skills, so teachers need to provide opportunities for children to talk to each other, to describe events in their lives and to express their feelings.

Most parents will also want to see sand, water, paint, playdough or clay, bricks, large toys for active play, a dressing-up box, a playhouse to encourage role playing and make-believe play. There should certainly be a corner for books, where children can feel comfortable looking at pictures or reading. A careful look at the displays in the room will give direct information about the level of creative activity.

The staff

Ideally the relationship between playgroup or nursery school staff and young children is an extension of the kind of good relationships children have with their parents. A caring and authoritative teacher, neither authoritarian nor permissive, will be best equipped to provide for small children the loving, secure environment they need.

When children are very young a high adult to child ratio is essential. In a toddler group, when children are under three, a one to three ratio is needed, in groups for three to five year olds the ratio should ideally not be less than one to eight. Parents may need to look a little further into the staff to child ratio quoted by the school. Remember that it is the availability of the adult to the child that counts. She or he needs to be working with the children directly, not employed as a cook or a cleaner or a 'special' teacher who visits the school irregularly. There should be at least one teacher who has professional qualifications plus experience.

When you hand over the care of your young child you need to feel personal confidence in the teacher. You must feel able to communicate with her or him: remember that you may have to share intimate details of your family life, so that the teacher will know why your child is behaving in a particular way, or is in need of special attention. You also need to be able to feel implicit trust in the teacher's discretion. Teachers are often members of the local community and they are necessarily in frequent contact with other parents. It is reasonable to expect that your child will be accepted with all his problems and flaws and will be in no danger of being gossiped about by his teachers.

Primary education

Whether or not a child has been going to some kind of preschool, the move to 'big school' is going to be a significant one for him; it may be, it should be, a matter of pride – but it can be daunting too.

Choosing a school

Some parents have quite a wide range of schools to choose from, others only a limited choice, but in either case deciding between the possible alternatives may seem a difficult task. All that has been said about choosing

Your child's teacher is very special to her, someone who makes her feel secure in the new and demanding world of school.

preschool groups also needs to be borne in mind when choosing a primary school, with some additional considerations as well. You may well want to visit the schools you are considering more than once, to talk to the teachers and watch the children in the classroom and the playground, to gain your own sense of the happiness and liveliness or otherwise of the children, how the school balances freedom with discipline, the quality and tone of the work displayed on the walls, and the many other indications you may pick up of the character of the school.

It helps to make a brief checklist of key factors that you will want to consider during your visits. Some suggestions have been made here, but different things matter to different families, and it is worth thinking for a while about the sort of questions you hope your visit will answer.

The staff

The headteacher is outstandingly more important than anyone or anything else in determining the atmosphere and philosophy of a school. He or she has the major part in setting goals and spelling out values and aspirations to staff and children, in developing and adhering to a fair and orderly system of discipline and in innumerable other facets of school life.

Your child's teacher will be the most important person in his daily life at school, so you will certainly want to meet and talk to him or her. If you have the opportunity to meet other teachers as well this is all to the good.

What have you liked
most about being in
Class 1 having

Miss Reddee ☺

thankyou Emily and I have liked having
you too

Respect and harmony between head and teachers is vital for the happy running of a school, and meeting teachers will help you to form an opinion of the relationships in the school.

Free and effective communication between home and school is vital. From the first interviews you can sense whether you will feel comfortable talking to the teachers and other school personnel. You have the right to check what feedback you will get from the school. How and when will you be informed if your child has problems with his work, or classmates? If he is upset on a particular day, will a note be sent home?

Academic standards

'Academic' may seem rather a large word to use in relation to a child about to start school, but most parents, quite rightly, are concerned that from their child's first days at school he should have the opportunity and encouragement to fulfil his academic potential. It is reasonable to ask the head to explain to you the aims and philosophy of the school in the teaching of reading, mathematics and other subjects.

Schools should be able to explain in some detail their approach to reading: most schools have a coherent programme which is then interpreted by the individual teachers. It is worth inquiring about the system or systems used in the teaching of reading (see pages 324–7) and also asking to look at any reading schemes. You will probably want to know if your child will

When story time at school is fun and interesting, children will want to explore reading for themselves.

bring books home. You may also want reassurance that he will be able to get individual help if he needs it. The reading programme should have a built-in evaluation system which provides regular feedback to school and parents.

In the same way, the school should have a coherent mathematics programme which provides for evaluation and remedial help if it is needed. It should have clear objectives for every year and the overall aim should be to impart basic mathematical skills and develop in children the ability to begin to think about mathematical problems. Children should be learning processes rather than rules and the school should attempt to make mathematics interesting and relevant.

Children do begin to learn some basic science, history and geography in their early years at primary school, and some schools also offer a second language; but reading and mathematics are, and must remain, the basic components of an academic curriculum at this age. Beguiling as a broad prospectus may seem, parents need to be wary of schools which offer a wide range of fashionable programmes but may lack depth in their teaching and commitment to them. There is only so much time in a school day and in primary school a lot of that time needs to be taken up with learning basic skills. Remember too that young children need time during the day to exercise freely and to be with their friends – aspects of school life that are quite as important as academic achievements.

If you are looking forward to your child taking specific tests or fulfilling entrance requirements at the next school, you need to be clear in communicating this to the head. You may also want to ask if many other children have achieved these goals. While no school can guarantee a particular level of achievement for your child, it is reassuring to know that he is attending a school which shares your expectations and has a past record of achieving similar objectives. If, on the other hand, goals which are important to you do not appear to be valued, or not considered appropriate, by the school you have in mind you may need either to look for another school, or to modify your own goals.

The right school for your child

A child's education at every stage is most likely to be successful if child, parent and school share the same goals and agree on how to achieve them. Often, having decided on a school for one child, parents take it for granted that any other children in the family will go to the same school. Indeed, it may be that the logistics of delivering and picking up children leave them little option. However, ideally, the school – whether primary or secondary – should be chosen to suit the particular child. And the best school for one child may not be the best for another.

For example, a child who is reticent and shy may be overwhelmed in a lively class with a lot of other children, in a big building with a large playground. He may have to face a large class eventually, but there is a greater chance of success if the challenge is taken in stages. For such a child it is probably best to try to find a small class where there are many opportunities for one to one interactions with the teacher, so he does not run the risk of being undervalued just because he is not very forthcoming. More active and outgoing or even aggressive children, on the other hand, may be restless in a quiet, highly structured classroom, but quite happy in a class that features active learning and allows for plenty of physical play and letting off steam.

It is by no means uncommon, within a family, to find one child who takes the extrovert, aggressive role, while another follows a quieter, less assertive line. Two such different children will probably benefit from quite different school experiences, especially at the beginning.

Trusting your intuition

In the end, our advice would be that, having weighed everything up, you should trust your intuition. There is a feeling about some classrooms that they are good places for children. The teacher may not correspond exactly to the way you expected your child's teacher to be, but still you feel instinctively that this is a warm, loving person, and the class seems happy and industrious, with children going about the business of learning with interest and independence. On the other hand you may find your intuition saying no to a classroom with an efficient teacher, many learning materials and children who are working almost too diligently. It may be worth making a second visit to check your first impression, but your initial intuition has its value. If you feel happy about the school, for whatever reason, your trust will be an important foundation for your child's confidence in his school.

The child at school

Parents sometimes feel, when they send their child to school, that they are handing him over to the experts and from now on they will be of only secondary importance. In fact, what happens is the handing over of children to teachers only for certain activities. Children continue to spend much more time at home than at school. More crucially, parents are still the main providers of support and guidance, and still have the most significant role to play in their child's development. Any teacher will testify to the impossibility of supplanting the parents and the home as the central determining factor in a child's happiness and progress. Many schools explicitly enrol the parents' participation in home-school study schemes, recognizing how much can be achieved by strong support from home even in the academic side of children's education.

Preparing a child for a new school

The most important part of preparation is giving children the feeling that they are going to enjoy their life at school, and that they can freely and easily turn to the teachers for help and information. The easiest way to impart such an idea is to believe in it yourself – which is one of the reasons you will

his normal behaviour, you need to question what is happening, at school and at home.

The first step is to talk and, what is more important, to listen to your child. Often, what helps children most is just talking about their worries – although they may need quite a lot of encouragement before they will say anything much.

Next you should talk to your child's teacher, to explain your concern, to find out her or his view of the problem and to enlist the help of the school.

There may be some cause which, when you begin to think and talk about it, becomes immediately obvious – perhaps your child has been unsettled by having a new teacher, or a friend has left. Or the child's anxiety may stem from an experience which he has found distressing but which has gone unreported or even unnoticed by the teacher. For example, some children wet their pants in the early days at school, perhaps from nervousness or because they are shy about going to the lavatory. Most teachers take these accidents as all in the day's work – they certainly don't punish the child. On the other hand, they may not realize that a child can find such an incident deeply humiliating.

Unfortunately, you may also have to consider the possibility that your child is being bullied at school (see pages 419–21).

If there is nothing clear-cut, it might be worth looking at the overall timetable. Is it perhaps too rigidly structured, so that the child is left with no time for play? Does he feel under pressure to fulfil expectations in too many directions? There is a whole world of after-school activities and classes which lure the parents of primary school children; but parents also need to recognize when children have had enough learning and new social situations for a while. It may be that what your child needs most now is some quiet talking and listening time with you after school; or the opportunity to get out and play with some friends; or both. Perhaps you could consider deferring certain activities for a few months or a year. You will not be depriving your child; on the contrary, he will enjoy them much more when he is ready.

Much has taken place in these years between three and seven. Development has been less dramatic than the almost daily changes of the earliest years, and at times you may not have realized how your child has been altering – but if you reflect on what the three year old can do and then observe your seven year old, you will see how remarkable the progress has been. In the years to come a whole new set of experiences unfolds. School friends and teachers become ever more important, new areas of thinking open up as children mature, attainments in and out of school become more sophisticated. Above all children become increasingly themselves, individual differences becoming more clearly delineated.

All that comes in the next chapter.

A WIDENING SOCIAL WORLD
seven to eleven

The years from seven to eleven are a time of dramatic social and intellectual advances, accompanying steady physical development. Contacts outside the family become ever more significant, school and friends constantly increasing in importance. None the less, children still need a secure base at home, and parents continue to occupy their central place in children's lives. And these are years when parents often greatly enjoy their children: with their growing individuality and creativity and their infectious enthusiasm, children in this age group make delightful companions, fun to be with and a pleasure to grow alongside.

Physical Development

Growth

Between the seventh birthday and the beginning of the adolescent growth spurt (see page 432), both boys and girls gain an average of about 5 to 7.5 cm/2 to 3 inches and 2.25 to 3 kg/5 to 7 lb a year. In both sexes there is during this period an increase in the amount of fat just beneath the skin. In boys the added fat will diminish in adolescence, while in girls it continues to increase, as their figures fill out.

In this age group it is possible to identify children according to three categories of body build: round and chubby (endomorphic); athletic and muscular (mesomorphic) and thin (ectomorphic). As with adults, very few children conform completely to these body types, though most will show the characteristic features of one.

During these years of middle childhood the facial bones develop and alter in shape: as the cheekbones and the bones of the forehead and chin become more pronounced, the face acquires a mature look. The growth of the head and brain is 95 per cent completed by the time a child is ten.

Precocious puberty

In some very rare cases, children of seven or eight, or even younger, may experience an abnormally early sexual development, known as precocious puberty. Girls may develop breasts and can even start to have irregular periods. In boys the penis and testes may enlarge, and they may begin to have erections. Their voices may deepen and they may grow pubic hair.

This situation is likely to be disturbing for both parents and children. Girls in particular feel isolated when they have to deal with periods at primary school, with no other children to share the experience. Both boys and girls tend to be treated inappropriately because they seem much older than they really are.

However, with the right treatment it is often possible to slow things down, and it is important for the child to see a pediatrician who specializes in growth and development. Expert counselling can help both parents and child to deal with the emotions involved. Of course, parents should explain the situation carefully to teachers and any other adults with whom the child may come into contact.

Overweight children

In many of the richer countries obesity is on the increase among children in this age group. In the United States, for example, obesity among six to eleven year olds has increased by about 50 per cent in the last twenty years. As it has been estimated that 40 per cent of those children who are obese at seven will become obese adults, and people who have been obese as children find it particularly difficult to maintain a normal weight in adult life, it is important to alter patterns that lead to obesity while children are still young.

Some people do seem to have an inherited tendency to put on weight easily, but the food taken in and the energy expended (or not expended) in exercise are at least equally significant. You can help your whole family to avoid weight problems by planning healthy family meals and by encouraging active pursuits. If you are concerned that your child is seriously overweight, you should discuss it with your family doctor: putting a growing child on a slimming diet is a serious step and you should not take it without medical advice. Not only is there the risk that the child will be deprived of essential nutrients, there is the additional danger that dieting may encourage her to become obsessive about food, which can lead to eating disorders.

It should be said, however, that there is a very real difference between obesity – where a child is at least 20 per cent above the weight expected for age and height – and a degree of plumpness. A lot of pre-adolescent children are a bit on the plump side, and this is nothing at all to worry about. It is certainly a good idea to encourage them to eat sensibly and to take more exercise, but do avoid making an issue of it.

Undernourished children

Underweight, like overweight, is usually defined in terms of weight for age and height, so children are described as underweight if they are 20 per cent below the average weight for their age and height. This is rather too simple, however, as a slender but healthy child may well be as much as 20 per cent below average weight. So long as a child is active, energetic and cheerful, and eats reasonably well, there is usually no need to worry.

However, parents should be aware that a child – even one of normal weight – who easily becomes tired, irritable or fidgety may be undernourished. Perhaps you need to watch more carefully what your child is eating. It may help if you offer three or four small but healthy meals a day, with nourishing snacks in between.

Another problem is that as young as nine or ten, occasionally even younger, some children become extremely conscious of their diets and may take to damaging slimming regimes. They may show the first signs of anorexia (see page 483), becoming extremely finicky about what they eat, even developing frequent stomach upsets. If you feel that this could be the case with your child, you should seek advice from your doctor. You may also need to look at the eating patterns of the family as a whole: children learn from those about them, and if other family members are very fussy about food, or are always worrying about their weight, a child may well copy this model.

Any child who suddenly loses a good deal of weight certainly needs to be checked by a doctor.

Good food

The chart on pages 496–7 outlines the nutritional needs of children in this age group. Once a child reaches school age it is not usually possible to control what she eats at every meal. She may be having her lunch at school; as she gets older she may be able to choose her own meal at a school cafeteria, and she may also buy sweets or snacks for herself, either at school or outside. You can, however, teach your child something about good food, and encourage her to make sensible choices.

You can also pay careful attention to those meals you do provide. You should make sure that a healthy breakfast is available every morning, and you can try to make sure that your child doesn't rush it or skip it. It's worth remembering that children are often very tired and hungry immediately after school, and need a snack to boost their energy level; you can ensure that the snack is a nutritious one.

Teeth

The first permanent teeth usually appear when a child is about six. Over the next five or six years she will acquire three or four permanent teeth a year, and by the time she is twelve or thirteen she will have twenty-eight permanent teeth (a full set, except for the wisdom teeth, which come later).

Various problems may become apparent as the teeth come through – for example, the teeth may be overcrowded, or crooked, or the lower teeth may be too far forward or too far back in relation to the upper teeth. Orthodontic treatment can correct most positioning problems: sometimes teeth are extracted to make room for others, often a brace is fitted to move the teeth into more regular positions. Children's attitudes to wearing braces vary a lot. For some a brace is a status symbol, to others an embarrassment. As with so many things at this age, much depends on how their contemporaries regard it. The family's attitude is important too, though: a matter-of-fact approach at home can be a great support.

Physical skills

At one time it was thought that there were considerable differences between the physical skills of boys and girls in this age group, but more recent research has questioned whether such differences really exist. An American study of over five hundred children aged eight to ten, carried out in 1984, indicated that girls and boys have similar abilities in such activities as sit-ups, short-distance sprinting and jumping.

By seven or eight most children have a well-developed sense of balance and good control over their movements. Most seven year olds have learned to somersault, possibly not very elegantly, and many perform well in school gymnastics. They are beginning to enjoy activities which involve precise movements – hopscotch, perhaps, or complicated skipping games.

Performing circus tricks on ropes – a new delight for seven year olds.

Swimming strokes may start to develop well by seven or eight. Stamina increases, and many eight and nine year olds can swim quite long distances. Some children as young as eight or nine may become involved in competitive swimming, but for most the important thing is that they should enjoy swimming for its own sake and have a feeling of well-being in the water. Children who feel confident can go on to other water sports, such as diving, canoeing and sailing.

Health and fitness

Despite all the opportunities available, towards the end of this period many children become less active: their interests change, and from spending long periods running around in the playground, kicking a football or riding a

373

bike, they begin to prefer sitting in front of a television set or playing computer games. Physical education activities at school sometimes place too much emphasis on competition, at the expense of personal satisfaction and enjoyment. Understandably, this can put some children off. It is up to parents to make sure their children are exposed to as wide a range of physical activities as possible.

Once the emphasis is put on health and fitness, rather than on organized games, the range of activities available is enormous. Dance, gymnastics, martial arts, swimming, riding, skiing, skating all require self-discipline and provide practice in learning complex skills and carrying out movement patterns; children should be encouraged to set goals for themselves and to enjoy improving their own performance. Other types of exercise, which are active and yet calm and without pressure, may suit some children better: walking and yoga, for example, both provide useful exercise, without being too taxing. Then there are adventure activities and outdoor expeditions of various kinds which can be carried out by the whole family or by children in groups organized and led by adults. It is worth remembering that at this age children will still find almost any activity more attractive if their parents are prepared to be involved as well.

Sports and organized physical activities

There is some controversy about whether children in this age group should be organized into team sports at all. Some people feel that they should simply be encouraged to take part in individual and group games spontaneously, as and when they wish. The psychologist David Elkind asserts that, 'Generally it is parent need, not a child's authentic wish, that pushes children into team sports at an early age. School-age children need the opportunity to play their own games, make up their own rules, abide by their own timetable. Adult intervention interferes with the crucial learning that takes place when children arrange their own games.'

Certainly it is a pity if children of this age become so absorbed in team games that they have no time left for more informal play. But many (though not all) seven to eleven year olds do enjoy team sports, provided that they can approach them in a relaxed way; that the rules and equipment are

Safety
You need to be certain that your children are fit to meet the demands of any sport they choose to engage in. This doesn't only apply when they first start to play; if they have been inactive over a long period – because of winter weather, illness, lack of interest, or for any other reason – they need to build up their strength and activity level gradually before they return to any demanding sport. Of course, you should make sure that whenever necessary they wear properly fitted, well-maintained equipment.

Always pay attention if your child is in pain and get a medical opinion immediately.

adapted to their age and ability level; and that they have sensitive coaches who understand their physical and emotional needs. From the time your child first begins to play organized games, you need to be alert to the sort of pressure which turns children into people who hate exercise and sport. A child can find it very humiliating to be told that she isn't a fast enough runner, or is useless at catching a ball, or to be constantly placed in situations where she just can't win.

You, as a parent, are well placed to give your child non-competitive opportunities. If she is keen to improve a particular skill you can encourage her to perform against herself: time her running, skipping or swimming a short distance and then see if she can beat her own time. Put her into situations where she can see her own improvement and give her praise for it. It is easier to do this at home, where children can't immediately compare performances.

Fine motor skills: writing and drawing

By seven, children are becoming more competent in their writing skills: the individual letters are more clearly differentiated from each other and capital and small letters are usually in proportion. By eight their words and sentences are clearly spaced and have a more uniform alignment and slant. At nine or ten most children have switched from print to cursive (some children do this much earlier – it really depends on how they are taught) and their writing is beginning to develop an original style. Many children can write quite quickly, and they may go on for quite a lengthy period before they tire; but most will still make a good many mistakes in letter formation. Nine or ten year olds can use their hands independently while writing: one hand can hold a book or a pencil while the other drums on a table or fiddles with the edge of the page.

Both the changes in children's drawings and their attitudes towards their

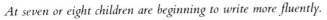

At seven or eight children are beginning to write more fluently.

Dear Sam,
Thank you for giving
Me the chocolate engine.
I am keeping it for a
special treat.

Getting the flow – an example of early cursive.

own work illustrate much that is typical of this age group. As their fine motor skills improve, so they have more control over a pencil. As their cognitive skills mature, so they begin to understand perspective, and start to draw from a particular viewpoint, with proportions worked out accordingly. Their pictures become more realistic and more conventional. Many children now draw or paint far less than they did when younger – probably, in part at least, because as their capacity for self-criticism increases they often find their work rather disappointing. It may also be that as they become more skilled in the use of language they feel less need for pictorial communication.

By seven, most children begin to use colour in a naturalistic way. Seven year olds tend to paint a band of green colour at the bottom of the page to represent ground or grass, with a blue band across the top of the page which indicates sky, and there is a gap in the middle. Between eight and ten the 'air gap' disappears and the colours meet, to form a horizon. This marks a significant development in the child's ability to understand and represent three-dimensional space.

Seven year olds are already drawing people with heads and bodies, possibly with hands, hair, fingers and clothes. By eight children are beginning to draw in perspective and are more aware of proportion; at this age they often draw an outline first and then fill in the details. By nine they may draw precisely what they see rather than their idea of it. If children under nine are asked to draw a cup when the handle is turned away from them, they will usually sketch in the handle anyway; by nine they are more likely to draw it just the way they see it, without the handle. Most children are eleven before they are able to draw overlapping figures, or to place one object in front of another in a drawing.

In drawing this mountain scene a ten year old is exploring perspective and proportion.

The Growth in Understanding

During the years from seven to eleven, children's understanding develops in subtlety, complexity and flexibility. As they grow older they acquire a greater comprehension of other people's feelings and motives and an ability to step back from immediate experience. They also learn to take an overview of a situation. An eight year old watching a football game will not only see the kick which has just been missed, but can consider the whole game, and put a single action into that perspective.

As children mature they are less easily distracted, and generally acquire a more systematic approach to problem-solving, realizing that they can be more successful if they approach tasks in an orderly way. At the same time, their thinking becomes more flexible – and more creative.

Learning to concentrate

Children's ability to select and assimilate appropriate information improves as they grow older – both because they are biologically more mature and because they have had more practice. Preschool children, asked to compare two pictures and find the differences between them, tend to dart their eyes all over the pictures, as if they are expecting the differences to jump out at them. From the time they go to school they become progressively less haphazard in their exploration and by nine or ten their search is planned and thought out systematically: they will explore the two pictures in an orderly way, pausing to focus on relevant details.

Remembering and learning depend on the ability to recognize and attend to relevant information. Right through this age group (and beyond), when a child is learning new information, she will need help to select out important details and focus on them. She will also benefit from being prompted to make links between her past memories and what she now needs to learn, so that she can build on the knowledge she already has. A child learning history, for example, will need help to focus her attention on relevant details of the past and draw attention to similarities and differences between the way people lived then and the way she lives now.

Logical thinking

By the time children are seven or eight they show a growing ability to deliberate on their experience and come to logical conclusions, which they can then apply in other situations.

A four or five year old child who is presented with ten sweets arranged in a line with wide spaces between them may become upset if they are pushed together in a shorter line – she feels that she has less than her original ten pieces. By seven or eight she will be quite happy with her ten sweets whether they are pushed together or spaced out: she is now more mature and has had a lot more experience, and so she realizes that things can be reorganized into different patterns and remain the same in quantity. The number of objects is independent of the way they are arranged – that is the rule which applies to this situation: the child now understands the rule, and is able to apply it.

According to Jean Piaget, it is through biological maturation and active exploration that children develop the power of logical thought. Through experimenting they construct concepts and learn gradually to apply them to new situations. How successfully a child does this is largely a matter of her own internal development and mental readiness. Parents and other teachers serve as facilitators. They supply the necessary materials or situation and the child, through solving problems on her own, increases her knowledge and skill.

Other theorists place more emphasis on the effect of teaching. A child may learn a certain amount through exploring an object or confronting a problem, all on her own; but teaching will make it easier for her to develop complex ideas. Jerome Bruner believes that quite young children can understand very complicated concepts, if they are presented at the children's own level. A child will not necessarily understand a particular concept precisely as adults do, but she can grasp it in a way that is appropriate to her own stage of development. If a child is taken sailing by her parents she develops a mental script of what a day of sailing is like, the kind of problems that are encountered and their solutions. A seven year old will not be able to navigate, of course, but she will learn from her own experience that the boat moves with the wind, and if she is taught she will also understand something of the function of the compass. Through a combination of experience and teaching she may come to realize that adjustment of the sails will change the speed and direction of the boat.

Sometimes, children just need to be provided with the basic scaffolding, and then they can build around that. For example, if you show a child how the first few pieces of a puzzle fit together, she may be able to work out the rest for herself.

If we look back we can see how the process of 'making sense' began in infancy. As babies, children were surrounded by routines and by words which they gradually mastered. Ever since then their conceptual understanding has been increasing in complexity, little by little. Children have been going shopping with their parents for years. Now, by eight or so, their script for going shopping has developed to a point where they can understand a chain of events and people which includes most of what is going on at the counter, and quite a lot about what happens behind the scenes. They are beginning to have a grasp of such subjects as the sources of food and some other goods, the relative cost of different items, what is value for money, how shopkeepers make a profit.

As a child in this age group gazes longingly at a bicycle in a shop window, you can see her thought processes working at tremendous speed: she begins to imagine herself riding down the street, and formulates plans for acquiring the new bike. She may think in terms of asking her parents for the bicycle, of saving her pocket money, earning money by doing chores, waiting until Christmas or her birthday. By seven or eight a child can reflect on the

Memory strategies

At this age children become increasingly able to call upon strategies to help them remember.

• One useful strategy is rehearsing – repeating a word or phrase over and over (see page 301). While only one in ten five year olds rehearses spontaneously, 50 per cent of seven year olds do so, and almost 90 per cent of ten year olds. Again, while younger children repeat one word at a time, older children group words, repeating each of the earlier items as they add a new one.

• Categorizing also helps children memorize. Most children of nine who are asked, for example, to remember the words 'car', 'boat', 'plane', 'shoe', 'bicycle', 'sock' and 'coat' will divide the words into two separate lists, one of clothes, the other of methods of transport. Having done this, they remember the words better than those children who try to remember word by word. The wider and richer a child's experience, the easier it is for her to form categories spontaneously: a child who knows the zoo well will have little difficulty in remembering a list of zoo animals. The more categories children are familiar with, the more agile they are at putting information together and finding a context for it.

• Creating a visual image is a device few children come to spontaneously, but once they have been taught the technique they often enjoy using it. This method involves forming a scene or story in the mind, incorporating the objects to be remembered: if, for example, we need to remember a shopping list including baked beans, fish fingers, cat food and shampoo, we might create a picture of a girl with shiny hair eating beans and fish fingers while the cat looks on longingly.

• Learning by rote (or 'by heart') is a traditional skill which is sometimes neglected, even disparaged, nowadays, but which provides useful memory training. You might like to encourage your child to learn a poem (or even the lyrics of a popular song) to recite to you.

• Mnemonics, as in 'Every Good Boy Deserves Favour' for the notes on the lines of the musical stave, can be helpful to children of seven and over, especially if they invent their own.

• External reminders such as making a list or tying a string around your finger have their uses too.

Once the teacher has initiated the discussion, the children can carry on; they enjoy learning to sort out problems and work with ideas.

strengths and weaknesses of alternative solutions, weigh her chances of success or failure and try several strategies. Her first attempt may be confined to simply asking over and over again in a increasingly whiny voice; but if this doesn't get her anywhere she can reflect that it may not, after all, be the way to succeed and try other routes, until she finally discovers a strategy that works.

What parents and teachers can do

Needless to say, some children extrapolate from their experience more readily than others. Some children are thoughtful by temperament, others more impulsive; but training is also significant. The more hands-on experiences a child had in the early stages, and continues to have now, the more flexible her approach will be as she begins to explore possible solutions in her mind. You can also help your child to develop skills in extrapolation and task analysis by presenting her with opportunities to practise: by asking thought-provoking questions and by encouraging her to try out her own solutions to problems.

Children, especially those who are not reflective by nature, may need lots of reminders from adults to stop and think, to contemplate the possible consequences of a decision or an action and to plan successful strategies. Parents and teachers provide for a child the bridge or link between what she knows and what she does not yet know. The adult needs to be conscious and reflective for the child until she is ready to take over this function herself. A good teacher has an overview of the subject she is teaching: she may, for example, set up an experiment and then, as the child begins to participate, hand over more and more, asking her to record her results or encouraging her to question what she has observed.

Deciding when a child needs to be supported in her thinking and when she must be given a chance to solve her own dilemmas is no easy task; learning is, and remains, an interactive process.

Creative thinking

Creativity involves flexibility, spontaneity, curiosity and persistence. It also requires an ability to combine ideas in a way that produces something new. The creative idea may result in a story, or a new ending to an existing story, in a picture in which everyday objects are depicted or combined in unusual or unexpected ways, in the construction of a machine, in acting, in experiments with musical instruments, in a joke. But creativity may be displayed in less obvious ways: in the way a child resolves an everyday problem, for example, or plans how to spend her Saturday.

It is the growing ability to think and act creatively that makes many children of this age so fascinating, amusing and exasperating.

All children are inherently creative, in that they are constantly absorbing and transforming the raw material of their experience. But some children do appear to be exceptionally original and inventive in their thinking, and are often referred to as 'creative' in a particular sense.

This kind of creativity is distinct from measured intelligence. Creative children may not do particularly well in academic subjects, especially those which require convergent thinking – the sort of reasoning that focuses on achieving expected answers. They are often divergent in their thinking, shooting off at unexpected tangents. For example, where a convergent thinker might answer the question 'What is a brick useful for?' with 'For building houses', the creative child might say 'To make a platform for a mouse giving a speech' – and enjoy the joke.

Encouraging creativity

Most parents enjoy their children's creativity, though they are perhaps more ready to encourage a young inventor or a budding writer than a child who removes the entire contents of the refrigerator in order to create a giant milk shake – and leaves the mess behind. And you can do much to foster, or to stifle, creative thinking in your child.

Creative clowning – how many funny ways can we wear these caps?

• A creative home atmosphere is not necessarily one in which chaos reigns. It is one in which space, time and attention are given to all family members, where each feels free to express him or herself and to challenge conventional ideas – and where each can learn to respect the opinions and activities of others. It is also a place where children are given time and encouragement to play and to explore. It is not just a question of providing paints, musical instruments or word processors, useful as these aids are.

• Children need to be encouraged to think creatively and to explore different situations. You might sometimes ask them to brainstorm family problems, encouraging a free flow of uncriticized ideas. Though it may not always be practicable to incorporate a child's ideas in the final solution, she will gain from seeing her contribution seriously considered.

• Children also need to explore their own creative solutions at times, even when you can foresee the consequences. Keep quiet where possible, and let them find out for themselves the disadvantages of the alternative route home from school, or what happens when they mix together all sorts of unlikely ingredients. Sometimes they may just invent a delicious new recipe, or devise a far more efficient way than yours of getting a job done.

It is reasonable, however, to impose some boundaries on creative forays. If the baby is recruited as a test pilot and flown down the stairs he is likely to end up in hospital; creative cooking is fun, but not just after the kitchen has been cleaned and your exhausted parent at last has a moment to relax; it is fun to decorate your room, but not by painting on the new wallpaper. Such constraints do not stifle creativity: unlimited possibilities are daunting; limitations make people feel safe, and working within them can provide a challenge in itself.

• Encourage discussion of entertaining and improbable situations too: 'What would we do if granny turned into a dinosaur?' Once started, the possibilities are endless.

382

Education

By the age of seven your child will be fully launched on her primary education. Once she is settled in school her progress there can be considerably enhanced if you, her parents, have a clear understanding of how children in this age group develop, and how the school works – and if you have realistic expectations of both the school and the child. You will be evaluating above all whether the school is helping your child to learn all she needs to know. This will depend both on the general effectiveness of the school and on how your child responds to what the school offers.

We look here at the structure and philosophy of schools, at the different ways the classroom may be managed, at teaching methods, and at what children are expected to learn in school during these years. Of course, where education is concerned there is widespread variation in the approach and practice of different countries and of individual schools within those countries. What follows is a discussion of key areas of concern, which acknowledges where differences exist between schools and how these may influence children's development.

What makes a school effective?

Some schools place the main emphasis on academic success; others are more relaxed, focusing on all-round accomplishment and paying particular attention to encouraging individual creativity; many, perhaps most, aim at a broad-based education that includes achievement in both the academic field and other areas. Whatever type of school your child attends, it is how effective that school is in helping its pupils that will most concern you.

Peter Mortimore and his colleagues, who made a thorough study of schooling for seven to eleven year olds in Britain in the 1980s identified some characteristics that contribute to effective schooling. They found, among many other things, that schools with about 160 on roll generally worked better than larger or smaller ones; that children in classes of fewer than twenty-four made more progress than those in larger ones – noticeably more than those in classes of over twenty-seven; that a good physical environment (buildings in good repair, no graffiti) was an advantage. They also found that the most effective headteachers had clear policies and good leadership qualities and that a high level of parental involvement in and out of school was beneficial. The most effective schools placed greater emphasis on praise and reward than on punishment and criticism, had enthusiastic and dedicated staff, plenty of extracurricular activities and a supportive environment in which children were happy and cared about the happiness of others. Of course, as Mortimore acknowledges, no one feature can ensure effective schooling – a school with small classes, for example, is not automatically better than one with larger classes. However, if a school is working well in even a few of these areas the children will benefit.

Recent reports indicate that schools which emphasize the acquisition of basic skills as an end in itself are generally less effective than schools which see those skills as tools to allow children to gain access to wider educational horizons.

Finally, remember that children are good judges. A child who is happy and enjoys school is her parents' best indicator that the school is effective. Children (like adults) work best when they are enjoying what they are doing.

Classroom structure

Classes for seven to eleven year olds are normally arranged according to age. In some schools year groups may be streamed – divided into different classes according to ability – but it is more usual in this age group for classes to include a range of abilities, the children within the class being put into small ability-related groups for some but not all of their work.

Though in some traditional schools children sit at desks arranged in rows, facing the teacher and the blackboard, in most primary schools children work in pairs or groups at tables, often helping or observing each other, and the teacher circulates among them.

Teaching methods: formal and informal approaches

Teaching methods vary from the formal, with the teacher standing in front of the class for much of the time and teaching children as a unit, to the informal, where the teacher helps the children either individually or in small groups. In schools where formal methods are employed children tend to be taught what to learn; in informal classrooms the emphasis is more often on guiding children into areas of study or exploration, and on teaching them the skills necessary to manage their work independently. Here, there is generally little emphasis on marks or competition; more attention is paid to individual achievement. Of course, many schools adopt elements of both approaches.

In this age group as in younger ones, children benefit from a 'hands-on' approach. They remember moderately well what they are taught simply through listening; better when they can both listen and watch; and much the best when they actually do something and learn from experience.

Teachers may use project or topic work to teach different areas of the curriculum through a central theme. A topic such as 'transport', for example, could include social history, science, maths and geography and, when it is written up and illustrated, language and art as well. It may also act as a springboard for school trips and visits, which often contribute much of value to children's education. A well-chosen project can motivate children to make discoveries, solve problems independently and communicate their results enthusiastically. But to be of value a project must be carefully planned, offer a wide range of skills and perspectives and be firmly related to the children's own experience. And the topics chosen need to be part of a whole-school policy: otherwise, a child may find herself covering 'transport' – for instance – two or three times in her school career.

Whatever teaching method is used, the aim is to achieve a quiet, busy classroom where pupils are clear about what work they are to do and how to go about it. The more time teachers spend communicating with children about their work the more progress is made on all fronts.

There is also evidence to indicate that children benefit from working together and helping each other. They profit from shared talents and experiences; what is more, working together helps them to think more clearly and to express their thoughts more cogently, develops their social skills and confidence and extends their patience.

The influence of teachers

The influence of the headteacher is all-important to the school's style and atmosphere and to its approach to both learning and discipline. According to the Mortimore study, in the most effective schools the head or principal has usually been in the post for between three and seven years. A newly appointed head can be very effective, but experience helps the head gain confidence – and the confidence of the staff – and in three years he or she will have had time to implement teaching programmes and philosophies. If they spend too long in one place, though, heads, like other people, can become set in their ways, and less open to new ideas; again, of course, there are exceptions.

It is also worth looking at how long teachers in general tend to stay at the school. A high teacher turnover usually – though not always – indicates that something is wrong.

Teachers undoubtedly provide role models for children: part of the hidden curriculum we discussed in the preceding chapter is to be found in the example teachers set, not only in the way they present a lesson or maintain order, but by the atmosphere they create in a classroom, the way they encourage children to behave, and the values they instil.

Closely related to this last point is the way in which a child's self-image develops as a direct result of what the teachers say and do. This process involves, to a very large extent, the child's response to a teacher's expectations, and the way those expectations are conveyed. Teachers who expect high standards do seem more likely to get them than those who do not.

An animated discussion around the globe – where everyone has a chance to contribute to the session.

Some schools, some teachers, regard it as essential that each child is encouraged to see herself or himself as excelling at something: they perceive that this can have far-reaching effects on a child's self-esteem. Excellence need not be confined to schoolwork, it can lie in something as simple as delivering messages efficiently or looking after a school pet.

Perhaps the most significant single test of whether teachers have contributed positively to children's self-esteem is the extent to which the children feel confident in asking questions which reveal their ignorance. As John Holt wrote, 'Most children in school fail . . . because they are afraid, bored and confused. They are afraid, above all else, of failing, or disappointing or displeasing the many anxious adults around them.'

When children are able to ask sensible questions to elucidate a point, they are revealing, first, that they are intelligent enough to realize what they do not know, second, that they are confident the teacher will not laugh at them, and, third, that the class has been so trained that other children will not laugh either. The teacher who creates an atmosphere in which children are not afraid to ask questions has succeeded, whatever the system the school uses, no matter how big or small, rich or poor it may be.

Discipline

Where the atmosphere of a school is happy, busy and considerate of others (including visitors), discipline problems are likely to be few. A positive school climate of this kind is achieved by an emphasis, not on rules and punishment (which have a negative effect on both learning and behaviour) but on praise and reward, on treating children with respect and encouraging them to take responsibility for their own behaviour. Such an atmosphere is an indication of effective and enthusiastic teaching and firm but fair classroom management; it has in turn a beneficial effect on learning and on the well-being of both pupils and staff.

An effective school will have worked out strategies for dealing with behaviour problems that do arise, and members of teaching and non-teaching staff will be aware of those guidelines and can expect the help and support of the head and other members of staff in implementing them. A consistent, fair and positive approach enables both staff and pupils to know where they stand.

The involvement of parents

Parents can contribute a great deal to the life of a school. Not only can you provide an extra pair of hands or ears in the classroom, but the fact that you demonstrate support for the school, the staff and your child by giving your time helps morale all round. You may also be able to supply a skill that the staff lack or have no time to indulge – you may be able to help with carpentry, cooking, needlework, pottery, or whatever you can offer and the school can use. And in addition to the practical help, everyone benefits from a breath of outside air: a different face, another approach.

What is your child learning at school?

Good teachers have a very definite idea about what they expect children to achieve during a school year and how that will relate to what they will be required to know in the years to come. The demands of national or local curricula (such as those of the National Curriculum in Britain) draw on good teaching practice of this kind and are designed to ensure that all children cover basic material at levels appropriate to their age, maturity and ability. This does not mean that children (or teachers) are restricted to the planned schedule, but it does help to ensure that in the early years the foundation is solid and that a child who falls behind can be recognized and helped.

Every effective teaching plan breaks down learning into small steps or objectives which the child can reasonably be expected to master. As children mature and are able to cope with more complex ideas and abstract thoughts, they are asked to tackle more difficult material. It can seem to some parents a slow process, but it is a painstaking one, and if the foundation is solid the child has something to build on throughout her whole life.

Different subject areas are discussed below. It should be remembered, though, that in the classroom the subjects frequently overlap.

Reading

Reading helps children learn to think. Books are not merely recorded conversations: they have order and structure and give a sense of sequence and of information unfolding. Children who read cannot help but be influenced by this when they come to organize information themselves.

It is usually not until children have been reading for several years that they can read well enough to extract substantial information from books. In the first few years of school what matters most is that they should enjoy what they read. By the time they are nine or ten, however, they can be expected to use books as a source of information, to be able to remember details and to interpret and evaluate what they read.

Encouraging reading

The most effective way to encourage your child to read is by reading yourself. Children of this age like to copy adults, especially their parents, and if your child sees that you enjoy reading she too will think of it as an everyday, pleasurable activity.

Sometimes parents stop reading to their children as soon as they have developed a basic competence in reading. This is sad. A child who is repeatedly told 'you can read it yourself' may be put off reading altogether. Most children appreciate being read to, right through primary and even into secondary school. Part of the fun is being able to share the experience. The other great advantage is that it enables the child to enjoy books that are still too difficult for her to read herself: this extends her experience and helps her develop her vocabulary and her ear for language.

Of course, children also need the chance to read to themselves outside school. A visit to a library or bookshop allows them to exercise choice. Not everything they read has to be of great literary merit: it is the variety and enjoyment that count. You are ideally placed to know what interests your child and to provide books which nourish that interest. If you feel uncertain you can enlist the help of a librarian or a good bookshop, or consult one of the guides to children's literature. And give your child the benefit of the doubt: if she says she wants to read a particular book let her try, even if you suspect that it may be too difficult for her. So long as she has a grasp of the story she will be able to use the context to help her guess the meaning of words she doesn't know. You can foster her reading skills by asking her to tell you what her book is about, so that you can see how much she has actually absorbed and understood and whether she needs help with words or ideas. And it is a good idea to encourage her to get into the habit of using a dictionary. But beware: if you insist on her checking every word, or interrogate her to make sure she understands every subtlety of a story line, you run the risk that she will come to consider reading a chore to be avoided.

Communication skills

Between seven and eleven your child will be rapidly improving her ability to communicate. This will include learning how to express herself in speech and writing, but she will also be helped to learn how to listen actively, which involves paying close attention and putting what she hears into practice or responding to questions.

In the earliest stages of writing the emphasis is on content and on getting the words down on paper, rather than on spelling, punctuation or grammar. As she gains confidence in expressing herself these things will gradually be introduced and she will be encouraged to present her work in a form which makes it easy for others to read. She will begin to understand that correct spelling and punctuation and clear handwriting will all help her to communicate clearly with others.

Creative writing becomes more demanding as stories begin to take on a structure and more attention is given to plots of greater complexity. Children who have a lot of stories told and read to them have a head start when it comes to writing. They are familiar with narrative: the idea that a story has a beginning, a middle and an end. By seven some children are beginning to produce accounts of their own experiences and fantasies. Gradually the sequential story – in which one thing happens and then another – is replaced by stories which convey a message or are organized to have dramatic impact and keep the reader's interest in mind.

When your child reaches eight or nine or so, she will be asked to write reports about things she has observed or subjects she has researched; writing tasks or assignments such as these can span several subject areas.

The author understands how to keep her reader interested – she likes dramatic touches, and has a strong awareness of narrative structure, probably acquired through having read and heard many stories.

> It's a hard life as a seamstress, working day in and day out. My son Alexander has a rare and bad fever. The doctor has come once or twice but I have no money to give him. My child needs oranges but I have no money to buy any. My husband died long ago of food poisoning and so I have no help with my work. The court ball shall be in two days time. If I have not produced a beautiful ball gown for Lady Andrea Carter, I shall lose my job. Then I will no longer be able to live in this cold and damp room but in the miserable streets of London.

Encouraging writing

When children learn to write they acquire a physical skill which gradually becomes a sophisticated means of communication. Parents are sometimes perplexed because children who are good at telling stories may not be able to write them down. To be able to write creatively, however, children need enough mechanical skill to write reasonably legibly and form letters without having to think about it (see page 375); if a child is struggling to write, tensely gripping her pencil, it is difficult for her to coordinate her thinking with the physical task. Some children may also become frustrated by the slow business of committing to paper the thoughts that flow so fast, while others may be daunted by not knowing what to write about, or what response their writing will elicit – in contrast to conversation, there is no listener and no immediate reaction.

Children benefit from having plenty of opportunities to exercise their new skills and sometimes they may need help with ideas for what to write about. One medium can stimulate another: photographs, music, a television programme can be used as a starting point for the child's own story or poem. Once a child has an idea, brainstorming is a good technique to help her develop it. Ask her to say whatever comes into her mind when she thinks of that particular subject and then encourage her to use these thoughts, words or ideas to help her writing flow. If a child gets tired of writing and ends abruptly, try asking questions to help her get going again, or suggest she stop for a while and take it up again later when she has had a rest.

Children who have real difficulty in getting words down on paper – either because they lack the manual skill or because they are not yet comfortable with the written word – can be helped by the use of tape-

Information technology

Children in this age group usually have the use of computers in school, and most have little difficulty in learning to keyboard information into a computer using simple word processing techniques – they often find they can write more freely using a computer because they don't have to worry about their handwriting. Children also learn how to use a computer to access a data base and acquire information; and they may be encouraged to devise simple programs they can use to solve, for example, mathematical problems.

Children may also have the opportunity to use tape-recorders, still and video cameras and projectors, and they will probably learn something about making newspapers, designing charts, creating advertisements. By the time they are eleven many of them have quite a sophisticated command of ways and means of presenting information and the ability to communicate using a wide range of media.

recorders. The child, on her own or with a group, can dictate the story for the teacher to type out later; the tangible evidence that she has 'written' a story will encourage her a lot. Children whose handwriting is less advanced than their cognitive skills may find it helpful to use a word processor for some work.

From ten or eleven on, children can begin to plan what they want to say. In the early stages too much insistence on perfect sentence construction, neat handwriting and correct spelling can dampen a child's enthusiasm, but between eight and ten children can be expected gradually to pay more attention to these aspects of writing. At any age, seeing your piece of work on the wall, properly mounted, with or without illustrations or decorations, is a great encouragement.

You will help your child most by encouraging her – getting her to read what she has written and listening with interest and enthusiasm, commenting positively on any part you have enjoyed or a word you find particularly appropriate. Avoid making negative comments, but you might sometimes suggest that she should try some new angle or different ways of saying something. If she is happy to try this, get her to compare the altered version with the original, and discuss with her why the second version reads better or is more interesting. Older children who write well constantly correct themselves, adjusting, clarifying and reorganizing their material to make what they want to say clearer. In this way, as they mature, they play a large part in teaching themselves.

Both the process and the mechanics of writing need practice. Encourage children to write letters, keep diaries and have pen friends. Ask them to help you with notes, shopping lists or any other writing you have to do, consulting them about how best to put things, or what you should say next.

Mathematics

The underlying principles of mathematics teaching and learning, which we outlined in the previous chapter (pages 311–15) are equally relevant in this age group. Learning mathematics involves both the acquisition of skills and an understanding of processes and concepts. The key to effective learning lies in the child's perception of mathematics as being useful – and fun. Maths teaching today is, to a large extent, based on investigation, and the best work takes place where teachers present real-life problems, help children to understand the processes required for a task, encourage discussion between children and with the teacher, and give children the confidence and the flexibility to apply the skills they have learned.

Progress in mathematics, perhaps even more than with any other school subject, is crucially dependent on a firm foundation. Any early problems or gaps in mathematical understanding will soon become apparent, as, from the age of seven or eight, children are increasingly expected to build on their basic skills to solve more complex problems.

By the time children reach the end of primary school at eleven, the basic number skills of adding, subtracting, multiplying and dividing have been established through routine practice, and children have learned how to apply them to practical problems and how to record the processes and their results. They will also, on the way, have learned their tables, which remain a useful tool. They will have been taught how to approach problems, and will be able to make confident and sensible decisions about which methods to employ – mental arithmetic, pencil and paper or a calculator, for example. As their cognitive skills develop, they learn to move easily between practical and theoretical areas and develop a growing awareness of the fascination of mathematics for its own sake.

Calculators do not remove the need for children to develop a sound basic number sense – quite the reverse. Children who have a good understanding of numbers are able to make sensible use of calculators, which can then be used to stimulate fresh ideas and new ways of looking at things.

In the early stages, children use learning materials to reinforce basic concepts; as they get older, similar materials may be used to clarify more complex concepts such as fractions and decimals. Objects from the natural environment may be used to introduce children to pattern and relationship; these concepts will later be extended on paper, and work in three dimensions will establish an important link with geometry. In learning about shape and space, children absorb the fundamentals and the language of geometry, and start to give explanations of why particular characteristics and patterns emerge: they are able to see how a folded tablecloth can become a triangle, a rectangle or a square, and how four triangles can fit together to make a pyramid. Gradually, children learn to predict a result, and to test the validity of generalizations.

Practical work on number, measurement and shape gives opportunities to practise mathematical skills, and introduces children to ideas of comparison in length, weight, angle, time, money, area, volume and capacity. A problem may encompass many of these elements: if the classroom is to be redecorated, how much paint will be needed and what will it cost? If there is to be a summer fair, what is the most economical way to arrange cars on the school playground?

Children are also likely to have experience of measuring temperature: they may, for example, predict and check the temperature, inside the school and in sunny and shaded areas of the playground, in a variety of weather conditions. Measurement of angles may be linked with map work and through that to an understanding of scale and symbols as well as of coordinates. As in most areas of mathematics teaching, practical experience is essential. The child who follows a map and successfully reaches the top of a local hill may pursue the academic aspects of the topic with redoubled vigour the next day in school.

One of the hardest measures for young children to learn is that of time. Repeated use of a working clock has been found to be more successful in teaching children how to tell the time than the use of paper diagrams, and the measurement of passing time is often combined with experiments in science. By eleven, most children can understand a twenty-four hour clock and are working with fractions of seconds.

By this age children will also have learned a good deal about handling and recording data. This begins in the early stages as sorting and classifying; higher up the school, perhaps with the help of a computer data base, children may learn to construct frequency tables, block graphs, pie charts, scattergrams and other forms of graphic representation.

The level of work achieved by individual children will, of course, vary according to their ability and the stage of development they have reached. While one eleven year old may be happily dealing with complex mathematical concepts, another may still be reinforcing her basic skills.

Encouraging mathematical skills

Many parents feel at a loss as to how they can best help their children with mathematics. Often, this is because they have little confidence in their own mathematical ability – a surprisingly high number of people describe themselves as 'no good at maths'. But these same people are, every day, exercising basic mathematical skills – we all have to add up, multiply, divide as part of our daily routines. Many opportunities arise for putting across fundamental mathematical concepts, in a simple, relaxed way, in perfectly ordinary situations at home: when cooking, gardening, shopping or just eating and drinking, for example.

You may also feel that it would help if you knew more about how your child is taught maths in school – which may well seem very different from the way you were taught. The maths workshops which many schools run for parents can be very useful here. They are often extremely successful in conveying how children are encouraged to acquire skills and understand mathematical concepts.

Science

Good science teaching builds on the everyday experiences with which children are familiar. They are encouraged to develop scientific concepts through practical investigation of their own surroundings. They learn first to observe carefully and to record accurately; they are then equipped to go on to the identification of patterns; from there they can progress to making predictions, drawing conclusions and communicating results.

Most children are fascinated by the real world around them. Good science teaching stimulates this curiosity and widens children's interests greatly. The value of children's experimental work is greatly enhanced if it is planned by the children beforehand; if the investigation is carried out in sufficient depth, with observations properly classified; and if findings are then discussed and recorded in the form of diagrams, sketches, written descriptions or computerized data. In this way each set of scientific skills reinforces the others, and children are helped to acquire both scientific knowledge and an understanding of systematic investigation.

Children enjoy learning about living things, about the world around them, and about themselves and their relationship with that world. By eleven or so they will probably have looked at plants and animals (including themselves); reproduction and genetics; human influences on the earth (pollution, for example); natural and man-made materials such as wood, metal or plastic, their make-up and uses; the earth and the atmosphere; magnetism and electrical forces; energy in its various forms; sound and music.

Much useful scientific work is done in schools through projects on themes such as transport, flight or water. Here, direct observation can be backed up by information from museum services and libraries, by visits to relevant places of interest, and by experiments on different aspects of the subject. Other skills, such as those of mathematics or communication, will be brought into play; ideally, many or all of the senses will be used; and the very acquisition of knowledge leads to further inquiry. Themes such as these can be used with any age group, and geared to provide valuable work for children of a wide range of ability.

Encouraging science activities at home

Many investigations can take place at home, where parents are in a good position to encourage scientific thinking. An important part of the process is simply allowing a child's natural sense of inquiry to emerge. For instance, follow up her interest in light coming in through a window, making shadows on the wall: observe it with her, talk about it and ask questions. You can investigate the answers together, perhaps getting books from the library, or, as the child grows older, encouraging her to read and find out for herself. Don't get anxious if you aren't able to answer questions immediately – children don't need to believe that their parents know everything; they often like to feel that parents share their curiosity, and are delighted if they can tell *you* the answer to a question.

Children can learn a lot about nutrition through preparing food with you and discussing the kinds of food needed for a healthy diet. They can observe and record the different findings while cooking, gardening or caring for pets. You can follow up what they learn about ecological issues through household activities such as organizing and collecting materials for recycling, or shopping for 'green' detergents and household cleaners.

Children can usefully record their observations of nature through painting, drawing or photography. All these methods help them to focus on interesting details, patterns or contrasts which may otherwise go unremarked. Photography, certainly, is easier to organize at home than at school – if you are interested in photography yourself you might even like to set up a darkroom where you and your child can develop and print photographs together.

Some children find commercially available junior chemistry sets, microscopes and telescopes very absorbing; others reject them entirely. Whether or not you choose to buy them, bear in mind that they are not at all necessary to stimulate scientific thinking in young children. Your own patience and responsiveness provide the best encouragement to inquiry.

History and geography

As children grow older they gradually become capable of seeing themselves in a broader context of time and place. At first children see history simply as an account of what happened and how people lived in 'the olden days' – and this can encompass almost any era, from prehistory to their parents' childhood and youth. As they begin to reason and to think in more complex ways, the focus gradually changes from simply knowing what happened to a consideration of why and how. Interpreting the past involves seeing events from different viewpoints, and this allows children to develop an imaginative understanding of the thoughts, feelings and actions of people who have lived in the past – which can in turn be of great value to them in understanding their own everyday experience. History also helps children comprehend abstract ideas such as those of change and continuity, cause and effect. It usually involves some of their first experiences of reading for content and develops their ability to memorize, absorb information and select relevant ideas and facts.

Like science, both history and geography are best taught as a process of inquiry. Most children begin learning about these subjects through work which is firmly based on their own experience, community and immediate environment. Their first experience of map work will probably come through making simple maps of their classroom, home and neighbourhood. They will learn about family and community history and start to gather information first hand – from looking at things in local museums, perhaps, or from talking to older people about their memories. As they progress, they may also consider their local economy: the kind of products their area is known for, whether the climate or local geography influences what is grown or manufactured. From there they can move out into a study of different societies.

History and geography are often most successfully taught through topic work. A Victorian project on the children's local town, for example, could include work on buildings, clothing, industry, commerce and transport. This could be supported by borrowing nineteenth-century artefacts, photographs and old newspaper reports from families, local traders and the local museum, as well as by researching other written sources. Children will be encouraged to consider different points of view and discuss their findings. Their curiosity will be aroused as they learn the skills of historical research. Dressing up and re-enacting some aspect of life of the period also provide valuable experiences, and in all these ways children's understanding of historical perspective is enriched. The value of such work is further enhanced by the variety of ways in which the experiences are recorded: illustrations, photographs, sketches, written work, art and drama can all help to consolidate and augment findings.

School visits can teach children a lot about how other people live and work, and get them involved in all sorts of new experiences.

In geography a simple beginning such as a pond study can act as a stimulating starting point for a much wider exploration of environmental issues that might include conservation and pollution and man's influence on the environment. Farm visits can illustrate the use of land, industrial visits can demonstrate the use of raw materials – steel, for example. Through observation of their own area, children may consider how places affect what people do, and how people have used and adapted their surroundings. Local field work with Ordnance Survey maps and compasses at seven can lead to quite sophisticated map work using globes and atlases later, and older children may happily extend their interest to other parts of the world. This in turn can lead to an understanding of cultural as well as geographic diversity. A topic on the polar region could include work on exploration, animal life, pollution and insulation. Through following the route of an explorer – Darwin or Magellan, for example – older children may learn to use Mercator projection maps as well as atlases – besides imagining for themselves what such a voyage must have entailed.

The creative arts

In art a wide variety of materials are used, from paint and clay to found objects. Which techniques are employed is determined in part by the expertise of the teacher, but children may be making pots, doing batik,

396

Playing the violin in a group is much more fun than practising alone – an encouragement when you are just beginning to learn the instrument.

printing on fabric, making collages, or painting their own portraits. Experience of using different materials is immensely valuable, as is the sense of satisfaction and self-esteem that comes with an achievement.

In music children are encouraged to explore their own means of music-making, using either traditional instruments or homemade ones. They may also be taught how to compose their own music on a keyboard. The emphasis is on discovering sound and rhythm and trying out their own creative abilities. Many schools have a choir, some run classes for learning an instrument, some have a school orchestra and many have a school band. Specialist music teachers may come in, perhaps once or twice a week, to supplement what the school staff can offer.

Designing and making

In most schools children are also introduced to technology, which covers a range of practical activities that will vary depending on the resources available but may include cooking, woodwork, metalwork, work with textiles, or the construction of working machines from a variety of materials. In all these areas, though children will be instructed in specific skills, the emphasis in primary schools today is not so much on teaching a particular craft, more on stimulating children to think creatively and to solve problems. They are encouraged to plan their working procedures and design their own work within the limits of their technical experience. Children may, for example, be put into small groups, given some basic materials and asked to make a machine with wheels that, powered by a balloon, will reach the other side of the room. Or they may be asked to make musical instruments to explore the variety of ways sound can be created. Some may need more help than others, but their ingenuity increases with experience.

Helping your child

The greatest help you can give your child probably lies in your own attitude towards the school and her place in it. Practical help in the classroom is valuable to the school and helpful in enabling you to see the everyday realities of school life, but this kind of direct involvement may not be possible if you are working or have smaller children, or it may just not suit your temperament. It is more important that your child should know that you listen to her and will try to understand her account of good days and bad days (and on many days you may well be told nothing); that you will support the teacher where you feel it is fair, and back her up likewise. The more children in her class you get to know the more meaning her experience will have for you, and it is good for her to feel free – within reason – to invite friends over after school and to visit them. And the more parents you know, the more satisfaction and interest you will probably derive for yourself. Comparing notes does help to give a more balanced picture of what actually goes on in the classroom from week to week.

If you are able to give encouragement and support and take a lively interest in the work she is doing, you will help your child, whatever her strengths and weaknesses, to feel secure, and to move forward.

If you think there are problems

At one time or another along the way many children feel themselves to be floundering. They may find the transition from reading for pleasure to reading for information daunting; they may experience difficulties in making the jump to more complex areas of mathematics. Or they may be having problems with friends or in the playground. Whatever it is, go and see the child's teacher. Most of the time he or she will be able to sort it out, or suggest ways in which you can help. In any case, if the teacher is going to help your child at all, he or she needs information about any difficulties that may be revealing themselves at home.

At the same time, remember that if there are upsets at home (family illness, job or money difficulties, an impending divorce – whatever the problem may be), the child may well show a reaction at school while maintaining a brave face at home. Do mention any such problems to the teacher, and enlist his or her support for your child. If for any reason you feel the teacher is not the person to talk to, go and see the head.

School refusal

At any time in her school career, a child may start refusing to go to school. Some children put up a fight every day; others do it every so often. Tears, tantrums, headaches, stomach-aches, vomiting at breakfast, may all manifest themselves in the struggle to persuade a parent that the child should stay at home.

In seeking to identify the reason for this, you will need to look at what is going on in your child's life. You must also talk, and listen attentively, to the child.

There may be some cause which quickly becomes obvious – perhaps she has been unsettled by having a new teacher, or a friend has left. Or you may have to go a bit deeper into things, to find, perhaps, that she has been frightened by some particular incident in the classroom or the playground, which she has never been able to tell you about. Perhaps she is being bullied (see page 419) by other children, or upset by a teacher who is coercive or aggressive.

Schoolwork may be the problem: a child may feel inadequate when academic expectations become more demanding, or if she is finding it difficult to keep up with her classmates.

However, while it is sensible to look first for an explanation in the child's experience at school, in many cases what happens in school is irrelevant; the root of the difficulty is to be found in an anxiety that is to do not with school, but with home.

Most often the anxiety is within the child and arises from her fear that something will happen to one of her parents. In this context school refusal often occurs when a parent has been sick, or after a divorce. Looked at from this point of view the refusal is an expression of misplaced love and concern.

Anxiety can also be found in parents. A parent who is depressed may unconsciously express a need for company; when the child meets this need by staying at home she is once again displaying a high degree of sensitivity. Indeed, school refusers (as opposed to truants, who skip school without their parents' knowledge) are more often than not rather quiet, thoughtful children.

What parents can do
The first step is to talk and (more important) listen to your child, and try to find out what is going on. Take complaints about school seriously, but give a clear message that you expect her to go to school and will not be persuaded otherwise without good reason. Explain that school problems can be sorted out only in school, and from the outset, do your best to enlist the help of the teacher and, if necessary, the head.

If the school staff are not prepared, or not able, to help, you may, after careful consideration, decide that the basic problem is that the school is the wrong one for your child. You will then have to try to find another school – but be wary of the danger of doing this only to find that the refusal is repeated in the new school.

If you come to realize that the problem does not lie directly in school, but elsewhere, you will need to encourage your child to talk about what it is that is really bothering her, so that you can help her to cope with it. Meanwhile, though, expect her to go to school. Enlisting a parent of one of her friends to pick her up on the way to school may help.

If, despite everybody's best efforts, the problem persists, you should seek help from a psychologist.

The underachieving child

Some children do not seem to do as well at school as their teachers or their parents might expect. If a teacher describes your child as 'not reaching her potential', you may find it difficult to know quite what is meant, and will need to ask. The teacher may be basing this assessment of the child's performance on the results of standardized tests, on uneven or badly organized work, on the child's apparent lack of motivation or simply on intuition and experience.

Or you yourself may believe that your child should be doing better. You may feel that she has suddenly lost interest in school, or that she doesn't care about her schoolwork any more. You may suspect that her attitude has something to do with the teacher's personality, experience or competence; or that she is having difficulties with new and more demanding aspects of her schoolwork; or that for whatever reason (perhaps an overcrowded class) she is not getting as much help and direction as she needs.

It is possible that your anxieties may be ill-founded: your child may be making steady progress, if rather more slowly than you would like. If this is the case, it is important that you do not convey your anxieties to your child and pressurize her unnecessarily. But if, all things considered, you are quite sure that she is not getting on as well as she could, you will want to help her do better.

Talk with the teacher (or the head) about your concern. It is important to make sure that the child has an adequate understanding of basic reading, writing and numerical concepts: if her grasp of these is shaky she will be left behind as schoolwork gets progressively more demanding. If she has real problems with basic skills she may benefit from some individual teaching. A special needs teacher may be able to give extra tuition, or advise the class teacher on additional aids; either will give you suggestions on how to help at home.

Talk to your child, and, what is even more important, listen to her. Encourage her to tell you how she feels about her experiences at school – her work and her relationships with friends and teachers. Keep your comments to a minimum, and avoid imposing your views (you may find the technique of reflective listening, described on page 366, useful here). You will want to avoid making her worried about how she is doing at school, for anxiety can only be counter-productive; but make sure she understands that you and the school are backing her and want to help.

You may need to learn how to encourage your child by building on her strengths. Try to look objectively at the way you handle her difficulties. With the best of intentions, parents can unconsciously undermine their children's efforts. Sometimes an outsider – a friend, a teacher, perhaps a therapist – may help to identify such patterns.

Try to give her all the home support she needs, in the way of reading with her, talking with her, watching television with her, and anything else her teacher may suggest. Explain to her what extra support she is going to get at school, and why (be positive about this); and tell the teacher what you have told the child, so that everyone is briefed.

Special educational needs

If we are to follow our convictions we must say that all children have special educational needs, since each has a unique set of attributes which she brings to school, attributes which require attention to the child as an individual if they are to be allowed to flower. However, in recent years the phrase 'children with special educational needs' has come to mean those who make demands over and above what is normally expected.

The British Warnock Report on the education of children and young people with special needs, published in 1978, estimated that one in five children will fall into this category at some point in their educational career. Included are children with moderate or severe learning difficulties, those with behaviour problems, with specific language impairments, with physical disabilities, those who have poor vision or hearing, autistic children, dyslexic children. Gifted children also have special educational needs, but they are usually considered separately.

Sometimes the needs are clear-cut: a child who is profoundly deaf or in a wheelchair is clearly going to make special demands on a school. At other times the definition may depend not so much on the child as on the system in which she finds herself. One school may be able to cope perfectly well with a child who is slower than others at academic work; in another staff may find that they do not have the resources to help as well as they think they should.

Equally varied are the ways in which systems respond to needs. An important area of debate in many countries now is whether or not to educate children with special needs in separate schools. There are three common alternatives. One is to keep the majority of the children within the mainstream of education, modifying school buildings if necessary, and providing additional classroom help in the form of an assistant or even an extra teacher. Another is to have special units within ordinary schools so that there can be, in theory at least, a mixture of integration and specialist provision. A compromise is to organize special schools in such a way that children can attend them part-time, going to mainstream schools for the rest of the school day. Much will depend on what is available locally.

At first glance it may seem that the phrase 'special needs' is a euphemism for mentally or physically handicapped – no more than cosmetic. In fact, it marks a radical shift in thinking, for it puts the child first, the disability or difficulty second. We now believe that rather than putting children into categories with crude labels we should ask ourselves what each child's needs are and then try to meet them. To this end parents, in Britain at least, have by law to be consulted as soon as there is any suggestion that a child will need something out of the ordinary, and they must make a statement as to their view of what is best for their child. Some have pointed out that it might be worth consulting the children as well, but so far this rarely happens at a formal level.

One point which parents sometimes fail to realize is that they can initiate the process that leads to extra educational help; another point is that educational decisions can be made well before a child reaches school age. Your doctor can put you in touch with the relevant department of your local education authority, or you can approach them directly for information.

The talented child

At the other end of the spectrum is another group of children who have special educational needs – those who are exceptionally talented, able, or gifted. There is no precise definition of any of these terms, but it is clear that there are some children who shine – at art, music, sports or mathematics, perhaps, or at schoolwork in general. It is often during these years that these special abilities make themselves known.

Some researchers have suggested that unusually able children can be divided into two groups. First, there are the all-rounders, children who are good at most things they tackle, but do not necessarily show phenomenal ability in a particular field. This kind of talent seems to be an unequivocal advantage. These bright children tend also to be taller and healthier than the average, and to have a wide range of interests. Even though they are cleverer than their classmates, they are not so sensationally clever that they seem 'different'. They are usually sociable, well adjusted and successful.

However, most people, when they talk about gifted children, are thinking about 'genius' – intelligence well beyond the normal range, or an extraordinary ability in one particular field, maybe mathematics, or music. Only a very few children have this kind of ability, and these children, just because they are so different, sometimes have problems fitting into a world of unexceptional people.

Outstanding ability, of whichever kind, is indeed a 'gift' – a quality the child is born with. But there are probably many extremely able or gifted children who do not develop their potential, while others, not perhaps so naturally talented, achieve more because they are more strongly motivated. If children are to make full use of their talents they need to have the self-confidence and the will to achieve.

Helping the talented child

Any child thrives best in a family which provides an appropriate level of challenge, encouragement and opportunity, with parents who work to enhance her feelings of self-worth. However, supplying appropriate stimulation for a talented child may involve a good deal of effort, and possibly sacrifice, on the part of the parents, and can put considerable strain on family resources.

Benjamin Bloom, a prominent American researcher on human growth and learning, supervised a large study of people who were talented in artistic, intellectual, musical and athletic fields. He found that one thing most of these people shared was an enriched home life with enthusiastic and appreciative parents. In the early years these parents devoted much of their time and energy to the children. This was particularly so with the children who were musical or athletic – the parents spent hours monitoring practice sessions, lessons, work-outs and athletics meetings. While some saw to it that their children experienced a wide range of other activities, most were more interested in the particular area of talent.

These parents also tended to pay a good deal more attention to the talented child than to other family members. Here, particularly, parents may need to make some very careful judgments – and, possibly, painful compromises. The talented child does not have an automatic right to the lion's share of her parents' time or money, and there are grave drawbacks to favouring one child at the expense of her brothers and sisters.

Whether or not you are able, or willing, to invest as much in one child as the parents in Bloom's study, you will want to help as much as you reasonably can. This will almost certainly mean putting effort into finding appropriate tuition. By seven or eight musically or athletically gifted children are often ready to move on to more rigorous and demanding coaches. If your child is intellectually gifted you may be concerned that her schoolwork is not stretching her enough – she may even complain herself that the work at school is too easy, or that there is not enough of it. You should certainly talk to her teacher about the possibility of planning a more challenging schedule of work. You can also ask for the child to be assessed by an educational psychologist. An assessment of this kind can be extremely useful in clarifying for you where the child stands and what kind of stimulus she needs; and discussion with the psychologist may also help the child's teacher to devise an appropriate work programme.

You can also help your talented child by making an effort to find other congenial children with whom she can work and play at her own level. This will not only provide stimulation, but will also give the child the opportunity to measure herself against equals. If comparisons are to be made – and experience shows that children will make comparisons, regardless of adult wishes to the contrary – they will be fairer and more useful comparisons.

But in the end the best preparation for growing up is to have a full and happy childhood – and this applies to all children, whatever their ability. A talented child is still a child, needing the same freedoms and restrictions as any other child. If your child shows outstanding talent you may well be particularly proud of her – but don't let this blind you to the fact that she is more than the sum of her gifts: she is a whole person, who needs to be loved and accepted as she is, with all her weaknesses as well as her strengths.

Emotional and Social Development

Who am I?

As, over these years, your child encounters more experiences and acquires more understanding, her idea of who she is, what kind of personality and what talents she has, will become increasingly complex and sophisticated.

Though children may start to talk about their feelings as early as six or seven, most continue to conceive of themselves and others largely in physical terms until they are at least nine or ten. When a six year old was asked if he could be changed into his friend, he said that would be impossible because the friend was shorter and could ride a horse. A seven year old girl, on the eve of plastic surgery, asked her father if she would be the same person after the operation. As they approach adolescence, children tend increasingly to describe themselves as much in terms of how they feel as of how they look.

I like sunny cold days,
I like the wind when it's pulling
and pushing me.
I like the rustle of leaves
I Like spiders' webs after the rain.
I like buying books in the town.
I Like my mums cooking.
Spag.hetti bolog naise,
raw mushrooms, carrots soft and dry
sweet tang erines and chocolate pudding

In this poem a nine year old girl demonstrates her growing sense of herself as an individual, with her own particular tastes.

Constructing a sense of identity

The American psychologist George Kelly developed ideas about how we see ourselves, in what he called personal construct psychology. He argues that we each build up a system of beliefs about our world which enables us to assess events, and also develop a central idea about ourselves which helps

404

us to maintain a sense of identity and purpose. These ideas form gradually, becoming more elaborate over the years, and any suggestion that this core of beliefs (the core role constructs) might be invalid brings with it a serious threat to our mental well-being. This explains why some children fly off the handle at certain insults, while taking others in their stride. For example, a child who has been brought up to believe that she is essentially and deeply honest will be far more hurt at an accusation of dishonesty than a child for whom the idea of honesty is peripheral.

While a child is developing a central core of beliefs about herself, she is also learning to see herself as a complex whole with a variety of roles: she is daughter, friend, pupil. Different people react to her in different ways, and she herself behaves differently in different situations. A child who finds it impossible to say in abstract terms what concept she has of herself, may reveal a clear sense of self-awareness when asked how she sees herself at school, at home, with friends or within the family – and each response may be slightly different.

Public and private selves

As we have seen, children as young as three may make a difference between private speech and speech for others. We cannot, however, say that they are conscious of making this distinction. It is usually not until they are eight or nine that they begin consciously to appreciate that what a person says may be quite different from what he feels. They can see through the bravado of a friend who protests that he doesn't care about not being in the football team. They begin to realize that they can keep their own thoughts private: they no longer believe that their parents always know what they are thinking. They can cover up emotions and put on a brave front, or cry 'crocodile tears'; when they tell a lie they now expect that it will be believed. They also begin to appreciate the fact that they can understand their own feelings better than other people's.

The ideal self

The notion of an ideal self begins to develop at around six or seven: from then on, children think in terms, not only of who they are, but also of who they would like to be. One might think that children whose ideal self and actual self showed close similarities would be those who were most comfortable in their own skins and therefore mentally healthiest. In fact, it is not quite as simple as that. One study at least has suggested that a moderate gap between the two concepts indicates a greater maturity, since it shows that the child realizes there is something to strive for. The higher standard set by the ideal self also exerts a certain control.

Self-esteem

When a child compares herself with her ideal self, when she reflects on how well she is matching up to her own or others' expectations, she is building a sense of self-esteem, which may be high or low.

Stanley Coopersmith, writing in 1967 with evidence from interviews with eighty-five American boys aged eleven and twelve, concluded that self-esteem is based on four criteria. His conclusions still have a ring of truth.

• The first of these four criteria is significance: if they are to think well of themselves, children must feel valued, loved and approved by the people who matter to them.

• The second is competence: children need to feel that they can do some things well, and that the people they care about appreciate what they do well.

• The third is virtue: children need to feel that they attain a certain moral standard – that they are good.

• The fourth is power: children need to influence their own lives and other people's lives.

The boys in this study who had high self-esteem were, not surprisingly, the most popular in their group, but – and this may be somewhat surprising – there was no association between self-esteem and physical characteristics. Position in the family was relevant: boys who were only or first-born children tended to have high self-esteem. How they were treated by their parents was certainly important: generally, the boys who had the highest self-esteem were those with emotionally warm parents who made strong but realistic demands for high standards of work and behaviour.

Who is in charge of me?

The answer to this question will depend on whether a child perceives herself as responsible for her own actions, or feels that others are in charge. This is related to the fourth of Coopersmith's criteria for self-esteem and has far-reaching consequences. Children who perceive themselves as being controlled from outside imagine that everything that happens to them is due to the actions of others; they feel powerless. On the other hand, children who perceive control to be internal may be led to think, unrealistically, that they know everything and can do anything. So children need to be encouraged to take responsibility for their own actions, but, at the same time, helped towards a realistic view of their powers and limitations.

In a laboratory study of the interaction between parents and children, where children were asked to complete a building task, the children's view of whether control of their lives was internal or external consistently reflected the way the parents reacted. Those parents who allowed their children to get on with the task, helping but not interfering, had children who felt responsible for their own actions; those who interfered, interrupted and directed had children who thought the world was controlled by forces outside themselves.

Taking responsibility for her younger brother increases her own self-confidence.

Understanding others

'Oh, *why* does she keep going on? Can't she see I'm upset because the baby is sick?'

The answer to questions like these is, 'Probably no, not if she is only six or seven years old.' Children are not always able to pick up on others' emotions as we might reasonably expect an adult to do. Before they can do that, they have to learn the rules of emotions and their expression, and that takes time and experience. If the situation is familiar, the recognition of another person's feelings is easier: a child who has lost a pet can readily sympathize with another in the same situation. But a six or seven year old is unlikely to have had any experience which will help her to understand what it is like to be the exhausted mother of a sick baby.

A simple response to an unfamiliar situation is to overgeneralize from what one does know. Children often do this, and in doing so may easily come up with an incorrect interpretation of the other person's feelings. As a child becomes less egocentric she can put herself in another person's shoes, and in assessing feelings she may be able to take into account factors which are outside her immediate experience. By the age of ten or twelve most children are able to consider different viewpoints.

However, the understanding and expression of emotion involve subtleties which it may take a lifetime to learn. In particular, children (and many adults) have difficulty in comprehending the possibility of a discrepancy between how people feel and how they act. Children have to learn that what people are thinking or wanting may not always be reflected in the action they take; before this stage is reached there can be distressing misunderstandings. Perhaps a brother or sister is in hospital: the parents may want to be at home looking after the healthy child but need to be at the hospital with the one who is sick. The child left at home knows only that her parents are not there and finds it hard to comprehend that there is conflict for them. At times like this it is important for parents to try to explain their feelings to the child – but also to realize that she still may not be able to understand, that she may in consequence behave in a way that they might consider unreasonable, and that they may need to make allowances for her.

Another form of inconsistency between feeling and action arises when feelings are displaced. Children need to learn that there are occasions when people appear to be angry about one thing when in fact they are anxious, cross or otherwise upset about something quite different. Parents may, for example, snap at a child when they have had a row, or are worried about work, or money. This can be confusing and distressing for the child. If you are aware that you have done this, it helps if you can explain later to your child, not necessarily what the underlying problem was, but that it was something other than her behaviour that made you cross.

How parents can foster an awareness of others

The best way to encourage your child to be considerate and helpful to other people is to let her see that you care about others. You can actively teach this kind of consideration for others by talking to her about other people's feelings, and by making a point of sometimes asking her to carry out a task because it will contribute to another's well-being, not just telling her to do it because she has to.

If you expect your children to behave with a consideration consistent with their level of maturity, they will take more responsibility for their own actions and will behave in a more caring way. It is worth remembering that considerate children also tend to have higher self-esteem, because they get positive feedback from the people they relate to.

How moral awareness develops

Seven year old children have a clear sense of right and wrong. Their moral code comes from a set of rules for behaviour outlined by their parents or other adults in authority and, on the whole, they do what is right because they need love and approval and fear punishment. As they get older and become progressively less egocentric, they are able to see another person's point of view; and they begin to realize that if you treat a person well he or she will probably reciprocate.

As they go through primary school and become more independent, children find themselves in situations where they need to determine what is right or wrong for themselves, and sometimes there will be confusions that they need to learn how to resolve. Children want to create and sustain relationships with their friends and very often their friends' values do not match the values of their family. Friends behave in ways that would never be acceptable at home – trespassing on other people's property, for instance, or fighting with another child. It may baffle parents that children who understand the basic rules, who are capable of feeling guilt and shame and who show that they can be helpful, generous and altruistic, sometimes behave in ways that are unthinkable in the family. They may, perhaps, be carried away on a wave of strong aggressive feeling, or need to be approved of by friends, or want the feeling of fierce independence that a moment of misbehaviour brings.

Young children believe that if they break a rule or someone else transgresses, they will be punished, regardless of the circumstances. By the age of eight or nine children have enough experience to realize that life is not always completely fair or just. They have seen people (both adults and children) do things which are clearly wrong and go unnoticed or unpunished. They know that they have a chance to get away with bad behaviour; they also bear the burden of knowing that someone might hurt them and not be caught and punished for it. Along with this new awareness of moral complexities, the child has a growing capacity to appreciate another person's situation. She can sympathize with a child who does not receive love and affection at home, as well as with a child who is in immediate pain and crying. As she moves towards adolescence, her growing sense of personal responsibility may lead her to feel guilty about the injustices and inequalities which exist in the world.

A child learning to see the grey areas of right and wrong is going to make mistakes as she begins to exercise her own moral judgment. She will find it helpful to talk through ways in which she might handle situations, real and imaginary, and be encouraged to see the consequences that could follow from her actions.

An eleven year old writer conveys her own sense of moral conflict with impressive clarity.

She wasn't very pretty and not many people wanted to look after her as she was new to the community. Everyone tended to say "oh someone else can do it." When I had agreed to look after her I had been in a particularly good mood and had wanted to do something to help an old person.
Mrs. Would (as she was called) was very lonely and I felt a bit sorry for her because she looked so sad staring out of the window or knitting for a jumble sale.
I was really cross with myself for saying yes

How parents can foster moral awareness

How can you help your child to think independently in a morally responsible way? It is not easy to say precisely why a child, when faced with a

A home where people treat each other with respect is the best place to learn about how to cooperate with friends and enjoy being part of larger groups.

choice, will make a 'good' rather than a 'bad' decision. One answer must be that she is motivated to do the right thing – she wants to do it. Faced with a choice between being home on time or going on playing, she goes home (or at least phones her mother, so she doesn't worry). She feels that she wants to do the right thing; as we say, her heart is in the right place.

How can you help your child have this feeling? It is not enough that she should feel love and loyalty for you, her parents, because she may find herself in a situation where her concern must be for someone with whom she has no personal connection. Neither is it sufficient that she be in touch with her feelings – if she is very angry, for instance, her strongest feeling may be that she wants to strike out.

Thinking about religion

To some extent a child's concept of religion depends on what she is taught. That is not the whole story, however, for the child will interpret what is told to her according to her own temperament and her ability to understand and to question. As Robert Coles points out in *The Spiritual Life of Children*, God can take almost any shape for a child: 'He can be a friend or a potential enemy; an admirer or a critic; an ally or an interference; a source of encouragement or a source of anxiety, fear, even panic.' Many children in this age group spend a lot of time thinking about God and religion. Up to the age of nine or ten they tend to wonder about practical, matter-of-fact questions – 'What does God look like?' 'Where does he live?' 'How does he look after so many people?' As they approach adolescence they may begin to reflect on concepts such as sin, heaven and hell, and what happens after death.

There are no guarantees; but there are certain conditions which foster moral awareness. The most effective teaching is, as usual, by example. Children not only follow the models set by their parents, but, more subtly, they adopt the values they absorb from the environment around them, and they are sensitive to an atmosphere even if they are not able to pinpoint any overt signs. Selfishness or unselfishness will be learned from parents going about their daily lives; hostility will be felt even when no violence is seen. It is easy to understand the confusion that can arise from such an example as that of a parent hitting a child for hitting another child.

So you will help your children here if you yourself are concerned for each other, for the family and for people outside the family. It also helps if you consider moral judgments important, and are prepared to discuss them; if you are ready to talk about your own moral struggles, however trivial; and if you are prepared to abandon the easy road of delivering orders, and will instead encourage children, through discussion and dialogue, to weigh the evidence.

Friends and friendships

The period between the ages of seven and eleven is one when friendships grow, become longer-lasting and deeper. Around two-thirds of these school-age friendships last as long as a full school year; many last much longer, and a few can be lifelong.

Friendships help children to learn: about others, about how society is ordered and, most importantly, about themselves. In sharing ways of solving a whole range of problems they discover the strengths and weaknesses of others; in discovering that successful cooperation brings with it mutual respect and emotional satisfaction they learn something of the way society works. As part of this process, they may also learn that not all behaviour accepted within the family is appropriate outside the home: the child who at home cries at the least frustration may have to learn to stand up for herself; the child who is used to getting her own way may learn to give and take. The confidence and stimulation provided by friendships also enlarge children's horizons; they will try out new ideas and explore avenues that would otherwise be closed to them.

In testing themselves against the yardsticks provided, not by adults, who are different from children in so many ways, but by other children, they learn to rate themselves. And, above all, true friendship conveys the message that the other person values you enough to want to be your friend. This kind of psychological support is vital to a child's self-esteem. Close friendship in childhood provides the basis for satisfactory long-term relationships in later years, and the lack of it may be reflected in emotional problems in adult life. The American psychiatrist Harry Stack Sullivan noted that his adult male patients who were socially ill at ease had all lacked the opportunity to form close pre-adolescent friendships.

Making friends

One of the reasons that friendships are formed more easily around this age is the child's growing ability to see another person's point of view: increasingly, children work or play together for mutual benefit and do more for each other. They also have a more sophisticated understanding of time and so have a concept of building a friendship which they expect to continue.

Friendships tend to begin with an exchange of information designed to explore similarities and differences and so establish common ground. If there are too many similarities children may become rivals rather than friends, or they may fail to develop a friendship because each finds the other predictable and therefore uninteresting. Too many differences and children may hold back from developing a friendship, or the friendship may fail when they find they have to compromise too often, or put too much effort into preserving their individual preferences and goals. If the balance is right they become responsive to each other. In responding in this way each changes and, while they retain their individual identities, they progress to becoming a more or less coordinated pair.

At seven or eight 'best friends' can change from one day to the next, but around nine or ten comes a growing loyalty and commitment to best friends, and these friends are expected to do certain things to keep the relationship going. By eleven or so children see best friends as people who may need help and support, who share their interests and values; they say they do things for each other's happiness. At this age best friends become more intimate, strive to dress alike, look alike and meet each other's needs.

Finding your own small group of close friends gives security in the ever-widening social world.

Romping about with a large group of children is fun and offers the opportunity to make new friends.

Relationships within the family remain an all-important influence. If a child has a close, secure attachment to her parents, she will expect to have satisfying friendships outside the family; if her family attachments are insecure and anxious she is likely to carry these feelings into relationships with other children. However, while in younger age groups friendships tend to be fostered by parents, as children become older the choice becomes more directly their own; and it is important for a child's self-esteem that she be given, within reason, the freedom to select her own companions and the feeling that her parents approve of her choice.

The rules of friendship
The underlying rules of friendship shift during this age group from rigid notions of reciprocity and fairness to a more complex, abstract concept. If a child of seven helps a friend she is likely to expect – or exact – prompt help in return; if she is hurt she will likewise retaliate immediately. As children grow older reciprocity may take longer and/or come in a more subtle form: help may be received on one day but not returned until an occasion demands it; hurt feelings may result in a discussion rather than immediate retribution.

The sex of friends
While in younger age groups up to a third of friends may be of the opposite sex, by seven or eight almost all close friendships are between children of the same sex. However, a small number of children continue to gravitate to the opposite sex throughout this age group. Some parents may be concerned by this, but they should remember that children gain from being given as much freedom as is reasonable to select companions according to their own wishes, not those of adults.

413

Sex differences and friendships

Boys' friendships tend to operate largely through activities they have in common, while girls prefer to talk, especially about relationships. The British psychologist Michael Argyle, who has studied children in the years leading up to puberty, watched what groups of pre-adolescent boys and girls did when asked to perform a task or play a game. He found that boys got straight down to it, while girls began by getting to know each other.

Exchanging confidences

However, while boys talk less than girls, good friends of both sexes often disclose secrets to each other and discuss quite intimate feelings; they provide emotional support, give each other advice and swop information; they may help each other with homework or tell each other about trends and fashions. This exchange helps them agree on values and test the validity of feelings. As children approach puberty and need to explore so many aspects of growing up, they often find it easier to confide in and learn from a friend, especially one of the same sex, rather than their parents.

From nine or ten on, friends spend a lot of time gossiping, insulting each other and teasing. They may engage in a good deal of negative gossip about other people: it seems that the more bad things they can say about a third person, the closer they feel in their friendship. Gossip also helps children to understand their own position in relation to others. Both boys and girls talk a lot about being embarrassed. An embarrassing situation can arise from being noticed, wearing the wrong clothes, sitting in the wrong place, from

Listen to this! Children love to tell secrets, to confide in one another.

a public reference to puberty or sexuality, from comments on your liking someone of the opposite sex – above all, from having your emotions exposed. Discussing the embarrassment with a friend helps take the sting out of it.

Groups and gangs

'I'll get my gang on to you!' is a common cry at this age, generally from boys, but girls have equivalent tightly knit groups with their own jokes, preoccupations and support for each other. A group can be anything from a loose cluster of children playing in the school playground to clubs which meet for a particular activity. Groups are usually formed at first by children who live close to one another; as they get older proximity is less important and shared activities become paramount.

Groups behave according to a well-defined code. They often have rules, perhaps even a uniform, and regular times and places for gathering together. Above all, the group implies a shared set of assumptions which somehow make the members feel superior to non-members who do not subscribe to them – though friends may in fact be far more critical of each other than they ever are of outsiders.

Among younger children, groups are composed of children of the same sex who taunt and tease each other if the sexual boundaries are crossed. By eleven or so groups are beginning to have mixed parties and there may be some attempts at kissing and cuddling.

Swimming and other out of school activities are a significant part of a child's social life.

Though, ideally, children will remain close to their families and continue to enjoy doing things with them for many years to come, one important function of the group is to help children towards independence. The safety of numbers enables them to take steps towards becoming independent of the family; it also helps them to defy adult authority and survive. Children who would not dare, or be allowed, to go out alone, will as part of a group go to the cinema, go swimming, go shopping, without adult supervision; they may also get up to pranks such as ringing doorbells and running away, but if the pranks remain comparatively minor, little serious harm is likely to be done.

Where defiance of adult authority takes a more extreme form, this may herald a serious rejection of society's authority and may even lead to true delinquency. However, while parents often worry about the pressure to misbehave put on children by their friends, most research has found that pressure is actually more likely to be against misconduct than for it.

There are also, of course, groups organized by adults that can provide similar support in the move towards independence: scouts, guides, youth clubs, athletics clubs, music clubs are some examples. As they get older, children can cope with being in several groups: an eleven year old may be in a drama club, a swimming team and a group of friends who just hang around together.

Losing friends

Adults often greatly underestimate the distress that a child may feel at the loss of a friend. Friendships end for many reasons: sometimes there is a simple drifting apart, perhaps because the children are at different stages of development, as when one girl is still playing with dolls, while her friend has become preoccupied with boys; sometimes a house move or a change of school precipitates the break. Sometimes a new friend comes on the scene, and then the children involved may suffer agonies of jealousy and guilt.

Occasionally parents insist that a friendship should end; this is a serious step to take, and can have damaging consequences. If you are convinced that it is essential to remove your child from the influence of a particular friend, you should explain the reasons carefully and give the child every opportunity to discuss the situation. If you simply forbid the friendship 'because I say so', the association is likely to continue on a clandestine basis; what is more important, you run the risk of damaging the relationship of trust between you and your child.

The most painful form of break-up is when one child ends a friendship before the other is ready for the break. 'I don't like you any more' can be a devastating thing to hear at any age, for it is an attack on one's self-esteem. However, distressing as it is, such an experience does occur very commonly, and may be seen as a normal part of growing up. What matters is how the break-up is perceived. As usual, there are differences in the ways children react: some seem to be very much better than others at coping with the loss of companionship and even the blow to self-esteem.

But whatever the cause of the break-up, and however well a child copes, there is likely to be some distress. A few children go so far as to show signs of clinical depression, going off their food, sleeping badly, and generally moping. It helps if a child has other resources: the child with another friend or group to fall back on will to some extent be cushioned against the worst effects of losing a friend.

The child without friends

Having laid so much stress on the importance of friendships, perhaps we need to emphasize that in this area, as in every other, there are enormous variations between children. While some prefer a wide circle of friends, others get along perfectly well with very few; some want 'a friend to play' every evening and weekend, others make firm friendships with brothers or sisters, while others prefer to play alone when they are at home, needing space for themselves, their fantasies and their constructions after being

Some children are naturally self-sufficient, and are quite happy to find their own occupations.

with other children all day at school. Some are loners by temperament, and enjoy reading, playing or working alone for long periods of time.

Again, while it is always upsetting for parents when a child comes back from school saying she has no friends, or has been ostracized by her usual group of friends, and the child certainly needs comfort and support, it is usually reasonable to regard the situation as no more than a temporary setback. What is worrying is the child who truly has no friends, of any description, anywhere. The key question then is whether or not the child is capable of making friends.

Sometimes there are obvious reasons why it is difficult for children to make friends. Children who live in isolated rural areas, children who have physical or mental disabilities or who suffer from ill health, all face special difficulties in developing relationships with other children. Sadly, as they grow older the problems may be compounded. A child who doesn't make friends easily may just stop trying, and withdraw.

Frequent moves may also have long-term effects on a child's ability to make friends. Writing of an American army family which suffered from such disruption, Vance Packard noted the way in which the frequent loss of companions caused one boy unwittingly to begin to shun close relationships. Similarly, but perhaps even more unfortunately, some children of divorced parents feel betrayed by the one who has gone away and become wary of any emotional closeness, even with children of their own age.

Another source of withdrawal is the failure to learn socially acceptable behaviour when young. The preschool child who, for whatever reason, fails to develop an adequate repertoire of social skills will not know how to react to early overtures of friendship and may rebuff them. She may fail to understand that friendship means sharing and commitment to another person. The longer this goes on the harder it becomes to move to appropriate interchanges.

Withdrawn children are more than just shy; they shrink from contact with others. They are often very lonely and unhappy. Their feelings of loneliness increase with age and they tend to feel more and more adrift. Often forgotten in the classroom because they do not cause trouble, they are likely to grow up still friendless.

What can be done to help the withdrawn child

A withdrawn child needs to be helped to make relationships, but if this is not done very gently and tactfully the child may simply panic and withdraw further. Here, parents will probably need to enlist the help of the school. A sensitive teacher might start by pairing the withdrawn child with one who is likely to make her feel comfortable. This could be a child who has characteristics similar to her own but is a little less shy; sometimes a younger child can seem less threatening. Through this first friend, there can be a gradual introduction to others.

Withdrawn children need to learn to listen, share and take turns. Again, their horror of exposure can only slowly be overcome. A teacher might begin by asking the child to read, work or play in partnership with another; from there she may be led step by step to contributing first to small groups and then to larger ones.

One useful technique which parents or teachers can employ is to act as a bridge between the withdrawn child and others. The adult will introduce a topic of conversation – the latest craze, a television programme, anything that is likely to catch the children's attention – and will then fade out once the children begin to engage.

It may also be necessary to teach a withdrawn child the necessary social skills: to provide techniques that enable her to approach other children and respond to friendly overtures. This teaching can be carried out by a parent or teacher, but expert advice may well be required from a psychologist experienced in helping withdrawn children.

Bullying

Teasing and insulting a friend is often part and parcel of friendship. It can be painful but is in the main not vicious. Bullying, like teasing, involves finding the chink in another child's armour and taking advantage of the weakness, either physical or emotional. But unlike teasing it is vicious in intent.

In boys bullying usually involves some form of physical attack or threat; girls generally use verbal means, often more damaging in the long run, because they attack the victim's self-esteem: 'No one likes you . . . you're ugly . . . no one will ever want to go out with you. . . .'

While some bullying goes on among younger children, it is generally more of a problem in this age group, when – out in the school playground or coming and going from school – children may no longer be under close adult supervision.

The bully

Children bully others for various reasons. Sometimes it is for material gain – money or sweets, for example. Sometimes it is to compensate for the bully's own feelings of inadequacy. When children have poor social skills, bullying sometimes seems to be the only way that they can make contact and relate to others. Sometimes jealousy at home can more easily be expressed by beating up a child at school; or, if children are bullied at home, bullying at school may be the only way they can get their own back. Or they may assume that bullying is a perfectly acceptable way to treat others. It is small comfort to the child who is being bullied, but it is often the one who is bullying who is more deeply disturbed.

Parents sometimes unconsciously encourage bullying by bragging about their children's physical exploits or encouraging them to resolve arguments by 'letting so-and-so have it'. Violence and aggression on television and in films may also encourage those children who have a tendency towards bullying (see page 424).

The victim

Some children are more likely to be bullied than others. Children who are seen to be different often attract bullying. They may look different – perhaps they wear glasses or are unusually fat or thin; perhaps their place in the pecking order has not yet been sorted out, because they are new to the school or the neighbourhood; they may be particularly clever or especially slow; or they may have a physical handicap or racial characteristics which make them different.

This is only part of the picture though. Not all children who are 'different' are bullied. Children who are vulnerable are also likely to be on the shy side, possibly physically weak as well; above all, they will show distress when attacked – so they give satisfaction to their aggressors.

A small minority of children readily accept the role of victim, either because they have already been cast in the role of scapegoat at home, or because this is the only way they know to get attention.

Signs of bullying

When children suddenly become reluctant to go to school, or unusually moody or withdrawn, or lack concentration at school, one of the first questions to ask is whether they are being bullied. There are, of course, various other reasons why this may happen, but bullying is always worth considering as a possibility. Another possible sign is increased requests for pocket money – or even some filching from a parent's purse.

What parents can do

When your child is the victim of bullying, the first step is the hardest: to establish that your child is being bullied and to find out who is doing it. Children who are being bullied are almost invariably reluctant to tell adults what is going on, partly because of the unwritten rule about telling tales and partly for fear of retaliation; they are also terrified of their parents telling the teacher. Patient, gradual questioning, with constant reassurance that both parents and teachers will support the child, will probably be needed to elicit any information.

Help can then be given in two ways.

• The first step is to discuss the problem with the relevant teacher or person in charge. The teacher may have been unaware of what was happening. Once given the information, he or she can often defuse the situation by keeping an eye on things and acting quickly at any sign of trouble.

• The second step is to teach the child techniques to avoid being bullied. It will help to stay in a group of other children when the bully is around and appear to be closely involved in what the group is doing, even if it is only talking – someone who is deep in conversation is far less vulnerable than someone who is hanging around. (Though this advice may of course be difficult to follow if the bully has whipped up support against the victim.) Pretending not to notice the bully will also reduce the opportunities for contact to be made, though again this may be hard to put into practice.

If your child has been bullying others, the chances are that you will find out from the school, which should at least make it easier to enlist their help in dealing with the problem. If it is other parents who complain, the position – an uncomfortable one for any parent – is even harder.

It is not easy to stop a child being a bully. The sad fact is that children usually become bullies because for some reason bullying makes them feel better – at someone else's expense. If you are going to achieve any lasting change you will need to look into what lies behind the bullying. It might perhaps be that your child has learned at home that bullying is a means of getting one's own way. If this is so, you will need to demonstrate that there are better ways of accomplishing one's aims. Or it may be that the child feels inadequate, and the bullying is a means of compensating. In this case you need to look carefully at your child and evaluate what he or she does well. Make sure that there are plenty of opportunities to demonstrate competence in these areas, and that achievements are appreciated and rewarded. If parents and teachers can work together to enable a child to feel effective in a constructive way, the need to make a destructive mark will usually diminish.

Play and pastimes

In this age group, as earlier, children develop their physical, linguistic and social skills through play, and play also helps them cope with new and often difficult situations. Acting out a painful situation, either directly or in a different form, can often help children to see the situation in a new light and come to terms with it. Though they may feel self-conscious about acting out their fantasies at this age, and turn to other forms of fantasy such as books or television, given the opportunity, many children will engage in dramatic play – taking part in an informal drama group, perhaps, and revelling in the opportunity for creative self-expression.

Once children have reached a certain level of competence, childhood toys can take on a new meaning. Real tools can be used to construct castles, garages, airports; an electric train set can be put into action, or a motorized Lego set made to work. The results of creative cooking can now actually be eaten and enjoyed; the baby being tucked up in his pram and walked round the garden may be a real one and not a doll. And many of these activities now involve discussion, cooperation and compromise.

Schools vary in how much they use play in this age group, but often the trappings of earlier play will be there, used in a different way: the Lego constructions help with technology; building bricks may still be used for maths work; dressing up will be involved in class assemblies and end-of-term plays.

Play at home will now depend a good deal on the kind of school the child is at – whether she has masses of homework or comes out of school at three o'clock with none; on the extent to which her evenings and weekends are occupied by organized activities; and on the kind of neighbourhood she lives in – a block of city flats with no park nearby or a suburb with plenty of garden space, an isolated farm surrounded by fields and cows or a village with plenty of safe meeting places. But children's own requirements also vary. Some need to expend physical energy, others will spend hours playing quietly with their toys.

Childhood cultures

This is the age of the collector. Children tend to begin by just keeping whatever comes to hand: all bits and pieces are treasures, pockets bulge and bedrooms begin to look like the local junk shop. Woe betide anyone caught throwing out the collection of bottle-tops from last year's holiday. Then, slowly but surely, they become more discriminating and more organized: books begin to fill with stamps, boxes with rock collections, walls with stickers, posters and badges; discs and tapes are each given a place and counted regularly. Some collecting is incomprehensible to the onlooker: what on earth is the point of writing down car numbers? But there are

This ten year old's room speaks clearly of his passionate absorption in aeroplanes.

underlying reasons: forming collections helps children to bring order to a world which often seems to be uncontrolled and chaotic; a room full of their personal paraphernalia provides a microcosm of everything which they find important in their universe.

This is also the age which finds magic tricks, board games, card and computer games exciting. Listening to certain radio programmes, watching certain television shows and videos, owning the right tapes becomes essential to the fabric of the child's life. Two children living thousands of miles apart can find they have a common culture in television and music. And pressure to conform is strong at this age: friends influence what is watched on television, what music is acceptable, what games are played. Children who do not follow accepted patterns tend to be rather isolated: this raises a query about whether they are out of step because they do not have friends, or whether they do not have friends because they are out of step. It may be a bit of both, of course. We should also consider the possibility that, at least sometimes, both problems may be brought about, or made worse, by over-controlling parents who fail to appreciate children's need to conform, and try to force their children into patterns of behaviour quite different from those of their contemporaries.

Television

Television watching reaches a peak in this age group and then declines in early adolescence. In most western countries children watch television for between two and four hours a day. This bald figure is, of course, an average: some children watch a good deal less than this, but many watch a lot more, and there are children who spend more time watching television than they do engaged in any other activity apart from sleeping. However, viewing does drop by half in the summer months.

The debate about the effects of television has been going on for almost as long as it has existed, and gradually some agreement seems to be emerging.

There is little doubt that television can have a beneficial effect. It is used widely in schools to show educational programmes, and learning is also provided, in the form of entertainment, by such programmes as *Sesame Street*. Children of the seven to eleven age group can learn much about the world they live in from natural history films and from programmes about the latest inventions and discoveries or other news topics. They can live their fantasies or develop their own ambitions by watching programmes about sport, ballet, music, exploration, archaeology or any other subject that interests them. They can also learn about the irrationality of prejudice, learn tolerance of men and women seen in non-traditional roles, learn to feel sympathy for and concern about children and others less fortunate than themselves, and learn, through watching children on the screen in predicaments similar to their own, that their own problems and anxieties are valid ones.

But, the difference between a child sitting in an unresponsive, passive state in front of the television and one who responds to and learns from what she is watching, depends largely on you, the parents. If television is used as a means of getting the children out of the way, or if it is used by the child herself as an easier option than thinking of something else to do, the gain is minimal and there is a great loss in terms of time that might more usefully be spent in thinking or doing. If, on the other hand, you show your interest in what the child is watching, respond to it and discuss what you have seen, there will be a significant gain. You will encourage your child to develop a critical response to what she watches, and to extract elements of value from it. She will also be less likely to absorb in an uncritical way what is bad about television.

For there is much that is bad. Nearly 80 per cent of prime-time television in the United States contains at least one violent episode, with an average of over seven per hour; by the age of sixteen the average American child will have watched over thirteen thousand killings on television. An analysis of British or Australian television presents a similar picture.

Experimental evidence shows some support for the view that children who watch a violent episode in a story are more likely to be violent themselves immediately afterwards, and that children who watch a lot of violent television when young are more likely to be behaving violently themselves by the age of eighteen. Of course, it may well be that such children watch violence on television because they are that way inclined already. However, it seems reasonable to suspect that a hefty diet of screen violence may increase children's tolerance of violence in general, and encourage them to assume that violence is a normal and acceptable part of life.

There are other negative aspects of television. Some programmes, and some advertisements, present distorted stereotypes of certain groups of people – giving the impression that all policemen are thugs, all blondes are brainless, all scientists are men, or whatever. There is still some advertising that suggests that good mothers are obsessed with getting clothes so white they dazzle. Here again, if parents watch with their children they can do something to counteract this kind of misapprehension.

From time to time it has been suggested that watching television makes children less able to think for themselves, and some people fear that it may make them socially isolated. In fact there is little evidence to support either supposition. There is, however, some evidence that television can influence family patterns, reducing the amount of time spent in talk, games, arguments, family meals and family festivals – through which much learning takes place. Perhaps the chief danger of television lies not so much in what it may encourage children to do as in what it may prevent.

Television is here to stay, and as children get older it is not possible for parents to monitor all the programmes they watch. The two essentials are for producers and distributors to recognize what power they have at their command, for good or ill, and for parents to participate as much as they can in their children's viewing and so encourage their active, thoughtful response to what they see.

Developing sexuality

At one time it was usual to describe the early years of this age group as a time of sexual latency, a stage when children's instincts are relatively quiet. However, although six to nine year olds have not developed the intense interest in sexual relationships that marks the teenage years, it is certainly not true to say that they never think about sex. What does seem to happen is a realization of sexual taboos. In many societies children discover, around six or seven, that they are not expected to go about with nothing on, that it is 'not nice' to talk about certain things, and even that it is not acceptable to be too friendly with children of the opposite sex.

At ten or eleven, as children approach puberty, they naturally (though not invariably) show an increasing interest in the changes, actual or impending, in their bodies.

Sex education

In deciding what information about sex to impart, and when and how to convey it, the guiding principle should be the readiness of the child. In general, pre-adolescent children want facts; a little later, as they approach the age of sexual activity, they need encouragement to talk freely about their feelings and about the emotional aspects of sexual experience. But no two children are alike and no two families have precisely the same approach.

Some families are entirely open with their children about sex. At the other extreme there are families where any mention of sex is forbidden and film and television viewing is strictly censored. Some parents find it easy to discuss sex with young children in simple terms ('You grew in mummy's tummy') but a shutter comes down when more difficult questions are asked about how the baby got there or how it gets out. Attitudes to sexual discussion often change as children grow older: both parents and children may become more reticent as the children approach puberty, and in general children may have less opportunity to ask casual questions than they had before they went to school.

Where children get their information

For children in this age group, the three principal sources of information about sex are parents, school and friends.

In Britain, the United States and Australia, schools are generally expected to make a significant contribution to sex education. In Britain guidelines from the Department of Education suggest that at primary level (up to the age of eleven), children should be given an elementary understanding of reproduction and help in coping with the physical and emotional challenges of growing up. In America policy on sex education varies, depending on the school and the community, but reproduction is usually covered as part of the science curriculum. Eighty per cent of a teenage sample questioned in Britain in 1985 said that they found sex education in school helpful; the remainder complained that it had been too limited or lacking in detail.

Children also get a good deal of information (or misinformation) about sex from their friends.

However, parents are really in the best position to impart information about sex to their children. They can give a more accurate picture than the children's friends; and where teachers may be limited by an official policy

Preventing sexual abuse

Child sexual abuse is any exploitation of a child under sixteen for the sexual gratification of an adult. Such abuse may involve obscene telephone calls, watching children undress, taking pornographic photographs, fondling them or actually having intercourse.

Naturally, parents feel very protective of their children, but by the time they reach school age they cannot be watched over every minute of the day. They need independence, and parents must teach them to take care of themselves.

Unfortunately, it is not enough simply to tell children to beware of strangers. It is often people they believe they can trust who present the most danger. About 75 per cent of the assaults on children are committed by people they know, often a family member.

The best way to protect your children is by encouraging them to communicate with you openly and easily. If you generally take what your children say seriously, you will be helping them to value their own judgment, the basis on which the self-assurance necessary to confide is built. As far as more specific guidance goes, you need to talk to your children about the difference between good and bad touching, teach them how to say 'no' and encourage them to tell rather than keep secrets. They should also be taught never to accept an offer of a lift in a car or go to anyone else's house without your

knowledge; and they need to know that they should react to assault by making a lot of noise and running away. Molesters often think children are helpless and are caught off guard by a child who is assertive.

Unfortunately, though, children who have been sexually assaulted are often frightened or ashamed to tell, so parents need to be alert to other signs. Children who have been assaulted often abruptly change their behaviour. They may suddenly start to do badly at school, begin lying, stealing or running away, or retreat into their own world and stop talking to their friends. They may become very preoccupied with sex, flirting or showing affection in a way which is inappropriate for their age. Sometimes, as a result of the abuse, children develop urinary infections or have pain in the genital area.

If for any reason you suspect abuse you should talk to your child again about touching, and gently encourage her to tell you about anything that has happened to her. Over a period of a few days she may start to answer direct questions. It is not easy for a parent to stay calm in these circumstances, but it is very important that you should not add to your child's anxieties by becoming distraught yourself. The lines of communication must be kept open so that the child can describe exactly what happened and can be reassured that she is not to blame.

on what should be taught and how, parents are free to approach the subject as they wish, using whatever books or other materials they find helpful. They also have continuity on their side and can impart information in small doses, as and when it is needed. At school discussions of sex have to be fitted into a rigid timetable, whereas at home the subject can be dropped and picked up again at an appropriate moment.

As part of a study of children between five and fifteen, researchers Ronald and Juliette Goldman asked children in Australia, Britain, Sweden and the United States where they got information about sex, what they would like to know and who they would like to tell them. Most said they wanted information from their parents but felt that the parents were uneasy about certain subjects, which in turn made the children feel embarrassed. Most children, boys as well as girls, preferred to ask their mothers rather than their fathers, because the mothers had babies and talked to doctors.

The majority did feel that they got most of their information from their parents. Often, however, this information was picked up indirectly from listening to adult conversations and was distorted and inaccurate. Even if they don't ask questions, children are alert to what they can overhear. 'One fact is abundantly clear,' say the Goldmans. 'Children perceive it is the adults who have hang-ups about sex and adults who deliberately or unconsciously withhold the information and knowledge the children seek.'

Towards a positive view of sex

Although children certainly need to be warned of the risks involved in sexual experience, it is important not to put so much emphasis on the dangers of sex that they come to distrust their own sexuality. Too often children coming up to adolescence are conditioned to protect themselves against disease and pregnancy, and against being 'used', by avoiding sexual encounters. This may lead them to see their natural desires as dangerous and destructive. As young people approach the age of sexual activity they need encouragement to talk freely about their feelings and about the positive and loving aspects of sexual experience.

Some people assume that eleven or twelve sees the end of childhood – after that comes adolescence, another world. This is far from true: childhood does not end suddenly. The process of change is gradual, with the child building on what has gone before in order to cope with new demands, both physical and emotional.

Demands there will certainly be. Although adolescence is not inevitably a time of storm and stress, there is no doubt that dramatic, major changes do occur, in mind and body. The more secure and confident the relationship you have by now established with your child, the better equipped you will both be to manage the years ahead.

Adolescence and Puberty

The terms 'adolescence' and 'puberty' are often used as though they were synonymous, but this is not so. Puberty comprises a series of physical and physiological changes which convert children into adults capable of reproduction. These include a growth spurt, alterations in body proportions, and the development both of the primary sex organs – in girls the ovaries, in boys the testes, prostate gland and seminal vesicles – and of secondary sexual characteristics, including the uterus, vagina and breasts in girls, the penis in boys, pubic hair in both sexes. All this normally takes between two and five years. Adolescence refers to the whole process of growing up, both physically and psychologically, which takes much longer.

The end result of adolescence is adulthood, something which is much harder to define; it clearly involves a lot more than just being capable of reproduction. We all know what we have in mind when we say someone behaves in a mature way; we all know people who are adult in years but emotionally adolescent; however, it is not easy to explain exactly what we mean.

In adolescence there is one overwhelming psychological demand: to become independent and in so doing to develop a sense of identity.

Adolescents have so much to do. In a very short time they have to learn how to look after themselves in a whole variety of ways – from taking responsibility for their own health care to becoming streetwise; they have to sort out friendships; learn skills; possibly take exams, with all the stress that involves; and become independent of their parents.

Differences between individuals become more evident than they have ever been before. We can, with some justification, generalize about two or three year olds' patterns of behaviour, we can make some reasonable guess at the kind of music, story or television programme that will appeal to a five year old; but in adolescence the range of tastes, skills and interests widens to adult proportions. One seventeen year old will find delight in a television soap opera, another in *War and Peace* (sometimes, of course, both).

Different timetables of development become more evident as well. Some children grow up fast and early, others are much slower.

Discussing ideas and events, comparing points of view – all part of finding out what sort of a person you are and what you think and feel.

431

The Changes of Puberty

The onset of puberty is not an abrupt event, but is preceded by several years of hormone adjustment. Hormones can be released at high levels in newborns but their activity is inhibited by a sensitive feedback mechanism. During the years leading up to puberty there is a gradual increase in the release from the pituitary gland, at the base of the brain, of hormones which stimulate the gonads, the sex glands. When the gonads produce sex hormones in sufficient concentration, the sex organs begin to develop. We refer to this as the onset of puberty, but it is important to realize that the process of hormonal adjustment has already been going on for years.

Although hormones are often described as male or female, each individual has a combination; it is the balance that makes the sexes different.

The timing of the onset of puberty depends on a number of factors: a person's genetic make-up and his physical condition, which includes how well nourished he is, combine with various psychological influences.

In developed countries the average age for the onset of puberty in girls is now approximately eleven, although a normal range lies between nine and thirteen. For boys the average age is around twelve, a normal range being between nine and fourteen. The extent of this range is well illustrated in a typical class of twelve to thirteen year olds, which will include the short and the tall, the gangling and the slight, the flat-chested and the well developed, the baby face and the incipient moustache, the high voice and the gruff, all in one room.

The growth spurt

As well as the variation in age, there is also variation in the order of events in puberty. However, girls generally begin their growth spurt (a sudden and rapid shooting up in height) at the same time as they start to develop secondary sexual characteristics, while boys' voices may break, and they may begin to grow pubic hair and show other signs of development, while they are still relatively small. For a brief time girls may be taller than boys of the same age and, because they also have a 'muscle spurt' earlier, they may also have more muscle than their male counterparts at this time.

Girls usually begin their growth spurt at about eleven, grow fastest between twelve and thirteen and slow down by fourteen. The growth of boys lags by two to three years: boys typically begin to grow quickly at about thirteen, grow fastest at fourteen or so and slow down at sixteen. During the growth spurt a child may put on as much as 10 cm/4 inches in one year. 'Goodness,' everyone says, 'hasn't he grown!' For the child concerned this can be quite gratifying to hear – the first few times; the child whose growth spurt is delayed – or who has growth problems – can find it wounding to hear others apparently praised for something over which they have no control. Nor is it easy for the child who is growing up much faster than others.

Physique

Before puberty boys and girls differ little in strength, but during puberty an increase in the flow of male hormones causes a boy's heart and lungs to

Disparities in size and physical maturity may be very marked in young adolescents.

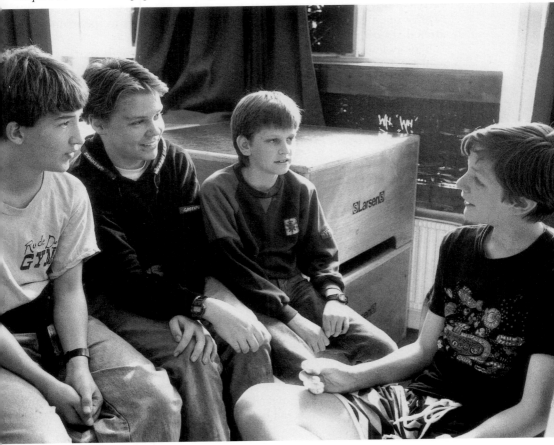

grow more than a girl's and leads to a proportionately greater increase in muscle; this increase in muscle mass continues after puberty and because of this adult men are on average stronger than women. Of course there are, as usual, exceptions to this general rule.

At the beginning of puberty, 20 to 24 per cent of the body weight of girls is made up of fat; this rises to about 28 per cent by seventeen. In boys, at the beginning of puberty, only about 17 to 20 per cent of body weight is fat and this declines to perhaps 10 to 12 per cent at seventeen. A girl who is extremely athletic – a dancer or a gymnast perhaps – will have a body fat level much lower than that of the average girl, perhaps even as low as the average boy's, but it will still not be as low as the fat level of a very fit boy.

Growth of the bones

Bone growth is rapid in the early and middle years of puberty, then slows and finally stops. As the bones grow the muscles stretch to cover them. The part of the bone where growth occurs is towards its end. In the late teens or early twenties (usually between sixteen and eighteen in girls, eighteen and twenty-one in boys) the growing part of the bone fuses to the main shaft; after that no further growth is possible.

The awkwardness of the adolescent during the growth spurt is partly explained by the order in which the bones grow. In a reversal of the proximodistal pattern of early growth, the lower parts of the arms and the legs begin their spurt before the upper part: first the feet and hands lengthen, then the calf and forearm, then the thigh and upper arm, followed by the hips and chest and shoulders.

In the early stages of puberty the bones of the legs and arms are growing

---

Growing pains

So-called 'growing pains' are common in early adolescence, but are rarely serious. Their cause is not known.

These cramp-like pains are deep in the body of the muscle, away from the joints. They usually occur in the shins, but can also affect the calves and the front of the thighs. They are commonly felt late in the day or at night, particularly following a day of vigorous activity (though this is not the cause). Attacks usually last only a few minutes, rarely more than an hour, but may occur on and off over several years. A child with growing pains will need reassurance, and heat or massage may help.

There can, however, be skeletal disorders associated with growth in early adolescence, so it is wise to have serious or prolonged aches and pains investigated. Pain in the hip is always to be taken seriously, and it is worth noting that pain originating in the hip is sometimes felt in the knee.

Pain in the arms or legs may also be the result of overuse or repetitive exercise: the joints are particularly sensitive when the bones are growing rapidly, and can easily become painfully inflamed. If this happens, it is important to reduce the level of activity and rest the affected part of the body, in order to avoid trouble in the future.

Sleep

Sleep takes on an added importance in adolescence because deep sleep is needed for efficient secretion of pubertal and growth hormones. The body is maturing and getting bigger and stronger, but it needs help. Children who, for whatever reason, do not sleep well, may not grow well. There have been few studies of the sleep patterns of normal adolescents in their home environment: what most parents notice is a decrease in the time spent asleep at night but a considerable increase during the day, with teenagers staying in bed, if they are allowed to, throughout the morning! Here again, it is necessary to achieve some sort of balance, this time between the desire to stay up all night and the need to be active during the day. Parents do need to realize, though, that teenagers will not be 'on the go' all day as they were when they were younger.

---

proportionately almost twice as fast as those of the trunk – which is why young adolescents look so leggy. However, as puberty advances the rate of trunk growth speeds up, and by the age when an adolescent is growing fastest overall (on average twelve for girls, fourteen for boys), trunk and limbs are growing at approximately the same rate. Within a year of this peak rate of growth, limb growth has slowed dramatically and within two years the legs and arms have almost stopped growing, while the trunk continues to grow. However, over the years of adolescent growth the ratio of limb length to trunk increases in most people – adults' limbs are longer, in proportion to the trunk, than young children's.

As children, boys and girls have much the same bone structure, but after puberty there are differences: boys' shoulders are broader; girls develop wider hips, and, because of the overlay of fat, their shoulders and hips are more rounded. During adolescence both the trunk and the limbs of a boy, but particularly the limbs, grow more than those of a girl, and, on average, men have proportionately longer legs than women.

The bones in the head continue to grow during adolescence: although the increase in skull circumference may only be about 2.5 cm/1 inch, the change can be noticeable. The overall shape of the face changes at this time, the length altering more than the width, and boys changing more than girls. In particular the lower jaw becomes bigger. Changes in the shape of the face can continue until the middle twenties.

Puberty in girls

For most girls, puberty is heralded by the beginning of the growth spurt and the first signs of breast development. Usually, an increase in weight is the precursor to growing taller. Hips broaden and a thin layer of fat develops under the skin, beginning to give girls their fuller, female shape. Then they start to shoot up in height.

Your daughter may watch the appearance of her breast buds and their subsequent growth with interest and pleasure or with anxiety, depending on fashion and her own point of view. The nipples get larger, become more sensitive and stand out more, and the areola – the circle of skin surrounding each nipple – gets thicker and darker. Uneven breast development is not at all uncommon – one breast may bud before the other, or they may both grow, but be of different sizes. They usually even out in time, and only occasionally is medical attention required.

In about 20 per cent of girls pubic hair starts to grow before breast development begins. For the rest, it follows soon after. At first pubic hair is straight and fine; it gradually becomes thicker and curlier, and spreads out over a larger area; it may even spread over the thighs. Body hair which is finer and less curly begins to grow in the armpits and on the arms and legs, and some girls have hair growth on their faces. The quality, quantity and distribution of hair is normally a matter of inheritance; some families and cultural groups have a good deal more hair than others.

The clitoris and inner lips of the vagina increase in size. Girls may suddenly discover the clitoris and explore it, finding a new pleasure in masturbation. At this stage, some girls explore each others' bodies and talk through their ideas on what it means to become women. This does not imply any tendency towards homosexuality.

Menstruation begins when the breasts are almost fully developed and growth is slowing down. For the majority of girls the first period occurs between twelve and fourteen – most often within six months of the thirteenth birthday. Sometimes, though, girls start to menstruate very early, and sometimes menstruation is considerably delayed. The determinants of the timing of menstruation are not fully understood, though we know that there is a high correlation with skeletal maturity. The age at which a girl begins to menstruate is in part genetically determined – the average difference in the age at which periods start is only two months for identical twins, while for fraternal twins it is eight months. However, there are various other influences at work.

One of these is nutrition. Some sources suggest that girls will not start to menstruate until they achieve a minimum weight of about 45 kg/7 stone, but it is not really possible to be so categorical. Food is, of course, essential for growth and for development, and successful reproduction demands a certain nutritional standard, but that standard varies from individual to individual. Adolescents need a good balanced diet and are likely to eat a lot, but, as in everything else, individual requirements vary. That having been said, malnutrition and low body weight, which can result from severe dieting of the kind that occurs in anorexia nervosa (see page 483), or from chronic illness such as poorly controlled asthma or diabetes, is likely to delay menstruation.

The association between emotional influences and menstruation is complex, and there are few hard facts available on the subject. However, the pattern of menstruation can undoubtedly be altered by stress produced by emotional problems.

Headaches, irritability and cramps – caused by hormonal changes – may announce the first period, but some girls begin with little warning. The first periods tend to be irregular, and are often a matter of light spotting rather than heavy bleeding. Most girls do not begin to ovulate until twelve to eighteen months after their first period. For the first year or so they menstruate without ovulating, shedding the lining of the womb without releasing a mature egg. However, it is important for girls to know that ovulation can begin at any time (even before the first period) and, of course, once ovulation has begun sexual intercourse can lead to pregnancy.

Girls need to be well prepared for their first period; otherwise, they may find it extremely upsetting. Even when girls know what to expect, there can be a degree of embarrassment and confusion in their reaction. This is especially likely if a girl matures earlier than her friends.

Preparing your child for menstruation

The best time to tell your daughter about menstruation is long before either she or her friends start their periods. She will probably already know quite a bit about reproduction, but now is the time to talk about human reproduction, and menstruation in particular, in more detail. Schools may have sex or health programmes, and primary schools often arrange for a nurse to come in and talk to their ten and eleven year olds about menstruation. There are various useful books about human reproduction available. But all this is best used as back-up and for reinforcing the information you can give her. For you, her mother, are the person closest to your daughter, you have your own personal experience of menstruation to guide you, and you can reassure her, inform her, and help her with the practicalities in a way that will make the whole business seem less daunting and indeed a normal – even gratifying – part of growing up.

Explain that because of the hormonal changes leading up to menstruation she may start to get occasional headaches and cramps. Reassure her that her first period is unlikely to entail a flood of bleeding, but that probably she will first notice a few spots on her pants. Show her some sanitary pads and tampons and discuss how they are used and the advantages and disadvantages of each. Tell her also how to dispose of them, both at home and elsewhere, and what to do if her pants or bedclothes are stained, and assure her that you will help her if accidents of this kind occur.

If she wants to use tampons, tell her that there is usually quite enough room for them in the vagina, but that inserting them takes a bit of getting used to. Reassure her that if she follows the instructions tampons will not cause pain. It is important to warn her to change tampons frequently – four or five times during the day – to avoid the risk of toxic shock, as this very rare but sometimes fatal bacterial infection has developed in some women when a tampon was left in too long. You might suggest that she should use pads at night.

It will probably be easier for her to use pads the first time, at any rate, so

Puberty in boys

The first sign of puberty in boys is enlargement of the testicles, which generally occurs around the age of twelve, though, as with girls, there is a wide variation in the age of onset of puberty; at first, one testicle often hangs lower than the other. Boys may also notice their nipples getting larger, darker and more sensitive, and many boys experience a temporary swelling in one or both breasts. In early puberty there is as much oestrogen available to boys as to girls, so it is only surprising that male breast development does not happen more often; it is probably prevented by the male sex hormone

Spots and acne

Spots are one of the problems adolescents dread the most. During puberty the sebaceous glands in the skin are stimulated to overactivity by the male hormone testosterone, which is at a high level in boys and quite high in girls too. Spots occur when these glands produce an excessive amount of their oily secretion sebum. The glands readily become clogged and the bacteria under the skin release toxins that cause spots to erupt on the skin's surface. They usually appear on the face, neck, chest or back.

Chronic acne, a more severe problem in which crops of pustules erupt on the face, neck, torso or thighs, affects more boys than girls (because of their higher level of testosterone boys have greasier skin), but many girls are afflicted too. It is most common between the ages of sixteen and nineteen in boys, and fourteen and seventeen in girls.

Scientists have found no direct link between diet and the eruption of spots: junk food, sugar, chocolate or dairy foods cannot be blamed, and the excess of oil in the skin is caused not by the fat in fried foods but by the secretions of the sebaceous glands. Skin problems can be aggravated by indigestion and constipation and teenagers certainly need a well-balanced diet, but there is no scientific evidence to justify badgering them to change their eating habits in order to control acne.

Emotional stress and fatigue do seem to trigger the eruption of spots in some adolescents.

Many teenagers find that their skin improves over the summer months when they are outdoors more and more active. Sunlight certainly helps. Cleansing the skin thoroughly helps too, and water-based cleansing lotions are best; alcohol-based preparations or those containing hexachlorophene have not been shown to limit or prevent spots or acne, and can dry the skin and cause irritation and peeling. Greasy cosmetic and hair preparations should be avoided because they may irritate the skin. It is also important not to squeeze spots, as this only makes them more inflamed and tends to spread infection.

If your child is suffering from a bad outbreak of spots or acne you should arrange an appointment with a doctor. Lotions, creams and gels based on a derivative of Vitamin A have proved effective in many cases. Doctors can also prescribe systemic antibiotics or other topical preparations which will improve the condition.

testosterone counteracting the effects of the oestrogen. If your son's breasts swell you can reassure him that such swelling is common, that it is usually only mild, and that it almost always passes spontaneously within a year or eighteen months.

Usually, fine, downy pubic hair appears at about the same time as the testicles begin to develop, with underarm and facial hair following about two years later. In a few boys, however, underarm and facial hair appears first. Hair on the chest and legs does not usually develop until late adolescence or early adulthood. The profusion, or otherwise, of hair growing on the chin, legs, chest and (often) on the back is an inherited family or racial trait.

Around thirteen or fourteen boys begin to put on height, weight and muscle and the shoulders start to broaden. The penis grows rapidly and erections become more frequent – they may be brought on by any kind of anxiety or excitement. Boys sometimes spend a lot of time investigating and comparing the size of their penises. (It may comfort them to know that there is much less difference in size when they are erect.)

Ejaculations begin about a year after the penis begins to lengthen. At first the liquid produced is clear and sticky; later, as the testicles start to produce sperm, it becomes milky. The first ejaculation sometimes comes in sleep, in association with a 'wet' dream.

Voice changes occur as the larynx increases in size and the vocal cords lengthen. This happens over a long period of time and a boy does not usually develop the deep masculine voice he will have as an adult until late adolescence. Along the way this development reveals itself when a boy's voice 'cracks' – often at an embarrassing moment – and he is unable to control the pitch. Occasionally the voice remains high, a condition known as puberphonia. A more acceptable pitch can be achieved with training, and a speech therapist will be able to advise on this. Singing voices also change, and many good boy singers find that they have to give up musical ambitions; sometimes, though, the adult voice is an improvement.

Early and late developers

The problems of precocious puberty were discussed in the previous chapter (see page 370). Those children who mature within the bounds of normal development but rather before or rather after most of their contemporaries also have particular situations to deal with.

Early development can result in pressure on children because they are not emotionally in tune with their bodies. Late developers also have problems related to the mismatch between social and sexual development, and may be made to feel deeply inferior if they do not show the bodily changes expected of them. It may be helpful to know that medical treatment for delayed maturation is available.

Developing earlier or later than friends may lead to complex, often opposing emotions. An early-maturing girl, for example, may feel proud of

Friends who develop physically at different rates may find that their interests diverge – but clearly these boys are still good companions.

her advanced physical development at home and in school, but awkward in ballet class. A late-maturing boy may be less distracted from schoolwork and therefore do better academically than his more mature contemporaries, but may be less successful in sports and feel left out socially.

Adolescents play many different roles, and these roles often conflict. Girls who mature early are often given more independence at home: they may be allowed to stay at home without supervision and be expected to make more independent decisions. But they may also be more often at odds with their parents over clothes, make-up, late nights and homework. It takes time and effort, not to mention emotional energy, to compete socially and try to succeed with boys when you are only twelve or thirteen, and schoolwork and other areas of achievement can fall by the wayside.

Adolescents who mature early tend to date or pair off with a partner earlier, and an early-maturing girl may find herself going out with older and more experienced boys. If, as she well may, she feels that she wants to be part of an older crowd, she may try to gain acceptance by wearing more sophisticated clothes, more make-up, and so forth. This can lead to squabbles with parents; at the end of the day, it is also likely to make the adolescent even more self-conscious and less confident because, appearing as she is in borrowed feathers, she will be treated as someone she is not.

Boys who mature early tend to feel more positive about their body image and have higher self-esteem than their companions who have not yet matured. They themselves are inclined to see their maturity as an advantage, because it leads to more social encounters with girls and to greater popularity in general. They may also feel more confident in their friendships. Like early-maturing girls, they are often given greater responsibility and freedom than their contemporaries. Again as with girls, however, early maturing may lead to a temporary falling-off in academic achievement.

The superior size and strength of early-maturing boys may give them an advantage in athletics. Within a few months or years most of their contemporaries will have caught up and the early maturers will find that they can no longer rely simply on size for athletic advantage. However, late-maturing adolescents may lose several years of practice by being excluded from competition and team sports in favour of their more mature contemporaries.

On the positive side, one study found that late-maturing boys have a stronger sense of who they are and where they are going in life, perhaps because they have more time to think about future plans and how to achieve them than their more physically mature friends, who may be absorbed in their more immediate physical prowess. These findings could well also apply to girls; they were not included in the study. And we should remember, too, that all these comments are generalizations and will not necessarily apply to your child or to children you know.

Physical skills

From adolescence onwards, boys' athletic performance differs from that of girls, for various reasons: their internal organs, including the heart and lungs, are larger than girls'; their muscles are stronger; and their endurance is greater, because male hormones enable a more efficient use of the muscles.

However, it is only in physical strength that boys and men have a natural advantage. Where skill is as important as strength girls will continue to do as well as boys. And in areas such as dancing, skating or gymnastics, the advantage lies with the girls. Both girls and boys are at their most agile between the ages of twelve and fourteen, but girls are more agile than boys (as, indeed, they have been from the age of five or six). And as muscles develop, flexibility decreases; girls, whose muscles do not increase dramatically in size and strength, remain better coordinated and more graceful. Women also have the edge when it comes to swimming, because their greater fat deposits make them more buoyant, and they do not get cold so quickly.

Ideally, adolescents, both boys and girls, should be participating in a wide range of physical activity. However, by twelve or so children are well able to evaluate their own performance at sport, and if they feel they are not doing well they tend to lose interest. One large-scale study showed that at around twelve 80 per cent of children drop out of all organized sport other than that which they are required to take part in at school. At any time during adolescence, poor performance, whether it is the result of natural lack of skill, or of poor coaching, or of an injury, can result in a teenager's feeling incompetent and disheartened, and may lead him to give up sport entirely. Even for those who are enthusiastic, there comes a critical moment when young adults move from sports readily available at school to an independent adult life. If they choose then to carry on with some form of exercise – whether or not this takes the form of an organized sport – it can be said that their physical education, at school and at home, has been successful.

Thinking

Adolescence is a time of rapidly increasing mental capacity. Young people's working memories improve a lot, as does their ability to relate components of a task one to another, and they become much better at finding effective strategies when faced with a problem and at planning ahead.

What is most exciting of all, during adolescence some children become scientists and philosophers: they develop the ability to reason in the abstract, and use this power not only to make startling progress in school but also to analyze broader issues of politics, ethics and religion. Being able to reason in the abstract means that one no longer needs to rely solely on the way things are but can contemplate how they ought to be. The ability to reason in this way underlies the preoccupation among some young people with rights and wrongs, philosophical conclusions about life based not on experience, which they have not had, but on theory, which they have just discovered.

As so often, we turn to Piaget as a starting point for a discussion of thinking, for his work forms the basis on which so much has been built. Piaget argued that the age of eleven or twelve saw the onset of what he called 'formal operations', the ability to follow the form of reasoning while ignoring its content. Children with this ability can reason from the general laws that lie behind the array of particular instances; they can think using formal systems such as those of algebra and physics. This enables them to incorporate hypotheses in their thinking in quite sophisticated ways: they can speculate,

Do they think in different ways?
There is some evidence that, from early adolescence on, boys and girls begin to show different aptitudes, with girls tending to move ahead of boys in areas related to language, while boys often do better at tasks requiring spatial ability, notably mathematics and science. There is much debate about whether this discrepancy in skills occurs because of a difference in structure between the male and the female brain or whether it is brought about principally by different expectations, specifically by attitudes common among teachers. There can be no doubt, however, that the differences between the mental abilities of boys and girls are by no means clear-cut (many girls are good at maths, many boys are good at language-based lessons), that teaching can make a difference, and that girls and boys alike need to have a strong grounding in both mathematics and language.

444

Voicing your ideas among friends helps to clarify your own opinions and values.

for example, on 'what would happen if no one died?' and can mull over a number of possible answers.

More recent research indicates, however, that Piaget may have under-estimated the age at which people become capable of reasoning in the abstract – and, indeed, suggests that many people may never reach this stage. Learning and experience play a part in this.

When Piagetian experiments were tried out on a large scale, it was found that only 50 to 60 per cent of eighteen to twenty year olds were capable of formal reasoning as Piaget defined it. Some researchers found that whole communities failed to demonstrate an ability to think about logical or mathematical systems at this level.

A weakness of Piaget's theory is revealed by the fact that those who failed to meet Piaget's criteria for the most advanced mental stage had

445

received far less formal education than those who did. Although Piaget defined 'formal operations' as a universal stage in intellectual development, people are actually more likely to reason at a sophisticated level if they have been taught the rules of a formal system such as physics. If an ability to apply formal rules such as those of physics is a hallmark of the most advanced intellectual stage, then, not surprisingly, those who have studied such a system will do better than those who have not. Learning to think about how they think undoubtedly increases children's all-round ability to reason. Children who are encouraged to discuss the mental steps by which they have reached their answers in one subject do better not only in that subject, but in others as well.

Moral reasoning

Amidst all the controversy surrounding the development of moral reasoning, at least one clear point can be made: adolescence is pre-eminently a time when many young people will relish moral problems put to them.

One way of assessing how people reason in this field is to present them with stories of moral dilemmas: for example, a man's wife is dying of cancer and the only way he can get enough money to buy her drugs is to steal; what should he do? Young children will define the morality of this case in rigid terms. They will say, for example, that it is always wrong to steal, apparently unaware that there may be powerful, morally defensible, overriding reasons for breaking a law. The adolescent, on the other hand, will appreciate the play of ideas and the conflicts of moral principles that have to be taken on board before an answer can be reached. The really sophisticated adolescent will be able to appreciate that there can be no conclusive answer to such questions, and that it might be moral to steal under certain conditions but not under others.

Of all theories on the development of morality those of Lawrence Kohlberg have perhaps been the most influential. Kohlberg put forward the idea that moral thought develops in a series of three levels. At the first level, children are bound by the inflexible rules imposed by external authorities, the seriousness of an offence depending on the magnitude of its consequences.

Adolescent egocentricity

The idea that adolescents are still to some extent egocentric thinkers has been revived recently by David Elkind, who has put forward the rather complex notion that as young people reach the level at which they can think about the thoughts of others they imagine that other people share their own preoccupations. For example, the adolescent is preoccupied with his appearance and he assumes that everyone else is similarly concerned about how he looks. The teenager constantly performs before an imaginary audience – hence the hours spent in front of the mirror.

The period of Kohlberg's second 'conventional' level of morality is when the individual has his own moral standards but these largely conform to the rules and precepts made for him by his parents and friends, and other groups to which he may belong.

Kohlberg's third and final level is entitled 'postconventional': the individual's moral principles are freed from the constraints of identification with a particular group; the basis for action is the conscience. In Kohlberg's view few people reach this level.

There is support for this theory from long-term studies which indicate that, when questioned along the lines suggested by Kohlberg, children do indeed pass through a series of stages consistent with his predictions. However, there have been a number of criticisms.

One is that his theories are based on information acquired by posing hypothetical dilemmas expressed by characters in stories, not by questioning people about real problems encountered in daily life. People often argue differently when asked about something to do with their immediate experience.

Another criticism is that he based his work on male interviewees being asked about male-oriented topics. Yet another is that he uses sophisticated terminology, abstract words such as 'justice' and 'equality'. If such terms are not part of people's everyday language it is hardly surprising that they do not use them when faced with a moral dilemma.

The most powerful, if most obvious, point to be made about theories of morality, however, is that there is not necessarily a direct correlation between how people say one should behave and how they actually do behave. Children's level of moral reasoning develops with age, but their moral behaviour may not follow. One of the most telling criticisms of Kohlberg is that he took no account of the fact that there is an emotional component to all our decisions. In the face of reality, our feelings will exert a powerful influence on what we do.

What parents can do

In the final analysis we should be most interested in what will actually help our adolescents to behave in a morally responsible way. Two main strands have emerged from research, allowing us to draw some conclusions. The first is, yet again, the importance of example. Parents, teachers, other significant adults, bear an enormous responsibility in this area. Adolescents are also, of course, greatly influenced by their peer group – and, in a more general way, by the values displayed in the society around them.

The second strand is the vital importance of discussion. As we have already seen in previous chapters, encouraging children to talk about moral dilemmas sharpens their moral sense. In the adolescent years, discussion of such issues becomes even more crucial. Through discussion we learn to step back from our own limited viewpoint, to open up to the idea that there can be two (or more) sides to a question; and that is really what morality is all about.

Education

School serves three critically important functions in the life of the adolescent. First, and at the risk of stating the obvious, it should help him to become skilled in certain areas. Whether the areas are academic or practical, theoretical or vocational, is of relatively little importance: what counts is that the young person should feel that he has reached an adequate level of achievement. Second, school provides an opportunity to encounter many others of the same age; observation of and discussion with his peers will help him to develop his individual value system. The third contribution school has to make lies in the provision of role models, in the head, the teachers, and sometimes older children.

The framework within which adolescents learn, encounter others of the same age and develop a sense of values is of vital importance. In most cases, the secondary school will be very different from the school the child attended when he was younger. It will have a more complex social system and a much broader academic and non-academic curriculum. Students may well be drawn from a wider social group, often representing a greater ethnic mix, and come from a wider geographic area.

Some adolescents thrive on this kind of complex social system while others resist it, but whether the adolescent conforms or rebels he will be acutely aware of the rules and expectations that operate both socially and academically within the school. A good school will increase a child's chances of achieving both academically and socially, and will provide experiences that help to develop confidence and self-esteem.

Which school?

Many parents are in no position to choose between schools, but where there is a choice it is worth finding out as much as you can about the various possibilities.

Schools with a good scholastic record, where attendance is good and discipline problems rare, are in general those where teachers are committed, have high standards themselves and expect high standards from their students; they spend most of their time teaching as opposed to disciplining. Classes are well planned and students are expected to listen, work hard and participate in class discussion. Students are praised when they do well, and

Look what's happening! Adolescents, like younger children, enjoy working together, cooperating in a task and sharing the excitement of the results.

are also given a large amount of responsibility in the practical running of the school. Parents are encouraged to become involved in the activities of the school and to support its aims.

It is not always easy to discover whether a school meets these criteria, but it is worth keeping them in mind when you investigate possible options. You can find out a certain amount from a school brochure and published academic results, but it is also always worth visiting a school. First impressions are important, from the secretary's response over the phone to the atmosphere in the corridors. Are the children friendly and polite? Is the school well cared for? Do the children in the classrooms appear lively and attentive? Is the work in their books interesting, well presented, carefully marked?

Ask to meet the head: he or she will set the tone for the whole school, and there will be questions you want to ask him or her about the school.

If possible, you should also talk to the parents of children who have been right through the school. Find out as much as you can about how the school operates before your child goes there; and if, once he is there, the system seems not to be working adequately, go and discuss it.

449

The academic framework

Learning at this time has various functions. One is the provision of a passport to a higher level of education or a desired workplace. The second is cumulative: successful learning leads to higher self-esteem; this in turn influences the student's willingness and indeed his desire both to press on in the area of success and to try his wings in other areas. The third is harder to pin down: it lies in the encouragement of learning for its own sake.

Differences in academic abilities and attainments between children become increasingly apparent and this can lead to immense pressure being put on children, sometimes to the point where it becomes counter-productive – children may see that they can never reach the goals set and give up altogether. Communities vary in the amount of pressure they put on their children – with, perhaps, nothing quite equalling the Japanese 'education mother', obsessed that her children should succeed in school. On the other hand, teachers despair when they see bright, once eager children, who receive no support from home for their school endeavours. There is also, of course, the frustration of children who long to learn, and who have supportive parents, but who find themselves in schools where learning is more or less incidental, where they are mocked by other children for showing enthusiasm, or where teachers struggle simply to survive.

At best, parents, teachers and teenagers will all be aiming in the same direction: to enlarge the student's horizons, increase his confidence and self-esteem, and provide him with adequate means with which to embark on the next stage, whether this be higher education or vocational work.

Homework and study skills

By the time they are twelve or thirteen children no longer need you to provide hands-on experiences; they can now think and reason in the abstract and work through their own ideas. However, with a few exceptions, they still need help to learn to study – to organize their work and use their time productively. This help can come in the form of parents' guidance, monitored study periods at school, or, in some cases, professional tutoring outside school.

Most secondary schools require homework, partly to extend the limited time that is available at school for children to consolidate the information they are given and to carry out independent research, partly so that they can learn to organize their own work. Some schools have supervised after-school study periods, while others rely on parents to oversee homework.

Every individual has his own way of working, a time of day he finds most productive and a span of time in which he can usefully concentrate. People also differ in the way they study: some people like a background of music and lots of posters on the wall; others find these distracting. Parents need to establish, with the child, a place and time for homework. Some basic policies need to be agreed: if, for example, you expect to check homework assignments and diaries, then make this clear from the beginning (though for the adolescent who is doing well in school this kind of checking up may not be necessary). If homework is going to be done at a certain time of day, other activities need to be fitted into the schedule and the rest of the family needs to be aware that the student must not be interrupted.

In general, teenagers need to learn how to get along academically on their own and to take responsibility for their own homework. However, if you are concerned about the amount, or the lack, of homework your child is being given, or want to know what level of participation is expected of you, do speak to the relevant teacher or tutor at school. It may be that your child is not writing down or understanding the assignments; it may be that the teacher does not check homework or accepts sloppy work and the child just doesn't feel it's worth making an effort; it may be that your teenager is testing your limits and interest and needs to have his homework checked for a time. Self-discipline is a hard lesson to learn.

So long as children are doing well at school, there is little reason for you to interfere with their system, no matter how idiosyncratic it may seem: that music may be helping to blot out family noises. (However, even the best students do not do their best work while sprawled in front of the television, and you can reasonably follow your instinctive urge to turn it off and send him to his room to study.)

Teenagers have a hard time balancing social life and school: some err on the side of too much time spent on fun and friends and the telephone, and others spend too much time studying. If a teenager is spending hours and hours trying to get homework done, or checking it obsessionally, there may be a problem. He may need reassurance that his work is adequate, and help to find a more balanced lifestyle.

Problems with schoolwork

Adolescents often go through a period when their work suffers at school. This may happen for many reasons. Health can affect performance at school, and parents need to be vigilant about hearing loss or problems with sight. Or perhaps your teenager is feeling anxious about life in general, perhaps a relationship has gone wrong, perhaps he has recently changed schools and left the security of friends and familiar surroundings behind, perhaps he is depressed – or perhaps he is anxious about impending exams and how they will affect his future. Whatever the reason, it is worth encouraging him to talk over his problems with you, or, if he finds it easier, with a sympathetic teacher, or with someone outside both family and school.

If one school subject in particular is causing problems, help from an outside tutor can often help restore confidence and performance all round. Where a teenager has persistent trouble academically, this often has its roots in learning difficulties which began much earlier – in poor reading skills, perhaps, or an inability to master basic mathematical concepts. Again, if the school is unable to help, a period with an outside tutor may improve the situation. And if anxiety about exams is a problem, it is certainly worth finding someone – an ex-teacher, perhaps – who can practise exam techniques with him and help reduce stress.

Examinations

Many teenagers experience anxiety about tests and exams, but getting good at exams is no different from acquiring other skills: the student needs to know what is required, to practise, to reflect on what he is doing, to analyze what he did and to alter strategies if there are areas needing improvement.

Teachers constantly admonish: see how many questions you are expected to answer, read the questions carefully, allow plenty of time, don't panic and don't rush at the first question on the paper. All this is excellent advice, though hard to follow if you are feeling anxious. Children are less nervous about tests when they are clear about why the test is being given and what it is designed to discover; they need to be told in advance what kind of test it will be, how long it will take and how it will be marked.

The more practice students have the better, and the results of practice exams and 'mocks' should be judged not just in terms of correct answers but

---

Coping with exam stress

Some anxiety about exams is useful. The student who is too laid-back may feel that he does not need to prepare. But when anxiety becomes crippling, when a teenager cannot concentrate or begins to make errors because he is anxious, he may need to learn some methods of coping with stress, to reduce the anxiety.

When you feel stressed your heart-rate becomes quicker and your breathing deeper (or you may arrest your breathing). You may feel cold and tremble. In an exam room you may feel cold or extremely hot. You may also have tension headaches, stomach upsets and need to go to the lavatory more frequently. Stress becomes distress when you can no longer think clearly and your concentration becomes focused on your surroundings and circumstances rather than on the work you are required to do.

Teaching stress management is really a job for a trained person, and the family might benefit from learning together. Relaxation forms a part of many exercise techniques from yoga to antenatal classes, and it comes with practice. Three simple methods are described below.

● One way is to visualize the tension draining out of your body and to focus on sensations of heaviness and warmth as you become more relaxed.
● Another method is to concentrate on each part of your body in turn, tensing and then releasing it.
● Or you can focus on breathing: take four or five slow, deep breaths and listen to them being slowly released as you relax.

Whatever relaxation method is used, it should be learned long before exam time, and practised until it becomes a habit. Your teenager will probably benefit from using it before exams rather than during them.

An art examination is in progress, but the atmosphere is relaxed.

even more in terms of the value of the techniques employed: did efficient note-taking prove of value; were the revision techniques satisfactory; what were the rewards, if any, of spending time planning the answers; and so on.

The social and emotional framework

Teenagers need the opportunity to develop socially and emotionally as well as academically, and a secondary school should provide the kind of atmosphere where development in all these directions can take place. The search for identity which can be seen as the main task of adolescence means trying out a number of roles, with constant changes of character, costumes and scenery.

In the space of twenty-four hours a teenage girl may find herself playing the roles of devoted daughter, sympathetic sister, *femme fatale* when she sees her current boyfriend or 'crush', good companion when she gossips with her girlfriends, serious student in her maths class, sports star on the tennis court. (It is partly this dilemma that keeps teenagers in front of a mirror in the morning, unable to decide what to wear to school.) The best schools and teachers are those that avoid labelling teenagers and allow them to play many different roles. When an adolescent is stuck with a label ('quiet' or 'assertive', 'slow' or 'brilliant'), it inhibits self-exploration; when schools pick out only the assertive students to fill posts of responsibility, give only the brightest students chances to excel academically, they discourage teenagers from trying out the wide range of roles that they need to experience in order to establish their own identity.

Teachers also need to give teenagers opportunities to learn to take responsibility. Teenagers need the chance to participate in the running of the school, but they can only do this in a school environment that is safe and secure. If the school is dominated by a group of anti-school non-cooperators or aggressive bullies, students who are trying to participate in the successful running of the school often become the butt of hostile behaviour

A network of schoolfriends provides the main social focus for many teenagers. Those who may feel quite uncertain of themselves as individuals derive security from the group.

The invisible child

School should ideally be a place where all children feel safe to express themselves and able to experiment with their identity. They should be given the opportunity to learn where their talents and their limitations lie; they should be given the chance to learn to be assertive and to disagree; they should feel safe from criticism and mockery and free to respond and to cultivate ideas. They should be helped to discover some activity at which they can excel.

The teenager who is most likely to be overlooked in the large secondary school is the reticent child who conforms and creates no waves. He is unassertive, shows no particular talents, and has no unpleasant habits to attract attention. He does average homework, gets average marks in examinations, seldom volunteers a contribution and rarely has anything original to say. His potential is never put to the test. As far as his teachers are concerned he is one of the many – not a cause for worry, nor a source of pride. He is the student who is instantly forgotten when the year ends.

Not all children seek the limelight. Many are quite happy being regarded as ordinary. However, if you as parents suspect that your child is being overlooked, and that he may be distressed about this, there are ways you can help. Simply recognizing that he is not flourishing or fulfilling his potential, even though he may be surviving the system, is a positive contribution in itself. You can go on to consider if there are special interests or talents that he has out of school and whether he can share in these interests at school. You may need to consult his teacher or tutor to find out if there is a way he could participate more actively in the life of the school, and the child may need help in learning how to build a bridge between home and school. The very fact that you have been to talk to the school could make them more aware of your child, and you can back this up by making sure you go to open evenings and report evenings so that the staff see your support and concern for your child.

from the other group, and in reaction may well choose to withdraw from school activities.

Secondary school is another rung on the ladder towards independence, and one that is hardly ever negotiated entirely without difficulty. Almost all the basic conflicts of adolescence have to do with the pull between dependence and independence. Internally, this conflict is felt by the teenager as an uncomfortable struggle between contradictory feelings; but the battle inside often manifests itself outwardly in the form of tussles with school rules, teachers or parents.

There is often a mismatch between an adolescent's capabilities and what the school enables him to do with them. To take an example, an adolescent may be extremely fit and strong, rippling with muscles and energy, and yet, not having made any of the school teams, have no outlet for his potential physical skills: there is a mismatch between the student's physical capability and the ability of the school to make use of it. On the intellectual side, an adolescent may read constantly and widely, or know every detail about, say, the music industry, but because his interests lie outside the school

Trying it on

Teenagers want to be in charge of their lives but they also want limitations. Limits and rules make them feel safer, both in the classroom and at home. The catch is that young people will rebel if rules are imposed on them from outside. They want to establish their own set of rules and they do this by testing the limits of the tolerance of those around them; they will endlessly 'try it on', seeing how far they can go.

Testing limits may seem like a long way round in establishing a set of rules for the classroom, but most children at this age have already experienced the fact that rules can be bent and that adults do not operate in black and white but in various shades of grey. Teachers may insist that homework be handed in on time, no excuses accepted, but few teachers will in fact refuse to listen to a reasonable excuse. Teachers may demand a quiet classroom but few would want or expect the class never to make a sound. Where do you draw the lines?

In most classrooms, only a few of the children carry out the function of testing limits for the rest of the class, and they may well find that they get into trouble for it. If you learn that your child is among them, you could point out that the class is using him in this way, and suggest that he might find a more constructive way of asserting himself.

curriculum he may encounter nothing to stimulate him intellectually at school: here there is a mismatch between the student's personal interests and the subjects offered at school. Social expectations can also cause trouble. Teenagers who are given responsibility and independence at home return at the beginning of the school year to find themselves monitored in the cafeteria, the corridors and the school grounds; those who are admired by their friends for the way they dress find themselves at odds with school dress codes. The discrepancy here between the culture at school and life outside school can easily make teenagers angry and rebellious; at the very least, they are likely to be confused.

We are not apportioning blame here. Life is full of such inconsistencies and growing up is, in part, a matter of learning how to deal with them. Once again it is a question of adopting different roles and learning how to play them: how to deal with the cultures of school, family, friends and society at large, with all their different requirements.

Discipline in school

When children talk more about behaviour than about what they have learned, it may be an indication that teachers are spending more time trying to control children than teaching them. If a teacher is using aggressive tactics, it is a clear sign that things have got out of hand. This may be because the school has a high proportion of disruptive children; or it may be that a particular teacher has a low frustration level or is suffering from personal problems; it may be because unreasonable and arbitrary rules are being imposed. Whatever the reason, the situation is preventing children from learning and should be discussed with the school.

Misbehaviour and delinquency have been found to be less common in schools where general expectations of behaviour are clearly set by the school and adhered to by the staff; where teachers work harmoniously towards these goals, care about the way the school functions, are punctual, fair and set and mark homework. Discipline is easier to maintain if students appreciate that it relates to these general expectations and does not rely on the whim of a teacher.

Trading and negotiating

It is not possible to impose rules and school learning successfully on teenagers without negotiation. There is little point in trying to teach a non-cooperative teenager something he does not see the sense of or refuses to learn; no amount of pressure will force someone to learn something unless he is prepared to participate and cooperate in the learning process – and for most teenagers this means negotiation on the part of the teacher. Teachers –

Adolescent humour

Adolescent humour is tough, down to earth, and often quite hard to take – though, on the whole, teenagers keep their fiercest and most bawdy side for their friends.

Sometimes teenagers use humour in the classroom (and at home) to relieve boredom and as a way of coping with yet another classroom activity or family event. Sometimes this humour is a way of taking control of a situation where they feel trapped – a group of students laughing during school assembly provides a classic example. Similarly, an adolescent compelled to endure a family dinner with adult visitors may engineer the younger members of the family into fits of giggles. Having a teacher who will share a laugh can save school for teenagers, relieving the tension that can build up during the school day. If the teacher can laugh at him or herself or with them (not at them) it creates a positive shared environment, and many teenagers say that having a good laugh is what they look forward to most in school.

While teenagers tend to be very sensitive to being mocked or teased themselves, they often relish sarcasm directed against somebody else: it helps them to define who they are and how they differ from people they don't like. Teenage humour can also be used as self-defence against an attacking or threatening group. If they label an academic group as 'swots' and laugh at them for studying all the time, they feel that much better about not doing too much studying themselves.

As teenagers become more sophisticated humour can take on a whole new dimension, with the realization that telling a funny story is a miniature performance involving a presentation of the self. The new-found ability to think about thinking is reflected in humour which relies on an ability to reflect on language, to use puns and jokes about jokes, to spin out a shaggy dog story not because there is anything funny in the components but because humour lies in the very lack of meaning of the whole.

and parents – who deal effectively with adolescents bargain and negotiate continuously.

The teacher as role model

A teacher who uses aggressive measures to control the class is giving students the message that violent, aggressive behaviour is acceptable. One who by negotiation establishes that the learning process is a question of mutual participation and shared aims will gain the respect and cooperation of the class. During adolescence, when young people are experimenting with different ways of being and behaving, they are very susceptible to the influence of the adult models they see before them; they are certainly likely to be influenced – whether for good or ill – by the models of behaviour presented by teachers.

Each child will respond in different ways to different teachers, but where there is a good relationship the teacher concerned will not only influence the teenager's achievement in school but also the way he will respond to others now and in the future. Students will be swayed both by the way a teacher handles the class and the individuals in it, and by how he or she interacts with colleagues and with parents.

The responsibility of the teacher is, for this reason – as for so many others – considerable. His or her example may set the teenager on the path he will follow into adult life.

Anti-school teenagers

In any secondary school there is going to be a range of students with differing attitudes. At one end are those pupils who participate cheerfully in school activities, conform to rules, work hard and have friends with similar values. They are orderly, interested and involved. At the other end are those who appear to define themselves by opposing everything that the school authority tries to impose. These students flout school rules, tend to shirk both academic and sporting activities, and are often insolent to teachers and disruptive in class.

The reasons why teenagers may be anti-school are many and various. Some of these young people come from a background where there is no expectation of success at school: neither their parents nor their teachers see any prospect of their doing well, so why should they themselves expect to achieve anything? It is a vicious spiral: the less people expect of them the less they achieve, and the less they achieve the less is expected.

Another group of anti-school teenagers are angry or depressed for reasons to do with home rather than school. Their parents may have had an acrimonious divorce, they may have had to move house against their will, there may be financial problems at home, they may get too little attention from their parents. Such children may feel that rebelling against the family would threaten what little security they have at home, and so they turn their anger on teachers, the nearest authority figures outside the family.

A further factor, which can affect a great many teenagers, is that much of what goes on in school is, to them, boring. Lessons are irrelevant, games of no interest and the regimentation of school life childish. Indeed, very bright teenagers may feel this way about school, and go on to do well in situations where the focus is on their work rather the trappings of an institution. These students shine when taught in small, informal groups and often excel when they reach higher education.

There are also those independent adolescents who are not actually rebellious: their behaviour is not directed *against* anything, rather it is an expression of their individuality, which brings them into conflict with authority. Such students, who, again, are often talented, seem to know deep down that for them certain aspects of school are a complete waste of time. They grow up to be self-confident, competent adults, looking back on school as a place that has to be endured on the path to adulthood. One such person described herself as a 'secret adult', unhappy in the company of most other teenagers, longing to be grown up.

Planning for the future

Parents often assume that teenagers will get all the career advice they need at school, and many schools, though by no means all, do now take this responsibility seriously. Where the system works well, teenagers will be encouraged to think ahead about the kind of jobs they might like to do, to discuss options, and perhaps to take some kind of aptitude test in order to help them determine whether they would be better suited to working with people, using their hands, going into academic work, or into one of the caring professions. They will be taught how to find information about possible jobs, and how to apply for a job and to handle an interview. They may have sessions arranged with local employers, and in addition may, before they leave school, do one or two weeks of 'work experience' or 'work shadowing', when they are placed with an employer – if they are lucky, in a workplace which does the kind of job they are considering for the future – and gain first-hand experience of the 'real world'. None of this ensures that school-leavers will know what they want to do – and it certainly does not ensure that they will be able to do it even if they do know – but it helps them to learn their own strengths and weaknesses, how to gather information and make choices; and discussion with teachers, parents and other adults will assist them in clarifying their ideas.

By the early teens some children have the idea (at this stage probably rather vague) that they might go on to university or polytechnic after school. If this is your child's general aim, and if teachers and exam results confirm his ability, it is important that entrance requirements are fully understood and that he follows a course that will enable him to fulfil these requirements. The school should be able to advise you here. Once this long-term goal of higher education is set, with child, parents and school all facing in the same direction, you can help most by keeping this aim in mind, by encouraging the child to seize opportunities for enhancing his education on all fronts, by bolstering confidence and by giving support. There will be things that get in the way: the teenager may change his mind or rebel; emotional and physical changes will take their toll; but your main aim will be to make sure that he acquires the results he needs to qualify for a university place if he still wishes to go at eighteen.

Similarly, teenagers whose talents lie in other directions – in design, perhaps, computer skills, art or home economics – should be helped and encouraged both to take their academic education as far as possible (the richer their general education, the more they will have to offer) and to pursue further training in their chosen field.

There are some teenagers for whom even the basic skills of reading, writing and numeracy are neither interesting nor easy. Learning difficulties may well have begun for these youngsters in primary school and never been properly resolved, but these basic skills are nevertheless important for a viable adult life today, and secondary schools must endeavour to provide them. An emphasis on vocational training rather than purely academic subjects is one way of giving these teenagers both a more rewarding school experience and more confidence – a confidence that can help a young person as he starts living his own life and can often spill over into more academic work as well.

If your teenager has plans that entail his leaving school before you really want him to, and he is prepared to tell you about them, listen carefully to what he has to say and remember that he is taking a big emotional risk in talking to you at all. Keep your mind open, encourage his expectations (there is plenty of time for realities to sink in, and they are often lessons better learned at first hand than from you), and help him to consider as many positive alternatives to school as you can. There is no point in hiding your own feelings, but make it clear that they are your opinions and do not invalidate his.

Then discuss with him how he can make best use of the remaining time at school – not forgetting that he may yet change his mind and decide to stay on. The very fact of seeing his future a little more clearly may provide the motivation he needs to apply himself to school-leaving exams with a greater sense of purpose. Find out, too, if there are out-of-school courses or activities which might be relevant to what he intends to do. Part-time jobs may help him to establish a serious interest. If he enjoys gardening, for example, he might put an advertisement in a local shop offering help at weekends or after school, or try and get work in a garden centre or florist's shop. Whatever he wants to do, find out all you can about further training or apprenticeship. The teenager may well change his mind, but your efforts will not have been wasted; you will have shown that you take his ideas seriously and are prepared to back him.

A Separate Identity

Adolescence is quintessentially a time of self-awareness. To outsiders young people may seem enviably attractive, but many of them, perhaps most, feel inadequate and uncomfortable in their new and changing bodies, bodies which somehow seem to have got out of control. Adolescents sweat, they blush, their feet smell, spots come no matter how much they wash, their hair seems greasy and unmanageable. Adults do not seem able to decide whether to treat them as grown-ups or children, and in any case they swing emotionally between mature self-confidence and a need to be mothered. (We should not, however, fall into the trap of imagining that all teenagers have to cope with all these pressures all the time. There is some selectivity and some spacing of events, which allows most adolescents to avoid serious levels of disturbance.)

In trying to answer the question 'Who am I?' the adolescent may come

Teenagers try on different roles – they may have to look and speak one way for their friends and be more formal with their parents and teachers. Through these conflicts and adjustments they work out who they are and who they want to be.

into conflict with parents, brothers and sisters, friends – and himself. One common response to this uncertainty is an aggressive adherence to a teenage group culture that may include lounging and giggling, hiding behind outrageous clothes, curious make-up and adornments and – less appropriately – excessive dieting, heavy drinking and drugs.

The aim and end result of adolescent activity is the development of a sense of oneself as an independent being, able to make decisions on values and beliefs, able to follow a personal lifestyle. Such is the complexity of this topic that it is probably better not to try to summarize all that happens but to examine the process from different theoretical viewpoints. None is in itself a complete explanation but each contributes to our understanding.

Who am I?

How psychoanalysts see adolescence

The psychoanalytic view of adolescence is that it is characterized by an instinctive upsurge of sexual drives and a central concern with the issue of who, what, how valuable and how together one is. Critical to this phase is finding a link between self-preoccupation and relationships with others.

The adolescent needs to separate from his parents and to seek both new people to love and a whole new world outside the family circle. When we lose a significant part of our life, we seek to replace it with an acceptable alternative. For the child, parents are the most important role models; parents can no longer fill that role for the teenager, and so he casts around for significant adults outside the immediate family, to take their place. Some young people find their new heroes in teachers ('crushes' on teachers are less common than they once were, but they still happen). More frequently, culturally appropriate idols fulfil this role. Whether they be pop stars, film stars or sports stars is no matter, what counts is their meeting the needs of the young person in his own mind.

However, pop stars or other idols may not be enough. The sense of loss, actual or anticipated, of the childhood relationship with the parents, may be too great to be filled with a hundred posters. One way of defending against the loss is to fill one's time and one's mind with other activities: hence the intense teenage preoccupations with sport, music, drugs, delinquency – with whatever is convenient and available.

The form adolescent behaviour takes depends almost entirely on what it is that the teenager is having to move from. If the background has been ultra-conservative then it does not take much to rebel: sitting on the floor instead of on a chair, staying up late and becoming a vegetarian may be quite enough to establish that one is moving away. However, the child who has been brought up in a relaxed, easygoing family may have to go to greater lengths to express individuality: in extreme cases, the teenager may become more conventional than the parents.

Testing limits

At some time during adolescence most teenagers need to test the moral code they learned in the family, and to try out the limits of their parents. Being confronted on a regular basis by an argumentative teenager can be irritating and exhausting, and it can be painful to see a child who was very close to you suddenly adopt another family member or an adult outside the family as a mentor. The questioning of a teenager may also force the family to look at their values and lifestyle in a new light. However, while all this might initially be distressing, often when the conflicts are resolved a new balance is reached, and by the end of adolescence a more mature relationship is beginning to form.

Some parents, when they feel their authority being challenged by their teenagers, become overly rigid, laying down laws and rules which are never going to be followed. Others seem to give up entirely and just let their child go his own way. Neither course is wise. You have to listen carefully to your teenager and you may have to make compromises, but adolescents do need limits. Sometimes the very fact that your child challenges your authority means that he wants you to set a limit. Even as he argues, he wants you to be firm. He *wants* to be able to turn to his friends in the middle of the party and say 'My mother says I have to be home by twelve – she's a real pain!'

Whatever form moving away takes, it is likely to lead to adolescent vulnerability: here he is, for the first time, on his own, seeking friends of the same age, not only in their own right, but also to replace the security of the family. Vulnerability has to be managed, and the way to control any stress, according to psychoanalytic thinking, is to erect defences. One such defence is flight into the fantasy of omnipotence. In their minds teenagers become pop stars, lovers, sports heroes. The aggressive component of the teenager's desire to be different from his parents, and also to be different from what he was before, but to be like his friends, can be seen as another form of defence.

Adolescents swing wildly from childishness to maturity and back. It is not just that they *seem* to be grown up one minute and babies the next – that is exactly what they are. Psychoanalytic thought says that they need to regress to the time when they were two years old, the time of 'me do it', in order finally to shed infant ties. They find themselves at once anticipating adulthood and harking back to a much younger emotional experience.

Achieving an individual identity

The need to establish a separate identity is clear: what is less obvious is the mechanism by which this aim is to be achieved. Do young people just start out wildly in one direction after another, until by chance they come upon one that suits? Or is the process more systematic?

Possibly the most influential theory, one that has been supported by much research, is that of Erik Erikson. Erikson sees the adolescent's main task as engaging in a decision-making process which leads to what he calls a

Checking out the latest styles and keeping up with the fashion can be a major concern for the adolescent.

crystallized sense of self, a self with the ability to decide on values, beliefs and life goals.

There are two principal dimensions to the process. The first is exploration: young people have to try out roles, identities and belief systems, either mentally or actually. The second is commitment: sooner or later they have to commit themselves to values, beliefs and a lifestyle.

The theory assumes that before this process begins all young people are diffuse in their thinking: they have not committed themselves to any one set of opinions and attitudes.

At the beginning of adolescence, some children simply adopt the value system of their parents or other significant adults with little or no exploration on their part; in Erikson's terminology they foreclose. Others, though, are less happy simply to follow in adult footsteps, they want to explore new ideas, on the understanding that they will, sooner or later, make up their minds about what kind of people they will be. Erikson called the time of exploration a moratorium.

Once the moratorium has run its course, there comes identity achievement, when past exploration is seen as having led to present commitment.

The more rigid the culture, the more adolescents foreclose; society does not tolerate stepping out of line. In other cultures, where exploration is encouraged, the process takes time: a review of five American studies of children up to college level showed that the majority had foreclosed or had still not committed themselves in any particular direction; only 17 per cent had achieved an individual identity.

Erikson's results were based on decisions concerning vocation, ideology and the family. Others have criticized his work as being too simplistic and have looked at sex role orientation, politics and religious beliefs, suggesting that instead of describing a person overall, we should think rather of his being possibly diffuse in one area, foreclosed in another, and so on.

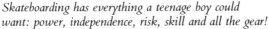

Skateboarding has everything a teenage boy could want: power, independence, risk, skill and all the gear!

465

Social theories

Social psychology takes a different stance. While it is accepted that adolescence is a period of transition from the family to a wider world, adolescent behaviour is explained in terms of role playing.

In childhood, roles are assigned by adults: there is an expected way to behave at home, at school, in the community. The roles may not be identical in all three settings but at least the child will know not only what is expected of him but also who expects what.

With adolescence role expectations become more chaotic. Either the impositions are lifted or, more painfully, children have to escape the previously imposed rules in order to establish their own identity as teenage members of society.

Usually, role conflicts in early adolescence are relatively mild, since the settings in which children operate, home and school, remain constant. However, once an adolescent has left school, there may be great differences between his home life patterns, former school patterns and those of the new society he has entered. The teenager going from the school to further education, to work, or to join the ranks of the unemployed, has huge adjustments to make. A familiar cry of the sixteen or seventeen year old is that he is expected to be an adult at work while at home his mother still treats him as child.

When sexual activity begins, even if at first it is confined to going out with someone as a boy or girlfriend, there comes another role conflict: how is a girl to be daughter and girlfriend at the same time?

The resolution of such conflicts is found in the search for reassurance: 'If others are like me then I'm all right.' Hence the pack mentality of adolescents, who are like each other but different from everyone else.

The adolescent and his parents

Theorists who base their explanations on how people think argue that adolescence is all about self-understanding and the sorting out of relationships with parents. It has been suggested that this involves four stages. In the first part of a child's life parental views dominate, with a characteristic urge towards autonomy emerging in late childhood.

The second stage (arriving usually in early adolescence) is a time when parents' needs and views are seen as separate from one's own but there is, as yet, no clear recognition that parent and child may be in conflict.

In the third stage, the conflict between parents and adolescents is recognized and gives rise to problems, because the adolescent is not yet able to encompass a system that can include himself, his friends and his parents. This is typical of mid-adolescence.

Finally, the relationship between self and parents becomes clear, and the autonomous self is perceived as a complex entity, separate from but related to the parents. This stage is most commonly reached in late adolescence.

Self-consciousness

Adolescence is the time when young people become painfully aware of their appearance, when hours are spent in front of a mirror, when wearing the right jeans, the fashionable trainers, attains an importance out of all proportion – that is, in the eyes of older people.

There are physical and psychological causes for this onset of self-consciousness, and as usual they are intertwined. Young people going through puberty are often unsatisfactory to themselves: they may be clumsy, have spots, be much taller or shorter than their contemporaries. Girls may be embarrassed by breast development, boys feel awkward as their voices break.

The psychological mainspring of self-consciousness is uncertainty. Because young people are so often unsure, not only of who they are but also of who they want to be, they frequently lack confidence to an extent that is psychologically painful. Support comes from others in a similar position – hence the truism that teenagers want to be like each other but different from everyone else.

There are times when parents need to be especially gentle with their children, and this is one of them. You can help first of all by being even more careful than usual about making fun of your child. The destructive force of mockery is often underestimated, and few teenagers have the confidence to cope with it.

The desire to be like other teenagers, and the need to cover up embarrassment, can lead some young people to dress and behave in ways that may seem, to some adults, outrageous. Here, as always, there is a need for balance and compromise. Each family has different areas of tolerance, but on the whole it is probably better to be forbearing about oddities of dress (most of the time). Experimenting with the way they look is important to teenagers. Where behaviour is concerned, however, they may need some reminders that other people too have rights, and deserve to be treated with consideration.

Self-esteem

A new period in a person's life will always bring with it a test of self against new yardsticks, and it is not surprising that some studies have suggested that there is a dip in general self-esteem as children enter adolescence. However, the overall picture, contrary to the belief of those who see this time as one of constant stress, is that throughout the period there is a consistent rise in self-esteem. Exceptions arise when the adolescent has too much to cope with at one time, or when changes come too suddenly: if, for example, a teenager is uncomfortable with his body and there are stresses within the family and problems in school or with friends, then self-esteem can take a hard knock. But the overall rise in self-esteem suggests that most teenagers do manage to overcome the much-discussed turmoils of adolescence. As we shall see later in this chapter, they find it easier to do this if they can take problems one at a time.

Sexuality

First sexual relationships are at once thrilling and troubling.

Each adolescent has to learn to come to terms with him or herself as a sexual being, with physical and emotional desires that need expression within the context of relationships with other people. How these desires are expressed, received by others and fulfilled largely depends on cultural values. For example, premarital teenage sexual activity is regarded as normal in some societies, condemned in others.

In many, perhaps most, western countries, a majority of teenagers do become sexually active during their teens. It has been estimated that in the United States about 50 per cent of boys and 30 per cent of girls aged fifteen to seventeen have had some sexual experience, and by the time they reach nineteen 75 per cent of boys and more than 50 per cent of girls are sexually active. British figures indicate that at seventeen around 50 per cent of boys and 39 per cent of girls have had sexual experience, these figures rising to 74 per cent and 67 per cent among nineteen years olds. The overall figures, however, conceal the fact that the levels of sexual activity in one social group may be very different from those in another, something borne out in a recent Australian study, where 78 per cent of Chinese-Australian girls and

60 per cent of boys aged seventeen to twenty were virgins, compared with 32 per cent of Anglo-Australian girls and 28 per cent of boys.

Although teenagers may be sexually active, the evidence suggests that they are not particularly promiscuous – and they are certainly not carefree about sex. They are more open about it than previous generations, and generally have a clear view that sexual behaviour is a matter of private rather than public morality. Most see premarital sex as acceptable in an affectionate relationship, and the double standards of former generations, by which behaviour admissible in a boy was unacceptable in a girl, have largely been abandoned. However, while teenagers may say when asked that sex should only be part of an affectionate relationship, exactly what this means in practice is difficult to define – and parents and teenagers may differ in their views here.

Adolescents often receive conflicting messages from their parents and society. A teenager's sexuality can trigger sensitive emotions in parents who remember their own adolescent conflicts (and may never quite have resolved them). Society proclaims its disapproval of early sex, and yet encourages teenagers to look sexy and dress provocatively. Films, television, newspapers and magazines constantly present images of sexuality.

In fact, teenagers themselves have said in recent American surveys that they think they began sexual activity a year or two too early. In a 1986 Harris poll over a thousand American teenagers chosen to be a representative national sample were asked why they began to have sex. About 75 per cent said that they were influenced by peer group pressure and curiosity. Love was mentioned by only 6 per cent of boys and 11 per cent of girls. So while teenagers may be clear in theory that sex should be confined to affectionate relationships, it appears that in practice their behaviour is motivated by a desire to do what their friends do and a wish to discover adult pleasures.

For most teenagers, exploring sexuality involves a wide range of sexual thoughts and fantasies, often including erotic thoughts about someone of the same sex. Many teenagers feel, at some time during their adolescence, that they may be homosexual – perhaps because they have powerful homosexual fantasies, perhaps because they are anxious about their lack of heterosexual experience. For most these feelings remain in the realm of fantasy, or, if they are acted out, it is in a playful, exploratory way, and homosexual attraction diminishes in importance as heterosexual relationships develop. There is no reason at all to assume, on the evidence of one or two episodes, that a teenager will be permanently homosexual.

Some adolescents, however, have a strong attraction to their own sex that continues into adult life. The causes of homosexuality are unknown; indeed, it is doubtful that a single cause will ever be identified. The most interesting recent work focuses on prenatal hormones which may indicate a genetic predisposition to homosexuality; however, other factors may also be involved.

Unfortunately, much of society is still hostile to homosexuals, and it can be difficult for young people to acknowledge their feelings. Often, their

Is he looking at me – does he like me? The familiar pangs of uncertainty and excitement we all know when sexually attracted to another person.

greatest fear is that they will be rejected by the family. If your teenager tells you that he or she is gay, you may find it hard to accept; but it is vital that you respond in a sensitive and loving way that allows your child to continue to confide in you. There is certainly no way that arguments, threats or protests will change a teenager's sexual orientation; and a hostile response will badly damage the trust between you. That trust is essential if you are to be of help to your child, and together find ways forward. Your aims for your child remain as they always were – that he or she should lead a well-adjusted life and create successful, loving relationships.

Contraception

Young people need to have information about contraception well before they embark on sexual relationships. Once a teenager is sexually involved any discussion of contraception easily becomes emotional rather than rational – and it may in any case already be too late to avoid a pregnancy. The evidence is that most girls don't actually seek contraceptive advice themselves until about a year after they have had their first sexual experience. In the months between they are at high risk of becoming pregnant.

Parents sometimes worry that giving teenagers contraceptive advice may make them more curious and precocious, but there is no particular reason, really, to think this will be the case. On the contrary, a reasoned discussion of contraception may help them to see sex in a broader perspective, and to consider more thoughtfully the implications and responsibilities of having sex. When thinking about what contraceptive advice they should give to their teenagers, parents should consider four guidelines:

- The fact has to be faced that in many societies the pressures on teenagers to experiment sexually are immense.

- Teenagers can be helped to anticipate pressures and to make calm, responsible decisions.

- Teenagers need information about the mechanics of contraception and the dangers of sexually transmitted diseases.

- It is reasonable to communicate that you are not happy about adolescent sexual activity, if this is your position. But you should also make it clear that if your son or daughter does encounter trouble of any kind you will be there to give support.

You need to get across the idea that both boys and girls are responsible for contraception and that both need to be aware of the alternative methods available. They should also be told how and where to obtain different devices (lack of access is frequently given as a reason for not using birth control) and, equally important, how to use the devices once they have been obtained. You should get the latest information about all of this from a reputable family planning clinic. Methods of contraception (and knowledge of the advantages, disadvantages and risks attached to various methods) change rapidly, so you need to be up to date.

Both boys and girls certainly need to know that using a condom is the only way to reduce the risk of infection with Aids during intercourse with an infected person.

The pregnant teenager

Teenage pregnancy is a good example of the need to look at the social context of an event in order to understand its meaning for the individual. In societies where teenage marriage is the normal pattern, a teenage pregnancy is likely to be welcomed. In others it can be a tragedy, for the baby and for the parents.

With figures of around 10 per cent for girls between fifteen and nineteen, the United States has one of the highest rates of teenage pregnancy in the world. In Britain the figures for 1988 indicate that the conception rate for fifteen to nineteen year olds was about 6.6 per cent. Not all pregnancies end in a birth, of course: abortion figures of about 60 per cent mean that the actual rate of births to teenagers is falling slightly. Not all teenage mothers are unmarried, although recent data show that many are.

When a pregnancy is welcomed by parents and grandparents, where the mother-to-be looks after herself and has good antenatal care, the baby is not at any special risk. However, not all young mothers are in this position and there are dangers for many babies.

Teenage mothers from deprived areas in western societies are at a higher

Friendships

All young people need in some measure to move away from their parents in order to establish their own adult identity, though the extent to which they distance themselves varies enormously. Many parents remain powerful influences on their children throughout this period and beyond. Even they, though, are rarely as dominant as they were when their children were younger. Others maintain some degree of influence, which changes in its intensity and nature as the child becomes older. A third group seem either to abdicate or to be rejected by their adolescent children.

Whatever the case, there is, for most adolescents, a gap, actual or antici-pated, left by the impending removal of parents as the main reference fig-ures. These young people are vulnerable: they need someone to share their anxieties, to give support and to provide a role model. Even those for whom parents remain important figures of support and guidance will look to some extent to their friends and contemporaries to supply their needs.

Several studies point to the way in which the young adolescent still

Gangs of teenagers often find a place where they can horse around. It's fun to act like the children they were such a short while ago.

A best friend is the essential confidante in matters of the heart.

focuses on shared activity as the main reason for friendship. By middle adolescence (fourteen to sixteen) the stress is much more on security. This seems to be a time when children feel especially vulnerable, when they greatly fear rejection, and dependability is the quality most valued in a friend. By late adolescence there is a more relaxed attitude to friendships, a greater appreciation of individual differences and an assessment of what the friend's personality and interests can offer the relationship. As teenagers begin to form close relationships with members of the opposite sex there may be a reduction in the possessive intensity of same-sex friendships. However, friendships in general tend to become increasingly stable.

There are some continuing differences between the sexes in their friendship patterns. For girls the satisfaction of emotional needs is of the greatest importance, and they express more anxiety about friendships; boys continue to lay more stress on a shared interest in an activity.

The structure of the family and the reasons for this structure exert some influence here. If the father is absent, especially if his absence has come about through divorce or separation, greater demands are often made, by both girls and boys, on friends of both sexes.

There has been quite extensive study of which qualities tend to make children popular with others of their own age. Earlier conclusions laid great stress on the importance of sporting prowess for boys and on cheerfulness, good looks and sociability for both sexes. Later studies, however, show that academic success is not to be ignored: in these studies, the most popular children were those who did very well in sport and moderately well in schoolwork. What is more, if boys show they are knowledgeable about sport, this can compensate for a lack of skill. However, those who are below average at sport or not especially beautiful can take heart: the British psychologist John Coleman, who has specialized in work with adolescents, points out that much of the published work focuses on the extremes of popularity and unpopularity: for those in between, good looks and sporting skills may be less salient. We should also remember that almost all the work on popularity has been done in the United States – perhaps reflecting the importance that North American society gives to its attainment.

Young teenagers are notorious for conforming to group norms; usually, in later adolescence they become less conformist. One classic method of studying the inclination to conform is to collect a group of people, all but one of whom are in league with the experimenter. They are then shown two lines and are asked whether they are the same length. After a few mock trials the confederates assert that two lines manifestly different in length are the same. The extent to which the person outside the conspiracy goes along with the rest gives a measure of his inclination to conform to group opinion. In a 1966 study agreement with the herd reached a peak among eleven to thirteen year olds, after which there was a steady decline to twenty-one.

The influence of the peer group

It is tempting for parents, casting around for a scapegoat when their children are in trouble, to complain that their friends have led them astray. Groups of children of the same age undoubtedly influence such matters as hair style and clothes, but there is no evidence that they can, on their own, exert an inexorable pull towards any particular type of behaviour.

The key to understanding the influence of the peer group and the part it plays in anti-social behaviour is to see it not in isolation but as an element in an interacting whole. If we consider the young person's temperament, his family background and the degree to which his emotional and social needs are met in other groups, we see how these interactions operate.

As we have seen earlier, the ways families function affect relationships both within the family and outside. Children whose families have set certain examples of behaviour tend, on the whole, to choose friends who reinforce the patterns with which they are familiar. However, when parental values have been forced on children with no recognition of their needs, it is more likely that, as adolescents, they will try to choose friends whose values differ from those of their family. Families with communication patterns that are either authoritarian or permissive have less effect when they try to influence their teenage children's choice of friends than those with more democratic patterns. Presumably, authoritarian parents ('Do this because I say so') have created such resistance in their children that their words fall on deaf ears; while the requests – if requests are even made – of permissive parents lack conviction and are also discounted. Where there is a pattern of open discussion and mutual support within the family, relationships both within the family and outside are likely to be more satisfactory.

Behaviour Problems

Substance abuse

The use of alcohol and other substances to relieve physical or psychological pain and to offset boredom has a very long history. However, when we consider why most people smoke, drink or take drugs we have to look at political and economic factors as well as at individual and group psychology. In most countries the price of alcohol and tobacco is determined by government decree via the taxation system. There is no reasonable doubt that cigarette smoking, for example, is harmful to health, yet no government in the world has taken serious steps towards reducing consumption – the economic implications are too inconvenient.

'Substance abuse' occurs when consumption interferes with a person's ability to lead a safe and useful life. It is sometimes difficult to define precisely when substance abuse occurs, but there are some obvious examples. Anyone who drinks and drives is abusing alcohol; anyone who is smoking cannabis and getting progressively lower grades in school is abusing cannabis; a drug taker who is unable to speak clearly, is stumbling around and subject to anxiety attacks, is abusing drugs. 'Dependence' is a little easier to determine: a person can be said to be dependent on something if he suffers physically or psychologically when it is withdrawn. 'Addiction' and 'addict' are overused terms. It is best to confine them to those people who compulsively use a drug over a period of time and would experience severe physical symptoms if the drug were withdrawn. The teenager who smokes cannabis regularly is not an addict because he would not experience physical symptoms if he stopped smoking. Parents need to use these labels judiciously: otherwise they risk giving their teenager the message that he is one of the down-and-outs dramatized on television as addicts.

When we consider teenage substance abuse we have to ask, first, why the habit is begun. One thing drinking, smoking and drug taking have in common is that any of them may be perceived as a marker of having moved from childhood to adulthood – a rite of passage.

It helps if parents state their views on smoking, alcohol and drugs as clearly as possible. If you do not want your child to smoke in the house, say so. Emphasize that he will not be allowed to use the family car if he is found driving when drunk or with anyone else who is drunk. Make it clear that you will confiscate any illegal drugs found in the house, that you will notify other parents if their children are involved and that you may call in the police if you suspect that anyone over eighteen has played a part.

Smoking

Many children find their first cigarettes by smoking the stubs in their parents' ashtrays. Children who try smoking usually have their first cigarette between the ages of ten and twelve, and as the development of a smoking habit takes three to four years, it is possible that such children may be dependent on cigarettes by the time they are fifteen or so. Having said that, it is generally the case that a person who is not smoking by the time he is twenty will never become a smoker.

The most important way of influencing your child against smoking is by example – don't smoke yourself. If children grow up watching their parents smoke, smoking becomes part of their script for adult life – and, of course, it is very difficult to ban a child from participating in something which your own behaviour condones.

If, however, your teenager starts to experiment with smoking, you will want to stop him before it becomes a habit.

The fact that smoking causes cancer and heart disease may not influence a teenager much. Cancer and heart disease are things which happen many years on – and teenagers are concerned about how they feel now, not what

Smoking a cigarette might be one way of feeling grown up – but it can all too soon become a habit.

will happen in thirty or forty years' time. There are, however, arguments which may convince a teenager that smoking will affect the quality of his life now. (You may need to be quite subtle in the way you put them, though – too much preaching and laying down the law and you may just turn an inclination to smoke into a determination to continue in spite of you.)

Being young does not counteract the unhealthy effects of cigarettes. Nicotine is a poisonous, addictive drug which reaches the brain within eight seconds. Tar from cigarettes builds up on the lungs and cannot be removed. Smoking lowers the level of oxygen that can be taken into the body and causes shortness of breath; it reduces stamina, decreases muscle tone and slows the reflexes. It increases susceptibility to coughs, colds and respiratory problems. These by-products of smoking are not attractive – and neither is having hair, clothes and breath which smell of cigarettes.

Most teenagers (like most adults) believe that they can control their smoking habits, and it is not until they try to give up that they realize they are dependent. If your teenager does develop a habit, and wants to stop, you can encourage him to follow one of the many programmes for giving up smoking and, if need be, help him to pursue other outside help.

Alcohol

As with so many other aspects of life, the way alcohol is consumed is to a large extent culturally determined. It may be associated with celebrations – from football matches to weddings – or with an evening's relaxation in a

Teenagers often have little difficulty in getting hold of alcohol.

pub; it may be seen as an essential part of a meal, or an integral part of a religious observance. Some young people (and adults) see alcohol consumption as bolstering a macho image; many teenagers see it as a way of joining the ranks of adults.

Taken occasionally, in small quantities, alcohol is usually not harmful. There can be no doubt, however, that excessive alcohol consumption can be extremely damaging, both to the individual concerned and to those with whom he comes in contact. Many children under eighteen drink, and some of them drink far too much. Alcohol is often readily available at home, and, though it is illegal to sell alcohol to under-eighteens, there are always bars where they can get it.

The long-term results of excessive drinking – the way, for example, that over time it damages and may destroy brain and muscle tissue – may not mean much to young people. They may be more impressed, though, by the fact that alcohol poisoning and accidents, aggressive behaviour and suicide as a result of drunkenness are significant causes of death and disability in teenagers. Girls should be told that they can't drink as much as boys: girls have more fat and less water in their bodies than boys, and so alcohol is less diluted in a girl's body.

After all that, if you suspect that, nevertheless, your teenager may be drinking socially, make sure that he has a good meal before he goes out, encourage him to drink beer or wine rather than spirits, and advise him to drink as slowly as possible. If he even thinks about driving when he has been drinking, remind him that drink driving is a criminal offence, and that if he drinks and drives, and the police don't take his licence away, you will forbid the use of the family car. If he is somewhere where he or his friends may be drinking, give him money to phone you to come and pick him up, or to get a taxi home.

Drugs

One of the deepest worries that parents of adolescents can have is that their teenager will become dependent on drugs. Taking drugs is something that it is difficult to talk about openly in the home. Parents are afraid, first, that in bringing up the subject they may tell their teenagers more than they already know; second, that they may find out their teenager already knows more than they do; third, that they may provoke a fierce argument. It is very difficult to talk about drugs and keep a cool head (and heart). It is even more worrying if you suspect that your teenager may be using drugs. Not knowing whether your child is involved with drugs and wondering what to do if he is can lead to a feeling of helplessness.

Often (perhaps too often) newspapers and television provoke worry and misunderstandings. Seeing a young drug addict portrayed on television can make parents feel that this is a prototype for most teenagers today. In fact, most teenagers do not even experiment with drugs and it is only a small number that become dependent on or abuse drugs.

Teenagers may have their own reasons for being attracted to (or for avoiding) drugs. You may need to work hard to see things from a teenager's perspective, but it will help a lot if you can hear what your teenager is saying. It is important not to panic or overreact if you find that your child has some experience of drug taking. Trying something out is not the same as becoming an addict; nor does experimenting with drugs necessarily lead to dependence. Many adolescents experiment with drugs and stop almost immediately because they do not enjoy the effects or are not interested in having 'druggie' friends. However, those teenagers who continue to use drugs certainly sometimes become dependent on them.

Although some children start glue-sniffing well before their teens, it is usually not until adolescence that experimenting with drugs like cannabis and cocaine begins. The peak age for the serious use of any illicit drug, in the United States at least, is between eighteen and twenty-five, although in one survey 25 per cent of the children questioned said that they had tried cannabis before this age. Evidence about who takes drugs and why is patchy and inconclusive. Young people are almost always introduced to drugs by others of more or less their own age, and it is with them that the activity is shared. But why youngsters start taking drugs is less certain: it may be because of encouragement from friends, or because of a fear of rejection if they do not go along with the rest.

Some patterns in drug use have been traced. Drug taking usually begins with use of cannabis, a relatively mild drug, usually introduced by children in the same age group. But what tips people over to the use of harder substances such as heroin or cocaine is more complex, and seems to be more closely related to personality and to influences within the family.

Male drug takers outnumber females, especially among addicts. The ratio for heroin dependency is 4:1 in Britain, although there is less difference in the figures for the use of milder drugs in adolescence. There is little clear evidence on social class differences, but the higher cost of some drugs tends to restrict their use to those who are better off. On the whole, town dwellers, particularly those who live in the big cities, have easier access to drugs than those who live in the country, and a certain amount of city crime has its origins in the need to obtain money to buy drugs.

What parents can do
If you find out that your teenager is taking drugs, do not panic. Try to communicate in a calm and rational way. This means listening to what he is saying, without making accusations. Try to find out how serious the problem is. Find out how long he has been taking drugs, what drugs he has been using and if he is an occasional or regular drug user. Try to find out what lies behind his drug taking: he may have tried out a drug because it was easily available or because a friend offered it to him at a party. He may also want to be part of a crowd that uses drugs and only accepts people who take drugs. Many teenagers take drugs because they think it will be fun and they want to see what happens. There is also the possibility that they want to rebel against you.

Most teenagers who take drugs for any of these reasons are simply experimenting. They take drugs as part of the process of growing up and they will soon learn to set their own limits. You can help by remaining calm and keeping the discussion open. While you need to accept that growing up involves making some experiments and mistakes, at the same time you should be definite about your own attitudes, beliefs and values and make them apparent to him. At this stage you may have to agree to disagree, but at the end of the discussion you should both be clear about each other's viewpoints.

There are other reasons for taking drugs which are warning signs of more serious problems. Some teenagers feel empty, rejected, isolated and out of place in every way. They may be arrogant, irritating, aggressive, even violent at home, but withdrawn and depressed at school or in other groups. Many teenagers experience depression from time to time; but when they are in this state for weeks at a stretch and take drugs to make themselves feel better, they need professional help. As a parent, you may be the last person to notice the fact that your teenager has become withdrawn or is acting in a strange way when he is not at home. If you are told about it by another parent or a teacher, there is no reason to feel defensive or think that you have failed. Find a counsellor or psychologist who can work with your teenager to enable him to feel better about himself, and help him to use his anger more constructively. Or it may be worth looking for a family therapist who can work with you all, helping you to understand your feelings and improve communication.

Combating abuse

Health education programmes have been singularly ineffective in campaigning against smoking, drinking or drug abuse. By definition, the rebellious, anti-authority teenager who is into drugs is not going to be swayed by a message which he perceives as coming from the establishment. Moreover, the ill effects are long-term, and teenagers are rarely inclined to think about the future. This is not to say that all campaigning against abuse should be given up; rather, the message should be given to society, not just to the teenager.

In the long run the example set by parents is likely to be the most powerful influence on young people's behaviour, in this as in so many instances. It is worth remembering, too, that if within a family a certain substance is invested with a magical quality, whether for good or ill, the teenager will naturally perceive that substance as having great power. If the family attitude is more matter-of-fact, the substance cannot be quite so enthralling.

However, some teenagers will indulge to excess. Abuse of any substance is a symptom and to try to treat it as a disease in itself is to waste time and money; if your adolescent child is dependent on alcohol, tobacco or any other drug, he needs skilled help, and your best course will be to seek that help from people who have had successful experience of dealing with similar problems. Some hospitals have addiction units, and there are extremely effective self-help groups for different types of abuse. Your doctor should be able to put you in touch with people who are experienced in the field.

Anorexia nervosa

This condition could almost be included in the previous section, as a form of food abuse, but it is far more complex than that. Anorexia nervosa may be literally translated as 'loss of appetite for nervous reasons'; however, this is misleading, because anorexics have not lost their appetite, but their ability to satisfy their appetite. Anorexics have a fear of being fat so extreme that they become totally obsessed with restricting their food intake, and often they eat scarcely enough to keep themselves alive. Anorexia occurs preponderantly among girls: female anorexics outnumber males at least nine to one during and after puberty, though before puberty the proportion of boys is much higher, at about 25 per cent. Sufferers frequently have a distorted body image, perceiving both their own bodies and the amount of food they are offered as much larger than is actually the case. In younger girls the start of periods is postponed; if a girl's periods have already started before she becomes anorexic, they will stop as her weight drops.

Anorexia can begin at almost any age (there have been reports of sufferers as young as six), but in the majority of cases it starts in the age range fourteen to nineteen. At a very approximate estimate it appears in western countries in about one girl out of a hundred. It used to be almost unknown in any but white races; however, it is now becoming increasingly common in Asian groups.

Its onset may be sudden – sometimes it seems to be triggered by something as simple as a teasing remark – or it may be gradual, perhaps the continuation of an episode in which a group of girls decide to diet together. An anorexic girl will go to great lengths to acquire or maintain what she sees as the correct shape: she will avoid eating at all costs, may push food around her plate, hide it, pretend to her parents that she has eaten at a friend's house. Anorexics often also take excessive amounts of exercise, in extreme cases never keeping still even when indoors. A curious feature is that they tend to wear loose, enveloping clothes: whether this is intended to disguise their real thinness or to hide their supposed obesity we do not know; it may be that the two apparently conflicting motives are both at work.

An associated condition is bulimia nervosa, a condition in which excessive dieting alternates with what the girl regards as excessive eating. (Although this binge may indeed consist of the consumption of large amounts of food, it may involve no more than normal food intake.) After a binge the girl will try to get rid of the food by making herself vomit or taking laxatives. Bulimia is rare in children and young adolescents – the peak age for its onset is between sixteen and eighteen – but bulimics often have a previous history of anorexia or other problems with eating or weight. Bulimics do eat more overall than anorexics, so they are not so dangerously thin, but the cycle of bingeing and purging may result in serious stomach, mouth or bowel problems.

There is what the London psychiatrist Gerald Russell describes as 'deep uncertainty' about the causes of anorexia, despite the many theories put forward. It may be that there is usually more than one cause to look for, and that the precise causes, or mixtures of causes, are probably different for different girls. Studies of twins indicate that there may be a genetic factor, and other evidence suggests that, sometimes at least, there may be some abnormality in the way the brain functions. Some psychologists believe the condition reflects a girl's fear of becoming a woman, although it is only rarely that an anorexic girl will accept this. Another theory is that through strict control of her eating and weight an anorexic is trying to establish control over her life.

Anorexic girls are frequently perfectionists, striving to conform, to maintain high standards in schoolwork and to please their parents and teachers, yet still, despite being so well behaved and academically successful, not satisfied with themselves. They often say that they would like to go into a profession where they can serve others. (A symptom of this condition, and one that is often infuriating for parents, is a delight in cooking for

Anorexia nervosa: warning signs
You may be alerted to the possibility of anorexia nervosa if your child shows any of the following symptoms.
- Weight loss
- Eating very little, especially if this is combined with an interest in discussing food, or in cooking for others
- Denial of hunger
- Hiding food, playing with it on the plate
- Insistence that she (or he) is fat, when this is clearly not so

other people.) Some authorities point out that in families where a child develops anorexia there is often a high degree of overprotectiveness and a strong desire to avoid conflict, on the part of one or both parents; however, it is possible that this family system has evolved in response to the condition rather than being a cause, and as it is often a year or more from the onset of anorexia before medical help is sought, it is hard to be sure.

In general, boys who are anorexic show much the same patterns as those described for anorexic girls, which makes it the more puzzling that anorexia is so much more common among girls. The clue probably lies in the fact that in countries where anorexia is common the ideal female figure is slender, while that of the perfect male is not. It is perhaps not so surprising, after all, that for girls living in such societies an uncomfortable combination of perfectionism and low self-esteem should manifest itself in an obsession with thinness.

The earlier anorexia is picked up the easier treatment is likely to be. If you think that your child may be anorexic, you should, first, consult your doctor, who will need to weigh and physically examine the child, and also to talk to you and to her. With a seriously underweight child the first priority will be to get her weight up to a reasonable level. It will probably be necessary to discuss with a dietician what she should be eating – and you will also need advice on how you can persuade her to eat it. If her weight has dropped to a dangerous level, she may have to be admitted to hospital.

In the longer term, before an anorexic can really recover she has to come to accept and to like herself, with her weaknesses as well as her strengths. She will need a lot of help and support, both from her family and, probably, also from people with experience in this area. A skilled psychotherapist can help a lot, and the family may also benefit from family therapy.

The process of recovery tends to be long and slow, and emotionally it can be extremely painful, not only for the anorexic girl herself but also for her family. You will have to face the fact that, for a time at least, your daughter is probably going to resist all your efforts to help her. You and she may also find that you need to express some angry feelings: this can be upsetting, but is often an essential step on the road to recovery. The whole issue of food and weight will have to be handled carefully. You do need to make sure she eats, but confrontations over food are rarely, if ever, helpful. Try, as far as possible, to reach an agreement with her about how much of what should be eaten and when. It is worth remembering that, since your child is frightened of being fat, any comments about the fact that she has put

• Might the child be behaving badly to cause a diversion – for example, to stop his parents from quarrelling with one another?

• Is the family system one of extreme permissiveness or extreme strictness, or, worse, does it swing between the two?

• Who is the child trying to impress by his behaviour? If this person is not a responsible adult, then why not?

• Does he feel a failure in school or in other areas? Perhaps the only way he can gain a sense of success is by delinquent acts. Schools have been shown to have a strong effect.

Whatever the answers to these questions, the best response to anti-social behaviour is to make it quite clear that you disapprove of the activity, but you value the child. What you do beyond that will depend on the severity of any underlying problem which may be revealed in your replies. If, for example, there is a great deal of hostility in the family, then family therapy may help. If tension is only mild, you can probably sort it out yourselves. Frequently, just talking openly about the topics raised by the questions can lead to a major change for the better.

Dealing with delinquency

Not surprisingly, given its complexity, there are no universal, simple solutions to the problem. The most immediately obvious technique to reduce delinquency is the apprehension and punishing of the offender. However, although many youngsters who are punished once do not repeat criminal acts, the customary methods of dealing with delinquents have by no means reduced for everyone the likelihood of offending again.

One generally reliable predictor of delinquency is the place where one lives: some areas of large cities, for example, have shown consistently high delinquency rates for at least two generations. Moving to a different neighbourhood alters these patterns. Two follow-up studies of delinquent boys who moved from high-delinquency to low-delinquency areas confirmed a decline in their anti-social behaviour.

One of the most powerful agents of change is marriage, provided that the partner is not delinquent as well. (This is not to recommend early marriage: but parents may have hope that once their teenager reaches adulthood, marriage may be a stabilizing influence.)

The last way in which change is effected is simply through the process of growing up. There is a bleak outlook for the seriously delinquent adolescent who comes from a disadvantaged background and had severe behaviour problems in childhood; but the majority, the relatively minor offenders, cease to be involved in criminal activity as they grow older. A 1982 American study of young people who had featured in police records in Wisconsin found that only 5 to 8 per cent offended as adults. Most early offenders outgrow the need to commit crimes: we are not always prisoners of our childhood.

Adolescent Vulnerability

Sometimes a sport such as rock climbing can satisfy an adolescent's need to take risks.

Sooner or later, for longer or shorter periods, most teenagers feel immensely vulnerable; they show it by being touchy, easily offended, self-conscious – and in the way they are constantly having to make their point. As we have seen, this vulnerability is due in part to the physical changes taking place, the awkwardness that comes with uneven growth. But there is more to it than that: the realization that parents will not, should not, be there to look after one for ever is daunting.

Some teenagers, though not all, seem to enjoy taking risks; it is as if they need to test their own physical limits, and their nerve. They may engage in dangerous sports, drive their cars too fast, scale perilous cliffs or climb high buildings. Some are interested in discovering what their mature bodies can do and how they perform under stress. They want to find out if they can control their bodies and their environment in a variety of situations. Sometimes they seem to want to provoke confrontation with the law, making law enforcement officers rather than parents responsible for setting limits. Sadly, some risk-taking ends in a serious, possibly fatal, accident.

In developed countries accidents account for more deaths in the fifteen to twenty-four year old group than all other causes put together. Children under thirteen constitute some 10 per cent of bicycle traffic, and sustain one quarter of bicycle injuries.

Car and motor cycle accidents are the leading cause of death among older adolescents. In the United States over 60 per cent of automobile-related deaths among adolescents involve passengers in cars driven by young people. (Most fatalities occur in the four hours around midnight.)

It goes without saying that adolescents should be expected to follow the basic rules of safety, like wearing seat belts and crash helmets, but this is only part of the story. Some seem to revel in danger, deliberately putting themselves at risk. This pattern can be seen as part of the growing-up process: 'I am experimenting in all sorts of ways, I frequently feel insecure and I want to show that I am not afraid of anything.' Or: 'I don't really understand where I am going, or quite what is happening to me, and I feel isolated and self-conscious much of the time, so I am going to extreme lengths to get excitement in a way that will make me feel superior to others.'

There is a more prosaic explanation for some of the accidents that occur at this time: adolescents are often clumsy and they lack experience in skills such as driving.

Suicide

In the last thirty years suicide in the fifteen to twenty-four age group in the United States has gone up from 4 per 100,000 to 12 per 100,000, the figures for the population as a whole being around 11 per 100,000. The suicide rate in Britain has also increased over the past three decades, though, at about 3 per 100,000 in the fifteen to nineteen age group, it remains considerably lower than the American figures. In both countries records indicate that around twice as many boys as girls commit suicide. However, all data about suicides have to be regarded with caution because of the widespread reluctance on the part of doctors and relatives to categorize a death as a suicide.

In a 1989 American paper it was noted that when an adolescent committed suicide there had often been difficulties at home, particularly problems of poor communication, or conflicts with parents over values. There was also frequently a disparity between the young person's perception of his academic success and the level that was expected of him. In a large number of adolescent cases studied in Britain, the suicide was triggered not by an actual family dispute but by one that was impending: the teenager knew that his parents were soon to learn about something of which he was ashamed.

Many had relatives or contemporaries at school who had been involved in suicidal behaviour and many had read books in which suicide figured and/or had indulged in suicidal thoughts. Previous unsuccessful suicide attempts had been recorded in 40 per cent of the cases where an adolescent succeeded in killing himself; and this figure may be an underestimate.

The emotions of those who kill themselves usually appear to be loneliness, inadequacy, shame, and a feeling of being unloved.

There is one group of suicides, small perhaps, whose deaths remain an enigma: no warning was given, no cause can be established. We can only speculate – from our partial knowledge of the workings of the brain – about some biochemical event leading to a sudden and severe distortion of perception.

Attempted suicide

Although the boundary between the successful and the attempted suicide is often blurred, there are some suicide attempts which, it seems, are obviously not intended to lead to death. In this connection it is interesting to note that, in Britain at least, attempted suicides present a pattern different from that of successful suicides. In the sixteen to nineteen age group, where about 400 among 100,000 adolescents at some time attempt suicide, the sex ratio is quite different, with three times more girls than boys either attempting to kill themselves or making suicidal gestures.

There are various possible explanations for such an attempt: the one most commonly given is that it is a cry for help; it is also sometimes said that it is akin to getting blind drunk in order to gain temporary respite from sorrow; another reason that is occasionally given is a simple indifference to life. It may sometimes be a sort of high-level risk-taking – a person deliberately taking risks to prove superiority over the fates.

The actual attempt may be triggered by a crisis in a relationship, either with family or with a friend. Not infrequently, a conflict with parents over discipline is involved.

Predicting and preventing suicide

It is tempting to hope that, if we knew enough, we would be able to prevent suicide. There are, indeed, some warning signs to look out for.

One American study indicated that as many as 42 per cent of teenagers who went on to attempt or actually to commit suicide had previously spoken of having serious thoughts of suicide. Over 50 per cent of those of all ages who attempt suicide in Britain have visited a medical agency of some kind, usually the family doctor, in the previous month, often in connection with the event that precipitates the attempt. Evidently their cries for help had to become louder before anyone would hear. About 50 per cent of all successful adult suicides are preceded by an unsuccessful attempt.

In many cases, though, it is impossible either to predict or to prevent a suicide. Those who are left will almost inevitably find themselves troubled, by guilt and self-recrimination; they will need help to work through these feelings and somehow to come to terms with what has happened.

The Myth of Adolescent Turmoil

G. Stanley Hall, writing in the early years of this century in America, saw adolescence as a time of inevitable storm and stress. Many parents today adhere to this view, assuming that all young people will be difficult, and find life difficult, that the generation gap is painful to both sides and that the years between eleven and twenty are, for parents and children alike, a time to be endured rather than enjoyed. It is true that adolescence can be an intensely painful time for some young people: progress towards independence is not always straightforward, and there are pitfalls along the way. But to describe adolescence in blanket terms as a time of turmoil is to talk in the language of the myth.

It can, of course, be a painful time for parents themselves, as they see their beloved child growing up and changing, moving away from them, perhaps underlining their own need to adjust to a new middle-life style; some of the much-vaunted turmoil can often be found within the parents themselves.

Some parents find it difficult to come to terms with the greater sexual freedom that their children have; it can also be difficult for parents to cope with what they see as weaknesses in their children, to accept that children are not going to fulfil their expectations of them, or indeed to turn into the kind of people they would wish or expect them to be. Parents' anxieties are also influenced by sex stereotypes: they tend to worry more about boys being irresponsible, because they see them as potential breadwinners, and to be more concerned when girls, future wives and mothers, misbehave socially. Perhaps this pattern will change with shifts in role expectations.

Evidence on the gap between generations was first collected systematically in the United States in the 1950s. Some writers described a totally separate youth culture – not, however, a universal phenomenon. The general picture was one of hostility between the generations.

However, a report of interviews with three thousand teenagers across the United States published in 1966 presented a different story; this showed minor conflicts between parents and adolescents over matters such as make-up and music but few major differences. In 1976 Michael Rutter and his colleagues reported on alienation between fourteen year olds and their

You may prefer her not to wear too much make-up,
but she needs to look right in her own eyes.

parents on the Isle of Wight. As in the American study, there were some areas of conflict and 25 per cent of the fourteen year olds voiced some degree of criticism of their parents, but only 4 per cent of parents and 5 per cent of the teenagers recorded serious difficulties in communicating.

Reports since then have been generally consistent: while there are often minor difficulties between parents and children, on the whole adolescents move relatively peacefully away from their parents' authority; any anxiety that exists is felt more by parents – especially by fathers. Nor are adults, as commonly believed, forced by suddenly recalcitrant teenagers into exerting more control; more often the opposite happens, with mutual trust developing between parent and child. Many parents enjoy their children's development into adults, appreciate their growing understanding and are proud of their achievements and increasing independence.

Why, then, is there so much emphasis on the traumatic and chaotic nature of this period of development? Perhaps some writers, professional psychiatrists or psychologists, have relied too much on the anecdotal evidence of their patients, who, by definition, have undergone or are undergoing a difficult time. Perhaps sociologists, themselves preoccupied with tracing social change, have read too much into the youthful need to make choices. Perhaps some parents, wanting to keep their children close to them, are unable to cope with their distress at the adolescent move to independence and have to rationalize this by putting the blame on the children. Perhaps the extreme antics of a minority of teenagers have coloured people's views of the majority.

The British psychologist John Coleman puts forward a theory based on practical observation not of the abnormal few but of the normal many.

Coleman looks at stresses associated with certain aspects of adolescence and argues that young people do not embrace them all at once; rather they focus first on one, then on another, so that although there are many changes, they are dealt with little by little. First might come anxiety over peer group membership, then the problems of sexual relations, then the break from parents, and so on. These areas of change are not of course entirely discrete, they overlap to some extent, but on the whole one crisis is dealt with before the next comes along.

Coleman's theory, based on systematic observation of what actually happens, rather than on scare stories, is convincing. A useful general reminder is that although undoubtedly there will be ups and downs between parents and children they can all (well, almost all) be coped with, given good will and patience. Above all, do not assume that trouble will escalate; like the adolescent himself, negotiate one crisis at a time and never assume that one row will make for a winter of discontent. Try to think of practical ways of helping your children towards achieving independence; offer an allowance before they ask; help them to find a part-time job, if that is appropriate; ask for their help and give them responsibility (and do not despair if they fail the first time – they may succeed the next); introduce them to as many new and challenging experiences as possible. And go on showing that you care.

The rock band in the back bedroom may be rather too loud – but every musician has to start somewhere!

The needs of adolescents

We can summarize this chapter by reminding ourselves of the basic needs of all adolescents. They all need the opportunity:

- to sleep – and take exercise
- to enjoy privacy
- to have the security that comes of knowing that there are boundaries set on their behaviour – and to be able to renegotiate those boundaries over time
- to have demands made upon them by others
- to explore new ideas in religion, politics and philosophy
- to explore new roles, either in fantasy or in reality
- to explore new lifestyles
- to relate increasingly closely to others of their own age – and to establish new, less dependent relationships with parents and a new role in the family generally
- to come to terms in culturally appropriate ways with emerging sexuality

The adolescent negotiating the crises of puberty has come a long way from the tiny being in the womb and has a long way to go in the journey towards old age. It used to be imagined, wrongly, that personality was fixed in youth and that change during the next three-quarters of life was largely a matter of ageing physically. Today there is a much more realistic concept of continuing development throughout life: we go on changing and adapting through early adulthood, parenthood and/or career growth to middle age and then old age. That continuity of change is now acknowledged; the adolescent emerging into adulthood is only on the threshold. The past will fashion the future but does not determine it irrevocably.

She is on the verge of adulthood, and a new, more equal relationship is developing between you.

Nutritional needs

	Sources	Eating well
Carbohydrate There are three types of carbohydrate: starch, sugar and cellulose or fibre. Carbohydrate is necessary for energy and fibre and decreases the time food takes to be processed through the digestive system.	Starch is found in many foods, especially cereals, pulses and potatoes. Refined sugar (sucrose) is found in sweets, cakes, biscuits, jam, canned fruit and sweetened drinks. Fructose is a simple sugar found in fruit, fruit juices and honey. Fibre is found in wholemeal flours, whole-grain cereals, fruit, vegetables, nuts and pulses.	Aim to provide a variety of starchy high-fibre foods and keep sugary foods for special occasions. If you allow your children to eat sweets, offer these at the end of a meal, and encourage them to brush their teeth afterwards.
Fat Fat is a source of energy. Small quantities of fat are needed to obtain the fat-soluble vitamins. Butter, for example, contains Vitamins A and D.	Fats include meat fats, dairy fats, (especially butter and cream) and oils from fish and vegetable sources.	Starting your child on a relatively low-fat diet will help to set up good eating patterns for later life. 28g/1oz of fat is sufficient for a child's daily requirement. Children under 5 years old should be given full-cream milk.
Protein Protein is needed for growth and repair of the body. It helps regulate body processes and transports nutrients and oxygen through the body. It is also a source of energy. Growing children need a greater proportion of protein in their diets than adults.	Animal protein is found in meat, fish, eggs and dairy products. Vegetable protein is found in whole-grain cereals, nuts, pulses and root vegetables.	Milk is a good source of protein as well as of calcium, so if your child enjoys milk, aim to give 0.6 litre/1pt a day from about 1 year onwards.
Calcium Calcium is important in the formation of teeth and bones. Good supplies of Vitamin D are required for the absorption of calcium.	The main sources are cheese, yogurt and milk, tinned fish, green leafy vegetables, almonds, soya beans and seaweeds.	If your child dislikes milk, make sure that you offer plenty of other calcium-rich foods.
Iron Iron is important in preventing anaemia. It builds haemoglobin which helps the transfer of oxygen to the muscle cells. Vitamin C helps the body absorb iron.	Good sources are liver, meat, eggs, bread, cereals, beans, pulses and green vegetables.	Serve plenty of fruit and vegetables at meals to help your child absorb iron.
Salt All body fluids contain salt; it is needed to maintain the water balance of the body and to regulate nerve and muscle activity.	Many foods contain salt. There is no need to add table or cooking salt to food, nor to eat especially salty foods.	Avoid adding salt to a young child or infant's food; this is particularly important for young babies since their kidneys cannot yet excrete excess salt.

In the everyday rush of getting and preparing meals and coping with your children's particular likes and dislikes it may be difficult for you to think in terms of grams, ounces, cups and appropriate servings – but the guidelines here should at least give you an idea of good nutritional practice and what to aim for.

Between the ages of 2 and 8 years, one serving is the equivalent of 15g/½oz for each year of the child's life: for example, following the guidelines opposite, a 4 year old child's daily requirements from the milk group would be a total of 3 (servings) × 4 (years) × 15g/½oz = 170g/6oz.

Between 8 and 12 years, depending on height, weight and enthusiasm for food, a child may be eating adult servings of 120g/4oz: for example, 3 (servings) × 120g/4oz = a daily intake of 360g/12oz from the milk group.

Between 12 and 18 years the daily requirements are the same as an adult's. These servings are a minimum and growing adolescents may eat more than the amounts indicated without putting on extra weight.

	Sources	Eating well
Vitamin A Needed to maintain a variety of body cells and to prevent infection. Helps vision, particularly night vision. Helps maintain healthy skin and enhances bone development. It is a fat-soluble vitamin.	Fatty fish, such as herring, sardine and tuna, fish oils, cheese, eggs, butter, chicken, liver, oranges, cantaloupe melon, carrots, tomatoes, cabbage, spinach, broccoli.	A varied diet usually provides enough Vitamin A, but vitamin drops or cod liver oil guard against deficiency. Excessive doses of Vitamin A can be poisonous.
Vitamin B complex The B vitamins play an important part in the chemical reactions that release energy from food. As they are water-soluble they are easily destroyed by cooking. Vitamin B12 also assists in red blood cell formation and helps maintain the central nervous system.	Milk, liver, whole-grain cereals, pulses, eggs, green leafy vegetables, nuts and seeds, yeast extract.	Sunlight destroys Vitamin B12 so avoid leaving milk out on the doorstep. Vegans should take a supplement of Vitamin B12.
Vitamin C Vitamin C is important for growth and bone development, promotes healing and helps resistance to infection. It is water-soluble.	Breast and formula milk; fruit and vegetables, especially citrus fruits, blackcurrants, strawberries, tomatoes, potatoes, green leafy vegetables.	Vitamin C is easily destroyed during storage and cooking. Buy your fruit and vegetables as fresh as possible and either eat them raw or cook them lightly.
Vitamin D This is necessary for the absorption of calcium. Adolescents need extra Vitamin D and should take a supplement in winter.	Fish liver oils, fatty fish, dairy products. The body can manufacture Vitamin D when exposed to sunlight.	As dark-skinned children create less Vitamin D from sunlight than light-skinned children, they may need to take in more Vitamin D from other sources.
Vitamin E The need for Vitamin E in humans is not proven though it is thought to protect red blood cells from becoming fragile.	Liver, vegetable oils, wheatgerm, oats, brown rice and other whole-grain cereals, nuts, seeds, pulses, green leafy vegetables.	A deficiency of Vitamin E is unlikely in a normal diet.
Vitamin K Vitamin K is needed for normal clotting of the blood.	Liver, egg yolks, spinach, cauliflower, peas and cereals.	Excessive doses of Vitamin K may cause anaemia.

Daily requirements		2–12 years	12–18 years
Milk group	Milk, yogurt, cheese, cottage cheese	3 servings	4 servings
Meat group	Meat, poultry and fish. High protein meat substitutes might include soy products, nuts and pulses	2 servings	3 servings
Vegetable/fruit group	All vegetables and fruits, including at least one good source of Vitamin C and one deep yellow or dark green vegetable	4 servings	4 servings
Bread and cereal group	Bread, cereals, pasta and rice	4 servings	4 servings

Bibliography

Although this book is based on technical and professional literature, the suggested general reading lists have been limited to books and articles usually available in good reference libraries. Also included are selected lists of academic sources. Readers wishing to go more deeply into the technical literature will find the research discussed in depth in the textbooks recommended below.

General reading

Bee, Helen. *The Developing Child*, New York, Harper and Row, 1989

Chess, S.M.D. and Thomas, A. *Know Your Child*, New York, Basic Books, 1987

Clarke-Stewart, Alison and Friedmann, Susan. *Child Development: Infancy through Adolescence*, New York, John Wiley and Sons, 1987

Cole, Michael and Cole, Sheila R. *The Development of Children*, New York, Scientific American Books, 1989

Franck, Irene and Brownstone, David. *The Parent's Desk Reference*, New York, Prentice Hall, 1991

Hughes, Fergus P., Noppe, Lloyd D. and Noppe, Illene C. *Child Development*, St Paul, Mn, West Publishing, 1988

Lansdown, Richard. *Child Development Made Simple*, London, Heinemann, 1984

Leach, Penelope. *Baby and Child*, Harmondsworth, Penguin, and New York, Knopf, 1989

Mussen, P.H., Conger, J.J., Kagan, J. and Huston, A.C. *Child Development and Personality*, New York, Harper and Row, 1990

New York Hospital-Cornell Medical Center with Rubinstein, Mark. *The Growing Years*, New York, Atheneum, 1990

Papalia, Diane E. and Wendeskolds, Sally. *Human Development*, 4th edn, New York and Maidenhead, McGraw Hill, 1989

Shaffer, David R. *Developmental Psychology*, 2nd edn, Pacific Grove, Ca, Brooks/Cole, 1989

Spock, Benjamin and Rothenberg, Michael. *Dr Spock's Baby and Child Care*, New York, Dutton, 1985

Academic sources

Beischer, N.A. and Mackay, E.V. *Obstetrics and the Newborn: An Illustrated Textbook*, Philadelphia and London, Bailliere Tindall, 1986

Graham, Philip. *Child Psychiatry: A Developmental Approach*, Oxford, Oxford University Press, 1987

Gregory, Richard L. *The Oxford Companion to the Mind*, Oxford, Oxford University Press, 1987

Levine, M., Carey W.B., Crocker, A.C. and Gross, R.T. *Developmental Behavioral Pediatrics*, Philadelphia and London, W.B. Saunders, 1983

Nelson Textbook of Pediatrics, 13th edn R. Behrman and V. Vaughan (eds.), Philadelphia, W.B. Saunders, 1987

Rutter, Michael, ed. *Scientific Foundations of Child Psychiatry*, London, William Heinemann, 1980, published as *Developmental Psychiatry*, Washington, 1st American Psychiatric Press, 1987

Books on specific topics from birth to adolescence

Physical Growth

Tanner, J.M. and Whitehouse, R.H. *Atlas of Children's Growth: Abnormal Variation and Growth Disorders*, London, London Academic Press, 1982

Tanner, J.M. *Foetus into Man: Physical Growth from Conception to Maturity*, rev. and enlarged edn, Cambridge, Ma, Harvard University Press, 1989

Nutrition

Gershoff, Stanley W., with Catherine Whitney and the editorial advisory board of the Tufts University diet and nutrition letter. *The Tufts University Guide to Total Nutrition*, New York, Harper and Row, 1990

Forbes, Gilbert B. and the Committee on Nutrition. *Pediatric Nutrition Handbook*, Elk Greve Village, Ill, American Academy of Pediatrics, 1985

Howard, Rosanne B. and Winter, Harland S. *Nutrition and Feeding of Infants and Toddlers*, Boston and Toronto, Little Brown, 1984

Pipes, Peggy L. *Nutrition in Infancy and Childhood Times*, St Louis, Mo, Mirror/Mosby College Publishing, 1989

Physical Skills

Cratty, Bryant J. *Perceptual and Motor Development in Infants and Children*, Englewood Cliffs, NJ, Prentice-Hall, 1979

Thinking

Bruner, Jerome. *Actual Minds, Possible Worlds*, New York, Harvard University Press, 1986

Donaldson, Margaret. *Children's Minds*, London, Fontana, 1978, and New York, Norton, 1979

Flavell, J. *Cognitive Development*, 2nd edn, Englewood Cliffs, NJ, Prentice-Hall, 1985

Meadows, Sara (ed.) *Developing Thinking: Approaches to Children's Cognitive Development*, London and New York, Methuen, 1983

Wood, David. *How Children Think and Learn*, Oxford, Basil Blackwell, 1988

Memory

Kail, Robert. *The Development of Memory in Children*, New York, W.H. Freeman, 1989

Schneider, Wolfgang and Pressley, Michael. *Memory Development between 2 and 20*, New York, Springer-Verlag, 1989

Language

Bruner, Jerome. *Child's Talk: Learning to Use Language*, Oxford, Oxford University Press, 1983, and New York, Norton, 1985

Crystal, David. *Listen to Your Child: A Parent's Guide to Children's Language*, Harmondsworth, Penguin, 1986

Weiner, Harvey S. *Talk with Your Child*, New York, Viking Penguin, 1988

Social Relationships

Argyle, Michael and Henderson, Monika. *The Anatomy of Relationships*, London, Heinemann, 1985

Dunn, Judy. *The Beginnings of Social Understanding*, London, Blackwell and Cambridge, Ma, Harvard University Press, 1988

Chapter 1 Influences on Development

General reading
The Biological Birthright/Genetics or Environment
Plomin, Robert, DeFries, John C. and Fulker, David
W. *Nature and Nurture during Infancy and Early
Childhood*, Cambridge, Cambridge University Press,
1988
Plomin, Robert, DeFries, John C. and McClearn,
G.E. *Behavioral Genetics: A Primer*, New York,
W.H. Freeman, 1989
The Social Context
Aldrich, Robert A., and Austin, Glenn. *Grandparenting
for the 90's: Parenting is Forever*, Rolling Hills
Estates, Ca, Robert Erdman, 1991
Close, Sylvia. *The Toddler and the New Baby*, London,
Routledge and Kegan Paul, 1980
Dunn, Judy. *Sisters and Brothers*, Cambridge, Ma,
Harvard University Press, 1985
Dunn, Judy and Ploman, Robert. *Separate Lives: Why
Siblings Are So Different*, New York, Basic Books,
1990
Fitzgerald, John and Murcer, Bill. *Building New
Families through Adoption and Fostering*, Oxford, Basil
Blackwell, 1981
Freud, Sigmund. *An Outline of Psychoanalysis*, in J.
Strachey (ed. and trans.) *The Standard Edition of the
Complete Psychological Works of Sigmund Freud*, vol.
23, London, Hogarth Press, 1955
Hetherington, E. Mavis and Arasteh, Josephine (eds).
*Impact of Divorce, Single Parenting and Steparenting on
Children*, Hillsdale, NJ, Lawrence Erlbaum, 1988
Lamb, Michael E. (ed.) *The Father's Role: Cross-
Cultural Perspectives*, Hillsdale, NJ, Lawrence
Erlbaum, 1987
Ross, R.D. *Fathering*, London, Fontana, 1981
Siegel, Stephanie E. *Parenting Your Adopted Child*, New
York, Prentice-Hall, 1989
Steiner, Judith M. *How to Survive as a Working Mother*,
London, Kogan Page, and Woodstock, NY,
Beekman Publishing, 1989
Stern, Daniel. *The First Relationship*, Cambridge, Ma,
Harvard University Press, 1977, and London,
Fontana, 1980
Wallerstein, Judith and Blakeslee, Sandra. *Second
Chances*, Boston, Houghton Mifflin and London,
Corgi, 1990
Resilience
Kübler-Ross, Elisabeth. *On Children and Death*, New
York, Macmillan, 1983

Academic sources
Baumrind, Diana. 'Child care practices anteceding
three patterns of pre-school behavior', *Genetic
Psychology Monographs*, 75 (1967), 43-88 'Current
patterns of parental authority', *Developmental
Psychology Monographs*, 4 (1, Part 2) (1971) 'New
directions in socialization research', *American
Psychologist*, 35, 639-52
Bowlby, John. *Attachment and Loss*, vols. 1 and 2,
London, Hogarth Press, and New York, Basic
Books, 1969
Dunn, J. and Kendrick, C. 'Young siblings in the
context of family relationships' in M. Lewis and
L.A. Rosenblum (eds), *The Child and Its Family*,
New York, Plenum Press, 1979
Kaye, Kenneth. *The Mental and Social Life of Babies*,
London, Harvester Press, and Chicago, University
of Chicago Press, 1982

Lewis, Michael and Rosenblum, L.A. *The Effect of the
Infant on Its Caregiver*, New York, John Wiley, 1974
Lewis, Michael and Rosenblum, L.A. (eds.) *The
Development of Affect*, New York, Plenum Press,
1978
Plomin, R. and Rowe, D.C. 'Genetic and
environmental etiology of social behavior in
infancy', *Developmental Psychology*, 15 (1979), 62-72
Robins, Lee N. and Rutter, Michael (eds). *Straight and
Devious Pathways from Childhood to Adulthood*,
Cambridge, Cambridge University Press, 1990
Weikart, D.P. 'A longitudinal view of preschool
research effort' in M. Perlmutter (ed.), *Minnesota
Symposia on Child Psychology*, vol. 16, Hillsdale, NJ,
Lawrence Erlbaum, 1983

Chapter 2 The Newborn Child: the first weeks of life

General reading
Kitzinger, Sheila. *The New Pregnancy and Childbirth*,
London, Michael Joseph and Penguin Books, 1989,
published as *The Complete Book of Pregnancy and
Childbirth*, New York, Knopf, 1989
Macfarlane, Aidan. *The Psychology of Childbirth*,
London, Fontana, and Cambridge, Ma, Harvard
University Press, 1977
Before Birth
Grobstein, Clifford. *Science and the Unborn: Choosing
Human Futures*, New York, Basic Books, 1990
Illingworth, Ronald S. *The Development of the Infant and
Young Child*, Edinburgh, Churchill Livingstone,
1987
Moore, Keith L. *Before We Are Born: Basic Embryology
and Birth Defects*, Philadelphia, W. B. Saunders,
1989
Sinclair, David. *Human Growth after Birth*, 5th edn,
Oxford, Oxford University Press, 1990
The Birth
Apgar, Virginia and Beck, Joan. *Is My Baby All Right?*,
New York, Pocket Books, 1974
Kitzinger, Sheila. *Freedom and Choice in Childbirth*,
London, Viking and Penguin Books, 1987,
published as *Your Baby, Your Way: Making Pregnancy
Decisions and Birth Plans*, New York, Pantheon, 1987
Pregnancy Day by Day, New York, Random House,
1990
Kitzinger, Sheila and Nilsson, Lennart. *Being Born*,
London, Dorling Kindersley, 1986
Leboyer, Fredrick. *Birth Without Violence*, New York,
Knopf, 1975, and London, Fontana, 1976
Nilsson, Lennart, and Hamberger, Lars. *A Child is
Born*, New York, Delacorte, 1990
Odent, Michel. *Birth Reborn*, London, Fontana, and
New York, Pantheon, 1986
The New Baby
Bower, T.G.R. *Perceptual World of the Child*,
Cambridge, Ma, Harvard University Press and
London, Fontana, 1977
Bowlby, John. *A Secure Base*, London, Routledge and
Kegan Paul, 1988, and New York, Basic Books,
1990
(with additional chapters by Mary Ainsworth). *Child
Care and the Growth of Love*, Harmondsworth,
Penguin, 1965
Chess, S.M.D. and Thomas, A. *Know Your Child*, New
York, Basic Books, 1987
Kitzinger, Sheila. *The Crying Baby*, Harmondsworth,
Penguin, 1990

499

Breastfeeding Your Baby, London, Dorling Kindersley and New York, Knopf, 1989

Klaus, M.H. and Kennell, J.H. *Parent-Infant Bonding*, St Louis, Mi, C.V. Mosby, 1982

Maurer, Daphne and Murer, Charles. *The World of the Newborn*, New York, Basic Books, 1989

Schaffer, H.R. *The Child's Entry into a Social World*, San Diego, Ca, Academic Press, 1984

Winnicott, D.W. *Babies and Their Mothers*, ed. Clare Winnicott, Ray Shephard and Madeline Davis, London, Free Association Books, and Reading, Ma, Addison Wesley, 1987

When All Is Not Well

Glover, Barbara and Hodson, Christine. *You and Your Premature Baby*, London, Sheldon, 1985

Jason, Janine and Van der Meer, Antonia. *Parenting Your Premature Baby: A Complete Guide to Birth, Postpartum Care and Early Childhood*, New York, Delacorte, 1990

Kitchen, W.A. *Premature Babies*, Wellingborough, Thorsons, 1984, and Emmans, Pa, Rodale Press, 1985

Pringle, Mia Kellmer. *The Needs of Children*, 2nd edn, London, Hutchinson, 1980

Thompson, Liz. *Bringing up a Mentally Handicapped Child: It's Not All Tears*, Wellingborough and Vermont, Thorsons, 1986

Academic sources

Coren, S. and Ward, L. *Sensation and Perception*, Orlando, Fla, Harcourt Brace Jovanovich, 1989

Field, T.M., Huston, A., Quay, H.C., Troll, L. and Finley, G.E. (eds) *Social Perception and Responsivity in Early Infancy*, New York, Wiley, 1982

Gibson, E.J., and Walk, R.D. 'The "visual cliff"', *Scientific American*, 202 (1960), 64-71

Gibson, E.J. and Spelke, E.S. 'The development of perception' in P.H. Mussen (gen. ed.), *Handbook of Child Psychology*, vol. 3: *Cognitive Development*, New York, Wiley, 1983

Weiffenbach, James M. (ed.). *The Genesis of Sweet Preference*, National Institute of Dental Research, DHEW Publication No. (NIH)77-1068, US Department of Health, Education and Welfare, 1977

Wolff, P.H. 'The natural history of crying and other vocalization in early infancy', in B. Foss (ed.), *Determinants of Infant Behaviour*, vol. 4, London, Methuen, 1969

Chapter 3 Towards Independence: up to eighteen months

General reading

Fogel, Alan. *Infancy, Infant, Family and Society*, St Paul, Mn, West Publishing, 1984

Green, Christopher J. *Babies! A Parents' Guide to Surviving and Enjoying the Baby's First Year*, New York, Simon and Schuster, 1989

Kohner, Nancy. *Birth to 5*, London, Harper and Row, 1989

Leach, Penelope. *Your Baby and Child*, Harmondsworth, Penguin and New York, Knopf, 1989

The Baby Kit: Everything You Need to Know About Caring for Your Newborn, New York, Simon and Schuster, 1990

Richards, Martin. *Infancy: World of the Newborn*, London, Harper and Row, 1980

Spock, Benjamin and Rothenberg, Michael. *Dr Spock's Baby and Child Care*, New York, Dutton, 1985

Physical Development

Sinclair, David. *Human Growth After Birth*, Oxford, Oxford University Press, 1990

On the Move

Aston, Athiina. *How to Play with Your Baby*, Charlotte, NC, Fast and McMillan Publishing, 1983

Brown, Laurie Krasney. *Baby Time*, New York, Knopf 1989

Evans, Judith and Ilfeld, Ellen. *Good Beginnings: Parenting in the Early Years*, Ypsilanti, Mi, The High Scope Press, 1982

Newman, Virginia Hunt. *Teaching an Infant to Swim*, rev. ed., North Ryde (Australia) and London, Angus and Robertson, 1983

Segal, Marilyn. *Your Child at Play: Birth to One Year*, New York, Newmarket, 1985

In Time and With Love: Caring for the Special Needs Baby, New York, Newmarket, 1988

Segal, Marilyn, and Adcock, Don. *Your Child at Play: Starter Set*, New York, Newmarket, 1986

Beginning to Understand the World

Bower, T.G.R. *The Rational Infant: Learning in Infancy*, New York, W.H. Freeman, 1989

Bremmer, J. Gavin. *Infancy*, Oxford, Basil Blackwell, 1988

Fields, Tiffany. *Infancy*, Cambridge, Ma, Harvard University Press, 1990

Stern, Daniel N. *Diary of a Baby: What Your Child Sees, Feels and Experiences*, New York, Basic Books, 1990

Social and Emotional Development

Douglas, Jo and Richman, Naomi. *My Child Won't Sleep*, Harmondsworth, Penguin, 1984

Dunn, Judy. *Distress and Comfort*, London, Fontana, 1977

Sisters and Brothers, London, Fontana, 1984

Ferber, R. *Solve Your Child's Sleep Problems*, New York, Simon and Schuster, 1985

Gregory, Richard L. *The Oxford Companion to the Mind*, Oxford, Oxford University Press 1987

Play Matters and National Toy Libraries Association, *The Good Toy Guide*, London, A & C Black, 1986

Rutter, Michael. *Maternal Deprivation Reassessed*, 2nd edn, Harmondsworth, Penguin, 1981

Schaffer, Rudolf. *Mothering*, London, Fontana, and Cambridge, Ma, Harvard University Press, 1977

Communication

Bruner, Jerome. *Child's Talk: Learning to Use Language*, Oxford, Oxford University Press, 1983, and New York, Norton, 1985

Academic sources

Condon, K.W.S. and Sander, L.W. 'Neonate movement is synchronized with adult speech: interactional participation and language acquisition', *Science*, 183 (1983), 99-101

Dunn, J. and Kendrick, C. 'The arrival of a sibling: changes in patterns of interaction between mother and first-born child', *J. Child Psychology and Psychiatry & Allied Disciplines*, 21 (2), 119-132

Field, T.M., Woodson, R., Greenberg, R. and Cohen, D. 'Discrimination and imitation of facial expressions by neonates', *Science*, 218 (1982), 179-81

Greenough, W.T. and Green, E.J. 'Experience and the aging brain', in J.L. McGaugh, J.G. March and S.B. Kiesler (eds), *Aging: Biology and Behavior*, New York, Academic Press, 1981

Grunau, R.V.E. and Craig, K.D. 'Pain expression in neonates: facial action and cry', *Pain*, 28 (1987), 28–34

Lewis, Michael and Brook-Gunn, Jeanne. *Social Cognition and the Acquisition of Self*, New York, Plennen Press, 1979

Lipsett, L.P. *Advances in Infancy Research*, Norwood, NJ, Ablex, 1986

Osofsky, J.D. (ed.). *Handbook of Infant Development*, 2nd edn, New York, Wiley, 1987

Rovee-Collier, C.K., Sullivan, M.W.K., Enright, M., Lucas, D. and Fagan, J.W. 'Reactivation of infant memory', *Science*, 208 (1980), 1159–1161

Schaffer, Rudolf and Emerson, Peggy. 'The development of social attachments in infancy', *Monographs of the Society for Research in Child Development*, 29 (1964)

Thomas, A. and Chess, S. *Temperament and Development*, New York, Brunner Mazel, 1977

Chapter 4 Out into the World: eighteen months to three years

General reading
Brazelton, T. Berry. *Toddlers and Parents: A Practical Guide to Your Child*, Harmondsworth, Penguin, 1976

Green, Christopher. *Toddler Taming*, London, Century, 1983

Kagan, Jerome. *The Second Year: The Emergence of Self-Awareness*, London and Cambridge, Ma, Harvard University Press, 1981

Leach, Penelope. *Parents A-Z*, Harmondsworth, Penguin, 1985

Physical Skills
Kellog, Rhoda. *Children's Drawings, Children's Minds*, New York, Avon, 1979

Keogh, Jack and Sugden, David. *Movement Skill Development*, London and New York, Macmillan, 1985

Thomas, Glyn V. and Silk, Angèle M.J. *An Introduction to the Psychology of Children's Drawings*, New York and London, Harvester Wheatsheaf, 1990

Thinking and Understanding
Donaldson, Margaret. *Children's Minds*, London, Fontana, 1978, and New York, Norton, 1979

McGhee, Paul E. (ed.). *Humor and Children's Development*, New York, Haworth, 1989

Language
Garvey, Catherine. *Children's Talk*, Cambridge, Ma, Harvard University Press, 1984

Emotional Development
Sarafino, Edward. *The Fears of Childhood*, New York, Human Sciences Press, 1986

Growing Independence
Herbert, Martin. *Discipline: A Positive Guide for Parents*, Oxford, Basil Blackwell, 1989

Play
Aria, Barbara. *Nursery Design: Creating a Perfect Environment for Your Child*, New York, Bantam, 1990

Day, Barbara. *Early Childhood Education: Creative Learning Activities*, New York, Macmillan, 1988

Millar, Susanna. *The Psychology of Play*, Harmondsworth, Pelican, 1968

Petrie, Pat. *Baby Play*, London, Century, and New York, Pantheon, 1987

Tizard, Barbara and Havey, David (eds.), *The Biology of Play*, London, Heinemann, 1977

Academic sources
Crystal, David. *Introduction to Language Pathology*, London, Cole and Whorn, 1988

Flavell, J.H. *The Developmental Psychology of Jean Piaget*, Princeton, NJ, Van Nostrand, 1963

Inhelder, Barbel and Piaget, Jean. *The Growth of Logical Thinking from Childhood to Adolescence*, London, Routledge and Kegan Paul, 1958

Salapatek, Philip and Cohen, Leslie (eds.). *Handbook of Infant Perception*, vol. 1-2, London, Academic Press and Orlando, Fla, Harcourt Brace Jovanovich, 1987

Turner, Joanna. *Cognitive Development*, London, Methuen, 1975

Chapter 5 Developing Skills and Relationships: three to seven

General reading
Kagan, J. *The Nature of the Child*, New York, Basic Books, 1984

Smith, Peter K. and Cowie, Helen. *Understanding Children's Development*, Oxford, Basil Blackwell, 1988

Sylva, K. and Lunt, Ingrid. *Child Development: A First Course*, London, Grant McIntyre, 1982

Meadows, Sara. *Understanding Child Development*, London, Hutchinson, 1986

Physical Skills
Gleeson, G. (ed.). *The Growing Child in Competitive Sport*, London, Hodder and Stoughton, 1986

Gardner, Howard J. *Artful Scribbles: The Significance of Children's Drawings*, London, Jill Norman, 1980, and New York, Basic Books, 1982

Richman, Naomi and Lansdown, Richard (eds.). *Problems of Preschool Children*, London, Wiley, 1988

Thinking and Understanding
Donaldson, M. *Children's Minds*, London, Fontana, 1978, and New York, Norton, 1979

Language
Evesham, Frances. *Help Your Child to Talk*, London, Cassell, 1989

Snowling, Margaret. *Dyslexia*, Oxford, Basil Blackwell, 1987

Social and Emotional Development
Kohlberg, Lawrence. *The Psychology of Moral Development: The Nature and Validity of Moral Stages*, San Francisco, Harper and Row, 1984

Kohlberg, Lawrence. *The Philosophy of Moral Development: Moral Stages and the Idea of Justice*, San Francisco, Harper and Row, 1981

Kohlberg, Lawrence and Lickona, Thomas. *The Stages of Ethical Development from Childhood through Old Age*, New York, Harper and Row, 1986

Leight, Lynn. *Raising Sexually Healthy Children*, New York, Avon Books, 1990

Maccoby, Eleanor E. *Social Development: Psychological Growth and the Parent-Child Relationship*, Orlando, Fla, Harcourt Brace Jovanovich, 1980

Rubin, Zick. *Children's Friendships*, Cambridge, Ma, Harvard University Press and London, Fontana, 1980

Sarafino, Edward P. *The Fears of Childhood: A Guide to Recognizing and Reducing Fearful States in Children*, New York, Human Sciences Press, 1986

Going to School
Bale, John. *Geography in the Primary School*, London, Routledge and Kegan Paul, 1987

Basham, Margaret. *Getting Ready for School*, Harlow, Longman, 1988

501

Blyth, Joan. *History: Five to Nine*, London, Hodder and Stoughton, 1988

Children's Television Workshop, *Parents' Guide to Raising Kids Who Love to Learn*, with preface by David Elkind, Children's Television Workshop Series, New York, Prentice-Hall, 1989

Children's Television Workshop, *Parents' Guide to Understanding Discipline: Infancy through Preteens*, Children's Television Workshop Series, New York, Prentice-Hall, 1990

Curtis, Audrey M. *A Curriculum for the Pre-school Child: Learning to Learn*, London, NFER-Nelson, 1986

Katz, Lilian G. and Chard, Sylvia C. *Engaging Children's Minds: The Project Approach*, Norwood, NJ, Ablex, 1989

Merttens, Ruth. *Teaching Primary Maths*, London, Hodder and Stoughton, 1989
Parent's Guide to Your Child's Math, New York and Harmondsworth, Penguin, 1989

Merttens, Ruth and Vass, Jeff. *Bringing School Home: Children and Parents Learning Together*, London, Hodder and Stoughton, 1990

Skemp, Richard. *Mathematics in the Primary School*, London, Routledge and Kegan Paul, 1989

Skemp, Richard. *The Psychology of Learning Mathematics*, Hillsdale, NJ, Lawrence Erlbaum, 1987

Tizard, Barbara and Hughes, Martin. *Young Children Learning: Talking and Thinking at Home and at School*, Cambridge, Ma, Harvard University Press and London, Fontana, 1984

Academic sources
Kohlberg, L. *Stages in the Development of Moral Thought and Action*, New York, Holt Rinehart and Winston, 1969

Chapter 6 A Widening Social World: seven to eleven

General reading
Elkind, David. *The Hurried Child*, rev. edn, Reading, Ma, Addison-Wesley, 1988

Williams, Joyce, W. and Smith, Marjorie. *Middle Childhood: Behavior and Development*, New York, Macmillan, 1980

The Growth in Understanding
Hughes, Martin. *Children and Number Difficulties in Learning Mathematics*, Oxford, Basil Blackwell, 1986

Taylor, E. *Hyperactivity: A Parent's Guide*, London, Martin Dunitz, 1985

Wood, Miriam. *Living with a Hyperactive Child*, London, Souvenir, 1984

Education
Bloom, Benjamin, (ed.). *Developing Talent in Young People*, New York, Ballantine, 1985

Holt, John. *How Children Fail* (rev. edn), Harmondsworth, Penguin, 1984 and New York, Dell, 1988

Liebeck, Pamela. *How Children Learn Mathematics: A Guide for Parents and Teachers*, Harmondsworth and New York, Penguin, 1988

Moon, Bob. *A Guide to the National Curriculum*, Oxford, Oxford University Press, 1991

Mortimore, Peter, Sammons, Pamela, Stoll, Louise, Lewis, David and Ecob, Russell. *School Matters: The Junior Years*, Berkeley, Ca, University of California Press, 1988 and London, Open Books, 1989

Pinder, Rachel. *Why Don't Teachers Teach Like They Used To?*, London, Hilary Shipman, 1987

Roberts, Geoffrey. *Teaching Children to Read and Write*, Oxford, Basil Blackwell, 1989

Science in the National Curriculum, London, HMSO
Mathematics in the National Curriculum, London, HMSO
(For specific subjects order updated material from HMSO, PO Box 276, London, SW8 5DT.)

Emotional and Social Development
Coles, Robert. *The Moral Life of Children*, Boston, Houghton Mifflin, 1987
The Spiritual Life of Children, Boston, Houghton Mifflin, 1990

Coopersmith, Stanley. *The Antecedents of Self-Esteem*, San Francisco, Freeman, 1981

Davies, Maire Messenger. *Television is Good for Your Kids*, London, Hilary Shipman, 1989

Greenfield, Patricia Marks. *Mind and Media: The Effects of Television, Computer and Video Games*, Cambridge, Ma, Harvard University Press, and London, Fontana, 1984

Hutt, Corinne. *Males and Females*, Harmondsworth, Penguin, 1972

Liebert, R.N. and Sprafkin, J.N. (eds.). *The Early Window: Effects of Television on Children*, New York, Pergamon, 1988

Open University. *Living with Children: 5 to 10*, London, Harper and Row, 1981

Academic sources
Kalata, G. 'Obese children: a growing problem', *Science* 232 (1986), 20–21

Chapter 7 Adolescence: eleven to eighteen

General reading
Coleman, John C. and Hendry, Leo. *The Nature of Adolescence*, 2nd edn, London and New York, Routledge and Kegan Paul, 1990

Petrie, Pat. *The Adolescent Years: A Guide for Parents*, London, Michael Joseph, 1990

Santrock, John W. *Adolescence*, Dubuque, Iowa, Wm C. Brown, 1990

Steinberg, Laurence. *Adolescence*, New York, Knopf, 1989

Adolescence and Puberty
Bell, R. *Changing Bodies, Changing Lives: A Book for Teens on Sex and Relationships*, New York, Random House, 1987

Buckler, John. *The Adolescent Years*, Ware, Castlemead, 1987 and New York, Springer Verlag, 1990

Madaras, Lynda (with Area Madaras). *What's Happening to My Body? A Growing-up Guide for Parents and Daughters*, New York, Newmarket, 1989 (with Dane Saavedra). *What's Happening to My Body? A Book for Boys*, New York, Newmarket, 1987

Vaughan, V.C. and Litt, Iris F. *Child and Adolescent Development: Clinical Implications*, Philadelphia, W.B. Saunders, 1990

Thinking
Flavell, J. *Cognitive Development*, 2nd edn, Englewood Cliffs, NJ, Prentice-Hall, 1985

Kohlberg, L. *Stages in the Development of Moral Thought and Action*, New York, Holt Rinehart and Winston, 1969

Education
Buzan, Tony. *Use Your Perfect Memory*, New York, Dutton, 1984
Use Your Memory, London, BBC Books, 1989

Carnegie Foundation for the Advancement of Teaching and Boyer, Ernest L. *High Schools*, New York, Harper and Row, 1985

Erickson, M.H. *Exam Revision Skills and Performance*, Birmingham, Birminham University Counselling Unit, 1989

Freeman, Richard. *Mastering Study Skills*, London, Macmillan, 1982

Harman, Carol A. *How to Study Effectively*, London, Macmillan, 1984

Rutter, Michael, Maughan, Barbara, Mortimore, Peter and Ousten, Janet. *Fifteen Thousand Hours: Secondary Schools and Their Effects on Children*, Wells, Open Books Publishing and Cambridge, Ma, Harvard University Press, 1979

Woods, Peter. *The Happiest Days? How Pupils Cope with School*, London and New York, The Falmer Press, 1990

Establishing a Separate Identity

Erikson, Erik. *Identity, Youth and Crisis*, New York, W.W. Norton, 1968

Sexuality

Bell, Ruth. *Changing Bodies, Changing Lives: A Book for Teens on Sex and Relationships*, New York, Random House, 1987

National Research Council. *Risking the Future: Adolescent Sexuality, Pregnancy and Childbearing*, Washington DC, National Academy Press, 1987

National Center for Health Statistics. *Vital Statistics of the United States*, Washington DC, US Government Printing Office, 1990

Friendships/Behaviour Problems

Coleman, John C. *Working with Troubled Adolescents*, London, Academic Press, 1987

Open University in Association with Health Education Council and the Scottish Health Education Group. *Parents and Teenagers*, London, Harper and Row, 1982

Steinberg, Laurence and Levine, Ann. *You and Your Adolescent: A Parent's Guide for Ages 10-20*, New York, Harper and Row, 1990

Institute for the Study of Drug Dependence. *Drugs: What Every Parent Should Know*, Institute for the Study of Drug Dependence, 1 Hatton Place, London EC1N 8ND. Also available from this address, *What everyone should know about drugs* by Kenneth Leech; and leaflets on different drugs.

Academic sources

Elkind, D. and Bowen, R. 'Imaginary audience behaviour in children and adolescents', *Developmental Psychology*, 15 (1979), 38-44

Jones, M.C. and Bayley, N. 'Physical maturing among boys as related to behaviour', *Journal of Educational Psychology*, 41 (1950), 129-48

Keating, D.P. 'Thinking processes in adolescence', in J. Adelson (ed.), *Handbook of Adolescent Psychology*, New York, Wiley, 1980

Mann, Leon, Harmoni, Ros and Power, Colin. 'Adolescent decision making: the development of competence', *Journal of Adolescence*, 12 (3) (1989), 265-278

Marcia, J.E. 'Development and validation of ego-identity status', *Journal of Personality and Social Psychology* 3 (1966), 551-8

Overton, W.F., Ward, S.L., Noveck, I.A., Black, J. and O'Brien, D.P. 'Form and content in the development of deductive reasoning', *Developmental Psychology*, 23 (1987), 22-30

Peskin, H. 'Influence of the developmental schedule of puberty on learning and ego-functioning', *Journal of Youth and Adolescence* 4 (1973), 273-90

Richardson, Ken and Sheldon, Sue. *Cognitive Development to Adolescence*, Hove, Lawrence Erlbaum in association with the Open University, 1988

Rutter, M., Graham, P., Chadwick, O., and Yule, W. 'Adolescent turmoil: fact or fiction?', *Journal of Child Psychology and Psychiatry* 17 (1976), 35-56

Index

Authors' Acknowledgments

This book was successfully parented by the editorial and design staff at Frances Lincoln, particularly by our editor, Jo Christian. Jo asked difficult questions which forced us to clarify our thoughts and to research even more deeply. Special thanks go to her family for providing the back-up she needed to work so intensively over several years. She was ably and intelligently helped by Judith Warren, who not only edited many sections but also coordinated all the various parts of the book. We would also like to thank Jo Durden-Smith, Erica Hunningher, Anne Kilborn, Sarah Mitchell and Mathew Reitz, who contributed to the editing.

Caroline Hillier gave special attention to layouts and chose the right pictures for the text every time.

Our thanks to Doreen Blake, who provided the meticulous and intelligent index.

Chapters of this book have also been read and checked by friends and colleagues, who contributed their expert knowledge and helpful advice: Professor Kathy Sylva, University of London; Alison Clarke-Stewart, University of California at Irvine; John Coleman, Director, The Trust for Adolescence; Audrey Curtis, University of London; teachers Kate Frood, Nora Groban and Richard Jones; Sheila Kitzinger, childbirth educator, author and social anthropologist; John Marr, of Greenwich Hospital, Greenwich, Connecticut. The staff at Great Ormond Street Hospital have been particularly helpful. Among them we would especially like to thank David Atherton, Consultant Dermatologist; Susan Bellman, Consultant Audiologist; Deborah Christie, Research Neuropsychologist; Richard Stanhope, Senior Lecturer in Paediatric Endocrinology; Marianne Tranter, Social Worker; Marie-Anne Urbanowicz, Research Psychologist; Faraneh Vargha-Khadem, Consultant Neuropsychologist; Marion Woodard, Chief Speech and Language Therapist.

Friends have also shared their experiences as parents, and their children have made their comments and contributions. We wish to thank Connie Booth, Elizabeth Christian, John Lahr and Chris, Richard and Val Morant and Tama and Jake, Lucia and Anthony Reynolds and Georgia, Susan and John Rothchild and Sacha, Berns and Chauncey, June Streets, and, most particularly, Rawle Adams and Dez Hallum. Special thanks must go to Kathy Sylva, not only in her role as an expert, but also as a friend.

Photographer's Acknowledgments

I wish to thank Janet Balaskas and Yehudi Gordon for giving me the opportunity to take the active birth photographs on pages 54, 59, 63 and 73. I should also like to thank Ackland Burghley School, Brookfield School and the Eleanor Palmer School, all in London, the American Community School, Cobham, Kent, the Central Primary School, Watford, and Summerhill School, Leiston, Suffolk, for allowing me to take photographs; and very special thanks to all the parents and children who appear in the book.

Publishers' Acknowledgments

The publishers wish to thank the following people for their help in producing this book: Nicky and Stephen Adamson, Sallie Coolidge, Yvonne Cummerson, Serena Dilnot, Katy Foskew, Sue Gee, Sue Gladstone, Gillian Greenwood, Susan Kennedy, Monique Maxwell, Helen Perks, Janet Swarbrick, Hazel Wood. We are especially grateful to Elizabeth Fenwick, Caroline Taylor and Deborah Thompson for their invaluable editorial contributions.

Our thanks to Nancy Durrell McKenna for the photograph on page 79; to Sandra Lousada for the photographs on page 178; to Roger Hillier for the photograph on page 308; and to The Dyslexia Teaching Centre, London for supplying the illustration on page 332. The photographs on page 48 are reproduced courtesy of Petit Format, Paris. The x-ray photographs on page 104 are reproduced from *The Radiographic Atlas of the Skeletal Development of the Hand and Wrist* by William Greulich and S.Idell Pyle, with the permission of the publishers, Stanford University Press, © 1950 and 1959 by the Board of Trustees of the Leland Stanford Junior University.

Our very special thanks to the children who contributed their drawings and writings: Elizabeth and Nicky Christian, Richard Dedomenici, Hannah and Beth Gladstone, Camilla Hickey-Brown, Oliver Hillier, Sebastien Kilborn, Emily and Joseph Sharratt, and Sophie Warren.

Editors Jo Christian, Judith Warren

Designers Niki Medlikova, Claudine Meissner

Editorial Director Erica Hunningher

Associate Art Directors Caroline Hillier, Tim Foster

512